**CONTRIBUTIONS
TO AN EDUCATIONAL TECHNOLOGY
VOLUME 2**

Contributions to an Educational Technology Volume 2

Edited by
JAMES HARTLEY *Keele University, UK*
IVOR K DAVIES *Indiana University, USA*

Kogan Page, London/Nichols Publishing Company, New York

In memory of George William Hartley

First published in Great Britain in 1978 by
Kogan Page Limited
120 Pentonville Road
London N1 9JN

First published in the United States of America 1978 by
Nichols Publishing Company
Post Office Box 96
New York, NY 10024

Library of Congress Catalog Card No 78-65915
ISBN 0-89397-038-7

Printed in Great Britain by offset lithography by
Billing & Sons Ltd, Guildford,
London and Worcester

ISBN 0 85038 129 0

Preface

This text is a sequel to the first *Contributions to an Educational Technology* (Butterworths, 1972). In that text, and in this one, our aim has been to put together a selection of papers, each of which has made a contribution to the field, and each of which represents a certain viewpoint or perspective for an educational technology. As before the contents are divided up into various parts (with inevitable overlaps) but this time there are fewer categories and longer papers. As before, each part is prefaced by a short introduction which explains why each of the contributions has been chosen and places each selection in a wider context.

In the first volume we found it difficult to define the nature of educational technology. Over the years this difficulty has increased. The scope of educational technology has widened in every area of endeavour since the early 1970s. To encompass this we begin with a prologue and conclude with an epilogue, both of which assess the nature of educational technology from different historical viewpoints. Between these papers we consider more recent theoretical developments, practical procedures and applications.

In putting this text together we have had to select from a great deal of material. Some papers have been written for the book. Some others we have had to edit firmly. Our aim, however, as before, has been to indicate the diversity of views and approaches that exist in this exciting and increasingly important area of educational inquiry.

Many people have assisted us in the preparation of this book, not least our fellow contributors as well as their editors and publishers. To all of them we would like to express our appreciation.

James Hartley
Ivor K Davies
April 1978

Contents

Preface   5

Prologue: Educational Technology: Archetypes, Paradigms   9
and Models *Ivor K Davies*

Part One: Theoretical Developments
in Educational Technology

    Introduction   27
1.1 **Learning Theory in Practice** *James Hartley*   30
1.2 **What Does it Take to Learn?** *Ference Marton*   47
1.3 **Conversational Techniques in the Study and Practice**   56
    of Education *Gordon Pask*
1.4 **The Psychological Principles underlying the Design**   73
    of Computer-based Instructional Systems
    J Roger Hartley and Kenneth Lovell
1.5 **Individual Differences and Instructional Design**   96
    Richard E Snow
1.6 **Some Aspects of a Theory of Advice** *Ivor K Davies*   104
1.7 **The Responsibilities of the Researcher** *Marten D Shipman* 123

Part Two: Procedural Techniques

    Introduction   131
2.1 **Objectives in Curriculum Design** *Ivor K Davies*   135
2.2 **Analysis for Training** *John Patrick and Robert Stammers* 152
2.3 **Principles of Sequencing Content**   165
    George J Posner and Kenneth A Strike
2.4 **They Teach Concepts, Don't They?** *Susan M Markle*   170
2.5 **Fifty Guidelines for Improving Instructional Text**   182
    James Hartley and Peter Burnhill
2.6 **Decision Making in Instructional Design**   195
    Bernard T Dodd, R J G LeHunte and C Sheppard

2.7   Evaluation as Illumination   205
      Malcolm Parlett and David Hamilton
2.8   A Story of Assimilation and Dissemination   219
      Richard Hooper

Part Three: Applications

      Introduction   233
3.1   Teaching Machines for the Severely Retarded: A Review   237
      John R Hegarty
3.2   Programmed Instruction for Creativity   250
      Robert E Williams
3.3   Teaching Children Thinking *Seymour Papert*   270
3.4   'Goodbye Teacher . . .' *Fred S Keller*   282
3.5   Educational Technology at the Open University: 296
      An Approach to the Problem of Quality *Brian N Lewis*
3.6   The 'McMaster Philosophy': An Approach to Medical   313
      Education *Victor Neufeld and Howard S Barrows*
3.7   An Approach to Rapid Problem Solving in Clinical   325
      Medicine *Brian J Essex*
3.8   Computer-assisted Instruction in British Airways   331
      Harry Butcher and Gerry Moult
3.9   Computers in Military Training *Roger Miles*   359

Epilogue: Next Year, Jerusalem! The Rise of Educational   370
Technology *David Hawkridge*
Authors' Addresses   395
Index   397

Prologue: Educational Technology: Archetypes, Paradigms and Models

> His Majesty's Ministers, finding that Gulliver's stature exceeded
> theirs in the proportion of twelve to one, concluded from the
> similarity of their bodies that he must contain at least 1728 (or 12^3)
> of theirs, and must needs be rationed accordingly.
>
> *Jonathan Swift*

Like education itself, educational technology has undergone
considerable change over the last twenty years. Although the old fears
about technology still exist, particularly when technology is narrowly
conceived, the basic concepts are gradually being absorbed into the
mainstream of educational thought and practice. Imagination and
technology, aided by a renewed sense of craftsmanship in teaching,
have together enlarged the possibilities of knowledge, action and moral
obligation. At the same time, however, whilst imagination and
technology have expanded the possibilities or range of choices available
to educators, they have also made it more difficult to foresee the full
consequences of the choices made and the actions taken.

Technology, contrary to popular belief, is not necessarily confined
to the *means* by which educators realise their ends. Technology also
raises anew questions about the nature of the ends themselves. It forces
us to reflect on the morality of what we are about, by its very
insistence on defensible choices. By opening up the range of possibilities,
technology in and of education has caused us to reflect upon, and
sometimes to reconsider, the manner in which selections are made, as
well as the purposes for which they are being considered. In other words,
the very richness of the alternatives now available to us, together with
potential for increased effectiveness, forces us to reflect on the ethical
nature of what we have in mind. Unfortunately, the deep satisfaction,
sense of creativity, and feelings of accomplishment that can be
experienced in the *doing* of educational technology are too often
preferred to the related, but very different, pleasures of *contemplating*
educational technology. Yet contemplation and responsibility go hand
in hand, one without the other is meaningless.

Problems of choice

The problem of the standard or criteria against which choices are made
from the range of technological alternatives available is, therefore,
becoming a matter of enhanced importance to both the theory and
practice of education. What is 'best' is not only a technological question,
but also an ethical one. A defensible choice, at the very least, involves
addressing both of these issues, and, in so doing, raises yet again basic

9

questions regarding the nature of education. Different sets of criteria reflect different values, and the idea of value is implicit in the very term 'education'. Richard Peters (1959) speaks of education as initiation into worthwhile activities, and goes on to suggest that:

> Education relates to some sort of processes in which a desirable (eg valued) state of mind develops. It would be as much a logical contradiction to say that a person has been educated and yet the change was in no way desirable as it would be to say that he had been reformed and yet had made no change for the better . . . something of value should be passed on . . . the truth is that being worthwhile is part of what is meant by calling it education.

Thus, tightly bound up with the idea of education is the underlying notion that education is implicitly worthwhile, and that what students learn should be valuable. Since educational technology should contribute to the worthwhileness of the experience, the issues of relevance and justification must constantly be addressed by the technologist. Judgements as well as decisions must be constantly made and questioned.

A *judgement* is a choice between 'right' and 'wrong'; a choice between 'good' and 'bad' or 'true' and 'false'. The goal is to determine who is 'guilty' and who is 'innocent'. This is achieved by weighing the evidence, having previously determined what information will be admissible, and then making a pronouncement or judgement. Implicit in the process is the role of an outside arbiter who forms an authoritative opinion one way or another, providing that there is a case to answer and that it is within jurisdiction. A *decision*, on the other hand, is a choice between a range of alternatives, none of which is probably more right than the others. At the very best, a decision is likely to involve selecting between alternatives that are 'almost right' and 'probably wrong', and, at the very worst, between a range of alternatives between which there is little to choose. Implicit in the process is the role of an inside person, who has the necessary authority to resolve the issue by making a choice appropriate to the circumstances.

In a very real sense, decisions are made prior to an event, before any action has been taken, whereas judgements are more likely to be made after the event when a course of action has been implemented. This distinction is important, in the context of educational technology, for all too often it is overlooked. An educational technologist chooses between the alternatives available by making appropriate decisions on the basis of a set of principles and procedures valued by the profession and founded in a theory or paradigm. The experiences and results that stem from these decisions, however, should subsequently be judged in terms of their worth in an educational endeavour. The question 'What is desirable, and why is it desirable?' is the fundamental and most far-reaching problem facing education. Yet, it is not a question that lends itself to a final answer. All that is possible is to consider it rationally, and for the technologist to attempt to identify the relative merits of the solutions that are proposed for meeting current educational demands. Care should be taken, however, to leave the door open, so that fresh solutions and new evidence can be considered as they become available.

As long as the question is constantly being raised, and educational judgements made, educational technologists will be better able to make decisions more likely to contribute to initiation into worthwhile and morally defensible experiences.

The nature of educational technology

The effectiveness of any form or organised activity largely depends upon an organisation's ability to achieve its goals, fulfil the needs of its members, maintain itself internally, and to adapt to its environment. If an organisation fails to realise these goals, it is 'unhealthy', or steadily ineffective. If an organisation realises them, it is 'healthy', and able to learn through experience, free to change, and free to respond to new circumstances. Educational technology is concerned with these problems in an educational context, and it is characterised by its disciplined approach to a creative organisation of resources for learning. In order to make this contribution to the 'health' of an educational institution, curriculum, programme, course or lesson, an educational technologist uses a body of established principles, know-how and procedures. Indeed, the original meaning of the word 'technology' was concerned with know-how or method, and it was only with the Great Exhibition of 1851 that the word became overly associated with machines.

Although in one very real sense there has always been a technology *of* education (teachers, for instance, use their voices to excite as well as to explain; chalkboards and books have become such commonplace items in classrooms that few think of them as a form of media; lesson planning is a form of systematic development, etc), its 'modern' antecedents are clearly discernible in the so-called educational revolution of the late 1950s. Sir Eric Ashby (1967) actually distinguishes four revolutions in education. The first occurred when society began to differentiate out varying roles, and the task of educating the young was partly shifted from parents to teachers and from homes to schools. The second occurred with the adoption of the written word as an alternative to oral instruction, whilst the third revolution came with the invention of printing which resulted in a wider availability of books. The fourth revolution, Ashby argues, was foreshadowed by developments in electronics, particularly developments in the area of radio, telephone, television, projectors, recorders (both sound and picture), and computers.

The term 'revolution', particularly in the context of education, is distasteful, but the four developments that Ashby identifies have certainly had, and are still having, a remarkable effect on educational practice. Each has brought along a set of problems, still largely with us today. Each has led less to an enlargement of the intellectual realm, and more to a reinforcement of existing traditional institutions and practices — but on a different scale. The problem of the respective responsibilities of the home and school still troubles us today, and the role of the teacher and of the learner in the theatre of education is a matter of continuing concern. The uneasy competition between

11

the written and oral traditions in education is with us still, whilst the present escalating prices of printed books are bringing renewed problems to classroom teachers and students alike. The developments of the fourth or electronic revolution (already in general use in educational research, in growing use in administration, and in some use in the information and library sciences) are now beginning to affect the teaching-learning processes. They are making possible independent study, an enriched variety of courses and methods of instruction, easier access to education, a lessening of routine teaching responsibilities and duties, as well as a more analytical and creative approach to subject matter. Unfortunately, the cost is a very heavy one, not only in terms of money, but even more importantly in terms of the centralising effects that each revolution has introduced into the organisation of education. Whilst some people are concerned with the problems that can come from de-humanising education, too few appear to be concerned with the greater problems which stem from the centralisation of education.

Ashby's four revolutions, if we must continue to use the term, also highlight another problem with educational technology, as it has been utilised. In each case, there has been a tendency, in most instances stemming from inertia, to use the fruits of technology merely to replicate, on a larger and grander scale, traditional institutions and practices (the Open University is a major exception to this rule, as are some of the curriculum development projects of the Schools' Council for Curriculum and Examinations). Instead of viewing educational technology as an opportunity for renewing educational practice, it has, too often, been conceived as a means of doing what has always been done — only more efficiently. Too few educators and parents, until perhaps the 'Great Debate' which took place in Britain in 1977, have overly concerned themselves with asking whether, what can undoubtedly be done more efficiently, ought to be done at all. Something else is needed, and educational technology ought to be a part of it, but this entails questioning the underlying assumptions we make about technology *in* education. Indeed, technology is probably considerably less self-limiting than our own perception or view of it.

The three new educational technologies

Some years ago, Francis Crick, winner of the Nobel Prize for his work on DNA, was asked why it was that only a few scientists made important discoveries. Professor Crick thought for a while, and then said that there were many reasons. Sometimes, it was due to an absence of the necessary resources, or even a lack of opportunity. A piece of experimental evidence could be wrong. Rarely, however, was the failure due to an absence of the necessary facts; usually they were there all the time. The most important reason, he went on to say, was usually that people were handicapped by assumptions that they were not aware they were making. So it is with the assumptions we make about the nature of the educational technology. Indeed, three different technologies can be discerned in the literature, depending upon the assumption made. They can be conveniently referred to as Educational Technology One, Two and Three (Davies, 1972).

EDUCATIONAL TECHNOLOGY ONE

Educational Technology One is essentially a 'hardware' approach, stressing the importance of aids for teaching. Its origin lies in the application of the physical sciences and engineering to the problems of education. This concept tends to dominate most of the classical writings on educational technology. It assumes that a technology of machines is intimately related to a technology of teaching, and that progressive views in education, therefore, are closely associated with possession of the latest projector, language laboratory or computer.

Technology is seen as a means of mechanising or automating the process of teaching with devices that transmit, amplify, distribute, record and reproduce stimuli materials, and thus increase the teacher's impact as well as widen the potential audience. In other words, teachers can use Technology One to deal more efficiently with larger and larger groups of students, increase the power of their teaching, and reach beyond the boundaries of the school or classroom — all without necessarily increasing the cost of students taught, and sometimes even reducing it.

EDUCATIONAL TECHNOLOGY TWO

Educational Technology Two is essentially a 'software' approach, stressing the importance of aids to learning. Its origin lies in the application of behavioural science to the problems of education. This concept tends to dominate most of the current writings on educational technology, particularly in the areas of curriculum, course and instructional development. It assumes that a technology of message design (founded firmly on goal setting, task analysis, motivational principles and evaluation) lies at the heart of efficient learning.

Technology is seen as a means of providing the necessary know-how for designing new, or renewing current, worthwhile learning experiences. Machines and mechanisation are viewed merely as instruments of presentation or transmission. The procedures of curriculum and course development (the predominant British terms) as well as instructional development (the current American term) characteristic of this approach largely revolve around: identifying appropriate aims, goals and objectives; selecting relevant content and subject matter; choosing contrasting learning methodologies, activities and experiences so as to make for a worthwhile and rewarding course of study; and then evaluating not only the success of the resulting learning experience but also the effectiveness of the very development techniques employed.

Teachers can also use Technology Two as a means of enhancing their own teaching. If they are inexperienced, Technology Two provides guidelines or procedures; if they are experienced teachers, Technology Two can be used as a springboard for further craftsmanship. Indeed, much of the curriculum and course renewal that has characterised European and North American education over the last ten years (at primary, secondary and tertiary levels), as well as a great deal of military and industrial training, is a product of the interest that has been taken in Educational Technology Two. The activity is also a testimony to the efficacy of the development procedures available, as well as a warning of the limitations that can be expected if enthusiasm and systematic development activities lose sight of the ultimate 'name of the game'.

EDUCATIONAL TECHNOLOGY THREE

Educational Technology Three combines the 'hardware' and 'software' approaches of the other two technologies. It rejects systematic development (ie step-by-step, rigidly mechanical or mechanistic procedures) as the *only* way of proceeding, in favour of a systemic (ie organic rather than mechanistic) set of procedures focusing rather more deeply on the processes as well as on the products of teaching and learning. It applies system analysis concepts to education, and its bias is somewhat less towards the individual *per se* and rather more towards the group or team within which an individual plays a role. The quality and relevance of the overall experience is one of the major concerns of Technology Three, and accordingly it assumes that the environment within which teaching and learning take place is as important as the actual processes themselves. Authority and organisation in the school, in so far as they are related to both curricular and pastoral matters, and as they affect individuals, groups, institution and community, are subjects of concern. No teacher or student is free to act in total isolation, and neither is an institution like a school or university able to carry on its business without affecting others (see Richardson, 1975). Everything is part of a whole or a living system, and the 'health' of that system is a matter of primary concern, not only for its continued well-being but also for its very survival.

Educators can use Technology Three as a means of enhancing the worthwhileness of what they are about. Whilst Technology One is largely concerned with transmission-reception problems, and Technology Two with purposeful shaping of behaviour, Technology Three is warmly human in its total and integrated approach. Its emphasis is on a range of contrasting skills, from which selections can be made depending upon the nature of the problem posed. It is fundamentally a problem-solving approach, heavy in its diagnostic interest and inquiry orientation. Technologies One and Two can be used, as appropriate, but the orientation and reasons for their use are wider and broader than might otherwise be perceived.

Educational Technology Three, with its primary orientation towards a systemic approach, is characteristically faced with one underlying question. Identifying the boundary of the system, within which problems are occurring, is a matter of enormous practical difficulty. What at first sight might appear to be a nice, self-contained difficulty, can soon become a matter of complexity involving a greatly enlarged context. It is as if 'everything nailed down is coming loose'. Whilst such a discovery might be intellectually exciting, it places an enormous burden of responsibility on the technologist. It is impossible, in the real world, to dismantle everything every time some change is required. Common sense, alone, suggests that there is an underlying advantage, in most cases, to a piecemeal approach, in which one moves by successive approximations towards some desired future. Indeed, this is likely to be one of the reasons why educators so dislike the term 'revolution' as applied to their professional area, with all its connotations of a utopian blueprint — desirable, perhaps, but so out of tune with the realities. Reality for Educational Technology Three is to identify problem boundaries, to deal with the immediate situation, but without always calling for too drastic a remedy. The problem is one of effectiveness, not necessarily one of efficiency.

The skills of effectiveness are particularly revealing as far as they reveal the underlying priorities of a Technology Three approach. They include:

☐ *sensitivity*, so that the needs of the total situation, both people and task, can be sensed
☐ *diagnostic ability*, so that the nature of the problem or difficulty can be identified and communicated
☐ *decision making*, so that appropriate actions can be selected from a wide range of possible alternatives
☐ *flexibility*, so that it is possible to implement whatever the situation demands or requires
☐ *action skills*, so that routine and mechanistic tasks of implementation can be efficiently carried out

Above all, to borrow from Peter Drucker (1966), Educational Technology Three requires an understanding of where a teacher's and student's time goes. It requires a knowledge of how to gear efforts to results, rather than to activities which generate only busy work; how to build on their own and their students' strengths, rather than on their weaknesses. It involves making the right decisions based on 'dissenting opinions', rather than on a 'consensus of the facts'. All this means focusing upon opportunities, rather than on problems, and on those few key areas that will produce outstanding results, rather than on trying to achieve everything and fail through lack of time (see Davies, 1976).

Archetypes, paradigms and models of educational technology

As in any area of disciplined inquiry, educational technologists never theorise in a vacuum. The way in which an educational problem is stated, the principles and concepts that are used, all provide a starting point. Empirical data, assumptions, professional perspectives are all used to illuminate the situation, as well as to suggest a range of appropriate strategies and tactics that might be employed. Other factors, as Phillips (1971) points out, can influence such theorising; factors such as simplicity, robustness, elegance and sophistication are often important, as is coherence with established theories in education and educational technology. In other words, educational technologists always have a theory, sometimes crude and at other times highly sophisticated, that shapes the way a situation is seen, and influences the values that

15

surround it. Since there is little currently in the literature that seeks to examine the theories of educational technology, it is important to use this opportunity to take stock — so that the papers making up this volume can be viewed in the light of the different positions they represent and the values that they espouse.

Three terms are often used in the general literature dealing with disciplined acts of inquiry, all of which have quite specific technical meanings. The three terms are 'archetype', 'paradigm' and 'model'. Since the term 'model' is often used in the literature of educational technology, usually with a lack of precision, it is important to consider what is being said and more often suggested when the term is employed. Indeed, the literature of educational technology, and more especially that of curriculum, course and instructional development, is replete with competing models, all of which suggest different ways of proceeding, and most of which appear to indicate values more appropriate to engineering than to an education.

AN ARCHETYPE

The viewpoint or perspective used by someone engaged in an act of inquiry is most often referred to as an 'archetype' or 'root metaphor'. It acts as a loose theoretical framework or prototype, a primordial image or pattern that seems constantly to recur throughout the professional literature. More importantly, it is consistent enough in its occurrence to be considered a universal principle or algorithm for thought and action.

The term, which was first used in English around 1605, is part of the vocabulary of historians, anthropologists and psychologists. Jung (1922) uses the term in the context of a 'primordial image', a 'psychic residue', which constantly tends to repeat itself in human experience. Frazer, in *The Golden Bough*, uses the word to trace elemental patterns of myth and ritual, which recur in the legends and ceremonials of diverse cultures. The term has also been used in literary criticism (by Wilson Knight, Robert Graves and Northrop Frye) to identify narrative designs, character types or images which are said to be identifiable in a wide range of writings. The term is also meaningful in educational technology as a descriptor for the myths, dreams and ritualised modes of professional conduct, which — rather than be seen for what they are — have often been taken for what they are not. They hold the profession together, offer a language of belief, and bind the community in a set of common acts and assumptions. The current myth of concern and the liturgy of action, as evidenced by the basic *engineering* archetype, threatens to become for educational technology a limitation to further creative efforts.

A PARADIGM

An archetype can serve a number of different paradigms, but more usually only one paradigm is involved — although the paradigm may be presented differently or in varying degrees of detail or complexity. In essence, a paradigm is a more concrete conceptualisation of an underlying idea or theory, involving definitions, statements and interrelationships between the statements. Some refining has taken place so that a coherent tradition of research and practice is possible. The paradigm, which is usually qualitative in nature, may be expressed in words, in numbers or in some other type of visual display. A diagram, illustrating important relationships by means of a series of boxes and arrows, is often used. In this way, a unique description of the phenomena can be portrayed, underlying methodologies indicated and research questions worthy of further study suggested. The paradigm may also be used to help explain events previously unexplained.

Unlike the archetype, a paradigm rarely represents a dramatic new orientation, nor does it attempt to offer a 'world view' or wide embracing perspective of the nature of reality. It is much too limited and applied for that. However, as in educational technology, a particular paradigm can be recognised in two important ways:

- □ it is sufficiently novel and appealing to attract an enduring group of adherents away from competing ways of proceeding
- □ it is sufficiently open-ended to allow adherents to pursue all sorts of problems in a manner that allows them to refine and define the details of the basic paradigm, as well as to attract new adherents.

To put it another way, it can usually be assumed that where there is a small group of people working together, with shared values and concerns, the liturgy and rituals of their activities indicate that there is likely to be a shared paradigm. The paradigm acts as a cohesive and binding force for their work.

Once a paradigm or series of paradigms has been proposed, there will still be details and ambiguities to be identified and resolved. This type of activity will commonly result in different variations of the basic paradigm design. The basic principle remains, but the emphasis, priorities and particulars may change. In fact, the number of paradigm variations can be endless, and often a new paradigm is promised when nothing more than another variation is proposed. So it is with educational technology, and even more particularly with curriculum, course and instructional development. The paradigms that are currently available are worryingly limited, although the variations offered seem endlessly lacking in anything creatively different.

A MODEL

Curriculum, course and instructional development is rich in so-called 'models', which in the manner of the preceding discussion are technically paradigms. A model, which usually has a quantitative dimension, is a much more specific and detailed representation of reality. Just as a child's model car bears a quantitative relationship to the real thing, so that the distance between the rear wheels on the model can be used to calculate the distance between them on the real car, so a model in science bears a quantitative relationship to reality. A map is a model, distances on the map represent distances on the ground, a mathematical equation is a model, and so is a photograph. Simulators are also models, as are some games.

The idea of modelling is hardly new. Early astronomers made models of the universe as they conceived it, engineers made models of the bridges and aquaducts they designed, and architects have long made models of the buildings they wished to build. What is new, is the recognition that is currently given to models, and the extent to which they are currently employed as a basis for intellectual activity. Three main reasons suggest themselves for this growth and ready acceptance (Starr, 1971). First, the deliberate manipulation of people and organisations is ethically questionable and in many cases now unlawful. Secondly, the amount of uncertainty with which professional people have to deal has been increasing rapidly, so that errors are more probable at a time when the costs (human and financial) associated with them are increasing at an alarming rate. Finally, as a result of developments in operations research, our ability to build models that are good representations of reality has improved to such a degree that there has been increased interest and confidence in their usefulness.

The underlying purpose of building a paradigm is to falsify it, so that it can be replaced with a more accurate portrayal. On the other hand, the underlying purpose of building a particular model is to exploit or use it in the solution of a particular problem. Models are usually specific to a particular phenomenon, and quite different models may represent the same phenomenon from quite different paradigmatic viewpoints. Exploiting Bohr's principle of complementarity in physics as a paradigm, for instance, it is possible to model 'light' both as particles travelling as straight lines, and as a series of wave trains without being inconsistent. The great property of the paradigm is its 'suggestive power', whereas the importance of the model lies in the manner in which it is possible to formulate associated hypotheses so that they can be tested.

In educational technology, few of the models — with the possible exception of the models of Aptitude-Treatment Interaction (ATIs) — have been tested, with the worrying result that so much of the empirical investigations have taken place without reference to an underlying theory. Instead, the field has been overly characterised by a vast amount of small pieces of self-contained research, which is often difficult to put together into a coherent framework useful as a guide for future action. An attempt to make such a contribution has been made in the area of pre-instructional strategies (Hartley & Davies, 1976), where the empirical findings concerning behavioural objectives, pre-tests, advance organisers and overviews have been reviewed in an attempt to indicate their several roles in a range of contrasting instructional situations.

Objective and subjective paradigms in educational technology

As we have already seen, the concept of educational technology implies for many people a systematic approach to learning 'in which one tries to develop means to achieve given ends and persists in one's attempts to find solutions to problems' (MacKenzie, Eraut & Jones, 1976). The basic and all pervasive archetype appears to be an engineering one, and the associated paradigms are heavily biased towards the kinds of objectivity traditionally valued in science as normally perceived (see Kuhn, 1970). This has led to a suspicion amongst educators that the notion of objectivity is the *only* paradigm possible in educational technology, especially in the areas of curriculum, course and instructional development. It is as if perception, consensually validated, is the only professionally acceptable way of knowing and understanding reality. Yet an alternative is available, and an alternative that is particularly valuable in the domain of educational technology. This alternative involves the notion that there is available a subjective paradigm, and that both objectivity and subjectivity are themselves assumptions.

The very process of observation, in an educational context, interferes with what is being observed, as it does in any other situation, so that the phenomenon observed is changed by the very act of observing it. Eddington (see Heisenberg, 1958) put the matter dramatically when he wrote:

> We have found that where science has progressed the farthest, the mind has but regained from nature that which the mind put into nature. We have found a strange footprint on the shores of the unknown. We have devised profound theories, one after another, to account for its origin. At last, we have succeeded in reconstructing the creature that made the footprint. And lo! It is our own.

The inescapable conclusion to be drawn would appear to be that there are limits to objectivity, and that knowledge leads back to the people engaged in the act of inquiry. Problems are solved by people, and the data they collect is contaminated by the people making the very act of observation and perception, analysis and evaluation. This thought, however, is so alien to some traditional ways of thinking developed by educational technologists, although not to many teachers in the humanities, that it has only been in the last few years that any attempt has been made to accommodate the idea by developing a new archetype based not on engineering but on creative problem solving. Lateral, rather than vertical, thinking (see de Bono, 1976), like Zen, has become a fashionable and useful archetype with associated paradigms.

A great deal of the present concern in education with morality and ethical matters can be viewed as a direct contribution of the subjective paradigm. Poole (1972), for instance, argues that since the 'body is the locus of all ethical experience, all experience is, because spatial, ethical. There can be no act which does not take place in ethical space. There can be no "flaccid" act, no act devoid of all significance, no unconditioned act.' In other words, knowledge and responsibility are both aspects of the subjective paradigm and ethical concerns have little or no role in a world seen from the viewpoint of an objective paradigm. Such a thought is of particular importance to educational technology, since the antecedents of so many of its procedures are clearly discernible in the principles of behaviourism. The very advantages claimed for behaviourism, as viewed from the perspective of the objective paradigm, raise important ethical questions for education when viewed from the alternative perspective of the subjective paradigm. Dogmatism and scepticism, however, are human failings associated with both paradigms, and at the very end technologists are still faced with the problem of making a judgement and a series of associated decisions about technology.

Three archetypes and three paradigms of educational technology

In the light of the preceding discussion, it is possible to identify three archetypes that have developed in educational technology. The first archetype is an audio-visual one, and although initially developed in the media field in the 1930s it became particularly important in the years following the second world war. The second archetype is an engineering one, which came into prominence with the emerging interest in programmed learning in the early 1960s and is still with us to a very large extent to this day. The third archetype is a problem-solving one, highly related to the creative process, which is currently emerging as a focal point of the more innovative curriculum, course and instructional development activities currently under way in both the United Kingdom and the United States.

Each one of these archetypes has led to the development of a series of related paradigms. Although more than one paradigm has developed for each of the 'root metaphors', the differences are more in detail than in substance. Accordingly, it is possible to indicate the major concerns and development procedures by looking at one paradigm for each of the three archetypes. For the sake of illustration, a metaphor is used for each paradigm in order to indicate the flavour of the underlying approach. As with all figurative language, the metaphors should not be taken literally or even too seriously. Figure 1 illustrates both the three paradigms of educational technology, and their associated metaphors. In each case, additional boxes, circles and arrows could have been added to the diagrams, as well as more labels. The aim, however, has not been to be as exhaustive as possible, but to convey the major thrust of each of the three contrasting approaches.

THE AUDIO-VISUAL ARCHETYPE

The Audio-Visual Archetype predates the other archetypes of educational technology, which perhaps explains why media departments in so many of our universities have associated with them, as an apparent anomaly, curriculum, course or development activities. The associated metaphor is one of a gum-ball machine, 'you put in your money and you are given something to chew on.' So it is with the associated paradigm. Educational technology or, more accurately, the associated audio-visual 'hardware' can be used to: aid classroom presentations and teaching; serve as a means of improving classroom demonstrations by allowing students to experience what normally would not be available to them; help solve logistical problems (as in the use of radio and television, films and sound tapes) by enabling teachers to deal with

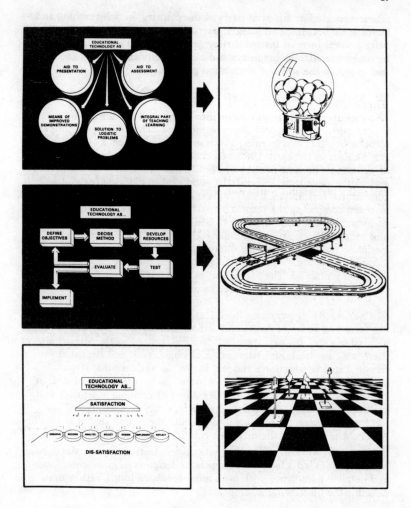

Figure 1. *Paradigms and metaphors of educational technology*

learners located in different parts of the country; enrich teaching and learning by becoming an integral part of both processes; and, finally, offer a novel form of instrumenting assessment and testing procedures by making available computers and other machines so as to automate and speed up the whole examination process.

THE ENGINEERING ARCHETYPE

The Engineering Archetype came into being with the advent of programmed learning, and the application of behaviouristic technology to both teaching and learning as a result of the influence of Professor B F Skinner in the early 1960s. Operant conditioning, and the shaping of behaviour, became part of a radically new technology in education and, at the same time, generated a good deal of emotion for and against educational technology itself. A great deal of the initial effort, therefore, involved comparing the respective performance of classroom teachers and teaching machines in order to demonstrate the advantages of the new methodology. It was a similar technique to that still used in medicine and pharmacology, where a new procedure or drug is tested in a comparative situation, with one group given the new treatment and the other a placebo. The metaphor, in both instances, is that of a slot-car race, in which one car is raced against another in order to see who wins.

The underlying paradigm in educational technology normally takes the form of a series of boxes and arrows, usually with a feedback loop, indicating a step-by-step approach to development work. Almost always there is a clear beginning (definition of objectives), and almost always a terminal step (evaluation). Indeed, the initial and terminal steps have become so threatening to classroom teachers that a great deal of emotion has been generated on the subject of defining objectives and evaluating teaching. The debate, however, really centres around the mechanistic character of the paradigm, and the notion that it is possible to regard each one of the different activities associated with development work as self-contained entities. Unfortunately, the debate has sometimes led a few technologists to design even more complicated and detailed paradigms, with even more feedback loops, rather than examine the underlying assumptions.

THE PROBLEM-SOLVING ARCHETYPE

The Problem-Solving Archetype began to be adopted around 1973 to 1974, and, although still not characteristic of the everyday activities of the majority of educational technologists, it is fast becoming an alternative way of seeing. The associated metaphor is that of a chess game, in which players engage in an intellectual activity for which there is no one set of appropriate moves. Intense concentration, ability to foresee the future consequences of current actions, flexibility, and acquired skill and learning experience are all essential prerequisites for success *and* a rewarding experience. So it is with educational technology. In the educational context some sort of dissatisfaction should preface development activities, and the overall goal should then be to reach a state of satisfaction as quickly as possible. In order to accomplish this, an educational technologist brings to the situation a range of skills (observation, analysis, synthesis, etc). The order, and manner, in which they are then used depends upon the character of the problem, and the aim in mind. There is no one best way, and no one way of proceeding. Neither is there one optimal solution. Everything depends upon the situation, and the skills available.

FOUR CLASSES OF PROBLEM

Generally speaking, four broad classes of problem can be recognised in the work of an educational technologist, each associated with a set of appropriate ways of tackling them. The four classes of problem can be identified as: problems of deviation, problems of improvement or renewal, problems of prediction, and problems of acceptance. Problems of deviation occur when there is a gap or deviation from some known standard, and the gap is of sufficient magnitude to warrant some form of corrective action. Examples of this will be found in the present concern amongst parents and teachers with the ability of children to engage in the fundamental skills of reading, writing and reckoning when they leave school.

Problems of improvement or renewal are basically concerned with situations where there is a perceived need to bring about some improvement. This may involve renewing what is being experienced, as well as improving what is being accomplished. Any programme or course can become, over the years, out of tune with the times, and reflection and development are necessary to bring it back into the mainstream. An example of this kind of activity in educational technology is to be found in the growing concern with needs assessment, and the importance of examining the source of many of the ideas underlying the curriculum. Where objectives come from is a much more important question than how they should be written or identified.

Problems of prediction are gradually becoming more frequent in the experience of educational technologists. They basically involve situations in which there is a need to anticipate emerging or future changes in society and the economy, which are likely to have significant effects upon education. An example of this might be found in industry, where the development of a new process entails training workpeople to operate a plant before it has even been constructed. Predicting the training needs, in such a situation, is a demanding operation, for one is really carrying out a task analysis before the event. However, the weight of the evidence is very strong in favour of such techniques, and work in this area has been carried out by the author and his students over the last three years in both the chemical and coke industries.

Problems of acceptance have always faced us. The problems of dealing with planned change are paramount, and the diffusion and adoption of ideas is a matter of prime importance in education. Although a wide range of strategies and tactics are available to the educational technologist, resistance and inertia often present seemingly insuperable barriers. Overcoming these is no mean task, and the educational technologist is intimately involved in their solution.

23

Conclusion

Educational technology is coming of age. Three contrasting archetypes are available, and each has had developed a set of related paradigms for future action. It has, at last, been generally realised that there is no one best way of proceeding, and that there can be no one educational technology. Scepticism and dogmatism have had their day, and for the educational technologist, as for Kant in his *Critique of Pure Reason,* 'the critical path is alone open.' Criticism, or evaluation, is becoming the underlying theory of educational technology, rather than merely a sub-component of the process. Educators devoting themselves to technology, however it is conceived, without a sense of distinctive purpose, can never be more than second-class citizens. Educators, on the other hand, who devote themselves to technology, with a conception of criticism, evaluation or reflection as the basic theory, place educational technology in its proper light as having a central rather than peripheral role in matters of educational concern. It is this point that we are fast reaching, but our success will depend upon our ability to develop useful models for action.

References

Ashby, E (1967) Machines, understanding and learning: reflections on technology in education, *The Graduate Journal* 7 2 : 359-73

Black, M (1962) *Models and Metaphors.* Ithaca, New York : Cornell

Davies, I K (1972) *The Management of Learning.* London : McGraw Hill (published as *Competency Based Learning* in the USA)

Davies, I K (1976) *Objectives in Curriculum Design.* London & New York : McGraw Hill

de Bono, E (1976) *Teaching Thinking.* London : Temple Smith

Drucker, P F (1966) *The Effective Executive.* New York : Harper & Row

Frazer, J G (1871) *The Golden Bough.* London : Macmillan

Hartley, J and Davies, I K (1976) Pre-instructional strategies: the role of pre-tests, behavioural objectives, overviews and advance organizers, *Review of Educational Research* 46 2 : 239-65

Heisenberg, W (1958) *The Physicist's Conception of Nature.* London : Longman

Jung, C (1922) On the relations of analytical psychology to poetic art. In *Contributions to Analytical Psychology.* London : Paul Trench and Trubner

Kuhn, T S (1970) *The Structure of Scientific Revolutions.* Chicago : University of Chicago Press

MacKenzie, N, Eraut, M and Jones, H C (1976) *Teaching and Learning: an Introduction to New Methods and Resources in Higher Education.* Paris : UNESCO Press

Peters, R S (1959) *Authority, Responsibility and Education.* London : Routledge & Kegan Paul

Phillips, D C (1971) *Theories, Values and Education.* Melbourne, Australia : Melbourne University Press

Poole, R (1972) *Towards Subjectivity.* New York : Wiley

Richardson, E (1975) *Authority and Organization in the Secondary School.* London : Macmillan

Starr, M K (1971) *Management: a Modern Approach.* New York : Harcourt Brace Jovanovich

Part One: Theoretical Developments in Educational Technology

Introduction

The relationship between theory and practice is a symbiotic one: theory contributes to practice, and practice contributes to theory. In the last decade, in the area of instructional technology, we have seen this very clearly. There has been a swing against the theory that guided the earlier practice and the present practice has influenced the latest theories.

In particular, there has been a marked rise and fall in the use of Skinner's operant conditioning approach to the design of instructional materials. Practice has shown us how human learning is much more complex. The notion that human learners are passive recipients of instruction who can be reinforced in a variety of ways has been replaced by the view that learners are active processors of information using varying strategies to remember and utilise knowledge (strategies which they can switch on and off in different contexts), and that they are very flexible. New theories in educational technology reflect this change of viewpoint. Educational technology today is seen as contributing to our knowledge about how to cater for the differences between individuals in various learning situations.

In accepting this, however, we must recognise that operant conditioning and reinforcement still play an important part in human learning. Behaviour is almost always affected by its consequences, and it would be foolish to cast out this baby with the bathwater. Reinforcement is one technique amongst many that can be used to let the learner know how well he is succeeding — itself a cardinal principle in successful learning, albeit one that requires careful explication (see Paper 1.4).

The aim of Paper 1.1 ('Learning theory in practice') is to review these older conceptions of learning theory that are being refined by modern practice in order to see what guidelines they have to offer for instruction today. The paper looks at guidelines stemming from stimulus-response, cognitive, and social learning theories. It examines how these approaches can still be seen separately, and in combination, in some present-day instructional situations. Some of these situations provide prime examples of today's educational technology in practice. Paper 1.1 thus provides the background for many other papers in this text.

Paper 1.2 ('What does it take to learn?') illustrates a cognitive

27

approach to learning. It is concerned with how university students grapple with complex text. The crucial matters being discussed are the different levels of understanding displayed by students, and how this understanding is arrived at. This notion is taken further by Gordon Pask in Paper 1.3. Here machinery is used to exteriorise the learners' thinking processes. The approaches described in these two papers take us far from operant conditioning: the authors are concerned with the nature of understanding, with the use of student strategies, with learning how to learn, and with what Lewis calls the quality of learning (Paper 3.5).

Pask's paper (Paper 1.3) is concerned in addition with how the organisation and the structure of complex material can be presented to learners. Should this be done for them, or should they (guided by computer-based learning techniques) organise it for themselves? This consideration — the organisation of material — is taken up further by Roger Hartley and Kenneth Lovell (in Paper 1.4) when they discuss psychological principles relevant to computer-assisted learning. The principles they discuss in detail are the use of feedback, the use of organisational aids, and the use of self — *versus* instructor — control. In all three areas they are concerned to indicate the possibilities available, and to suggest in which situations which alternatives seem most viable. Hartley and Lovell suggest that few computer-based programs fully exploit the possibilities available, but that development along these lines is possible.

Paper 1.5 by Richard Snow examines more explicitly the problems posed by individual differences for instruction. He notes that four aptitudes are specially important. These are intelligence, achievement motivation (whether through independence or conformity), anxiety and prior knowledge. What he argues in his paper is that these variables interact with different teaching methods, and that it is one of the aims of educational technologists to develop a theory of individual differences.

In Paper 1.6 Ivor Davies takes up the point that introducing new methods of instruction invariably involves making an intervention of some kind into an already ongoing system. Such an activity presents its own special problems — as noted in the Prologue. Paper 1.6 argues and develops the view that careful management is required for any intervention to work successfully. A similar theme is addressed in more practical terms by Richard Hooper in Paper 2.8.

Part 1 concludes with a brief paper written by Marten Shipman for a conference not related to educational technology. Nonetheless, Shipman is making an important point, and it is one that is expounded in detail in his book *The Organisation and Impact of Social Research*. This paper is included here to indicate (with Paper 1.6) the growing awareness of researchers that research does not take place in a social vacuum and that researchers have some rather special responsibilities. Education in general, and educational technology in particular, provides a multi-faceted set of theoretical, practical, social, small and large educational and political problems. No single answer, however well presented, will be a final solution. Shipman, however, suggests some ways in which some of the mistakes of the past might be avoided.

Finally, we need to note here that the papers in this introductory section, and indeed throughout the text, assume a certain familiarity with terms like teaching machines, programmed learning, operant conditioning and educational technology. If the reader is a novice in the field, we suggest that it might be best to read first the final paper of this book — the Epilogue — for in this paper David Hawkridge traces the history of the development of educational technology from its earliest days. Reading this paper will bring back fond memories for *aficionados*, and it will sketch in the background for the beginner. For completion, however, Hawkridge's paper needs to be supplemented by an account of the development of computer-assisted learning: for this the reader might like to refer to the paper by Bunderson and Faust (1976).

Suggested further reading

Bunderson, C V and Faust, G W (1976) Programmed and computer assisted instruction. In N L Gage (ed) *The Psychology Teaching Methods.* Chicago : NSSE, University of Chicago Press

Eggleston, J (1977) *The Ecology of the School.* London : Methuen

Entwistle, N and Hounsell, D (eds) (1976) *How Students Learn.* Lancaster : Institute for Research and Development in Post-Compulsory Education, University of Lancaster

Gagné, R M (1977) *The Conditions of Learning* (3rd edition). New York : Holt, Rinehart & Winston

Glaser, R (1977) *Adaptive Education: Individual Diversity and Learning.* New York : Holt, Rinehart & Winston

McDonald, B and Walker, R (1976) *Changing the Curriculum.* London : Open Books

Shipman, M E (ed) (1976) *The Organisation and Impact of Social Research.* London : Routledge and Kegan Paul

1.1 Learning Theory in Practice

JAMES HARTLEY

Introduction

In this paper I want to examine the application of theories of learning to instruction. I want to examine the limitations of the theories in this respect, and I want to suggest that dissatisfaction with theories of learning in the mid 1950s and 1960s led to a number of divergent responses. Two of these responses were first, an interest in theories of instruction and secondly, a move away from laboratory studies of learning with animals to classroom research involving meaningful subject matter, realistic learning situations and actual teachers.

The paper is divided into five parts: part one presents the 'laws' or 'principles' of learning as they existed in the 1950s; part two shows how the influence of these principles is still present today; part three examines some criticisms of the principles; part four indicates reactions to these criticisms; and part five points out some recent trends and problems in the field of educational research. To do all this properly and in detail is beyond the scope of such a short paper so some of the points made and some of the examples given will necessarily be brief.

The principles of learning

Hilgard and Bower (1975) conclude their text *Theories of Learning* with a chapter entitled 'Theory of instruction'. In this they list a number of principles drawn from theories of learning which they consider to be potentially useful in practice. The list contains twenty-one items and, as an aside, it is interesting to observe that it is very little different from an earlier list produced nearly twenty years ago (Hilgard, 1959). Of course different writers have produced different lists and different writers have classified the literature in different ways: Bugelski (1964), for example, lists fifty-eight principles, mainly drawn from conditioning theories, and Knowles (1973) provides interesting illustrations of the many different ways of categorising major learning theories. However, I have chosen to base this discussion primarily on Hilgard and Bower because (i) it is an authoritative text, and (ii) it makes my task simpler!

Hilgard and Bower divide their principles into three categories:

(i) principles emphasised within stimulus-response (S-R) theory;
(ii) principles emphasised within cognitive theory; and (iii) principles
from motivation, personality and social psychology. The following is
a shorter account than their own, and I have rewritten some items,
particularly section (iii), rather differently. What then are these
principles which are potentially useful in practice?

PRINCIPLES EMPHASISED IN S-R THEORY

Activity. Learning is better when the learner is active rather than
passive. As Hilgard and Bower put it, ' "Learning by doing" is still an
acceptable slogan.' This does not imply that people do not learn
anything if they are passive but rather that they are likely to learn more
if they are actively involved in the learning.

Repetition, generalisation, discrimination. If learning is to become
appropriate to a wide (or narrow) range of stimuli, then these ideas
imply that frequent practice, and practice in varied contexts, is
necessary for it to take place. Skills — of any kind — are not acquired
without considerable practice.

Reinforcement is the cardinal motivator — the effects of the
consequences on subsequent behaviour are important — whether they
be extrinsic (reward from a teacher) or intrinsic (self-reward). As
Hilgard and Bower put it, 'While there are some lingering questions
over details, it is generally found that positive reinforcers (rewards,
successes) are to be preferred to negative reinforcers (punishments,
failures).'

PRINCIPLES EMPHASISED IN COGNITIVE THEORY

Organisation and structure. A hallmark of efficient instruction is
that it is well organised by the instructor (although one man's
organisation may be different from another's). Organised material is
easier to learn and to remember than unorganised material. Relatedly,
subject matters are said to have inherent structures — logical
relationships between key ideas and concepts — which link the parts
together. Well-structured materials are more easily understood and
better remembered than are poorly structured ones. Organisation —
how the teacher sequences the material — and structure — the inherent
logic of the material — are thus closely related issues.

Perceptual features. Human beings attend selectively to different
features of the environment, so the way in which a problem is
displayed to the learner is important in helping him to understand it.
(Procedures which convey in advance the structure of a topic to learners
provide appropriate illustrations.)

Learning with understanding is better than learning by rote, or
without understanding. For a person to acquire something new it must
fit in with what he already knows. The job of the teacher is to show
how the new material fits in with what has gone before, and to
indicate in what ways it is new or different.

Cognitive feedback. is the provision of information to the learner
about his success or failure concerning the task in hand. This feedback

may be intrinsic or extrinsic. The information is only of use, of course, if the learner understands it — ie if it is appropriate to the task which he has set himself. In S-R theory the term 'reinforcement' is often used largely in this sense of 'providing information' rather than simply 'reward', and another term commonly used here is 'knowledge of results'.

Differences between individuals are important in how they affect learning. As well as differences in intellectual ability and personality (such as extraversion, need for achievement and locus of control), differences in 'cognitive style' also affect learning. A 'cognitive style' signifies an individual's preference and ability for certain kinds of information selection and processing. Some main contenders for inclusion here are differences in flexibility, impulsiveness, and styles of thought (such as convergent-divergent and serialist-wholist). Individual differences are relevant, of course, to both cognitive and personality theories.

PRINCIPLES EMPHASISED IN PERSONALITY THEORY AND SOCIAL PSYCHOLOGY

Learning is a natural process. Human beings have a natural propensity for learning — one cannot stop them doing it. People by nature are curious beings who constantly absorb information: they are natural decision makers and problem solvers. Learning is not something that is 'done' at school, and nowhere else.

Purposes and goals. Learning is not conducted in a vacuum. Learners have needs, goals and purposes which provide important motivators for learning and for the setting of future goals. Many decisions about what to learn result from long-term goals which may have been decided on much earlier. (The importance of goals is, of course, also relevant to cognitive theories.)

Choice, relevance and responsibility. Learning is better when the material to be learned is personally relevant, and when the learner is responsible for his own learning. Significant learning, it is argued, only takes place when the learner chooses what he wants to learn, how he wants to learn it, and when he wants to learn it.

The social situation. Learning is rarely an isolated event. The group atmosphere of learning (competition *v* co-operation, authoritarianism *v* democracy, the value systems of teachers and pupils) will all affect both success and satisfaction in learning.

Anxiety and emotion. Learning which involves the emotions and feelings as well as the intellect is the most lasting and most pervasive kind. Significant learning only takes place in a non-threatening environment.

COMMENTS

These three groups of principles are, of course, not mutually exclusive and it is difficult, in fact, to envisage a learning situation in which they do not all apply simultaneously in varying degrees. What has happened, in practice, as we shall see below, is that the influence of the three major categories is still strong in new teaching methods and many of the principles are now being used in combination. Theories that actually attempt to combine content, cognition and individual differences are rare, although some (ambitious) attempts are now being made in this direction (eg Pask, 1975; Scandura, 1977).

Modern applications of the principles of learning

In this section of the paper I want to describe modern teaching methods in which the influence of the early principles can still be clearly seen. In examining these modern applications some examples, because of space limitations, will be mentioned very briefly (with appropriate references) but others will be developed in more detail.

APPLICATIONS IN THE STIMULUS-RESPONSE TRADITION

There are today several examples of teaching methods which demonstrate an application of the traditional S-R approach. Behaviour modification schemes including token economies have been used with schoolchildren of varying ages, with the mentally retarded and with juvenile delinquents (eg see Azrin, 1977; Howe, 1972; Kiernan & Woodford, 1975; Thoresen, 1974).

The example I would like to mention more fully in this section is that known as the Keller plan (see Paper 3.4) or PSI (personalised system of instruction) or just simply as behavioural instruction (Robin, 1976). The main feature of this kind of instruction — which has been widely used in introductory courses at the tertiary level of education — is that students work on their own at their own pace with units (or chapters) of text. Each student has to demonstrate mastery of the unit (by taking a test) before he is allowed to proceed to the next unit, and most of the organisation and testing is carried out by fellow students or 'proctors'. Lectures are occasionally given as a source of motivation rather than instruction. Many different procedures are possible within this general framework (eg the mastery of the units may be paced, contracts may be established for various amounts of work done, and so on) but, in general terms, behavioural instruction combines the ideas of the student doing the work when he wants to do it, learning with peers, self-paced mastery performance and immediate knowledge of results. Assessments of behavioural instruction by Kulik *et al* (1976) and of variants on it by Robin (1976) have shown it to be remarkably effective. Kulik *et al* conclude their review by saying, 'In our judgement, this is the most impressive record achieved by a teaching method in higher education. It stands in stark contrast to the inconclusive results of earlier comparisons of college teaching methods.'

MODERN APPLICATIONS OF COGNITIVE THEORY

The principles drawn from cognitive psychology are not as clear cut as those from stimulus-response theory, and they have to some extent become absorbed in common practice. It is not unusual, for example, for modern programmed texts to have overview summaries (or 'maps') and indexes — although such approaches scarcely featured in the earlier examples of programmed learning. Thus in this section I shall report influences rather than direct applications. Work on the importance of meaningful verbal learning is best exemplified by the work of Ausubel (Ausubel, 1963, 1969; Ausubel & Robinson, 1969). Work on the design of typographical layouts for conveying the structure of complex text has been described by Hartley (1978). Work on various so-called 'cognitive styles' and their interactions with different teaching methods has been summarised by Glaser (1973) and Cronbach and Snow (1977). Work on teaching *via* problem solving — and the difficulties this causes for different individuals — has been discussed by Barrows (1976) and Cowan (1977). As the main illustration in this section, however, I would like to mention again the importance of the notions of sequence and structure and to indicate how two psychologists, with widely different orientations, are tackling these topics.

Robert Gagné (1977) claims that much subject matter is organised *hierarchically*, and that this has implications for the sequencing of instruction. Figure 1 shows some schematic diagrams of topics with different structures. All that one has to do to discover this structure is to ask, 'What skills does a learner have to have in order to do this task when given only the instructions to do it?' Answers to this question provide material to which one can apply the same question, and so on, producing a sub-set of skills, or more technically a cumulative hierarchy of sub-tasks. Figure 1 shows different examples, but basically the argument is the same: success at the task on one level below, and so on reading down the figures. The phrase 'cumulative hierarchy' simply argument is the same: success at the task on one level requires the ability to perform successfully at the task on the level below, and so on, reading down the figures. The phrase 'cumulative hierarchy' simply implies that in order to learn successfully the learner must be able to succeed at one level before he can continue to the next.

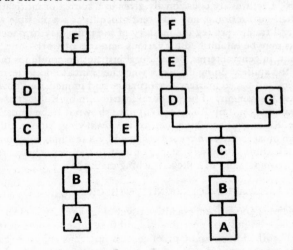

Figure 1. *Simplified examples of the hierarchical nature of topics (after Resnick, 1973)*

In his earlier work Gagné stressed that in order to achieve full mastery of a skill a pupil should master each sub-skill in order up the hierarchy, and he applied the hierarchical notion to all kinds of subject matter. Today these views are not so strictly held. Gagné (1968) for instance distinguishes between the presentation of topics and the skill inherent in them. He states: 'Regardless of presentation sequence, if one is able to identify the intellectual skills that are learned he will find them to generate positive transfer in an orderly fashion.' Others have argued (eg Hawkins *et al*, 1975) that if situation D requires knowledge of A, B and C some teachers would prefer to present D as a problem-solving situation involving A, B and C, rather than start straight away with A.

Gordon Pask (1975) talks more about a *network* of connections forming an 'entailment structure' to describe the structure of a topic. Paper 1.3 (by Pask) provides examples to show that in some respects the end result is very similar, but Pask draws more attention than Gagné to the logical interrelatedness of all the elements in the structure and to how the interrelations match the cognitive structures of the learners involved. The figures given in Paper 1.3 oversimplify the problem: the more detailed networks provided by Pask (1975) are extremely complex.

The aim of both of these workers, however, is to try and determine the nature of subject matter in order to devise teaching sequences from it. Again Gagné and Pask differ on how the sequences are to be derived from the structure. Oversimplifying once more, we might say that Gagné would be more prescriptive than Pask — deciding the sequence for learners in general on the basis of the hierarchy, whereas Pask would be more likely to show the structure (in a simplified way) to particular learners and let them, by means of computer-assisted instruction, determine their own way through it. Gagné is thus more concerned with probable sequences for groups of learners: Pask with individuals. In passing we may note here again that there are many more ways of sequencing than the ones just suggested: Posner and Strike (1976), for example, describe seventeen different possibilities. This paper is summarised in Paper 2.3.

Task and subject-matter analysis are important features of computer-assisted instruction, and the reader may have observed that computer-assisted instruction has been placed in the context of cognitive rather than stimulus-response psychology. This position, of course, is different from that taken by some commentators but I believe this approach to be justified on at least two grounds: (i) most of the personnel involved in computer-assisted instruction are not behavioural psychologists, and (ii) the research conducted by workers in the field of computer-assisted learning is, by its very nature, more complex than that done originally in the field of programmed learning (see Hartley, 1974). In computer-assisted learning it is not unusual to be tackling complex problem-solving skills, or even allowing children to write their own instructional programmes (see Paper 3.3). Cognitive styles are also considered to be of importance (see Pask, 1976).

MODERN APPLICATIONS OF PERSONALITY THEORY

Modern applications of personality theory as outlined above are perhaps best illustrated in an extreme form in the work of the deschooling movement. Goodman, Holt, Illich, Reimer and others have all described how organisational forces acting in the classroom can markedly affect how children learn and teachers teach (see Lister, 1974). Speaking more generally we can view the debate about 'traditional *versus* progressive' primary teaching (eg Bennett, 1976) as related to the personality principles described earlier. How these principles tie in with attitudes and value systems in education is summarised in Table 1.

S-R theories (Classical perspective)	Cognitive theories (Modern perspective)	Personality theories (Romantic perspective)
class teaching	flexible grouping	individualised learning
autocratic	participative	*laissez-faire*
conservative	liberal	abdication
subject emphasis	process emphasis	method emphasis
teacher dominated	inquiry centred	child centred
teaching aids	learning resources	audio-visual
discipline	experience	freedom
skills	creativity	discovery
active	transactive	reactive
certainty	probability	confusion
competitive	growth	co-operative
other directed	self-fulfilling	inner directed
discipline	responsibility	freedom
doing things to	doing things with	doing things for

Table 1. *Some contrasting value systems behind different perspectives towards the curriculum (after Davies, 1976)*

Note: Most teachers subscribe to some values in all three categories. Van Horn (1976), for instance, found with fifteen teachers that when they were teaching they spent 66 per cent of their time in activities associated with processing information, 14 per cent in social interaction and personalised instruction and 20 per cent in behaviour modification. Bennett's (1976) text is important for distinguishing between *twelve* teaching styles.

At university level there have been a number of attempts to be more 'progressive' and to offer more freedom to the student than that which is normally available. Hartley (1972a) described thirteen different studies which indicated how more freedom of choice could be given to students studying psychology. The data from an experiment by Faw (cited by Rogers, 1969) are of interest in this connection. Faw compared a traditionally taught introductory course in psychology with a system in which the students were free to choose the method and the content of their study. Faw found in terms of written work (i) that no students wrote about the same thing in the optional course and (ii) that the amount of reading was far wider in the optional course. (In the conventional system each of the thirty-eight students involved handed in a term paper: in the optional system only eight (out of the thirty-eight) students did so, but eighteen more handed in original experiments.) In the conventional system no student reported reading a journal article, whereas in the optional system one hundred and sixty-five articles were reported. Faw's experiment, and several others, are cited in greater detail in Roger's *Freedom to Learn* — in itself a testament to student-centred learning. Paper 3.6 in this text shows this approach in the unusual context of medical education.

Criticisms of the laws of learning

I have tried, so far, to list principles of teaching derived from theories of learning, and I have tried to illustrate how far the influences from these theories can still be seen in operation in modern educational practice. I want now to return to consider some of the objections that were raised in the mid-1950s and 1960s to the principles listed above. The discussion so far has made it clear, I hope, that the principles have withstood both the criticisms and the test of time to some extent. However, the criticisms themselves led to new and active lines of educational research which I shall consider further below. First, however, what were the criticisms of the 'laws' of learning? To indicate that there was great debate, I have posed the criticisms as questions.

DO STUDIES OF HOW ANIMALS LEARN TELL US ANYTHING ABOUT HOW HUMANS LEARN?

Much vigorous debate has taken place on the issue of how far the results obtained in animal learning experiments are relevant to the understanding of human learning in general and classroom learning in particular. The simple notion that there would be a general law of learning which could be applied from animals to humans has simply not stood the test of time. The work of Bitterman (1960, 1964), Seligman (1970) and others has shown that different animals respond differently to different stimuli, different levels of reinforcement and different contexts (eg see Hinde & Hinde, 1973). These results do not imply that the laws of learning discovered in animal work are totally wrong, but they do imply that learning is more complicated than was once imagined. As far as classroom learning is concerned, putting it simply, 'The methods of learning employed by animals in mazes do not necessarily correspond to methods of learning children use in grappling with verbal materials in classrooms' (Ausubel, 1963).

ARE RESULTS OBTAINED IN LABORATORIES RELEVANT TO NATURAL LEARNING SITUATIONS?

A standard practice, if one wants to investigate something complex, is to simplify it, and to carry out investigations on it in a laboratory situation under controlled conditions. Such a procedure, it is argued, allows one to discover and to manipulate the crucial variables and to assess their effects. A consequence of this procedure, however, is that one either has to generalise from the findings in the controlled and simplified conditions to the more variable natural conditions, or one has to do further experiments in natural situations in order to see if the laboratory findings still hold true. Many commentators today, however, consider the laboratory approach to be misguided (at the very least) and they favour more naturalistic descriptive and analytical observational studies. The argument — in the context of learning — is that laboratory studies lead to an inappropriate simplification of the material to be learned and that they ignore the complexities that characterise human learning. Putting it another way, experimental studies make certain questions tractable, but the simplification is self-defeating because it excludes that which is more characteristic and interesting about human learning. Today many investigations favour realism over experimental control.

HAVE SOCIAL FACTORS BEEN IGNORED?

As noted earlier, learning is rarely an isolated event, conducted in a vacuum: people learn a great deal from other people. Nonetheless most experimental studies examine single organisms solving particular problems in isolation: there is pitifully small literature on group learning and on imitation.

A remarkable study which showed that the same animal might behave differently with other groups of animals was carried out by Box (1967, 1973). Box first trained rats individually to operate a Skinner box with a lever at one end and a food delivery chute at the other (three feet away). Each rat would press the lever, run up to the food chute, consume its reward, run back and press the lever again, and so on. Box then placed three such trained rats together in the box. She found that two of the rats quickly became 'parasites', and sat and ate at the food chute, whereas the other became a 'worker' and did all the lever-pressing for the other two. Box next showed that if she took *either* three 'workers' *or* three 'parasites', and put them together then the same pattern would result — one would work whilst the others fed. Finally she showed that an individual rat might behave as a 'worker' in one situation and as a 'parasite' in another *depending upon which two other rats formed the trio*. I have cited this experiment in detail because it is an *animal* experiment which shows that behaviour can be tailored to social situations. Other examples are cited by Hinde (1974). It does not require a great deal of imagination to infer that similar things happen when children (or adults) learn.

WHAT ABOUT THE ROLE OF PAST EXPERIENCE?

Not only did much of the early animal and human laboratory work on learning ignore social factors, it also ignored developmental ones. Animals (and humans) were studied learning to carry out isolated tasks and no account was taken of their prior experience. The work of Harlow (1959) provided a notable exception. Harlow demonstrated that if you provided an animal with sufficient examples of, for instance, three objects two of which were the same and one different (the 'oddity' problem), and rewarded the choice of the odd object, then eventually, over time, the animal would come to choose the odd object on the first trial, irrespective of the nature of the objects. In other words the animal had learned the underlying concept of oddity. Harlow called this process 'learning to learn' and clearly it is of fundamental importance in the realm of human learning.

The question of how a child learns to do something that he couldn't do before, and how his knowledge builds up over time is an important question, both theoretically and practically. The assumption that knowledge is somehow incrementally and linearly acquired is questioned by the findings of Piaget and of other developmental psychologists (Bower, 1974; Hunter, 1976). It seems clear, to summarise recent work, that development involves the building up of a multiplicity of different kinds of skills and resources and a multiplicity of strategies for using them which can be deployed appropriately to the task in hand. Often, say at seven or eight years old, a child can do each of certain things independently (ie he has the sub-skills), but he cannot put them together into an appropriate higher order skill (ie he has not the appropriate strategy). Because learning involves building on past experience in order to deal with future contingencies this omission of developmental work by learning theorists reveals a serious limitation.

ARE THERE DIFFERENT KINDS OF LEARNING?

An interesting source of controversy was provided by the question of whether or not there were different kinds of learning, and if so, how could they best be described? So far, as we have seen, learning was originally studied in rather narrow contexts, and possibly this resulted partly from a lack of definition. Hilgard and Bower (1975) *still* write that 'The definition of learning is not a source of controversy between theorists. The controversy is over facts and interpretation, not over definition.' It seems that because a variety of activities were given the same name, psychologists attempted to account for them by single unified theories. However, if one looks closer at the work of different theorists, it is clear that the different investigators between them used different species of animals, they used different types of apparatus, they used different kinds of problem, and they employed different explanatory hypotheses to describe their results. (It is indeed a wonder there is any unity at all!)

For investigators of classroom learning, however, the notion of a single general law of learning has become untenable. Gagné (1965) for instance remarked, 'to begin with the premise that "all learning is the same" would be quite unjustifiable.' Different investigators have now postulated many different kinds of learning (see Table 2). Once again as work has proceeded, learning has been seen to be more complex than was initially envisaged. Gagné, for instance, has revised his thinking at least five times (see Gagné, 1965a, 1965b, 1968, 1970, 1977).

ARE THE PRINCIPLES OF ANY USE TO PRACTISING TEACHERS?

A major criticism raised about the principles listed in the first part of this paper is that they are descriptive rather than prescriptive. What this means is that they adequately describe how learning takes place but they do not tell teachers what to do about it. Teachers all recognise the principles and remark, probably with some justification, that there

Investigator	No of types	Labels given
Lewin (1942)	4	Changes in cognitive structure, changes in motivation, changes in group belongingness, changes in control of body musculature in skilled performance
Tolman (1949)	6	Cathexes, equivalent beliefs, field expectancies, field cognition modes, drive discriminations, motor patterns
Melton (1964)	6	Conditioning, rote learning, probability learning, skill learning, concept learning, problem solving
Belbin (1969)	5	Comprehension, reflex learning, attitude development, memorisation, procedural learning
Gagné (1970)	8	Signal learning, S-R learning, chaining, verbal associations, multiple discriminations, concepts, rules, problem solving
Leith (1974)	10	Stimulus discrimination, response learning, association, response integration, learning to learn, concept learning, concept integration, problem solving, learning schemata, self-evaluation
Gagné (1977)	5 and 10 (interrelated)	Intellectual skills, cognitive strategies, verbal information, motor skills, attitudes. Signal learning, S-R learning, chaining, verbal associations, discriminations, concrete concepts, defined concepts, rules, learning hierarchies, problem solving

Table 2. *Some different kinds of learning*

is nothing new in them, or that they know them all already.

To make descriptions valuable each description has to be turned into a prescription. We know, for example, that activity is important in learning, but what sort of activity? when? and how much? Are there occasions when activity hinders learning? Like the principles of learning from which they are derived, prescriptions will turn out to be generalisations in need of refinement for specific situations. Still, we might agree, some progress in this direction would be better than none.

Reactions to the criticisms

The criticisms described above led to new and active lines of research. In this part of the paper the reactions to the last two objections are examined first and in more detail than the reactions to the earlier ones.

It was the last major limitation — that learning theories were descriptive rather than prescriptive — that led investigators in the mid-1960s to try and develop theories of instruction. And, in creating theories of instruction, the second criticism had to be borne in mind: not only were there different kinds of learning but, relatedly, there were different kinds of teaching. The problem was how to intermesh the two.

A booklet published in 1966 illustrates the point. Wallis *et al* listed on one axis of a table eleven training areas considered appropriate for the training of military personnel, and on the other axis thirteen teaching methods. The interesting thing about this table was that in 1966 Wallis *et al* did not feel they were able to cross-tabulate which methods were appropriate for which aims: all the cells remained blank.

Theories of instruction are attempts to remedy this deficiency in knowledge. 'Theories of instruction are statements about what instructors should do in order to teach, or more precisely in order to obtain a given educational objective with maximum efficiency' (Annett, 1964). Four names spring to mind in connection with such theories: Gage, Bruner, Gagné and Atkinson. Gage (1964) suggested that different theories of instruction would develop from different combinations of four areas — teaching activities, educational aims and objectives, learning components and learning theories — and that 'no single unified general theory of instruction should be sought for the various processes by which teachers engender learning.'

Bruner (1966), on the other hand, considered that theories of instruction should have a high degree of generality. He stated that a theory should specify (i) the experiences which most effectively implant in the individual a predisposition towards learning; (ii) the ways in which a body of knowledge should be structured so that it can most readily be grasped by the learner; (iii) the most effective sequences in which to present materials to be learned; and (iv) the nature and pacing of rewards and punishments in the process of learning and teaching.

Atkinson (1972), too, argues that four criteria must be satisfied in a theory of instruction, but his approach, stemming from mathematical learning theory, is rather different. The four criteria that must be

41

satisfied are (i) a model of the learning process; (ii) a specification of the instructional objectives; (iii) a specification of the admissible instructional actions; and (iv) the existence of a measurement scale that will permit costs to be assigned to each of the instructional actions, and values or payoffs to the achievement of each overall objective. The argument is that when a precise definition can be given for each of these four elements then it is possible to derive an optimal instructional strategy.

Of the four instructional theorists, Gagné has been the most influential (if not necessarily the best), although his theory has not been so explicitly stated as a theory as the others. Gagné has been influential because his theory makes a number of broad assumptions about learning and teaching which are testable in practical situations. Gagné's contribution has been to tie together the following three ideas: (i) that subject matter has a hierarchical structure, (ii) that there are different kinds of learning (which are also hierarchically arranged) and (iii) that there are different kinds of teaching methods which can be linked up appropriately with the different kinds of learning. Thus Gagné suggests that operant and classical conditioning techniques are appropriate for teaching at the lowest level of his hierarchy of teaching types (signal-learning and stimulus-response learning). He suggests various chaining techniques for teaching chains and associations, and simultaneous-contrast techniques for teaching multiple discriminations. Practice, simultaneous-contrast techniques, verbal exposition, discovery and guided-discovery methods, are suitable for the teaching of concepts, rules, learning hierarchies and problem solving (Gagné, 1977; Gagné & Briggs, 1974). These suggestions have been fruitful in the sense that they have generated a great deal of research — much of it conducted in the context of programmed and computer-assisted instruction.

The systematic approach of programmed instruction (first state your aims; next decide how to measure the achievement of them; then do the teaching; next assess your teaching success; and finally, revise your teaching to make the instruction better next time) in itself implies a general theory of instruction. Although this approach may be pragmatic it has produced instruction which works in a variety of situations (Hartley, 1972b). Many different strategies have been developed in order to help achieve each of the different stages listed above, but the problem still remains of interrelating them successfully (Hartley, 1972c). Nonetheless, the pragmatic approach underlying programmed instruction has had an enormous impact on educational research. In particular it has forced research workers to consider practical issues.

Some recent trends

Although the development of theories of instruction — in both general and in more limited forms — is likely to continue, there have been other reactions to the list of criticisms stated earlier. Areas of research which have expanded enormously in the last decade have been:

(i) pre-school provision and education; (ii) research stemming out of Piagetian notions; (iii) work on the personalities of learners and teachers and the interaction between the two; (iv) studies of different teaching methods; and (v) research on the effects of organisational structures on learning. (Summaries of these developments can be found in Glaser and Resnick [1972] and McKeachie [1974].) In short, what we have seen is a much greater interest in classroom learning than ever before. In the United Kingdom this interest is reflected in studies on streaming (Barker-Lunn, 1970), on teaching styles (Bennett, 1976) and in the process of schooling generally (see Hammersley & Woods, 1976).

I think it important at this point to pay tribute to work carried out by sociologists in the field of education — despite the criticisms that this work sometimes evokes (Flew, 1976). The sociology of education has been dramatic in its impact: it has drawn attention to how the organisational structure of the classroom affects interests, motivation and learning and it has shown the schoolroom to be a mini-society in which are acquired the rules of society itself. Work on classroom learning has received a new impetus from this approach (eg see Hammersley & Woods, 1976) and, in my opinion, research on teaching at university level is likely to stagnate until such perspectives are also applied there. A little work has been done in the area of assessment and in learning from textbooks which does seem to reflect what students actually do but it is a pitiful amount (see Miller & Parlett, 1974; Marton & Säljö, 1976a, b; Parlett & Simons, 1976; Coles, 1977; and Paper 1.2 by Marton in this text).

Bitterman (1960) estimated — by counting journal papers — that ninety per cent of the studies of animal learning reported to that date had used the laboratory rat as the subject of the investigation. Today, as noted above, the range and style of learning studies is wider than ever before. Hilgard and Bower (1975) describe seven kinds of educational research which span the narrow, classical laboratory studies with animals to the broad large-scale research involving, for example, the evaluation of new curricula. In the 1960s and 1970s we have seen a shift in emphasis across this continuum to redress the balance of the earlier years.

It is important, nonetheless, in considering learning to recognise that there is a place for *all* seven types of research: the problem is to recognise the strengths and the limitations of the different approaches and to maintain an appropriate complementary balance. (Animal studies, for example, may not seem to be of immediate practical relevance to classroom learning, but they can tell us a great deal about the biochemistry of learning, and indeed about the different ways in which animals learn.)

We need also to remember that we research workers are not the only contributors to knowledge about education and that perhaps we overestimate our own importance. The role of a researcher, as I see it, is primarily to assess the evidence for what we and others do and to do this as dispassionately as possible. It would be foolish to pretend that we can do this in an entirely neutral way, however much we strive for it. The more applied our work is, the less hidden are the political, the personal and the ideological pressures that we bring to bear upon it. There is no need to be over-dramatic about this — provided that we recognise the difficulties. *The Organisation and Impact of Social Research* (edited by Marten Shipman, 1976) is a salutary book to read in this connection. This text contains retrospective accounts by the authors of six major educational studies carried out in Britain (J W B Douglas, J and E Newson, Julienne Ford, C Lacey, Joan Barker-Lunn and R R Dale). The authors present accounts of how they did their research, what problems they had to face and overcome, and how their findings have been used — and abused — since publication. The book is a testimony to the personal commitment of the researchers involved and to how practical limitations guide research. It also makes clear that educational research cannot be free from value judgement. Shipman's text shows how researchers are interested in improving existing situations and how they adopt different strategies in order to do this.

These difficulties, together with the methodological ones that must accompany new approaches to educational research (see Snow, 1974), present the educational researcher with formidable problems. The worlds of teachers, learners and researchers are almost separate realities. Trying to link them presents a daunting, but stimulating, challenge.

References

Annett, J (1964) The relationship between theories of learning and theories of instruction. In *Programmierter Unterricht und Lehrmaschiner*. Berlin : Pedagogische Arbeitselle

Atkinson, R C (1972) Ingredients for a theory of instruction, *American Psychologist* 27 : 921-31

Ausubel, D P (1963) *The Psychology of Meaningful Verbal Learning*. New York : Grune & Stratton

Ausubel, D P (ed) (1969) *Readings in School Learning*. New York : Holt, Rinehart & Winston

Ausubel, D P and Robinson, F G (1969) *School Learning*. New York : Holt, Rinehart & Winston

Azrin, N H (1977) A strategy for applied research: learning based but outcome oriented, *American Psychologist* 32 2 : 140-9

Barker-Lunn, J (1970) *Streaming in the Primary School*. London : NFER

Barrows, H S (1976) Problem based learning in medicine. In J Clarke and J Leedham (eds) *Aspects of Educational Technology X*. London : Kogan Page

Belbin, R M (1969) *CRAMP: A systems approach to training*. Cambridge : Industrial Training Research Unit (32 Trumpington Street)

Bennett, N (1976) *Teaching Styles and Pupil Progress*. London : Open Books

Bitterman, M E (1960) Toward a comparative psychology of learning, *American Psychologist* 15 11: 704-12

Bitterman, M E (1964) The evolution of intelligence, *Scientific American* 212: 92-100

Bower, T G R (1974) *Development in Infancy*. San Francisco : Freeman

Box, H O (1967) Social organisation of rats in a 'social problem' situation, *Nature* 213: 533-4

Box, H O (1973) *Organisation in Animal Communities*. London : Butterworths

Bruner, J S (1966) *Toward a Theory of Instruction.* Harvard : Belknap

Bugelski, B R (1964) *The Psychology of Learning Applied to Teaching.*
Indianapolis : Bobbs-Merrill

Coles, C R (1977) Course designing: some suggestions following observations
of undergraduate medical courses. In J Gilbert and P Hills (eds) *Aspects of
Educational Technology XI.* London : Kogan Page

Cowan, J (1977) Individual approaches to problem-solving. In J Gilbert and
P Hills (eds) *Aspects of Educational Technology XI.* London : Kogan Page

Cronbach, L J and Snow, R E (1977) *Aptitudes and Instructional Methods.*
New York : Irvington

Davies, I K (1976) *Objectives in Curriculum Design.* London : McGraw Hill

Flew, A G N (1976) *Sociology, Equality and Education.* London : Macmillan

Gage, N L (ed) (1964) *Theories of Learning and Instruction.* Chicago : NSSE

Gagné, R M (1965a) The analysis of instructional objectives for the design of
instruction. In R Glaser (ed) *Teaching Machines and Programmed Learning*
(vol II). Washington : NEA

Gagné, R M (1965b) *The Conditions of Learning.* New York : Holt, Rinehart
& Winston

Gagné, R M (1968) Learning hierarchies, *Educational Psychologist* 6: 1-9

Gagné, R M (1970) *The Conditions of Learning* (2nd ed). New York : Holt,
Rinehart & Winston

Gagné, R M (1977) *The Conditions of Learning* (3rd ed). New York : Holt,
Rinehart & Winston

Gagné, R M and Briggs, L J (1974) *Principles of Instructional Design.* New York :
Holt, Rinehart & Winston

Glaser, R (1973) Intelligence, learning and the new aptitudes. In R Budgett and
J Leedham (eds) *Aspects of Educational Technology VII.* London : Pitman

Glaser, R and Resnick, L B (1972) Instructional Psychology, *Annual Review of
Psychology* 23: 181-275

Hammersley, M and Woods, P (eds) (1976) *The Process of Schooling.* London :
Routledge & Kegan Paul

Harlow, H (1959) Learning set and error factor theory. In S Koch (ed)
Psychology: A Study of a Science (vol 2). New York : McGraw Hill

Hartley, J (1972a) New approaches in the teaching of psychology: an annotated
bibliography, *Bulletin of the British Psychological Society* 25 89: 291-304

Hartley, J (1972b) Evaluation. In J Hartley (ed) *Strategies for Programmed
Instruction: An Educational Technology.* London : Butterworths

Hartley, J (1972c) Preface. In J Hartley (ed) *Strategies for Programmed
Instruction: An Educational Technology.* London : Butterworths

Hartley, J (1974) Programmed instruction 1954-1974, *Programmed Learning
& Educational Technology* 11 6: 278-97

Hartley, J (1978) *Designing Instructional Text.* London : Kogan Page

Hawkins, S, Davies, I K, Majer, K and Hartley, J (1975) *Getting Started: Guides
for Beginning Teachers.* Oxford : Blackwell

Hilgard, E R (1959) Learning theory and its applications. In *New Teaching Aids
for the American Classroom.* Washington : US Department of Health,
Education and Welfare, 1962

Hilgard, E R and Bower, G H (1975) *Theories of Learning* (4th ed). Englewood
Cliffs : Prentice-Hall

Hinde, R A (1974) *Biological Bases of Human Social Behaviour.* New York :
McGraw Hill

Hinde, R A and Hinde, J S (eds) (1973) *Constraints of Learning.* London :
Academic Press

Howe, M J A (1972) *Understanding School Learning.* New York : Harper & Row

Hunter, I M L (1976) Memory: theory and application. In V P Varma and P
Williams (eds) *Piaget, Psychology and Education.* London : Hodder & Stoughton

Kiernan, C C and Woodford, F P (eds) (1975) *Behaviour Modification with the Severely Retarded.* Amsterdam : Elsevier

Knowles, M (1973) *The Adult Learner: A Neglected Species.* Houston : Gulf Publishing Co

Kulik, J, Kulik, C C and Smith, B (1976) Research on the personalised system of instruction, *Programmed Learning & Educational Technology* 13 1: 23-30

Leith, G O M (1974) Programmed learning in science education. In *New Trends in the Utilisation of Educational Technology for Science Education.* Paris : Unesco

Lewin, K (1942) Field theory and learning. In N B Henry (ed) *The Psychology of Learning.* Chicago : NSSE

Lister, I (1974) *Deschooling: A Reader.* Cambridge : Cambridge University Press

Marton, F and Säljö, R (1976a) On qualitative differences in learning: I — outcome and process, *British Journal of Educational Psychology* 46 1: 4-11

Marton, F and Säljö, R (1976b) On qualitative differences in learning: II — outcome as a function of the learner's conception of the task, *British Journal of Educational Psychology* 46 2: 115-27

McKeachie, W (1974) Instructional Psychology, *Annual Review of Psychology* 25: 161-93

Melton, A W (ed) (1964) *Categories of Human Learning.* New York : Academic Press

Miller, C M and Parlett, M (1974) *Up to the Mark: A Study of the Examination Game.* London : Society for Research into Higher Education

Parlett, M and Simons, H (1976) *Learning from Learners: A Study of the Student's Experience of Academic Life.* London : Centre for Research and Innovation in Higher Education

Pask, G (1975) *Conversation, Cognition and Learning.* Amsterdam : Elsevier

Pask, G (1976) Styles and strategies of learning, *British Journal of Educational Psychology* 46 2: 128-48

Posner, G J and Strike, K A (1976) A categorisation scheme for principles of sequencing content, *Review of Educational Research* 46 4: 665-90

Resnick, L B (1973) Hierarchies in children's learning: a symposium, *Instructional Science* 2 3: 311-61

Robin, A C (1976) Behavioral instruction in the college classroom, *Review of Educational Research* 46 3: 313-34

Rogers, C (1969) *Freedom to Learn.* New York : Merrill

Scandura, J M (1977) A structural approach to instructional problems, *American Psychologist* 32: 33-53

Seligman, M E P (1970) On the generality of the laws of learning, *Psychological Review* 77 5: 406-18

Shipman, M (ed) (1976) *The Organisation and Impact of Social Research.* London : Routledge & Kegan Paul

Snow, R E (1974) Representative and quasi-representative designs for research on teaching, *Review of Educational Research* 44 3: 265-92

Thoresen, C E (ed) (1973) *Behaviour Modification in Education.* Chicago : NSSE

Tolman, E C (1949) There is more than one kind of learning, *Psychological Review* 56: 144-55

van Horn, R W (1976) Effects of the use of four types of teaching models on student self concept of academic ability and attitude toward the teacher, *American Educational Research Journal* 13 4: 285-91

Wallis, D, Duncan, K D and Knight, M A G (1966) *Programmed Instruction in the British Armed Forces.* London : HMSO

1.2 What Does it Take to Learn?

FERENCE MARTON

This is a shortened version of a paper prepared for the Council of Europe
Symposium 'Strategies for Research and Development in Higher Education',
University of Gothenburg, 7-12 September 1975, which first appeared in
N Entwistle and D Hounsell (eds) *How Students Learn*. Lancaster : Institute
for Research and Development in Post-Compulsory Education, University of
Lancaster, UK. It is reproduced here with permission of the author.

The purpose of this paper is to summarise some observations and
reflections made during a research project which has recently been
completed. This project was concerned with higher education in the
social sciences (eg economics, education, political science, sociology)
and the major goal was to arrive at a description of differences in the
process of learning underlying the differences in the outcome of
learning in students.

Before describing this research it is important to place learning in a
wider perspective. There are, of course, different forms of learning. In
early childhood, for instance, learning by direct experience is
predominant. Learning takes place by doing and by observing. By far
the most common form of learning, however, in formal schooling and
in adult life in a literate society is of a different kind. Learning takes
place through reading and through being told, and it is this type of
learning with which we were mainly concerned in our investigation.

A written or spoken discourse (the sign) can be considered as a
medium for the expression of what the discourse is about (what is
signified). In the kind of learning that concerns us here the crucial
problem is, in our opinion, the grasping of what is signified by the
sign (ie understanding what the discourse is about). Since we are above
all interested in the comprehension of what is read or what is heard,
the exact wording is of minor importance. The object of our research
has thus been labelled 'non-verbatim learning'.

Differences in the outcome of learning are usually described in
terms of how much is learned, both in research on learning and in
written university examinations. A number of questions are
constructed in order to cover the content of a passage, a book or an
entire course. From the answers to these questions we conclude how
much of the content has been acquired and retained by the learner.
This is usually expressed in terms of a total number of right answers.

There are two tacit assumptions behind this quantitative view of
learning. The first of these is the notion that knowledge is 'evenly
spread', ie the idea that what is learned (and what is to be learned) can
be described as a sum of a number of independent pieces of knowledge,
equal in value. The second tacit assumption is that learning can be
equated with a transfer of unaltered pieces of knowledge from the book

47

to the inside of the learner's head. It is to this view of learning that we should like briefly to outline an alternative.

As far as the first presupposition above is concerned, it is fairly obvious that in most instances there is a variation in depth in written or spoken discourse. There are generally certain central underlying phenomena, concepts, principles or lines of thought for which to a large degree the discourse serves as a means of expression (clarification, exemplification, etc). It is principally the understanding of the central or deep aspects of the discourse that should be of interest, since the understanding of these usually accounts for an understanding of the rest also.

As regards the second presupposition above, it is also fairly obvious that conceptions of one and the same thing will probably vary between individuals. Even in this case, it seems reasonable to assume variation in depth: some of the learner's conceptions will bear a closer resemblance to the conception the author intended to express than others. The real problem is thus not 'how much is learned' but rather 'what is learned'. This implies a description of the outcome of learning in terms of the different forms in which the same phenomenon, concept, principle or line of thought may appear in a group of individuals.

Our starting point was thus that a study of learning should originate from a close analysis of 'what is to be learned'. A study of learning should preferably concern the learning of something and not learning in general. The content of learning is considered to be of primary importance. Furthermore, we are interested in the depth dimension as regards both the material to be learned and the learner's comprehension of it. We think that variation in the latter can be described in terms of the extent to which it approximates to what the discourse is about (ie what is signified).

We combined two methods in our research project. On the one hand we carried out a series of individually administered experiments. In these we let the subjects, who were students in the social sciences, read parts of their set books, or material of the same kind, under fairly well-controlled conditions. In some of the experiments the conditions were approximately equal for all subjects. Our purpose was to observe and describe the process and the outcome of learning, and the relationship between the two. In other experiments we introduced different conditions for different groups of subjects in order to manipulate the process of learning. Our hypotheses about what was going to happen were checked against the results as regards the outcome of learning. Qualitative differences were described for both immediate and long-term retention in all experiments. The differences in the process of learning were described on the basis of the subjects' answers to our questions about how they had experienced the process of learning.

The second approach comprised interviews about how the students set about their studies. Details of the students' academic performance were collected, and additional investigations were carried out in order to describe certain long-term effects of their studies.

In the research design used, we had thus investigated the relationship between process and outcome of learning in experimental settings on one hand and in the context of normal studies on the other. Since the same students served as subjects in both kinds of studies we could also examine the relationship between the corresponding components (ie outcome-outcome and process-process) in the two different contexts (ie in experiments and in normal studies).

As mentioned above, our starting point was the description of the outcome of learning in terms of variation in depth (ie in terms of levels of outcome). What comparable description could be made of the process of learning?

It is a common experience that there is a variation in intensity of attention. This notion usually refers to the fact that one may pay more or less attention to various parts of what one reads. This variation in attention corresponds to the quantitative aspect of the outcome of learning. In both cases it is a question of, so to speak, horizontal variation. When we analysed the subjects' answers to our questions concerning their experience of learning, it appeared, however, that there was also a variation between individuals in attention in what we may call a vertical dimension (ie variation as to depth). Some subjects had the discourse itself (the sign) as the object of attention, and others were more concerned with what the discourse was about (what is signified). Corresponding to the variation in depth in the outcome of learning (levels of outcome) there is thus also a variation in depth in the process of learning (levels of processing). The two levels (deep and surface) identified are, of course, not to be considered as two distinct and separate categories. Rather they imply a dimension along which individuals vary.

The subjects who were considered to have a 'deep' approach had stated that in reading the text they

'thought about'	'the point of it'
'got a grasp of'	'what it was about'
'tried to get at'	'the conclusions'
'remembered'	'what it meant'
'got a clear impression of'	etc
etc	

In other words, they concentrated on what the discourse was about.

This attitude was in general associated with an active approach in which the subjects

> '... made connections between various points ...'
> '... went back to find the connections ...'
> '... kept the previous page in mind while reading the next ...'
> '... drew conclusions from the tables ...'
> '... went back to the tables to check the conclusions ...'
> '... thought over the logic of the argument ...'

and so on.

The subjects thus appear to have been actively attempting to connect what they were reading with what had gone before and utilised their own capacity for logical thinking.

What the 'surface approach' subjects say about their reading differs considerably from the above. They state, for example,

'. . . I didn't remember what I read, because I was just thinking of
hurrying on . . .'
'. . . I was thinking about the fact that I was going to have to repeat all
this . . . I didn't think about what I was reading . . .'
'. . . The whole time I was thinking "now I must remember this" and
"now I must remember this" . . .'

In other words these subjects concentrated on surface aspects of the
situations: on the discourse itself, on subsequent achievement
requirements and so on. This attitude seemed to be associated with a
passive approach:

'. . . It was words . . . you didn't have to think about what they meant,
it was just a matter of reading straight through.'
'. . . I just read straight through without looking back at anything . . .'
'. . . It wasn't so much that I drew conclusions . . . and reacted to
them . . . but that, well, that I read it sort of because I was supposed
to read it . . . and not so as to react to it.'

These subjects were confronting the discourse passively. It was treated
as an isolated phenomenon, and they touched only its surface (without
making any contact with what it was about).

To sum up, we may say that the subjects varied as to their
conception of 'what it takes to learn'. For some, learning is the grasping
of what the discourse is about, ie learning is learning through the
discourse, and for others, learning is learning the discourse (ie
memorising it). The former appear to experience an active role (ie
learning is something they do); the latter do not appear to do this
(learning is something that happens to them).

In the experiments, we found a very close relationship between what
we call level of processing and level of outcome. Simply, subjects who
focused attention on what the discourse was about (what was
signified) to a great extent also grasped it, and those subjects who did
not think about it, could not answer the questions correctly.

The next problem was whether we could find the counterpart of
levels of processing (identified in experimental settings) in the students'
everyday academic work. And if they were found, how did 'deep
approach' students manage in an educational system frequently accused
of putting a premium on surface aspects of learning and regurgitation of
facts? In several subjects we did find a concentration on:

'the central point . . .'
'the point of the whole thing'
'what the basic idea is'
'basic concepts'
'the actual set-up'
'what lies behind it'
'the whole thing'
'the total picture'
'what it boils down to'
'what the author actually means'
'what's at the bottom of it'
etc

All of these indicate a deep level of thinking about the content of the studies.

In normal studies too this attitude appears to be associated with an active approach:

You try to
- connect
- relate
- set in relation to each other

- the new and the old
- what you read
- what you know
- what you have read before
- different books
- books and teaching

You
- build up
- draw

- a connecting line of thought
- the major outline
- the structure
- the construction
- the conclusions

You
- reflect on
- question
- find out

- the logic of the argument
- the conclusions
- the truth of the statement
- points that are not clear

In the case of normal studies, there is a further aspect of the 'deep' approach besides those represented in the experimental setting. The subjects who are judged to have this approach frequently state that they internalise (absorb, make a part of themselves) what they learn in their studies. They grasp the fact that the university subjects they are reading have to do with the same reality as that of their daily lives. This means that they make use of their knowledge and skills. Students of education, for instance, when asked their opinion of university studies in general, draw partly on what they have learned in their subject. Similarly, students of political science or economics make use of what they have learned in these subjects when they observe and analyse the political and economic reality in which they live. This is by no means as self-evident as it may seem. In the experimental settings several students were not especially interested in (or aware of) what the discourse they read was about. As regards university studies many students did not even seem to assume that their subjects had anything to do with reality. What you study and 'reality' were seen as two quite separate matters.

So far we have shown that students do differ in their depth of processing the material they meet in their everyday studying. The next question is: how do students who aim at learning something about an outside 'reality' manage in an educational system which to a large extent is governed by an artificial internal situation made up of examinations and pass-rate requirements? In the cases that we studied, the students who adopted a 'deep' approach (and had better qualitative results) in our experiments also adopted this approach in their normal studies and achieved better examination results (in the quantitative sense) than the others. According to an interpretation based on a detailed analysis of the data (Svensson, 1975) most examination questions do not necessarily demand a 'deep' approach, but reading a large amount of material (which is a part of the course requirements) without such an approach is a fairly soul-destroying activity. This perhaps helps to explain why students using a 'surface' approach generally adopt rather poor study habits (among other things they read less) and thus achieve worse results. In this way a strong statistical correlation between attitudes to learning and time actually spent on study and between both of these and examination results can be obtained. This interpretation is supported by, for example, Poulsen's (1970) findings that successful and less successful mathematics students not only differed in the total amount of time devoted to study during one term, but that the former category showed a rising and the latter a falling trend in this respect during the course of the term.

As regards the connection between 'learning strategy' and success in studies, Goldman (1972) has demonstrated a positive relationship between grades in statistics and 'logical' learning strategy in a group of undergraduates. This strategy was defined as 'trying to learn the underlying reasons for the technique in a verbal way'. The opposite of this, called 'mnemonic-concrete strategy', was defined as 'trying to learn the computational technique by observing examples often without worrying about reasons for the technique'.

Biggs (1973) '. . . found that success in Arts was related to two rather different types of strategies: (i) reproductive, where the student gives back prescribed material intact, and (ii) transformational, where the student ranges widely over material and injects his own meaning and interpretations'.

To sum up, it would appear that a decisive factor in non-verbatim learning, both in experimental settings and in everyday academic work, is the learner's approach to learning. Those who succeed best (both qualitatively and quantitatively) seem to have an approach that aims beyond the written or spoken discourse itself towards the message the discourse is intended to communicate. These students feel themselves to be the agents of learning; they utilise their capacity for logical thinking in order to construct knowledge.

We argued above that the crucial question in non-verbatim learning is the grasping of what is signified by the sign (ie to find out what the given discourse is about). To grasp what is signified is simply to discover (or to create) meaning. In our opinion, this is precisely 'what it takes to learn'. And — we may add — to teach is to facilitate this learning. This formulation certainly represents no new view of learning. Many of the most influential thinkers in the field of education have stressed the role of meaningfulness in learning and teaching, probably in accordance with the views of a majority of educational practitioners today. Nonetheless, this view of learning seems to be at variance with several decades of research on rote learning in psychological laboratories, and it seems also to be largely at variance with current educational practice. But how can this be if, as we have good reason to assume, most teachers, especially in the field of higher education, freely admit the decisive role of meaningfulness in learning and teaching? The difficulty is that this agreement in principle seems to be restricted to the verbal level, but the real problem is how meaningfulness is to be translated into concrete terms in the actual learning/teaching process. It is here that the main weakness is found at present.

In our modern society we are used to looking for technical solutions to our problems. We use the term 'technical solutions' in a wide sense to include the introduction of algorithmic procedures (ie procedures where one can explicitly state the specific routines to be carried out). No such solutions seem to be possible, however, in the case of learning and teaching. In every specific case of insight the entire complex of the individual's knowledge of the world is involved more or less directly, since the understanding of something new is always dependent on the previous understanding of something else. A necessary prerequisite of ease of learning on the part of the learner is that the teacher himself has sufficiently clearly understood what is to be learned (and taught). Another necessary prerequisite is that the teacher has a clear conception of what lack of understanding looks like and can recognise the absence in the student of those prerequisites on which it may depend. Some teachers have acquired a good insight into these matters through experience, but in most cases we find ourselves powerless in the face of lack of comprehension in students. What assistance can educational research give in this respect?

We mentioned above that in the experiments on learning we applied a qualitative model of description of the outcome of learning. This means simply that we described the subjects' various conceptions of the phenomena, concepts, principles that the discourse was about. Such a description illustrates the different ways in which something can be understood or misunderstood, and it also gives clues as to what prerequisites for comprehension are lacking in a given case.

Across different academic disciplines and subdisciplines, and across different 'schools' of thought within the same discipline, research has been conducted with a view to describing qualitative variations in people's conception of the world around them, their interpretation of various concepts, their methods of problem solving, etc. This has been common practice in anthropology, for instance. Within the *Gestalt* school of psychology many very detailed analyses of various problems have been made of which the best example is the work of Wertheimer (1945). Piaget's empirical work has been of this kind, even if the attempts at describing general characteristics in intellectual development have possibly overshadowed his mapping out of the psychological structure of individual concepts (see, for instance, Flavell, 1963).

Two decades ago Schatzman and Strauss (1955) carried out a study aimed at describing functional differences between groups with varying educational and professional backgrounds concerning how they apprehended and described certain phenomena in the world around them. After a devastating storm in a town in Arkansas several hundred people were asked what had actually happened. The differences between the various groups were not only differences in ability to give a clear and sufficiently detailed description of the course of events. Nor was it merely a matter of varying degrees of grammatical correctness or of a more or less elaborate vocabulary. The most significant find was:

... a considerable disparity in (a) the number and kinds of perspectives utilized in communication; (b) the ability to take the listener's role; (c) the handling of classification; (d) the frameworks and stylistic devices which order and implement the communication.

More recently, in various contexts, examples of qualitative analysis in terms of the content of learning and thinking have been given by Smedslund (1963), Gruber (1966) and Greenfield *et al* (1972). Karplus and Peterson (1973) have described different conceptions of proportionality (ie of the concept of ratio) and demonstrated that many high-school pupils lack the necessary prerequisites for comprehension of many of the scientific principles dealt with in their textbooks.

A question which can be raised here is whether qualitative variation in thinking between various age-groups, between various cultures and between individuals within the same culture and the same group can be described in similar terms (ie whether we can assume commensurability between the different sources of variation). If there is such a common dimension of variation, it could possibly be thought of as representing a variation in complexity of thinking. The only way of finding an answer to this question is, of course, to pay more attention to the phenomenon in itself (ie to learning and thinking) than to the limited aspects of it which have traditionally been treated within separate scientific disciplines and subdisciplines.

Research on learning and thinking has, in our opinion, too often concerned itself with the wrong questions. There has been an attempt to establish general properties of learning and thinking without consideration of content. In all the examples mentioned above, however, an attempt has been made to describe how certain specific concepts, problems and phenomena are understood by different people. We believe that it is precisely the content of man's view of the world around him that is the proper subject of research on learning and thinking.

This is true both of basic research and of applied research. As far as the learning-teaching level in higher education is concerned, we must identify the basic concepts and principles in various academic subjects and describe the variation in how these concepts and principles are understood or misunderstood. In this way we can discover both what the individual acquires and what he fails to acquire. The idea is simple enough: in order to help the students understand, we must first understand their way of thinking about the topics with which we are concerned.

References

Biggs, J B (1973) Dimensions of study behaviour: another look at ATI. Paper presented at the Annual Conference of the Australian Association for Research in Education, Sydney, 9-11 November

Bruner, J S (1960) *The Process of Education.* Cambridge : Harvard University Press

Bruner, J S (1971) *The Relevance of Education.* New York : Norton

Flavell, J H (1963) *The Developmental Psychology of Jean Piaget.* Princeton : Van Nostrand

Goldman, R D (1972) Effects of a logical versus a mnemonic learning strategy on performance in two undergraduate psychology classes, *Journal of Educational Psychology* 63: 347-52

Greenfield, P M and Childs, C P (1972) Weaving, colour terms and pattern representation. (Unpublished paper)

Greenfield, P M, Nelson, K and Saltzman, E (1972) The development of rulebound strategies for manipulating seriated cups: a parallel between action and grammar, *Cognitive Psychology* 3: 291-310

Gruber, H E (1966) Factors controlling the rate of conceptual change: a study of Charles Darwin's thinking, *Proceedings of the 18th International Congress of Psychology,* Moscow

Karplus, R and Peterson, R W (1973) Intellectual development beyond elementary school II: ratio, a survey. In K Frey and M Lang (eds) *Cognitive Processes and Science Instruction.* Bern : Huber (pp 314-21)

Perry, W G (1970) *Forms of Intellectual and Ethical Development in the College Years: A Scheme.* New York : Holt, Rinehart & Winston

Poulsen, S C (1970) Study skills and mathematics achievement, *Report from the Danish Institute for Educational Research,* no 2

Schatzman, L and Strauss, A (1955) Social class and modes of communication, *The American Journal of Sociology* 60: 329-38

Smedslund, J (1963) The concept of correlation in adults, *Scandinavian Journal of Psychology* 4: 165-73

Svensson, L (1975) Study skills and learning. (Manuscript)

Wertheimer, M (1912) Ueber das Denken der Naturvoelker, Zahlen und Zahlgebilde, *Zeitschrift fuer Psychologie* 60: 321-78. Translated and reprinted in abbreviated form in W D Ellis (ed) (1938) *A Source Book of Gestalt Psychology.* London : Routledge (pp 265-73)

Wertheimer, M (1945) *Productive Thinking.* New York : Harper

1.3 Conversational Techniques in the Study and Practice of Education

GORDON PASK

Pask, G (1976) Conversational techniques in the study and practice
of education, *British Journal of Educational Psychology* **46**: 12-25.
Reproduced here with permission of the author and the editor.

Introduction

The intention of this paper is to introduce some of the basic ideas and
techniques used in a series of recent investigations of learning involving
realistically complex learning materials. It has proved impossible to give
a full description here, and this may lead to misunderstandings about
both the theory and the methods used. However, the ideas have been
developed more fully elsewhere (Pask, 1975a, 1975b) and further
details may be obtained from the author.

The starting point is the idea that the fundamental unit for
investigating complex human learning is a conversation involving
communication (see McCulloch, 1965) between two participants in the
learning process, who commonly occupy the roles of learner and
teacher. In an experimental situation, such as that used, for example,
by Piaget, one of the participants is the experimenter who plays a less
active role than that of teacher. Evidence of learning may come from
comments or answers from the learner, or from the use of materials
which demonstrates understanding more unambiguously than do verbal
responses. In the research reported here the mental processes used by
the learner in reaching an understanding of a topic are exteriorised by
providing apparatus which controls his learning and also allows records
to be made of the steps taken.

An essential part of the apparatus is a subject-matter representation —
a diagram of the relationship between concepts which need to be
grasped before the topic as a whole can be fully understood. The
student is provided with materials and practical demonstrations to help
him understand the concepts and relationships and is allowed to explore
the concept structure with a good deal of freedom, provided certain
fundamental principles are not violated. The student progresses through
his learning sequence generally by making a series of electrical contacts
which show, by means of lights, what are his immediate learning tasks.
The electrical contacts are also linked to a computer which monitors
and records the steps taken. The computer thus provides a permanent
record of the learning strategies adopted by the student and also
prevents the student from making forbidden moves or attempting to go
further than his present level of understanding allows. This procedure
provides an effective learning environment for the student and also data

for the research worker which allow him to examine learning strategies which are normally only accessible through introspection (as in the work described by Marton in the previous paper in this text).

These experimental methods represent an entirely different research procedure from those commonly used in investigating human learning. Conventional laboratory investigations (such as those by Wason, 1968) and factor-analytic studies (Guilford, 1960) provide important evidence about certain types of intellectual activity or structure, but it is argued that conversational theory, as developed later in this paper, provides important evidence about how students learn realistic bodies of subject matter over appreciable intervals.

In fact, the theory takes us much further than that. It permits the investigation of other important, but elusive, aspects of human learning which have educational implications — notably, the nature and control of understanding; the nature and use of analogical concepts; learning style; innovation; and learning to learn. The chief drawback is that it becomes necessary, in developing conversational theory, to redefine common terms (such as understanding) to have a restricted and more precise meaning and also to introduce new terms in describing the operation of the apparatus used in these studies. These various terms are italicised when they are introduced and the sense in which they are being used is explained. Another problem in describing this approach to learning is that it no longer is possible to make a clear distinction between learner and teacher in describing the two participants in the conversation which leads to learning. It soon becomes clear that the brain of the person who is learning can operate in two distinct modes which can be viewed as 'teacher' (directing attention to what needs to be done) and 'learner' (assimilating the subject matter), when a student is using structured learning materials and appropriate heuristics.

It is, of course, risky to set up a new theoretical structure. Most traditional theories are well founded in experimental work and have demonstrated their value in some applied fields. However, the current approach rarely, if ever, contradicts well established ideas on learning; rather it reinterprets them in a way which has greater educational utility and which also unifies ideas and evidence derived from other experimental procedures. Conversational theory basically sets up a *system* within which to view learning. In this it resembles the information processing approach to perception and learning described by Broadbent (1957, 1971), Miller *et al* (1960) and Welford (1968). The methods adopted, however, draw from a wide variety of approaches. It makes use of, for example, the experimental procedures and ideas of Piaget (eg Flavell, 1963; Vygotsky, 1962; and Luria, 1961); personal construct theory (Kelly, 1955); transactionalism (Laing *et al*, 1966; Bateson, 1972); behaviourism; and eclectic functionalism (Bartlett, 1932; Poulton, 1953). Moreover, conversation theory accommodates the structural psychology of Scandura (1973) and, as a bonus, can draw on ideas from the fields of artificial intelligence and computer-aided instruction.

PREVIOUS RESEARCH USING CONVERSATIONAL TECHNIQUES

The techniques of observation and recording of conversations in the study of learning are not, in themselves, new. The themes pervading conversation theory have been voiced repeatedly. There are also methodological precedents in the approaches of Piaget, of Vygotsky, or of Papert (see Paper 3.3) which represent conversational methods for probing, observing and exteriorising normally hidden cognitive events — notably, 'the paired experiment' and the 'questioning interview'. Both techniques rely upon a participant experimenter in the role of a tutor, interviewer or interrogator, who shares in the mental activity of the respondent but who still obeys certain pre-specified, though conditional, rules. Several aspects of these methods are of special interest: the eliciting of explanatory responses, the notion of agreement between participants, and the representation of thoughts and discoveries. The problem situation is embodied in a physical artefact, such as a puzzle, a mechanical gadget, or else a concrete situation (water jars, metric rods and other means of depicting conservation of quantity, volume, etc). Whatever the apparatus may be, it is jointly perceived by the participants (respondent and experimenter) and is open to external observation.

The experimenter poses problems (some of them designed to place insuperable obstacles in the respondent's path) concerned with the function of the artefact or extensions of its function. The respondent replies, either verbally or by manipulating the artefact. Typically, the questions involve 'how' and 'why' and the answers, if forthcoming, are explanations or constructive responses. Since some inquiries are designed to pose insoluble problems, the respondent sometimes appeals for help and, in this case, the experimenter performs a demonstration or points out a principle or suggests some way in which the artefact could be modified. All explanations, whether verbally uttered or not, can be interpreted in relation to the problem situation. Thus, the participants are able to reach an agreement and the basis for their agreement is exteriorised for impartial scrutiny. Parallels with conversational theory will subsequently become apparent.

The development of conversational theory

Conversational theory, as already stated, represents a systems approach to learning. It has certain basic postulates and definitions through which its properties are described. Learning is seen as taking place through *interpreted formal relationships*, such as 'next', 'adjacent', 'periodic', 'dual', 'sum' or 'product'. These formal relationships are interpreted in terms of a context (societal, electrical, mechanical, statistical) and appear as sets of connected propositions (physical laws, social theories) which will be called *topics*. The *specific* meaning of this, and subsequent terms, must be noted. The *concept* of a topic is seen as a way of satisfying the relationship embodied in that topic, rather than simply a stored description. Similarly, a *memory* of a topic becomes a procedure which reconstructs or reproduces concepts. Within conversation theory learning develops through *agreements* between the participants which subsequently lead to *understanding* by the learner. Again the terms have a specific meaning which depends on the apparatus used for controlling learning and demonstrating understanding.

In normal conversation understanding of a topic is demonstrated if the learner provides a verbal explanation of its meaning in accord with an accepted standard definition. In the typical Piagetian experiment understanding is demonstrated by both verbal and non-verbal means. The experimenter questions the child, but also observes manipulations of the apparatus, and ultimately agrees that a valid explanation is given. In our own work, extensive use is made of modelling facilities in which the student's model building behaviour provides non-verbal explanations of a topic and thus exteriorises some of his thought processes. While agreement can be reached at a verbal level between student and teacher and is a necessary condition for understanding, within conversational theory additional evidence of understanding is required. Not only must the student be able to describe the concept (which may reflect only rote or temporary learning), he must also be able to *use* the underlying relationships by operating on appropriate apparatus to demonstrate understanding.

A concept of, say T, has been defined as an internal procedure which brings about and satisfies T. The procedure is a class of what may be thought of as 'mental programs' which satisfy the relationships embodied in T and there will be many ways, using a modelling facility, in which T can be represented. 'Teacher' and 'student' may choose different ways of representing T in practical terms, but the concepts will be equivalent if both representations, when executed, lead to the same outcome, or satisfy the same relation. *Agreement* will then have been reached about the concept, but understanding may still not have been satisfactorily demonstrated.

Within conversation theory *understanding* depends on the ability to reconstruct the concept of T. The only demonstrably stable or permanent concepts in the memory are seen as those which can be reconstructed *ab initio* by applying certain common cognitive operations to topics which are initially understood. For the present it is convenient to group a variety of cognitive operations under a single term *discovery* (Belbin, 1969). This 'shorthand notation' carries with it a recognition that the underlying mental operations are psychologically and formally distinct, and that students will differ in their competence to use different kinds of 'discovery' operations.

To ensure that a demonstration of understanding is unambiguous it is required to be carried out in a particular way, using modelling facilities in conjunction with a subject-matter representation which summarises the relationship between topics within the subject matter. This leads to the next crucial part of conversation theory — that the student should see in advance the 'map of knowledge' through which he is to work.

SUBJECT-MATTER REPRESENTATION

In the Piagetian interview or the paired experiment, the particular experimenter probes the respondent in order to draw out his concepts of the problem situation — for example, by asking why or how an event takes place or what would happen if some feature of the situation changed. In this type of learning the experimenter must have a comprehensive knowledge of the learning *domain* to provide appropriate corrective assistance. The experimenter can thus be assumed to have a mental 'map' of the subject matter, against which to compare the respondent's responses. Such an internal representation of knowledge has the defect that only the verbalised parts brought out through the conversation are made accessible to the respondent, or to an external observer. It seems clear that there must be great advantages in providing *both* participants with an external representation of the subject matter through which topics can be identified and discussed. In this way, explanation can be initiated by either participant.

Allying this idea to the earlier formal definitions of concepts and topics, it becomes necessary to develop a network of topics and concepts which represent the chosen subject-matter area. It is also necessary to ensure that the formal relationships between the concepts are made explicit within the network. The final network within which the student works is called an *entailment structure*, which is developed initially from discussions with a subject-matter specialist and later through working out more precisely the logical relationships involved.

The starting point is a thesis on the chosen subject area expounded usually by a subject-matter expert, although it can be done by a student. The thesis is then broken down into a series of derivations bringing out the various topics, concepts and relationships involved. Each topic relation stands for a class of valid explanations of the topic, or it can be thought of as a series of abstract programs which would satisfy the topic relation if they were compiled and executed. Again, to meet the requirements of the narrow meaning of *understanding*, the entailment structure developed must have the type of 'cyclicity' which allows a student to reconstruct a concept and also have 'consistency', implying that all the topics can be separately identified and connected by derivation paths.

DEVELOPMENT OF AN ENTAILMENT STRUCTURE

The techniques which have been developed for enabling subject-matter specialists to expound a thesis within the constraints imposed by conversation theory involve interaction with a computer which stores the information already provided and also provokes the expositor(s) to further clarification of the underlying relationships. It is important to stress that the resulting structure, describing say 'optics', is merely the expositor's thesis on optics. It is not 'optics' in any ideal sense; the thesis represents only the personal construction of one or more expositors.

Initially, the subject-matter specialist is required to cite topics which are involved in his thesis — say P, Q, R, S and T. Next he is asked to construct a thesis on the assumption, which is later checked, that he can explain each topic by saying how it is derived from the others. Suppose his thesis is that T is derivable from P and Q. In terms of conversation theory, this means that an explanation of T can be derived from an explanation of *P* and *Q*, provided that the student is capable of the cognitive operations which have been labelled *discovery*. The expositor's derivation is accepted if, and only if, an explanation of *P* and *Q* can also be derived from the explanation of *T*. This requirement provides the necessary cyclicity or 'getting back' property which can later be used to demonstrate understanding.

There may be, and nearly always are, different ways of deriving *T* — from *P* and *Q*, say, but also perhaps from *Q, R* and *S*. Such derivation paths are kept distinct and are conveniently exhibited to the expositor in the form of a diagram, or directed graph, in which the *nodes* stand for topics, the *arcs* for parts of a derivation and the *arc clusters* (eg the pair of arcs linking *P* to *T* and *Q* to *T*) for derivation paths. Figure 1.1 shows the structure '*T* derived from *P, Q*', while Figure 1.2 shows '*T* derived from *P* and *Q* or from *R* and *S*'.

The term *entailment* is used as shorthand for the whole relation represented by 'derivable from . . . given the necessary cognitive operations involved in discovery'. To codify entailment it is necessary at least to discriminate between axiomatic, purely formal, derivations and *correspondences* (morphisms, such as isomorphism) which depend upon the potential, but not yet identified, universes of interpretation. For example, no such distinction is shown in Figures 1.1 or 1.2 but one does appear in Figure 1.3 (which is explained in simplified form in Figure 1.4 and its footnotes) where electrical and mechanical universes of interpretation are identified.

As a thesis is expounded under the constraints demanded to maintain cyclicity and consistency, its representation burgeons into an expanded version showing a whole series of topics (nodes) and interconnecting lines (arcs). At this stage the diagram is called an *entailment mesh*, which must later be simplified and tightened up to form the final entailment structure. As the mesh develops the expositor is urged to expand the thesis by saying what the peripheral topic relations are, and these additions cause the mesh to widen and produce more interconnections between topics.

At this stage the structure, as stored by the computer, contains nodes with names, but only a 'formal' or abstract meaning. Subsequently the expositor provides adjectives or *descriptors* which give ordinary meaning to the topics within the entailment mesh. But, once this is done, we move away from the abstract graph, towards the practical descriptions of the concepts later developed within the ancillary modelling facilities.

Most studies which employ explicit representation of subject matter take it for granted that a description is given and understood by the participants. Commonly, this description is just sensibly chosen, as in Bruner, Goodnow and Austin's (1956) study of concept acquisition. Sometimes it is based upon a factor analytic resolution of semantic scales, as in Osgood's (1962) semantic differential techniques. Among the exceptions to this rule is work by Thomas (1970) and his associates in which exploratory conversations, often concerned with learning, are based upon mutually generated descriptions. Such descriptions are obtained from one respondent (here an expositor) by

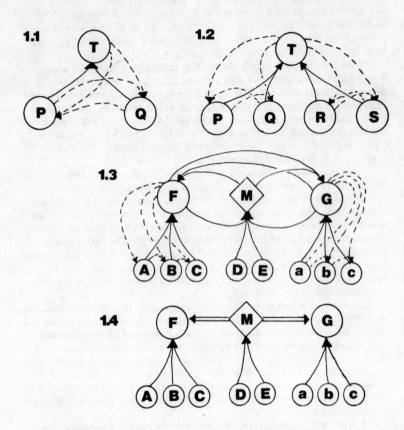

DERIVATIONS.

1.1. topic T derived from topic P and topic Q.
1.2. topic T derived from topic P and topic Q, or from topic R and topic S.
1.3. a correspondence, M, between topics F and G, depending upon D and E (see explanation below).
1.4. a shorthand notation for Figure 1.3. when interpreted (see text) to represent an analogy.
One plausible interpretation of Figs. 1.3 and 1.4 is as follows :

F = Mechanical Oscillator.
G = Electrical Oscillator.
A = Mass.
B = Friction.
C = Elasticity.
E = laws of simple harmonic motion.

a = Inductance.
b = Resistance.
c = Capacitance.
D = Properties (predicate name) distinguishing electrical and mechanical universes.

M = Analogical Topic containing the formal similarity (E) which is common to F and G as well as the class of property—value distinctions (D is only one of any) which express differences essential to any analogy relation.

Figure 1

applying the repertory grid sampling procedure technique (Bannister & Mair, 1968) to elicit descriptors and their values which are Kelly's (1955) 'personal constructs'. If the situation warrants serious attention to the description (construct) schemes of several expositors a more sophisticated routine, exchange grids (Thomas, 1970), is used to compare individual views and obtain a mutually shared description.

Within conversational theory we opt for descriptors which are personal constructs and which are also compatible with the formal structure already laid out. (This approach allows students to become expositors.) The description process can be shown briefly by the following stages:

1. The expositor chooses a *head node* which is the topic he believes his thesis is about. Many head nodes may be produced in the formation of an entailment mesh, as expositors often recognise the 'true' head node fairly late in the process.

2. The mesh is now pruned (by removing the dotted 'black linkages' in Figure 1) to yield a structure that is hierarchical apart from the introduction of correspondences (as in Figure 1.4) which become analogy relations, once they are interpreted.

3. The putative analogies are ordered and groups of them are used as though they were 'objects' in repertory grid administration. Each group of nodes is used to generate at least one construct (or descriptor name) having real values (+, −; or rating scale numerals) that discriminate the topics which are related by the analogy and the value NULL (' * ' or 'irrelevant') on the analogy itself. For example, in Figure 1.4 the descriptor name, 'Scientific Discipline' may be entered as D and has values 'Electrical' and 'Mechanical'on topics F and G ('electrical oscillator' and 'mechanical oscillator'). D is the difference part of an analogy relation (node M). The systemic or formal similarity preserved by the analogy is expressed by the equations for simple harmonic oscillation (node E). All constructs so far elicited are given values on all the nodes (as in rating constructs over all the objects in a set, not just the triple selected for construct elicitation in Kelly's approach).

4. The process continues until all topic nodes can be *uniquely* identified.

5. At this stage the main descriptors divide up into independent universes of interpretation for each of which an independent part of the modelling facility is required. The lowermost nodes, which refer to a particular part of the modelling facility, specify the kinds of formal relations that are to be modelled in it when (non-verbally) explaining topics with nodes at a superordinate position in the hierarchy. For example, in Figure 1.4, two partitions of the modelling facility are required — one is a simple 'electricity bench', while the other is a simple 'mechanics bench' both of which would be found in any school physics laboratory. In this case, it is necessary to model both electrical circuits and mechanical devices (with springs, weights, and so on), some of which act as simple harmonic oscillators.

6. The entire pruned and described entailment mesh now created forms the *entailment structure*.

7. Finally the expositor is required to do what was originally described as necessary, namely to use the modelling facility, which has

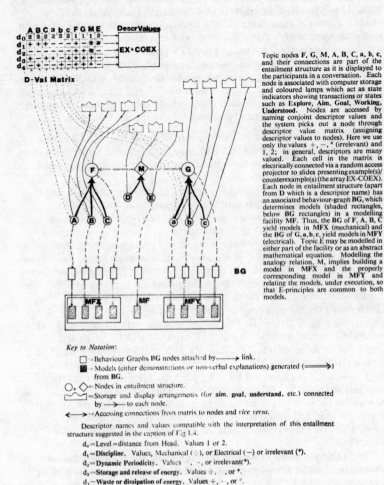

Topic nodes F, G, M, A, B, C, a, b, c, and their connections are part of the entailment structure as it is displayed to the participants in a conversation. Each node is associated with computer storage and coloured lamps which act as state indicators showing transactions or states such as Explore, Aim, Goal, Working, Understood. Nodes are accessed by naming conjoint descriptor values and the system picks out a node through descriptor value matrix (assigning descriptor values to nodes). Here we use only the values +, −, * (irrelevant) and 1, 2; in general, descriptors are many valued. Each cell in the matrix is electrically connected via a random access projector to slides presenting example(s)/counterexample(s) (the array EX+COEX). Each node in entailment structure (apart from D which is a descriptor name) has an associated behaviour-graph BG, which determines models (shaded rectangles, below BG rectangles) in a modelling facility MF. Thus, the BG of F, A, B, C yield models in MFX (mechanical) and the BG of G, a, b, c, yield models in MFY (electrical). Topic E may be modelled in either part of the facility or as an abstract mathematical equation. Modelling the analogy relation, M, implies building a model in MFX and the properly corresponding model in MFY and relating the models, under execution, so that E-principles are common to both models.

Key to Notation:

☐ =Behaviour Graphs BG nodes attached by ——→ link.

▨ = Models (either demonstrations or non-verbal explanations) generated (===⇒) from BG.

◯, ◇ =Nodes in entailment structure.

〰 =Storage and display arrangements (for aim, goal, understand, etc.) connected by ——→ to each node.

◀——→ =Accessing connections from matrix to nodes and *vice versa*.

Descriptor names and values compatible with the interpretation of this entailment structure suggested in the caption of Fig 1.4.

d_0 =Level =distance from Head. Values 1 or 2.

d_1 =**Discipline**. Values, Mechanical (+), or Electrical (−) or irrelevant (*).

d_2 =**Dynamic Periodicity**. Values +, −, or irrelevant(*).

d_3 =**Storage and release of energy**. Values +, −, or *.

d_4 =**Waste or dissipation of energy**. Values +, −, or *.

Figure 2

now been specified, to express the class of valid explanations for each topic of the entailment structure in a standard form which can be represented unambiguously in a computer. Perhaps the most suitable name for such a standard form of explanation is a *behaviour graph (BG)* meaning the (many different) prescriptions for building models that act as non-verbal explanations; not to be confused with the behaviour produced if the model is executed (either externally, in the facility, or 'internally' in the student's brain). Elsewhere, the BG has been termed a *task structure.*

THE CONVERSATIONAL DOMAIN

The result of the efforts of the expositors to fulfil the conditions imposed by conversational theory on the description of a thesis is a *conversational domain* (such as that shown in Figure 2), which represents in diagrammatic form the apparatus necessary to explore the relationships between such topics as the laws of simple harmonic motion and the behaviour of electrical and mechanical oscillators (as shown in Figures 1.3 and 1.4). This conversational domain consists of:

(a) an entailment structure;
(b) the associated collection of BGs indicating acceptable explanations;
(c) the modelling facility, partitioned into appropriate universes such as mechanical or electrical apparatus with which to test understanding of topics;
(d) descriptors which explain in everyday language the subject matter contained formally and symbolically in the entailment structure;
(e) various signalling and information storage arrangements that are attached to the topic nodes (lamps to guide the student and pulses passed to the computer indicating the step being taken by the student); and
(f) examples and counter-examples, usually displayed graphically, that provide the context for the descriptors and hence give meaning to the thesis.

The example given in Figure 2 is much simpler than entailment structures used in actual experiments. For example, a thesis on heat engines involved 60 nodes; reaction kinetics involved 180; meiosis and mitosis 275, probability theory 320, while the maximum used so far has been 500 nodes (statistics).

Tutorial conversations and transactions

The student using a conversational domain is able to undertake various learning activities or *transactions* either with an experimenter who responds verbally, or by relying on information provided in pamphlets under computer guidance within the framework of the entailment structure. In order to give a clear idea of what might take place in a conversational domain consider a tutorial conversation in which one participant (B) is the teacher, while the other (A) is the learner.

Participant A is ignorant of some of the topics and ultimately intends to learn the head topic. He has access to the modelling facility, the entailment structure, and its description scheme. *B*, in addition, is given access to and control over the descriptive examples and counter-examples, the various *BG*s and the state-markers which indicate the transaction taking place. *B* can take advantage of this polarity to act in the role of a teacher. *B* may use all kinds of acumen; he may learn about *A*, give good advice and so on. All we require is that the assistance he gives and the agreements he reaches are compatible with and derived from the entailment structure and its *BG*.

The following types of transaction may take place:

(a) *A* can ask *B* about the values of descriptors in general, and he can point out topics by citing topic descriptions, ie combinations of descriptor values. For example, referring to Figure 2, *A* can access the node encoded as *G* by conjoint statements like '*Level* $(d_0) = 1$ and *Discipline* (d_1) = Electrical' or by 'Periodic $(d_2 = +)$ and Discipline (d_1) = Electrical' or by any other combination that identifies this node. If he can uniquely point out a topic, he can ask what other descriptors (if any) have other than null values on these topics and, if so, what the values are. These questions are efforts to make sense of the domain, and if *B* answers the questions by providing examples and counter-examples of descriptor values to which he has access, they form part of what are called *explore transactions*.

(b) *A* can state his intention to come to grips with any topic that he can point out uniquely, using a combination of descriptor values. Such a statement is an intended immediate aim in learning. If *B* is wise he will check *A*'s sincerity (for *A* might point at topics haphazardly) by determining that *A* appreciates the meaning of the descriptors used to specify the intended aim. Assuming this precaution has been followed, we then refer to the original intention statement as an *aim request*.

(c) *B* validates the aim by asking *A* multiple-choice questions spanning the values of these descriptors and *B*'s reply is evaluated by confidence estimates over the response alternatives, to questions about the descriptors. If *B*'s certainty about the correct alternatives is high enough to make learning feasible (appropriate indexes, $\theta*$, are described by Baker [1969], Shuford *et al* [1966] and Dirkswager [1975], then the topic node is instated as the current *aim*; failing that, *A* is requested to engage in further *explore* transactions to obtain further information and so to increase the value of $\theta*$.

(d) Once an aim is instated, its node is marked by a signal light visible to both *A* and *B*. Then *A* can ask *B* questions like 'How am I permitted to learn about the aim topic?' and *B* is in a position to reply either by a gross display of all derivation paths or by delineating permissible derivations from the aim topic to topics which appear lower in the hierarchy and are marked *understood*, or else to topics which are lowest and simplest nodes.

(e) Given this information, *A* is also able to indicate the topic or topics he immediately wishes to learn about. The topics *A* desires to learn about are called *goals*; and these are marked with a goal signal to this effect. There may be one goal or several; if there is only one goal it may, in fact, be the aim topic.

(f) If B is wise he will check A's ability to learn about the selected goals by seeing that: (1) the goals are all situated on allowable paths; and (2) each permissible goal satisfies the condition that, for at least one derivation path leading to that goal (and usually there are many paths), all immediately subordinate topics in this path are marked as being understood. Any goal satisfying these criteria is called a *working topic* and the goal signal is changed to a working signal.

(g) If A disputes B's evaluation of his understanding or if no topics are currently marked as understood (which is the starting condition) then A can engage in an 'explain and derive' transaction. First A must show that he can explain the outstanding topic (an A, B agreement over models for the topic). If so, then A must show that he can also explain the immediately subordinate topics on some allowable derivation path. Then the outstanding topic can be marked as understood.

(h) All the transactions leading up to the selection of working topics are components of a 'higher level' agreement, namely, an agreement regarding the derivation of the topic.

(i) For any working topic A can, if he wishes, attempt a non-verbal explanation. On the other hand, he can request information by asking, for example, 'How do I explain this topic?' B is in a position to reply by recourse to the BG of the topic which generates the accepted non-verbal explanations of the topic. These model building behaviours are called *demonstrations* since they are delivered as though by a laboratory demonstrator. After each demonstration, B asks A the question 'How do you explain this topic?' and B keeps a record of all the demonstrations so far delivered.

At some stage, either A constructs an explanatory model for the topic or else the topic is discarded. Explanation (model building) often involves trials and self-corrected revisions. When A is satisfied with his 'final version' he submits the explanation (or explanatory model) to B who checks it to make sure it is not a replica, parrot-wise, of a demonstration already seen by A. It is accepted as understanding if this condition is satisfied and if there is 'agreement' in the sense explained earlier.

Generally, the explanations are non-verbal (models) and B's model will be found, like a demonstration, among the BG of the topic in hand. Under these circumstances, agreement and correctness are both secured, if both models do, on execution, satisfy the same relation. If so, the topic is marked *understood*. If not, A may opt for more demonstrations or revise his approach (*aim* and/or *goal* selection).

The crucial point is that an understanding in the present strong and special sense is determined by a two-level agreement: A and B agree about a derivation and, in the context of this derivation they also agree about an explanation of each topic.

Once a node is marked as understood, its state does not change during the rest of the conversation. The justification for this rule is our postulate (and experience) that understood topics have concepts that are stable.

(j) The transactions which lead up to the 'higher level' agreement about a derivation are exteriorised, physically, as a series of node-state distributions displayed throughout the learning process, both to A and B. These diagrams, showing the distributions of explore, aim, goal and understood markers represent learning strategies, which show how the student tackled his attempts to reach and understand his learning goals. Examination of the paths shown in these diagrams has led to the identification of characteristic learning strategies which will be described in a subsequent paper, together with systematic individual differences in competence to learn and discover.

Computer controlled conversations

In the tutorial condition described so far, B provides the answers to A's questions and gives appropriate demonstrations. His actions may involve help and encouragement, but the basic core of these activities depends only on the conditions imposed by conversation theory within the particular domain being explored. It is thus possible to replace the tutorial arrangement with what is called the *standard experimental condition* in which the tutor's control is handed over to a computer, or to an experimenter who has no teaching function.

Operating in this condition the student is required to accept certain rules. He must:

(a) intend to learn the head topic;
(b) obey the transaction rules (as described earlier);
(c) have only one aim at a time (except those which are being explored);
(d) not already understand the head topic; and
(e) undertake some transactions until the head topic is finally understood.

Under these conditions the computer is able to direct the student to appropriate information and demonstrations available in pamphlets and on tape/slide presentations. The student can carry out tests of his understanding and the computer will check which of the derivations are correct, in terms of the BG. The student thus progresses as he did with the tutor present and again it is important to realise that the variety of paths and demonstrations available means that students have considerable freedom to learn within the constraints of the system as a whole.

This standard condition shows why it was stressed originally that the distinction between teacher and student can no longer be maintained. In the tutorial arrangement A interacts with B through the conversational domain within the defined restrictions. But under the standard condition what happens? A does not converse with the machine, although the computer checks the moves made. In fact, A behaves in the two ways described earlier. One part of his brain (A_1) works out the moves to be made, asks questions, seeks answers, while another part (A_2) is trying to understand the topics.

OPERATING SYSTEM USING CONVERSATIONAL THEORY

To date two pieces of equipment have been developed within which conversational domains can be established. CASTE (Pask & Scott, 1973) is a computer controlled laboratory installation. A portable version, INTUITION, has been used for research in schools and colleges and is relatively inexpensive. Both systems contain a board showing a diagram of the entailment structure with electric sockets at the nodes surrounded by coloured lamps which indicate the transactions being undertaken and the stage the student has reached in learning the topics. The student uses wires to connect sockets according to the rules laid down, and the computer checks that each move is acceptable. The modelling facilities and ancillary descriptive materials are also part of the equipment. Figure 3 shows INTUITION as it has been used in schools for a thesis on probability theory.

A variant of these systems which does involve a tutor has also been used. This has been given the name TEACHBACK. In this system the tutor (B) attempts to maintain a neutral role by acting the role of a student and asking the learner (A) to provide an explanation of his own for each topic selected. He must also explain how he derived that explanation. TEACHBACK is important because it provides additional information about how students learn from (stilted) verbal transactions, as well as providing the standard behavioural information. The method has been used successfully in conjunction with tests, but only over short learning periods. The neutral role is hard for the tutor to maintain, particularly in large subject-matter domains. One-and-a-half hours has proved the maximum period for TEACHBACK to operate at a time.

Conclusion

Conversational theory is built up from stringent definitions of commonly used terms such as understanding and memory. It is associated with a system of learning in which the subject matter is broken down into its basic elements and reconstructed into an arrangement of topics which provides a 'map' for the student. Rules cover the transactions made within the system, but the student is able to follow different paths and obtain various demonstrations before testing his own understanding of topics. He is also free to adopt his own learning strategy within defined limits.

It is possible to view other experiments on learning as approximating to the conditions described here. For example, in TEACHBACK the student is involved in free learning, exploratory behaviour, and is guided by a neutral onlooker. The experiments of Luria and Piaget follow a similar approach, but lack the demands for proof of understanding built into the standard condition of conversational theory. Of course, the test of the theory will be in its explanatory power on the one hand, and in its effectiveness in bringing about understanding on the other. Some indication of explanatory power has already been given and a subsequent paper will provide evidence of the effectiveness of the systems so far developed, in which students learn, understand and remember complex subject matters.

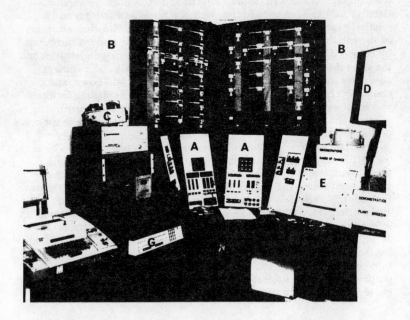

The 'INTUITION' Conversational system as used for learning about 'probability theory.'

A = Modelling Facility for topics in Probability theory: a 'Probability laboratory' in which demonstrations are given by instruction cards laid over fascia and in which non-verbal explanations are elicited.

B = Entailment Structure. Each topic has node with group of 'state' signals. Entailment connections shown by lines and descriptor values by colour and alpha-numeric coded regions.

C = Random Access Projector, Displaying examples and counter examples as required in explore transactions.

D = Screen.

E = Confidence Estimation console and questioning device.

F = Controller and recorder.

G = Minicomputer (can service several student stations).

Figure 3

Acknowledgements

The research reported in this paper is supported by the SSRC under Research Programme HR 2708/2 'Learning Styles, Educational Strategies and Representations of Knowledge: Methods and Applications'.

References

Baker, E (1969) The uncertain student and the understanding computer. In F Brisson and D De Montmollin (eds) *Programmed Learning Research.* Paris : Dunod

Bannister, D and Mair, J (1968) *The Evaluation of Personal Constructs.* New York : Academic Press

Bartlett, F C (1932) *Remembering.* Cambridge : Cambridge University Press

Bateson, G (1972) *Steps to an Ecology of Mind.* New York : Intertext Books

Belbin, R M (1969) *The Discovery Method in Training.* Training Information Paper H5, Department of Employment. London : HMSO

Broadbent, D E (1957) *Perception and Communication.* London : Pergamon

Broadbent, D E (1971) *Decision and Stress.* London : Academic Press

Bruner, J, Goodnow, J and Austin, G (1956) *A Study of Thinking.* New York : Wiley

Dirkswager, A (1975) Computer based testing with automatic scoring based on subjective probabilities. Pre-print for the 1975 IFIP Congress on Computers in Education

Flavell, J H (1963) *The Developmental Psychology of Jean Piaget.* New York : Van Nostrand

Guilford, J P (1960) The structure of intellect, *Psychological Bulletin* 53: 267-82

Kelly, G A (1955) *The Psychology of Personal Constructs* (vols I and II). New York : Norton

Laing, R D, Phillipson, S and Lee, A R (1966) *Interpersonal Perception.* London : Tavistock

Luria, G R (1961) *The Role of Speech in the Regulation of Normal and Abnormal Behaviour.* London : Pergamon

McCulloch, W S (1965) *Embodiments of Mind.* Cambridge, Mass : MIT Press

Miller, G, Gallanter, E and Pribram, K H (1960) *Plans and the Structure of Behaviour.* London : Holt

Osgood, C E (1962) Studies on the generality of affective meaning systems, *Journal of American Psychology* 17: 1-10

Papert, S (1970) Teaching children thinking. *Proceedings of the IFIP Conference on Computer Education, Amsterdam.* Reprinted as Mathematics Thinking, *Bulletin of the Association of Teachers of Mathematics,* no 58, 1972

Pask, G (1975a) *Conversation, Cognition and Learning.* Amsterdam and New York : Elsevier

Pask, G (1975b) *The Cybernetics of Human Learning and Performance.* London : Hutchinson

Pask, G and Scott, B C E (1973) CASTE: a system for exhibiting learning strategies and regulating uncertainties, *International Journal of Man-Machine Studies* 5: 17-52

Poulton, E C (1953) Two channel listening, *Journal of Experimental Psychology* 46: 91-6

Scandura, J M (1973) *Structural Learning.* London : Gordon and Breach

Shuford, E H, Massengill, H and Albert G (1966) Admissible probability measurement procedures, *Psychometrika* 31: 125

Thomas, L F (1970) *Kelly McQuittie: A Computer Program for Focussing the*

Repertory Grid. Centre for the Study of Human Learning, Brunel University

Vygotsky, L S (1962) *Thought and Language.* Cambridge, Mass : MIT Press

Wason, P C (1968) Reasoning about a rule, *Journal of Experimental Psychology* 20: 273-82

Welford, A T (1968) *Fundamentals of Skill.* London : Methuen

1.4 The Psychological Principles underlying the Design of Computer-based Instructional Systems

J ROGER HARTLEY AND KENNETH LOVELL

Hartley, J R and Lovell, K (1977) The psychological principles underlying the design of computer-based instructional systems. Reproduced from A Jones and H Weinstock (eds) *Computer Based Science Instruction.* Groningen : Noordhoff International, with permission of the editors.

1.0 Introduction

The last ten years have seen considerable developments in computer-assisted learning (CAL). Whilst most of this activity has taken place in the USA there have been significant projects in Canada and Western Europe, and in 1972 the British Government set aside £2 million for a five-year National Development Programme. Many reports of these projects have been published so there is sufficient data to justify a review of progress, to consider profitable lines of activity and to debate the difficulties which are, and will be, encountered in present and future work. In general, this paper will take the view that teachers themselves do not make the most efficient use of the CAL materials which have been produced, and that many of these materials do not make the most use of the languages and authoring systems which are available. Of course it is accepted that in the foreseeable future it will not be possible to mimic or replicate the type of instructional dialogue which can take place between the human teacher and student. On the other hand the computer programs can calculate and carry out instructions of data retrieval and processing extremely rapidly; they can also keep detailed records of students' performances and methods. Thus, many facilities and teaching modes become available which can be related to the knowledge which the system holds of the student, and this level of control and adaptivity cannot be matched by the human teacher faced with a group of students. It is also accepted that teachers will find it difficult to integrate computer-based methods within their normal teaching schemes. The former emphasise individualisation and the adaptive nature of teaching, whereas the latter tend to favour minimal variation in the conditions under which individuals are expected to learn.

In providing individualised modes of teaching, efficiency will come from managing those factors which influence learning and so it might be expected that educational psychology would have a central role in CAL. This is not the case in practice. Much of educational technology has tended to neglect psychology and to concentrate upon techniques of task analysis and the diagnosis of task structure. This analysis has been logical rather than psychological, and the program designs have been simplistic in their methods of individualisation. They have often been pragmatically imposed and rarely controlled by valid theories which underpin individual differences.

The purpose of this paper is to redress this balance to a small extent and to indicate some of the psychological work which should be taken into account in designing CAL materials. Before reviewing this evidence a brief synopsis of the main features of developments in CAL is set out, and this provides a framework for the criticisms of program designs which are made in later sections. The principal arguments are for a more comprehensive representation of the student's knowledge state on which to base decision making, and for a richer form of dialogue between the student and the computer programs. These factors suggest the design of more 'knowledgeable' teaching programs and the paper concludes with some examples and some observations on their potential.

2.0 Summary of some styles of application

2.1 TUTORING

A glance through the catalogues of CAL materials will show a wide variety of program design and subject areas to which they have been applied. However, many of them envisage the computer as a tutoring machine, although there has been a move away from large-scale objectives in which the programs are seen as a complete or major replacement of the teacher. A more typical objective is to provide a framework or support for initial teaching by textbook or lecture. The programs check the student's understanding, provide feedback or supplementary instruction where necessary and allow him to apply and extend his knowledge in different contexts. For example, a large-scale CAL project in teaching applied statistics has been established at Leeds University (Abbatt & Hartley, 1976). Over a dozen departments in three institutions are co-operating in the work and approximately one thousand undergraduates per week receive instruction at the terminal. Some of the materials are used for tutoring, and over one hundred small modules deal with topics which occur in a year's course in elementary statistics. The modules have several features. A virtually unlimited number of performance counters are available for representing the student's knowledge state and decision rules can be based on these. The learner can have some control also. He can ask for definitions and help if he is unable to answer a problem or a particular question, and he can request a more detailed level of explanation if he is dissatisfied with the feedback. If he were so inclined, the student could go back to earlier sections, explore different routes through the material and return to his original place in the program when he wished. Calculation and simulation facilities are also available and can be called from the teaching programs.

The tutoring modules act under the command of control programs which are specified by teachers and macrogenerated. The control programs select sections of the pre-stored teaching material, link them together with continuity comments, and specify decision rules which refer to the performance data stored by the modules. The rules usually specify minimum performance standards, and when these are met, the student is given choice over the amount and type of any further instruction he wishes to receive. Through their individual control programs, lecturers can place different emphases on the tutoring programs and alter their prominence within the overall statistics teaching.

The student performance data is collected in files specified in size and identifying name by the author. The data is used by the control programs to guide the dialogue and teaching decisions, and by assessment routines which print advice and guidance in further study for the individual student. A third use is by teachers who can process the files to find out which students are having particular difficulties and which topics are proving difficult for the class as a whole. Further teaching or revision can then be given through lectures, textbooks or remedial teaching at the terminal.

This application has many features which are typical of computer-based tutoring. The teaching initiative and control rests largely with the program. This selects tasks and provides feedback contingent upon completed responses; the learner can only exercise some control through an extremely limited set of commands. The material is designed by experienced teachers who try to specify their objectives, undertake task analyses, sequence the content, set out responses which are anticipated at each point in the program and the routing decisions which are then to be carried out. This detailed and particular teaching specification has to be pre-stored in the computer and this implies that the student can only have limited control over the teaching dialogue. In general he cannot propose his own methods of solution, or comment on the materials, or ask for explanations, or pose supplementary questions unless they have been anticipated by the course author. Thus the teaching modes, though useful, are limited.

Usually tutoring programs are written using general purpose author languages. These consist of commands and conventions which the writer follows so that, when his material is stored in the computer, the author language processor can retrieve and print labelled portions, accept, process and evaluate responses, update student histories, and apply routing instructions. The advantages of author languages are that they are easy to learn, and can be used with any subject area. However they do have several limitations, a principal one being the ways in which they deal with typed responses. Whereas numbers and symbols can be retrieved from the response, and processed arithmetically and algebraically, words are treated as character strings and are matched or compared with exemplars specified by the author. To make this exercise in anticipation manageable, he must carefully limit the command words which can be used by the student and restrict the size of task, question or dialogue step put to him.

2.2 SIMULATION AND THE ILLUSTRATION OF CONCEPTS

In the sciences many concepts are not only difficult to illustrate, but the relations between them are represented in formal and symbolic terms. Many students find it difficult to link these theoretical terms with the conventional language which describes everyday experience. Thus, to make scientific phenomena accessible to the intellect the teacher must illustrate the concepts, build up the student's knowledge structures and allow him to elaborate them in ways which show the nature of the underlying principles. For these reasons providing 'simulation' exercises through computer programs has proved a useful and popular development in science teaching. The idea is that the programs provide a 'working model' of the scientific system. In fact it is the formal representation of the system, ie a set of equations or a quantitative data base, which can be sampled, which is embodied in the programs. Usually the student cannot edit or amend the program itself but he can manipulate the input values and observe the effects on the output displays.

An example of such work is an emergency patient simulation program which has been implemented by Taylor and Scott (1975). The patient is represented at any current time as the state values of a set of vital signs such as temperature, pulse rate, respiration, coma and cyanosis, which are appropriate to the working context. Functions act on these values and so govern their change through time. The student is given a situation, for example a car accident patient with fractures and airway blockages, and he can ask for investigations and tests to be made and treatments to be carried out. In general the tests do not affect the patient's state directly, but they have a time penalty and during this time his condition could deteriorate. The user can monitor the changes and the rates of change in the values of the vital signs, and the results are shown graphically. To improve the patient's condition, the student can propose treatments. To each of these a time increment simulates its administration, after which functions attached to that treatment alter the patient's counter values. If threshold values are exceeded the patient dies. The treatments can be classified into those which are fatal at any point, and those which have good or bad effects in the short and in the long term. The aim, of course, is to hasten the patient's improvement and achieve a stable condition, and the sole feedback given to the user is the patient's state vector.

The objectives are to ensure that the student realises the need for comprehensive monitoring and for having several ongoing treatments. (Thus, in the particular example given above, cortisone will resolve the problem of falling blood pressure but unless the airway is cleared in some way, the cyanosis will be fatal.) The student must also learn to evaluate the various effects of the treatments. (For example, although phenobarbitone has a bad effect on respiration, coma and cyanosis in the long term, it has a good effect on pulse.)

This exercise has many of the features which justify simulation as a teaching device. First, the learner can operate with a simpler system than he would encounter in reality. He has greater control and so it is easier for him to appreciate the relationships, ie the patient's requirements and the effects of treatments. Secondly, the student can see the effects of his decisions without detrimental consequences, and the 'real' time scale is also compressed so that many exercises can be worked through in a relatively short period of time. However, there are some difficulties. Building simulators to serve as teaching devices is not an easy task and requires careful analysis. The dialogue also is limited. In the example above, the student can merely select the investigation or treatment, he cannot discuss his decisions, nor can he ask why or how the treatments have their various effects. There is no discussion of methods of handling such emergency patient situations, and no general teaching guidance is supplied directly with the program. Further, no records are kept of the learner's protocols and so the program is not able to become adaptive on subsequent runs of the simulation exercise.

2.3 TEACHING PROBLEM-SOLVING SKILLS

These deficiencies become more important in teaching problem-solving* skills when experience in developing appropriate heuristics is crucial. By presenting varieties of related tasks the student can learn to pick out those characteristics which indicate the economical methods of solution. Some workers have attempted to use the computer for teaching such skills either by incorporating extended dialogue facilities within the simulation programs, or by allowing simulation modules to be called from author language programs. For example, Bork and Robson (1972) devised a simulation/teaching program for the study of waves. The computer program simulated an experimental investigation of a pulse in a rope, and the student was provided with a measurement facility by which he could enter time and position and be told the rope displacement. There was a definite aim — he had to discover enough about the disturbance to be able to answer numerical questions about its behaviour. On request, the program would summarise the values and plot them graphically. In order to help those students who were working unsystematically and to little effect, Bork and Robson designed the program to retain the student's requests for measurements, make certain checks on them, and print advice based on these evaluations. For example, the program could check if the student had encountered non-zero values; if not the comments would suggest where they might be found. If data collection was haphazard, the program might advise that time should be fixed and the detailed behaviour of the rope studied at a number of different places, or that measurements should be gathered at a particular position for different intervals of time. These hints become progressively stronger so that if a student was performing poorly, the program almost instructed him how to proceed on a step-by-step basis.

In another example, taken from the applied statistics project at Leeds University, simulation modules are called from dialogue programs written in the author language. The topic area is that of experimental design, and for more experienced students a short background synopsis of an actual experiment is taken from the research literature. The

---

* 'Problem solving' is a term which is even more loosely defined and ill-used than 'simulation'. This paper will not attempt a technical definition of either term, but their meanings should be clear from the specific contexts. Problem solving implies a novel situation for the student; he has the requisite knowledge and sub-skills to solve the problem, but he has to sequence his reasoning and/or develop heuristics which take him from the initial to the goal state.

student has to construct a satisfactory experimental plan. He must identify the variables, define hypotheses, set out the methods of measurement, the organisation and design of the experiment and his proposed techniques of data analysis. Populations of data which replicate those reported in the literature have been stored in a simulation program, so the student can try out his decisions, process the data and draw his own conclusions. After a group of students has undertaken the exercise individually an interesting seminar can result. Some details of this experience have been described elsewhere (Abbatt & Hartley, 1974). Ayscough (1973) has developed other applications which help undergraduates to plan laboratory experiments in physical chemistry.

While simulation programs can provide illustrations which it is difficult to give by any other means, and although teaching dialogue can allow more extended problem-solving types of exercises, the student cannot, in any real sense, place his own construction on the problem and set out his own methods of solution. Practically, the program languages which are used do not permit this. All author language material must be pre-stored and the student responses anticipated; the author cannot set out the full range of solutions. Again, simulation modules do not permit direct insight into their structure; the student cannot amend the programs, neither is he involved in their designs. Accordingly some workers have attempted to devise programming languages in which students can write their solutions to problems. The exercise of writing and debugging such programs is claimed to be interesting, to provide deeper insights into the subject matter and to aid general thinking skills. The language itself should be easy to learn, provide immediate and lucid feedback on errors, have a structure which matches that of the subject area, and permit sophisticated programs to be built up from simple procedures.

The most interesting example of this approach is the language LOGO, which can be learnt by schoolchildren and which has suggested interesting developments in the curriculum and methods of teaching mathematics (Papert & Solomon, 1972). For example, the pupil might devise programs to draw geometric shapes on a crt terminal. The simplest procedure is to instruct the cursor to move forward n steps, rotate through an angle and repeat these instructions recursively. By labelling the parameters and altering the values, the pupil can study the shapes produced. Simple additions of an extra step length will cause spiralling, putting in tests to control the sequence of commands will allow the shapes to 'roll' along, or round themselves. Such programs can be extended and can be generalised as the child develops his notions of the properties of shapes and symmetry. (See, eg, Paper 3.3.)

At the university level, Brown and Rubenstein (1972) have used this language with psychology undergraduates, to explore topics in linguistics and grammars. The language APL is also becoming more popular for these problem-solving type objectives and Berry *et al* (1973) have set out some examples for teaching topics in mechanics and in computer science. Again, it should be noted that the dialogue is largely one-sided, with the computer responding to the instructions of the student and providing feedback on syntax errors, or displaying the output of a satisfactory program. The student is strictly limited to the command and syntax structure of the language, and any instruction on formulating the problem or on methods of generalising or correcting programs has to be supplied by a teacher or by the student himself. At present, experience in using these techniques is largely undeveloped and there has been little evaluation of their effects.

3.0 Factors influencing learning

Having summarised some applications in CAL, and considered the advantages and limitations of the techniques, it is appropriate to consider psychological research which shows some of the factors which influence learning. Hopefully this might suggest ways of improving the designs of computer-based teaching programs.

3.1 THE FUNCTION OF FEEDBACK

It is now generally recognised that feedback, ie the message or compound statement which follows the response made by the learner, should not be regarded as a reinforcing stimulus, but as information which will locate error and which may inform the student how to correct it. The word 'may' is used for two reasons; first the feedback information may not be assimilable to the student's ongoing intellectual structures and secondly, the giving of feedback messages assumes a certain level of attention and motivation. These conclusions must not be considered trite. Although the facilitating effects of feedback are often proposed in psychology, experimental demonstrations of the value of immediate feedback using actual lessons have been rare. Further, it will be argued that few CAL programs take full account of the value of feedback, and are not structured so as to control systematically the amount and type of feedback by managing such variables as task type and difficulty. So there are doubts about the importance of feedback in conventional learning situations which are reflected in the structure of many CAL programs.

The cause of this might well be the influence of initial work in programmed instruction. Following Skinner (1954), it was supposed that the learning task should be analysed into steps or tasks small enough to ensure that the probability of a successful response was almost unity. Thus the immediate knowledge of correct results (KCR) would reinforce the learner and strengthen the stimulus-response bond. However, when Grundin (1969) reviewed over thirty-five studies, of which thirteen were concerned specifically with feedback, not one showed a significant increase in learning.

Anderson, Kulhavy and Andre (1971, 1972) have provided some answers to this puzzle. The teaching material they used in their experiments was a linear program on the diagnosis of myocardial infarction from electro cardiograms. This was presented and controlled by computer and subjects were randomly assigned to several different teaching treatments in which knowledge of correct results was given on several different schedules. These included: (i) no KCR; (ii) one hundred per cent KCR; (iii) KCR given only after right answers; and (iv) KCR given only after wrong answers. The students were given pencil-and-paper post-tests. The results of the experiment showed that all other groups did significantly better than the 'no feedback' group. KCR given after wrong responses only was almost as effective as one hundred per cent KCR which was the most successful treatment. In a second similar experiment one group was shown the correct response before having to type it at the terminal (ie a cheat condition). This time the post-tests showed significant differences between the feedback procedures, with the cheat group performing significantly worse than all other groups, even the one which was not given feedback. The interpretation of the results is that the effects of feedback are beneficial, and that whereas in textbooks and programmed texts students can short-circuit the instruction and look ahead to the right answers (ie a cheat condition), presentation by computer means that it is possible to ensure that feedback is unavailable until after the student responds. Checks can also be made on his processing of this information. A second conclusion is that the main function of feedback is not to strengthen or reinforce correct responses, but to locate errors and provide information so that the learner can put them right (for KCR following wrong responses only was almost as good as the hundred per cent feedback treatment). Guthrie (1971) has also given a persuasive demonstration of this. Thus CAL tutorial programs should not necessarily be small step but have tasks large enough to expose the student's misunderstandings and correct them.

As well as the emphases on activity and control which computer-assisted methods can place on learning, the type of information which is provided by the feedback message is important. Further, these variables are likely to interact with the student's abilities. For example, in one experiment carried out at Leeds University, twenty-nine second-year undergraduates in physical chemistry were randomly allocated to three computer-based teaching treatments. In the first the student was merely told if his responses were correct or not. In the second treatment the program evaluated the student's response, located the error and provided information by which the student could see how the correct answer had been derived. However, there was no check that the student had attended to or comprehended the feedback message. The third treatment was similar to the previous one except that the student had to demonstrate his understanding by typing in a satisfactory response. The teaching material was to guide students in planning laboratory experiments in physical chemistry. (More specifically, the experiments concerned reaction kinetics and the determination of equilibrium constants.) Students came to the terminal on the three occasions which were necessary to complete the material. Retention tests and other pencil-and-paper post-tests on planning experiments were given. The results showed significant gains in performance. Not unexpectedly the first teaching treatment was the least satisfactory for learning but took less time. However, the more able students (as measured by performances in the traditional chemistry examinations) from this group learned almost as much as students of similar ability in the other two groups. Thus the results argue for adaptive teaching decision rules which relate type of feedback to a student's competence.

In general, type of feedback information is also related to the type of task which is determined by the educational objectives. A discussion of these matters is contained in Pask (1975). He distinguishes between feedback which relates to the answer itself, to the methods of determining the answer, and to techniques of learning. So it should be noted that giving a central role to feedback does not imply that educational objectives should be limited, or that the teaching mode should be tutorial and directive.

3.2 STRUCTURE AND ORGANISING FRAMEWORKS

Several experiments involving feedback tend to show that for a given set of tasks the greatest learning gains are made by the less able students. This is understandable for frequency of errors, and therefore feedback is a decreasing function of competence. A first inference then, is that task difficulty (a function which relates the student's working levels of success to task or subject-matter characteristics) will be a determining factor in learning since, as well as affecting motivation, it will control the quantity of feedback the student receives. Also, since educational aims are often concerned with the transfer of learning, it is expected, even required, that the feedback messages given to students will have a wider generality than the particular questions to which they refer. Hopefully the student will be stimulated to make these associations with previous experience. Thus methods of sequencing material and tasks are likely to be important in learning, and providing generalising frameworks within which new material can be subsumed might be beneficial also. This section will briefly consider these three aspects of organisation, namely task difficulty, the sequencing of material, and the provision of organisers.

In some circumstances, for example in the learning of algorithmic practice tasks, specific models of task difficulty can be set up. The sub-operations which make up the algorithm can be identified, error factors associated with each of them, and by making some simplifying assumptions of mathematical independence the overall probability of obtaining a successful outcome can be calculated. The student is then represented by his proficiency in the sub-operations and from this, estimates of his working level of success can be made for any future task which requires their use (Woods & Hartley, 1971). In other circumstances such models cannot be proposed even when the material has repeated applications. In this case certain classes of task are chosen and difficulty estimates of them are made from experimental data with a sample of students. Then computer programs can select and mix tasks together so that a specified working level of success is ensured.

It is now necessary to produce some evidence that task difficulty will influence the improvement of performances, and ask the subsidiary question of which levels of difficulty should be set in various tasks. If they are too easy, the internal search process the student uses to produce the response will become impoverished. If they are too difficult, as well as lowering student motivation, the quantity of feedback might be such that it cannot be assimilated within the ongoing cognitive structures of the student. In an experiment at Leeds, concerned with arithmetic practice with schoolchildren, such a hypothesis was proposed. It was predicted that a curvilinear relationship would be obtained with tasks of intermediate difficulty producing the most improvement. The difficulty of the questions was altered by computer programs so that a pupil worked at a high (95 per cent), moderate (75 per cent) or low (60 per cent) level of success. Subjects were given an arithmetic pre-test, stratified and randomly assigned to one of the three treatment groups.

The results were clear. Post-test performances showed that the intermediate group had the advantage in speed and accuracy over the high group, which in turn was significantly better than the low group. A three-way analysis of variance using pre-test level, treatment group and difficulty of items in the post-test showed that those pupils who were low on pre-test scores were more sensitive to the differences in the teaching treatments. It was also possible, from the analyses, to propose quantitative models which allowed feedback and time factors to explain these results without needing to consider subsidiary hypotheses about motivational factors.

Controlling task difficulty is one method of sequencing the educational material by means of decision rules which are based on models or hypotheses of student performances. A general, but less well defined, method is to use the educational objectives and task analyses to subdivide the course into a set of concepts and techniques which have to be learned. These can be partitioned into a series of levels depending on their complexity, and usually checks are made to ensure that the student has reached a satisfactory standard of mastery before he is allowed to continue to higher levels. Some workers, for example Gurbutt (1975), have used graph theory to work out more detailed arrangements within the various levels. Thus devising and managing such material has two components. The first is an analysis and arrangement of the subject-matter skills, and the second the performance standards required of the learner within the different curriculum levels.

Robert Gagné has been most influential in proposing and developing these methods of analysis. For him a hierarchy is the relationship between the behaviours of students as they interact with subject matters. It is a classification of student intellectual skills from making discriminations through the learning of concepts to the assimilation of higher order rules (Gagné, 1968). In 1961 and 1962, Gagné *et al* reported studies which showed the value of such an analysis. The experiments were set in mathematics and the materials were hierarchically arranged with the seemingly simpler behaviours appearing first in the instructional scheme. One result was that the best predictor of performances on the higher level tasks was the degree of mastery shown by the individual learners at the lower levels of the task hierarchy. Thus it might be expected that computer programs would be good decision makers in these situations, for detailed performance data would allow hypotheses to be made about the student which could be used to bias his future instruction.

However, there has been argument about whether such a rigid and, in some respects, logical organisation of learning is necessary or even desirable. Merrill (1974) maintains that a Gagné-type analysis is insufficient, and that for developing instructional materials a content analysis of the material is also required. More controversial is his assertion that such an analysis can proceed independently of student behaviour or instructional strategy. He organises subject matter into concepts (a set of symbols, objects or events which share a common attribute or attributes) and operations (the ways concepts can be described, related or transformed). The results of this analysis do not imply an instructional sequence directly and Merrill argues for showing the student the content structure and allowing him to develop his own performance algorithms (Merrill, 1973). Similar ideas for the use of 'maps' of objectives and content by learners have been taken up by several workers, including Grubb (1968).

Pask (in Paper 1.3 in this text) also acknowledges that there are advantages in providing both the expert and the student with some external representation of the material so that topics can be identified and discussed, and explanations initiated by either teacher or learner. However, the methods of content analysis proposed by Pask are somewhat different from those of Merrill, and re-establish the individuality of the teacher and, indirectly, the influence of teaching strategy on the structuring of educational material. In Pask's view the teacher projects his own arguments and interpretations of the subject matter so the external content map is obtained by the individual subject-matter expert analysing the various topics and relations which are involved in his own theses.

The teacher is required to show these are valid by constructing explanations, ie by showing how one topic is derived from others. The statements are set out as a network with the nodes representing topics, the arcs for parts of a derivation and the arc clusters showing the various derivation paths. To give direction and definition to his particular lesson, the teacher chooses a head node, ie the main topic, and a pruned, hierarchical topic map is obtained. On the basis of this structure tutorial conversations are planned, and for Pask a crucial point is that understanding is reached when teacher and student agree both on a description and on an explanation of a particular topic. Thus the conversation explores the nodes, arcs and arc clusters which make up the network, and the computer is able to control and assist the student in collecting information and in testing his understanding. Examination of the paths students take has led Pask to identify characteristic learning strategies and systematic individual differences to learn and discover (Pask, 1976).

A theory of the role of organisation in learning has been developed by Ausubel (eg Ausubel, 1968). He states that the degree of meaningful learning of new material is related to its interaction with the student's cognitive structures. If his existing knowledge can be used to provide 'ideational scaffolding' or anchorage for the new material, then learning becomes facilitated. To ensure this Ausubel suggests that, prior to the instruction, relevant organising material of greater generality and inclusiveness should be studied by the learner. Several studies set in the sciences have tried to test these ideas but the characteristics of 'good' organisers have not been thoroughly worked out, and research results of their effects have been equivocal (Hartley & Davies, 1976). However some work has shown that organisers are more beneficial when given before rather than at the end of the instruction, although several studies are in disagreement as to whether most benefit is enjoyed by students of low, intermediate or high verbal ability.

There are several plausible arguments for incorporating organisers within computer-based teaching programs. For example, the organiser need not only be given prior to instruction but can also serve as a teaching framework for the interactive program. In a preliminary study at Leeds, two teaching programs with differing degrees of organisation were used. The objective was to study their effects on students' ability to plan laboratory experiments in chemistry, and a pool of six experiments formed the material of the programs. The organiser was a three-page document which gave general rules and methods for use in planning experiments. The on-line tutorial treatments differed in the level of generality of the questions they asked the student and in the organisation of the questions themselves. In one treatment, after the students had studied the organiser, general questions taken from it required the learner to contrast the six experiments before making a response. The organising themes, eg control of variables, cut across all the experiments rather than concentrating on each experiment in turn. The questions were sequenced to follow the order of the organiser. In the second treatment the organiser was not studied; the questions were made specific to each experiment and were essentially unordered. The content of both programs was equivalent. The examination grades of each participating student were taken as a measure of his general ability in chemistry. Eighteen undergraduates participated in the study; these were paired on chemistry grades and then randomly allocated, one to each of the two teaching treatments.

Both groups showed significant learning gains on all the planning post-tests, but the first treatment showed significantly better results on the test of detecting flaws in given experimental plans. This result was repeated on the knowledge of planning post-test, but there was little difference between the groups on retention of material. Also there were positive correlations between chemistry grades and most of the post-tests, and the values of the rank correlation coefficients were usually higher for those students who followed the second 'unorganised' treatment. Thus it appeared that lack of structure penalised the less able students. Examination of the on-line performance data showed that the groups were approximately equivalent in the time they spent on the programs and the quantity of feedback they received. A questionnaire completed by all students clearly distinguished between the treatments. The first group gave significantly higher ratings as they reported on the amount they thought they had learnt, their confidence in their ability to plan experiments, the interest of the program and its continuity.

Pask has provided further evidence that organisation of material is an important variable in learning and one which he believes should be

matched to a student's cognitive style (Pask & Scott, 1972; Pask, 1976).
He distinguishes between 'serialists' and 'holists'. It is maintained that
the former habitually learn, remember and recapitulate a body of
information as a series of items related by simple links. Holists, on the
other hand, work in more global terms, using higher order relations and
grouping material in more complex structures. In an experimental study,
using relative small numbers (N=8) in each group, and with tasks which
require the students to learn taxonomies, Pask showed that teaching
was most effective when the sequencing of material was matched to the
individual's particular type of cognitive competence.

The importance of the type of organisation of material and its effect
on assimilation by students has been further reinforced in an interesting
paper by Mayer and Greeno (1972) which should be read by anyone
wishing to experiment in education. They argue that different teaching
materials and feedback comments activate and become assimilated
within different cognitive structures. They maintain that although the
mix of final performances on post-tests may not reveal a significant
difference overall, the detailed test profiles of the treatment groups
can be very different. Mayer and Greeno devised two teaching
treatments for topics in probability theory. The first emphasised the
interrelations between the tasks themselves, and concentrated heavily on
formulae and quantitative relations. The second tried to relate the
structure of the subject matter to the existing cognitive structure of the
student. This teaching organisation was therefore more thematic; it
emphasised meanings and relations and their attachment to common
experience. Various criterion post-tests were used. One set contained
numerical calculations and problems requiring algebraic techniques. A
second set included problems which looked plausible but had no
solution, and other questions emphasised the non-computational
aspects of probability measures. Overall there were no significant
differences between the groups on the combined sets of tests, but the
first 'formal' treatment produced superior results on the first set of
quantitative problems whereas the second treatment group had the
better profiles on the other tests.

3.3 TEACHING MODE AND LEARNER CONTROL

In the learning situation the problem of transfer involves the type of
feedback which is to be given to the student, and this is related to the
type of task he is set, the facilities and help he is allowed, and the
freedom he has to direct his own learning. This type of variable will be
referred to as 'teaching mode' and used to contrast techniques which
allow different amounts of initiative by the student. For example, the
mode may be highly directed and tutorial in which the computer
programs ask all the questions to which the learner must respond.
Alternatively, the style might be more open-ended and allow the student
access to facilities of help, example and explanation with some control
over the course of his own instruction.

It has been argued that when computer programs closely control the
content and sequence of pre-stored teaching, students have little
opportunity for taking responsibility and developing their own learning

strategies. To counter this, the American TICCIT system (Merrill, 1973) has implemented a type of command language which allows the student to regulate both content and teaching strategy. He will need to decide on his learning goals and the methods of accomplishing them by using the resources and materials which have been provided. So the command language should enable the learner to review material, explore fresh subject matter and set required performance levels. To help him form his learning strategy an adviser program should provide feedback and give guidance on content sequence, presentation mode, item difficulty and remedial instruction. The resources include the teaching material with content maps, practice and test items, examples and graphics support. Thus in the TICCIT system there are three levels of discourse dealing with answers to specific questions, the instructional process and the language to control it, and the modification of this control under the adviser program. The subject-matter expert performs a content analysis and divides the material into concepts, operations and rules which can be presented at two levels (as generalisations or as instances) and in two modes 'asking' and 'telling'. The quantity of instances determines the amount of practice and examples/non-examples are classified as hard or easy on an abstract-concrete dimension. The command language allows the student to control the presentation in content, sequence, quantity and difficulty. For example, in order to help his choice of a particular lesson unit he can ask for a content map of the course to be displayed. Response buttons are then used to ask for rules, examples or further practice. Pressing the 'hard' or 'easy' key regulates the difficulty of the material. The adviser function operates either on student request or when the student's choices appear non-productive. However, although the rationale underlying the design of the programs has been thoroughly worked out, there has been no large application of the methods and no independent evaluation of the project.

There are several experiments which suggest that students in such a free learning situation do not make a good appraisal of their abilities, and do not make such effective decisions as a program controller. For example, Pask (1975) reached such conclusions after studies which used a variety of tracking and concept learning tasks. However, he noted that a compromise strategy in which the control programs allowed student decisions where they were judged reasonable, maintained motivation and produced equally good results. A similar experience occurred at Leeds, where three teaching modes varied the controls which they placed on the learner. The subject area was teaching the planning of laboratory experiments in chemistry, and in the directed mode the planning questions were put to the student in a predetermined sequence. Failure to respond correctly resulted in active feedback being given in which further responses had to be made to sub-questions which located and corrected his errors. The second teaching treatment had intermediate control and allowed the students to access chemistry facts/definitions and teaching. These facilities were stored in three indexed files named, CHECK (for testing the planning decisions), HELP (for giving teaching), and FACTS. Students could use and browse through these files as they wished but they had to enter the CHECK file before leaving the program and, if they made an incorrect response in this file, the program did not give feedback or remedial teaching explicitly but routed them to the HELP or FACTS files. The third teaching mode only allowed access to CHECK and FACTS files. If he made an unsatisfactory response to a CHECK question, the correct information was printed. The chemistry content was equivalent in all the programs.

Some thirty students from the physical chemistry laboratory took part and, after pre-tests, they were randomly assigned to the teaching treatments. The results of post-tests showed overall improvements for all the groups, but the post-test scores for the second group were significantly lower than the others. An inspection of the ways in which students used the teaching files suggested an explanation of these findings. In the third treatment students tended to check all parts of the plan in an acceptable sequence and feedback was given to them when their responses were unsatisfactory. In other words, the teaching they received was very similar to that of the first mode except that feedback was printed and required no further response. In the second teaching treatment students generally collected insufficient teaching or facts before entering the CHECK file. When incorrect responses were made, they were routed to the teaching files again where they had to decide which parts to access. For this treatment there was also a significant correlation between chemistry ability and post-test performances. Thus, in the initial states of learning a complex skill, the teaching treatment which required decision making and information collection was not used efficiently, particularly by the less competent students. However, in a further experiment which used an extended series of laboratory experiments, the performances of the second group improved on subsequent occasions so that eventually the method produced equivalent learning gains and took a shorter time. It was also the method which students seemed to prefer. Similar results were also obtained in teaching the planning of statistical investigations with psychology students (Abbatt, 1972). Again the evidence argues for adaptive decision rules in which more responsibility is given to the student to direct his own learning as he becomes more competent.

Similar difficulties in student learning were observed by Bork (Bork & Robson, 1972) when he used the wave simulation program referred to earlier, with forty undergraduates from the Department of Engineering and Science. Ratings showed that half the students liked the program, half did not. It became clear that, for the weaker students, the program did not sustain interest long enough for them to make sufficient discoveries about the behaviour of the wave-pulse in the rope. When more advanced students used the program (many of whom understood the basic physics and so had a frame of reference) they became more involved, were more successful with the program, and the ratings of this group were enthusiastic.

4.0 Some design problems of CAL programs

The preceding research suggests some general principles which are important in learning. A central place is given to the informational role of feedback and its control by the computer-based teaching programs. The tasks which are given to the student determine the type of learning activities and the type of feedback he receives. The complexity of the task governs the quantity of feedback. When the educational objectives involve transfer of learning, the program organisation (through task sequencing, and by using previous knowledge or advance organisers to provide conceptual frameworks) is likely to be important. For aims which also require the student to develop learning strategies, the degree of learner control will be influential.

Two general comments should be made about this summary. First, all the experiments show that these variables interact with student knowledge and abilities, hence none of them can be efficiently used in CAL unless the programs have adequate information of the student's knowledge space. This is particularly true for determining the type of feedback, the degree of task difficulty, the use of organisers and the amount of learner control. Secondly, the educational interaction occurs through the dialogue which is transmitted at the terminal. The differing types of task, levels of feedback and degree of learner control require a student command language and a dialogue which not only permits answers to questions, but methods and explanations, lines of arguments and teaching/learning strategies.

An examination of current CAL programs will show that few systematically contain or exploit these principles in their designs. Many are put together in a pragmatic way, sometimes without any systematic statement of objectives or analysis of learning tasks. These comments apply to both tutorial and simulation programs; superficially the latter might appear to have clear underlying models, but incorporating these into learning packages for the student is deceptively difficult. Of course, there are many constraints imposed by the computer languages. Essentially author language programs rely on keyword matching, so that responses of the students have to be anticipated and pre-stored. So either the program takes the initiative and asks small-scale questions, or arranges a small number of commands to serve as a learner control language. These allow him access to facilities, eg HELP or CALCULATE, and to select material which is arranged in labelled files. With author languages other forms of educational dialogue are not practical. In simulation programs the dialogue is also restricted. For example, in the rope-pulse simulation program of Bork and Robson referred to earlier, although the teaching dialogue enhanced the program, the comments were pre-stored and could not respond to any type of data collection which had not been anticipated. The teaching sub-program had not the capability of directing the simulation routines to discover the wave characteristics, hence it could not evaluate student strategies in any general sense, nor respond to suggestions from him. Again, although the student has control over the input values which he selects, and can see their effects, he is unable to inspect, amend or discover (because of its complexity) the inner structure of the program by which these results are produced. Thus its function is limited to illustration for the naive student and elaboration of knowledge for the student who understands the underlying principles.

In order to individualise teaching, the programs must retain data of a student's performance so that hypotheses can be held about his knowledge state. Typically author language programs do this by a register of counters which summarises evaluations made of the student's responses. Since, in many programs, the decision to branch from one teaching element to the next is largely determined by the quality of the last response only, the student records which are retained are meagre, and usually consist of a few broad indices of performance. In simulation programs the data is even more sparse. Generally, no records of the learner's protocols are retained, although some 'tag' the facility or type of material which is currently being explored. Hence some advice can be given if the student asks questions, but even this information is unlikely to be retained between occasions so that no advice can be given individually on subsequent runs of the program.

If the dialogue from the student is restricted so that he can only respond to questions, or use a limited set of commands, he will not be able to set out his methods or lines of reasoning, and data about his information processing cannot be obtained. After answering small-step questions, knowledge of the correct response might be adequate feedback, but to give feedback of method and explanation requires knowledge of the student's working procedures, and advice on learning strategy needs information of students' goals.

Therefore the general argument is that current CAL programs have not given sufficient attention to a design for learning, and that some improvements could be made within present author languages and simulation packages. However, a full exploitation of psychological principles in design requires the programs themselves to have a more general 'knowledge' of the teaching tasks, of the student and of teaching strategy.

5.0 The design of knowledgeable programs

In order to increase the teaching power of CAL materials, it is necessary that the programs have three data structures. The first is a representation of the task, ideally in terms which will allow the programs to generate problems and undertake their solution. The second is a representation of the student. This should include not only counters, ie hypotheses which are held about his competence, but computer programs which can replicate to some extent his information processing. A knowledge of teaching is the third data structure. This is probably best represented as control programs which are ordered sets of condition-action statements. The conditions relate to characteristics of the task and to programs which model the student's working methods and performances. The teaching actions can select teaching mode, task complexity, facilities of help and type of feedback. The conditions which are met determine which of the actions are applied.

The advantages which come from having programs with these data structures are interesting, but it must be admitted that, at present, they can only be designed in a limited number of well structured subject areas, and that the costs of their development are large. A first example is taken from Brown *et al* (1974, 1975) who have developed a program, SOPHIE, to teach fault-finding in electronic circuitry. The papers also give ideas on how some of the current teaching and simulation programs in science could be redesigned and supplied with sufficient information of the subject area and techniques of problem solving to be able to respond to students' inquiries about working strategies. SOPHIE works with specific pre-stored circuits, but the routines which control the fault diagnosis and the help which is given to students are designed to operate over a variety of electronic circuits. When the student comes to the terminal, he is presented with a circuit diagram and the program automatically selects and inserts a fault of some specified degree of difficulty. The student can then ask for specific circuit readings, for components to be replaced, for hypotheses to be evaluated, and for help. In this case the system suggests plausible hypotheses which are consistent with the readings the student has taken. When he is ready, the user can specify the nature of the fault. The system is fully operational and is an 'intelligent' teacher in the sense that it can generate hypotheses about malfunctioning circuits, evaluate the student's hypotheses during his fault-finding and allow him to communicate with the system in relatively unconstrained English.

Many of the program's logical and inferencing capabilities are derived from using simulation models of the circuit. For example, in fault evaluation the programs modify the circuit to contain the fault suggested by the student's hypothesis. This model is run to repeat the readings gathered by the student. These values of the faulty circuit are compared with the values of the unmodified circuit, and the program decides if the readings are sufficiently close to be considered equivalent. If the hypothesis is not acceptable, the student is given the reasons for its decision. The system is also capable of generating hypotheses about faults. From output voltage measurements taken by the student, possible hypotheses are generated which are capable of explaining these measurements. Each hypothesis is evaluated in turn by using the simulation programs in the manner outlined above. The interesting feature is that the program answers the student after running an experiment on-line.

Although SOPHIE does not produce or store an adequate representation of student performances, it does provide a framework from which such models can be developed. The student has to use a language to request help and to state his hypotheses and lines of reasoning. An examination of his print-out will show the various reasoning operations which he employed and the knowledge which he used. When supplemented with individual interviews, the programs become a research tool for investigating problem solving.

A second example is taken from programs which have been designed for the learning of diagnosis skills of the sort which are encountered in medicine. Typically, information is collected sequentially from a patient by interview, examination and medical tests, and these symptoms and signs have to be summarised so that a course of treatment

can be given. Preparatory to this a diagnosis is usually made in which
the patient is assigned with some probability to a limited disease set.
Several simulation and tutorial programs have been written (eg Weber
& Hagamen, 1973; Harless *et al*, 1971). A 'diagnosis' program has also
been developed at Leeds, and the data base includes six diseases and
some seventy attributes or symptoms. The data include the relative
frequencies of the diseases, and for each disease the probability of
occurrence of each symptom state. Provided certain mathematical
assumptions of independence are met, probability theorems can be used
for 'diagnosis'. In addition, anticipated questions and the patients'
comments which are appropriate for each of the symptoms have to be
stored. This is the underlying knowledge base which is used by the
teaching programs. There can be arguments about validity, for it is
statistical and not strictly medical, but the educational aim is the limited
one of illustrating the underlying relationships between patterns of
symptoms and diseases.

Consider the advantages which come from such a task representation.
First, random number generators operate on probabilities to select a
disease and then generate a 'patient' ie a set of attribute states. The
program can easily restrict or expand the disease set so that suitable and
individual curricula can be built up on-line for students. A plausible
teaching strategy would be to start with a limited number of well
discriminated diseases and add to them as the student improves his
performance. Since material is generated by the program when it is
needed by the student at the terminal, it makes economic use of store
and an unlimited number of 'patients' are potentially available.

A second advantage is the variety of teaching modes and types of
feedback which can be developed. Examples of specific diseases can be
generated and printed on request, the student can be asked to diagnose
the complete case history, or be required to collect the information
sequentially by conducting his 'interview' at the terminal. Alternatively,
the student can specify a disease set, and symptoms. The computer
replies by calculating the disease probabilities for that symptom set.
By allowing the student to backtrack, and alter symptoms he had
previously typed, their effects on the disease probabilities can be
explored. These and other facilities arise because the programs can
undertake a statistical diagnosis. Since the data base allows generation
of 'patients', it is essential for the programs to be able to diagnose or
they would give misleading information or be unable to proceed. Since
they can solve the tasks, it is straightforward to have them output the
stages of solution. Similar routines can monitor the student's work at
the terminal and be used to provide feedback and help. For example,
the programs can calculate how the current diagnosis would be altered
by further attribute states. These calculations allow the programs to
advise the student on the sequence of his information collection. The
computer can withhold such help if the learner is competent, and other
controls can be used to prevent him making a premature diagnosis.
Finally, if the programs disagree with a student's conclusions, he is
asked to list the symptoms which support his decision. For comparison,
the computer calculates the support level of each symptom for his

diagnosis, and then recalculates their support for the correct diagnosis.

Of course these programs have their limitations. They are specialised, can only be used in classification tasks which have probabilistic data bases, and the effort which is needed to provide such data is considerable. There are also educational difficulties. Although the programs can use the different facilities of teaching mode, help and feedback to maximise learning, such decision rules are pragmatically stated. Also the representation of the student is extremely limited. It consists of a record of the facilities which he uses and his overall performance levels of correct diagnosis. This lack of knowledge is being remedied by studying the methods and strategies individual students use in selecting the patient information and processing it. Models, ie programs which distinguish between groups of students on the basis of these skills and which give significant predictions, have been developed and are described in an introductory paper (Hartley *et al*, 1972). This knowledge of the student can be stored as procedures and run on the teaching tasks to test hypotheses about the likely ways he would perform. This information can then be used to decide on the task and type of feedback which should be given.

A more serious criticism is that the program uses mathematical methods for diagnosis which the student or physician does not replicate and perhaps does not understand. Thus the dialogue is limited, for the computer program cannot explain its decisions or recommendations; the student must accept or reject the mathematical conclusions. However an interactive program, MYCIN, has been designed which uses the clinical decision rules and methods of experts. It advises physicians in selecting appropriate antimicrobial therapy for hospital patients with bacterial infections (Shortliffe *et al*, 1975). The aim of the program is not to teach students but, since the system has to explain its recommendations when queried and in terms which the physician can understand, the dialogue itself is educational. The knowledge base is a set of approximately two hundred decision rules (if-then statements) which permit an action to be taken (eg a drug treatment) or a conclusion drawn if the set of preconditions of characteristics or organisms taken from the patient is met.

After being given some patient data the MYCIN consultation program has to select those decision rules which apply to the patient. If, during the search, a condition (ie a clinical parameter) is not known, a sub-program attempts to find it. If it is not in the records, the user is asked to supply this data. In order to discuss the decisions which are made by the consultation program, an interactive explanation program has been developed. The initiative is taken by the physician who can ask various types of question. For example, if, during the consultation, the program asks the user for certain data, he can ask WHY it is necessary to obtain this. In reply the MYCIN explanation program has to state its goals, and show how the current decision rule set is to be used to establish that conclusion. Thus statements are printed which show how the data will satisfy the preconditions of those rules and so enable the conclusion to be drawn. The question WHY can be repeated during this line of reasoning so that inquiries can be made further into the sub-goals. If the physician wishes to examine other ways by which the goals can be achieved, he asks the question HOW. The program replies by giving alternative connections of rules through any part of the reasoning network. In these ways the user can question both goals and methods. The program also keeps a trace of its consultation so that any element which contributes to the final treatment decision can be examined or re-examined. Although the language of the program is stilted and largely composed of If/Since <conditions> Then <conclusion> statements, the decision-making processes are clearly shown.

6.0 Some conclusions

The teaching potential of MYCIN would be increased if a similar language were devised so that the student could set out his own goals, lines of reasoning and conclusions. The computer programs would need to evaluate this information, ask questions if the steps were too large or incomplete and provide feedback. The implementation of mixed initiative teaching dialogues will be difficult to achieve, but some attempts have been described (Carbonell, 1970; Collins *et al*, 1975).

Providing and using student models which can manage these dialogues is another distant but necessary objective, and Self (1973) has provided a small but useful illustration. Furthermore, even in so-called adaptive programs, the decision rules have been followed in a fixed way. Although the estimates of students' performances can be improved as more learners work through the material, this only enables decision rules to be applied more accurately. The programs must operate in the same way and continue to apply the same rules for a student even if they are not proving satisfactory. In other words, the programs are not self-critical and cannot alter their teaching strategies at run time. To accomplish this, programs need to be able to make assertions which relate student performances to teaching variables in order that larger-scale goals will be attained. These might be to maximise performance objectives or to minimise time at the terminal. The programs then need to be capable of running experiments which test these assertions. This work is still in its infancy, but such a system has been implemented for teaching the solution of quadratic equations by the 'discovery' method (O'Shea & Sleeman, 1972).

The researches of learning theorists and the techniques of artificial intelligence might appear somewhat remote from practical problems of writing CAL programs which are to be used regularly by students. In these circumstances the work of the program designer is shaped by practical considerations of computing facilities and development costs. However, the suggestions which have been made could be profitably taken into account and at least partially implemented within present designs of CAL materials. Hopefully the progress in research will be maintained and its ideas more readily assimilated so that the teaching roles of the computer will continue to be extended, particularly in the teaching of problem-solving skills.

Acknowledgements

Many of the experiments referred to in this paper were designed and carried out by the staff of the Computer Based Learning Project at Leeds University. In particular, acknowledgements should be made to: F Abbatt, A Cole, J Green, C Macrae, M Rawson, D Sleeman and K Tait. Much of this work has been supported by grants from the Social Science Research Council, and the National Development Programme in Computer Assisted Learning.

References

Abbatt, F R (1972) Preliminary experience in using a computer to teach the planning of experiments in the social sciences. Internal Report *P1,* Computer Based Learning Project, University of Leeds

Abbatt, F R and Hartley, J R (1974) Teaching planning skills by computer, *International Journal of Mathematical Education in Science and Technology* 5: 665

Abbatt, F R and Hartley, J R (1976) Teaching applied statistics by computer, *Aspects of Educational Technology X.* London : Kogan Page

Anderson, R C, Kulhavy, R W and Andre T (1971) Feedback procedures in programmed instruction, *Journal of Educational Psychology* 62: 148

Anderson, R C, Kulhavy, R W and Andre, T (1972) Conditions under which feedback facilitates learning from programmed lessons, *Journal of Educational Psychology* 63: 186

Ausubel, D P (1968) *Educational Psychology — A Cognitive View.* New York : Holt, Rinehart & Winston

Ayscough, P B (1973) Computer-based learning in the teaching laboratory, *Chemistry in Britain* 9: 2: 61

Berry, P C, Bartoli, G, Del'Aquila, C and Spadavecchia, V (1973) *APL and Insight: The Use of Programs to Represent Concepts in Teaching.* IBM Bari Scientific Centre Technical Report Number CRB 002/513-5302. Italy

Bork, A M and Robson, J (1972) A computer simulation for the study of waves, *American Journal of Physics* 40: 1288

Brown, J S and Rubenstein, R (1973) *Recursive Functional Programming for Students in the Humanities and Social Sciences,* Technical Report 27. Irvine: Dept of Information and Computer Science, University of California

Brown, J S, Burton, R R and Bell, A G (1974) *A Sophisticated Instructional Environment for Teaching Electronic Trouble-shooting,* Report 2790. Cambridge, Mass : Bolt Beranek & Newman Inc

Brown, J S and Burton, R R, Multiple representations of knowledge for tutorial reasoning. In D G Bobrow and A Collins (eds) *Representation and Understanding.* Academic Press, p351

Carbonell, J R (1970) Mixed initiative man-computer instructional dialogues (PhD thesis, MIT), Report No 1971. Cambridge, Mass : Bolt Beranek & Newman Inc

Collins, A, Warnock, E H, Aiello, N and Miller, M L (1975) Reasoning from incomplete knowledge. In D G Bobrow and A Collins (eds) *Representation and Understanding.* Academic Press, p383

Gagné, R M (1968) Learning hierarchies, *Educational Psychologist* 6 : 1

Gagné, R M and Paradise, N E (1961) Abilities and learning sets in knowledge acquisition, *Psychological Monographs* no 518

Gagné, R M, Mayor, J R, Garstens, Helen L and Paradise, N E (1962) Factors in acquiring knowledge of a mathematical task, *Psychological Monographs* no 526

Grubb, R E (1968) Learner controlled statistics, *Journal of Programed Learning* 5: 38

Grundin, H U (1969) Response mode and information about correct answers in programmed instruction. In A P Mann and C K Brunstrom (eds) *Aspects of Educational Technology III.* London : Pitman, p65

Gurbutt, P A (1976) *Thoughts on graphs in physics,* UCODI Working Paper 14. Belgium : IMAGO Centre, Batiment Sc 16-B, 1348 Louvain-la-Neuve

Guthrie, J T (1971) Feedback and sentence learning, *Journal of Verbal Learning and Verbal Behavior* 10: 23

Harless, W G, Drennon, G G, Marxer, J J, Root, G A and Mill, G E (1971) CASE: a computer aided simulation of the clinical encounter, *Journal of Medical Education* 46: 443

Hartley, J and Davies, I K (1976) Pre-instructional strategies: the role of pretests, behavioral objectives, overviews and advance organisers, *Review of Educational Research* 46: 239-65

Mayer, R E and Greeno, J G (1972) Structural differences between learning outcomes produced by different instructional methods, *Journal of Educational Psychology* 63: 165

Merrill, D M (1973) Premises, propositions and research underlying the design of a learner controlled computer assisted instruction system: a summary for the TICCIT system, *Working Paper No 44.* Provo, Utah : Division of Instructional Sciences, Brigham Young University

Merrill, D M and Gibbons, A S (1974) Heterarchies and their relationship to behavioral hierarchies for sequencing content in instruction. In J M Scandura *et al. Proceedings of 5th Conference on Structural Learning,* Penn : MERGE Research Institute, Pennsylvania 19072, p140

O'Shea, T and Sleeman, D H (1973) A design for an adaptive self-improving teaching system. In J Rose (ed) *Advances in Cybernetics and Systems.* London : Gordon & Breach

Papert, S and Solomon, C (1972) Twenty things to do with a computer, *Educational Technology* 12: 9

Pask, G (1975) *The Cybernetics of Human Learning and Performance.* London : Hutchinson

Pask, G (1976) Styles and strategies of learning, *British Journal of Educational Psychology* 46: 128

Pask, G and Scott, B C E (1972) Learning strategies and individual competence, *International Journal of Man-Machine Studies* 4: 217

Self, J A (1974) Student models in computer-aided instruction, *International Journal of Man-Machine Studies* 6 2: 261

Shortliffe, E H, Davis, R, Axline, S G, Buchanan, B G, Green, C C and Cohen, S N (1975) Computer-based consultations in clinical therapeutics: explanation and rule acquisition capabilities of the MYCIN system, *Computers and Biomedical Research* 8: 303

Skinner, B F (1954) The science of learning and the art of teaching, *Harvard Educational Review* 24: 86

Taylor, T R and Scott, B (1975) Emergency patient simulation program. Internal report, Department of Computing Science, University of Glasgow

Weber, J C and Hagamen, W D (1972) ATS — a new system for computer mediated tutorials in medical education, *Journal of Medical Education* 47: 637

Woods, Pat and Hartley, J R (1971) Some learning models for arithmetic tasks and their use in computer-based learning, *British Journal of Educational Psychology* 41 1: 35

Woods, Pat, Hartley, J R and Sleeman, D H (1972) Controlling the learning of diagnostic tasks, *International Journal of Man-Machine Studies* 4: 319

1.5 Individual Differences and Instructional Design

RICHARD E SNOW

Snow, R E (1977) Individual differences and instructional design, *Journal of Instructional Development* 1 1, Winter. Reproduced with permission of the author and the editor.

One of the oldest facts about human learning in educational settings is that individuals differ, profoundly and multiply, in how they learn. Individual differences in school learning have been apparent since Greco-Roman times, but it is only in recent years (perhaps the last decade or so) that research has begun to show the real significance of this fact for education. Until now, information about individual differences has been used in education primarily to select people *out*, that is, to reject college applicants, or to identify students needing slower or special education which often turns out to be no education at all.

However, three points about individual differences in learning from instruction now seem clear:

1. Individual differences are far more *complex* than the single rank order conception of intelligence usually manifest in popular personal thinking, and they are also more *fundamental* as human characteristics than usually assumed in popular social and educational policy.

2. Individual differences in various aptitudes not only predict individual differences in learning outcome; they also *interact* with alternative instructional treatments; that is, they relate differently to learning outcome under different instructional presentations or methods. This kind of interaction between individual differences and instructional conditions is called 'ATI', standing for 'aptitude-treatment interaction'.

3. Individual differences (and ATI) can be used by the instructional developer to understand and *improve* instruction for everyone.

First, the popular misconception that biological differences do not exist and psychological differences can be easily erased is partly our own fault as instructional communicators. It stems in part from plagiarism among educational illustrators and audio-visualists. Roger Williams (1956, 1967) stressed this point some years ago, but little notice seems to have been taken of it. He showed pictures of a variety of normal stomachs, for example, compared with a typical textbook version. Medical illustrators rarely show this kind of range of individual differences; when asked to make a new picture of a stomach for some instructional purpose, they just copy from existing textbooks. It is a bit frightening to think that our conception of the human stomach may be based on the shape of the stomach of a single seventeenth-century murderer. Williams gives many other examples of striking individual differences in livers, kidneys, heart and brain tissue, nerve cells, spirograms, blood chemistries, etc. Beyond this, there are now bits of evidence of correlations between biological and psychological measures. One, noted by Cattell (1971) for instance, is between measured intelligence and cortical evoked potential of the brain. Time in milliseconds from onset of the stimulus to the third wave crest is simply and inversely related to IQ. Rimland (1977) has recently noted several other psychobiological correlates.

In short, people are not created equal biologically or psychologically. It is their right to equal opportunity to learn, among other things, in spite of individual differences. And this makes adaptation of instruction to individual differences between students an imperative. Instructional development thus needs to aim at particular kinds of student, not at the mythical average student.

Now to the second point. Although all of the possibly thousands of individual difference variables are not relevant to instruction, some consistently correlate with learning and also give consistent ATI results. If ATI can be captured and understood, they will make possible the design of adaptive instruction. Only rarely, however, are these underlying ATI ideas properly evaluated in work on individualised instruction. All attempts to individualise instruction, it turns out, rest explicitly or implicitly on some kind of ATI idea.

But what does an ATI look like and how do we find one? Figure 1a shows the traditional outcome of instructional development attempts. Instructional Treatment A is judged better than B because average student achievement is higher after A than after B. A and B could be alternative instructional methods or media, or A and B might represent average effectiveness of the same course, film, program, textbook, etc, both before and after some instructional development work. Student individual differences are not considered here.

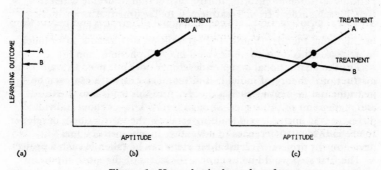

Figure 1. *Hypothetical results of (a) traditional instructional comparisons (b) studies including an aptitude variable and (c) studies testing for aptitude-treatment interaction*

97

Adding student aptitude scores (Figure 1b) gives the traditional picture an abscissa. Now we have a regression line, that is, a running average, showing the learning outcome level attained by students who come into instruction at different levels of aptitude. Pre-test measures of general mental ability and of prior knowledge often give this kind of positive slope in conventional instruction. It is obtained simply by measuring an aptitude before instruction, achievement or some other valued outcome afterward, and then plotting each student as a point in the graph using his or her two scores. The line can be thought of as the running average across different aptitude levels, but it is usually estimated statistically. When results look like this, attempts at instructional improvement should concentrate on the lower aptitude students, ie the question is: what instructional changes will improve things *for them* particularly? It is possible that iterative instructional developments might raise the low end of the regression line, realising more learning for the lower aptitude students while maintaining a high level of learning for high aptitude students.

But much research now suggests that Figure 1c is the more likely result. A new and different instructional treatment often gives a regression line that is sloped differently, even crossing the line for the first treatment. By improving instruction for one kind of student we have reduced its effectiveness for another kind of student. This happens often enough to suggest, only partly in jest, a first law of conservation of instructional effectiveness. It goes like this: 'No matter how you try to make instruction better for someone, you will make it worse for someone else.' Findings of this sort indicate ATI. If further attempts at instructional improvement fail to change this pattern, then the best one can do is to assign higher aptitude students to Treatment A and lower aptitude students to Treatment B. The two kinds of student do best with different instruction. This sort of adaptive classification of students into different instructional treatments is one important form of instructional development that can come from investigating student differences. And there are many variations on this theme, including periodic aptitude monitoring during instruction to decide when to switch each student from Treatment B to Treatment A as aptitude develops or knowledge accumulates. One can even imagine local instructional theories (Snow, 1977a) built on such results, after much more research is done to understand the ATI phenomenon fully.

But the instructional designer-developer does not need to wait for an instructional theory of individual differences. His work can even be instrumental in creating such a theory. And this leads into the third and main point of this paper. Enough is now known about individual differences in aptitude and learning to allow the instructional developer to use individual differences to advantage in any instructional development project. At least three steps can be taken in such a project.

The first step would be to choose measures of the most important student aptitudes, based on the accumulated ATI literature as well as on whatever hunches are available about the kinds of student who seem to do well or poorly in the particular instructional condition of interest. A recent book (Cronbach & Snow, 1977; see also Snow, 1977b) that summarises much of the voluminous ATI literature could serve as one guide, but there are several other summaries as well. The aptitude variables recommended for measurement at the start of almost any kind of high school or college instruction are the following:

G is a measure of general mental ability, otherwise known as intelligence (and sometimes divided into fluid, crystallised and visualisation ability; see Horn, 1976). G seems to relate to learning increasingly as more of the information processing burden of learning is placed on the student. As the treatment is made to do things for the student that he cannot do for himself, G relations are often reduced. No instructional designer should today fail to include a measure of G in a formative or summative evaluation study, because instructional conditions almost always vary in cognitive processing demand.

$A_i + A_c$ stands for general achievement motivation or orientation, but the distinction between its two parts may be more important. $A_i - A_c$ is achievement *via* independence *v* achievement *via* conformity. Many instructional treatments vary in the degree to which they encourage independent student action *v* conformity to instructor-set norms. Relative need for one or the other often turns out to be a critical student difference, particularly at the college level.

A_x is anxiety, another student difference that seems to be fundamentally involved in learning, both on its own and in combination with G. That is, there are higher-order ATI between A_x, G, and Treatment.

These four aptitude constructs deserve to be included in all instructional evaluations. Measures exist for each, and test administration time totals about one to two hours. There are also other individual differences of special interest. Among these are: *MS* (memory span), *PS* (perceptual speed), *MV* (visual memory), and *CS* (for various undifferentiated cognitive style measures). These aptitude variables may be important for some kinds of instruction; they deserve attention, but are optional in this general list.

Finally, a measure of prior achievement is obviously a requirement; one simply has to know what students already know, in order to develop instruction further. These measures may be pre-tests specific to the content to be taught, or they may be measures reflecting achievement in earlier courses, or even past grade-point-averages. One would hope, in any event, that they reflected not only variations in factual knowledge but in knowledge organisation. All such differences in prior knowledge are differences in aptitude.

These are recommendations, but it should be clear that they are based only on hypotheses. While supported by some strong prior research, they remain to be tested anew in each new instructional situation. For reasons too numerous to detail here, generalisations across diverse instructional settings are difficult, perhaps even impossible to make. Nor should measures of such aptitudes be taken blindly. While measures of G and A_x have been fairly well developed, any specific test may not always fit the student population of local interest. Measures of A_i and A_x have seen less development and validation, and are thus even less trustworthy. But progress should come from cautious iterative exploration. One should not throw out an aptitude measure after a single failure, nor should one institute a rigid instructional prescription after a single success.

The second step is to evaluate instructional effects by drawing scatter-plots and regression lines as demonstrated earlier, to determine which students do well and which students do not in a given condition. Take each aptitude-outcome pair and investigate it separately as before. Or, use two or more aptitudes at once in multiple regression. Statistical methods for this are discussed by Cronbach and Snow (1977).

Some example pictures of results involving two aptitudes in each of two or more instructional treatments are given by Snow (1977b) and so are not reproduced here. Each shows a bivariate regression plane for G and A_x, or for $A_i + A_c$ and $A_i - A_c$, as joint predictors of achievement in each of several treatments. The findings represented are those of Peterson (1976) and Porteus (1976). They are complicated, but they do make sense. The results suggest that high school students who are able, conforming and anxious, seem to need more step-by-step structure in the progress of instruction. They do better when teachers provide explicit objectives and sequences of instruction, with clear outlines, reviews, and emphases of the essentials. Students who are able, independent and non-anxious seem to need less teacher structure of this sort. They seem to provide their own organisation for learning. So also, apparently, do less able students who can nonetheless work on their own and are motivated (anxious) to do so.

Consider a hypothetical next step now. Suppose that an instructional designer pursues these earlier findings, administering the same aptitude measures in evaluating a new audio-visual tutorial course in college science. A study is conducted in which the new course is compared with the conventional lecture-demonstration format. Some student sections receive the individualised treatment, going to stalls in the AV library for work with films, tapes and slides to guide their own study and laboratory work. Others get the regular treatment. (Or perhaps aptitude and outcome data are available from the conventional treatment of previous years.)

Figures 2 and 3 give the hypothetical results. The ordinate in each case is end-of-course achievement. The aptitudes in Figure 2 are $A_i + A_c$ and $A_i - A_c$; in Figure 3, they are G and A_x. Comparison with the previous results shows our instructional developer that his data in the first figure conform closely to Peterson's (1976) and those of the second are only slightly different from some of Porteus's (1976).

With these results, one might think of establishing both kinds of courses and assigning students to whichever course their aptitude scores suggest will be best for them. But our instructional developer is mainly interested in improving the new course. The ATI results also give clues to help understand instructional effects because they focus attention on particular kinds of student who seem not to be well served by some particular condition. Why is the new course not effective for students high in achievement *via* conformity or either low or high on *both* ability and anxiety? Students in these groups have aptitude scores falling in the shaded regions of the aptitude base planes of Figures 2

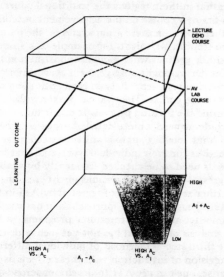

Figure 2. *Hypothetical results of a comparison between
a conventional treatment and a new audio-visual laboratory treatment,
showing a bivariate regression plane for each treatment,
with $A_i + A_c$ and $A_i - A_c$ as aptitudes*

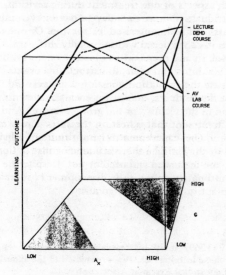

Figure 3. *Hypothetical results of a comparison between
a conventional treatment and a new audio-visual laboratory treatment,
showing a bivariate regression plane for each treatment,
with G and A_x as aptitudes*

and 3. Notice that in these regions the traditional course is better (higher) than the new course on the achievement outcome. Task analysis can then focus on these groups, and on the parts of instruction that give them trouble. We might, for example, ask students with these particular aptitude profiles what aspects on instruction bothered them or were helpful. Or we might observe them at work, or conduct item analyses of criterion tests separately in each aptitude group, to identify weak features of the course. Then we can tinker with these aspects of instruction during the revision process. It might turn out that conforming students need a more detailed procedural outline to follow in the AV lab, that able but anxious students need more clearly specified objectives for their individual work, and that less able, non-anxious students need to be checked frequently by a lab assistant to motivate progress. Making such revisions might erase the ATI effects, or perhaps further revisions will be suggested by ATI in further tryouts. Bunderson (1969) suggested this approach, and has used ATI this way in revising computer-assisted instructional programs. But aptitude-focused task analysis of this sort has not yet seen wide use. This then completes the third step — diagnosis of individual difference effects and focused revision of instruction with these effects as guide.

To summarise, one can use ATI to develop macroadaptations of instruction, assigning different kinds of student to different treatments aimed at the same outcome goal. Treatments are then designed on broadly different models to fit different classes of students optimally. Or, one can use aptitude information to make microadaptations by tinkering with aspects of one treatment during revision, so that it becomes individualised more on a day-to-day or even minute-to-minute level, as is possible in computerised instruction. Or one can do both: microadaptation can proceed within broadly differentiated streams at the macro level. In any event, what I believe one must do is to collect and use aptitude information in all instructional evaluations. This is required because the evaluation question is always: did the instruction work well for the students, that is, for each student, not just for the few who stand in the vicinity of the group average? And an instructional treatment that is best on the average may still serve some students poorly. One can choose to ignore student individual differences, but they will be there influencing instructional effects whether they are measured and used or not. Despite the fact that education is ultimately an aptitude development program, individual differences in aptitudes will never go away.

References

Bunderson, C V (1969) Ability by treatment interactions in designing instruction for a hierarchical learning task. Paper presented to the annual meeting of the American Educational Research Association

Cattell, R B (1971) *Abilities: Their Structure, Growth, and Action.* Boston : Houghton Mifflin

Cronbach, L J and Snow R E (1977) *Aptitudes and Instructional Methods: A Handbook for Research on Interactions.* New York : Irvington

Horn, J L (1976) Human abilities: a review of research and theory in the early 1970s, *Annual Review of Psychology* 27: 437-85

Peterson, P L (1976) Interactive effects of student anxiety, achievement orientation, and teacher behavior on student achievement and attitude. Unpublished doctoral dissertation, Stanford University

Porteus, A (1976) Teacher-centered vs student-centered instruction: interactions with cognitive and motivational aptitudes. Unpublished doctoral dissertation, Stanford University

Rimland, B (1977) Applying psychobiology, *Naval Research Reviews* January : 9-16

Snow, R E (1977a) Individual differences and instructional theory. Paper presented at the annual meeting of the American Educational Research Association, New York

Snow, R E (1977b) Research on aptitudes: a progress report. In L S Shulman (ed) *Review of Research in Education* (vol 4). Itasca,Ill : Peacock

Williams, R J (1956) *Biochemical Individuality*. New York : Wiley

Williams, R J (1967) *You Are Extraordinary*. New York : Random House

1.6 Some Aspects
of a Theory of Advice

IVOR K DAVIES

Davies, I K (1975) Some aspects of a theory of advice: the
management of an instructional developer-client, evaluator-client,
relationship, *Instructional Science* 3: 351-73. Reproduced with
permission of the editor.

Introduction

Instructional development and evaluation are essentially art or design
forms involving some type of planned and systematic intervention into
an ongoing organisational system. As such they involve the giving and
taking of advice, for most organisations tend to develop some kind of
functional blindness to many of their own defects. As John Gardner
(1965) once remarked, it is not so much that organisations cannot solve
their own problems, the difficulty is that they usually cannot see them
for themselves. This, of course, is as true of schools, colleges and
universities as it is of industry and business, and instructional
development and evaluation are really nothing more than two strategies
concerned with increasing the effectiveness of an instructional system.
As such, they are powerful weapons in organisational self-renewal; a
means of combating the processes by which teachers become prisoners
of their own instruction.

Instructional developers and evaluators, therefore, need to develop a
special relationship with their client organisation — whether it be a
complete school, college within that school, division, department or
small team of instructors responsible for teaching a specific course.
This relationship, if it is overlooked or undervalued, can threaten,
undermine and even nullify the very accomplishment of the task itself.
Creating and nurturing healthy, helpful and enriching relationships
between developers/evaluators and their clients does take a great deal
of time and effort, but the investment yields a very high return indeed
in the form of good will, co-operation and general feelings of
satisfaction. Helpful and rewarding relationships, however, rarely occur
by chance, they need to be deliberately entered into and consciously
managed as an important resource.

SPECIAL PROBLEMS

In considering the kind of special relationship that instructional
development and evaluation seem to require, three primary questions
need to be considered:

☐ How does a client enter into and manage his relationship with a
developer or evaluator, and how does the developer or evaluator

enter into and manage his relationship with his client?
- [ ] What steps can a client take in his relationship so as to ensure that the objectives that have been agreed are indeed realised, and what steps should the instructional developer or evaluator take in his relationship so as to realise these objectives?
- [ ] How can a client appropriately reduce or terminate his relationship with a developer or evaluator, and how can a developer or evaluator appropriately reduce or terminate his relationship with his client?

More than one client, of course, is usually concerned and more than one developer or evaluator is usually involved in any one project. The addition of more people, however, serves to increase the complexity of the character and nature of the relationships, so that even more care needs to be exercised than when one has a one-to-one relationship. The assumptions, styles and expectations become so much more various that it is often difficult, if not impossible, to reconcile the many forces at play. As Kurt Lewin is once reputed to have remarked: 'If you want to understand something, try to change it.'

A theory of advice

The three primary questions that have been identified are in fact facets of a larger and even more complex phenomenon — the nature of advice. Unfortunately, any analysis of advice is as yet tentative and fragmentary, for the literature is surprisingly thin and sporadic. Yet the giving of advice is one of the oldest and most problematic of human activities, involving as it does the very roots of authority and freedom of action. What is needed is a *theory of advice*, which can serve as a yardstick or criterion against which decisions can be made and priorities allocated.

In giving advice — for that really is the fundamental role of the instructional developer and evaluator — great care needs to be exercised so as to ensure that it is advice and not decisions that are offered. Developers and evaluators are usually called in to help their client make a decision; it is not really their function to make that decision for him. It is also important to remember that every other member of the client organisation also has the responsibility of offering advice, but their advice is rarely politically innocent. The advice offered by developers and evaluators, within their areas of professional expertise, can have objective standing provided that it is offered in an acceptable and constructive manner. However, it is important to bear in mind that the very expertise of developers and evaluators can often be unconsciously viewed as a criticism of their client's competence. It need not be so, but there is always the possibility that this factor will emerge as a destructive force in their relationship.

In terms of a theory of advice, the instructional developer and evaluator are caught up in a client's decision-action process, in which specific roles are expected of them. As with all decision processes, their client is involved in a sequence of activities (see Drucker, 1966), of which only three need concern us here — problem analysis, interpretation of data, and the generation of alternatives.

PROBLEM DEFINITION

When developers and evaluators are invited by clients to advise on some particular problem, the client's decision to make the invitation suggests that the problem is already partly described in his mind. In other words, the invitation is often less concerned with defining the problem, and rather more with filling in the detail and coming up with possible solutions. Such prior definition can be at once helpful and unhelpful, and it is not surprising that this first contact with the client can be what Bryson (1951) has called 'the locus of profound conflict and misunderstanding'. As all experienced developers and evaluators know, the problem you are initially presented with is usually not a problem at all in the real sense of the term, but a symptom of a more general malaise.

Instructional developers and evaluators, therefore, have to decide whether or not to accept the problem as it has been defined for them. They need to consider very carefully whether they have a right to reformulate or change it, or whether to go along with the situation as it has been defined for them. These are very real problems that affect the nature of the relationship as well as their client's expectations, and it is foolish and irresponsible to let events take care of themselves. Comfort, at least, can be taken from the fact that it is a fairly common phenomenon. John Gardner, for instance, pointed out some years ago in an entirely different context that the expert is traditionally challenged at the very beginning of his task by the question of who has the right to say what the problem is. Once developers and evaluators come to terms with this challenge, the dilemma can be accommodated. They have a moral obligation to state the facts and define the situation as they see them, and to do this in a way that is useful and relevant to their client's needs. In other words, if there is a discrepancy between the problem as viewed by their client, and the problem as they see it, then some sort of dialectic or debate is essential.

INTERPRETATION OF DATA

The function of interpreting data is not clearly formulated, and it can be viewed from entirely different points of view by different people. It is a natural human activity, common to all people, and inevitably there are many ways of interpreting any body of data. Interpretation depends upon the assumptions that are made: different sets of assumptions lead to different sets of interpretations. It is not surprising, therefore, that it is in the interpretation of data that client and expert typically run foul of each other.

Developers and evaluators often feel that they have *professional* skills that allow them to 'rightfully' interpret the data they have been given or that they have collected. Similarly, members of the client organisation — although they expect their developers and evaluators to interpret the data for them — also feel their *pragmatic perspective*, deep knowledge and wide experience adequately fit them for the task of interpreting data about their own situation. If their interpretations are different from those that they expect the developer and evaluator to make, and this is usually the case, a rupture is likely to occur in the relationship unless it is very carefully, tactfully and sensitively handled. Even when the matter has been thrashed out, and an interpretation agreed, the delicate relationship is most likely to have been damaged — but hopefully not beyond repair. It is important, therefore, for developers and evaluators to remember that their ideas and their 'facts' will *always* be interpreted by their clients. They should also bear in mind that the people who most welcome their ideas are most often the ones who will interpret them in a way that was never intended by their originator!

GENERATION OF ALTERNATIVE SOLUTIONS

A theory of advice is not only descriptive but also prescriptive, and an adviser has a very definite responsibility to ensure that he presents his client with a range of possible solutions to the situation with which he has been presented. At the same time, an adviser ought to suggest the range of advantages and disadvantages that can be expected from each possible alternative. His job is to give a client a new perspective of the situation, and to offer him new dimensions of freedom of action. Unfortunately, too many advisers fail to do this, for typically they offer their client just one solution in the form of a very clear recommendation. What they have done is take over the decision-making function of the client for themselves. Some clients prefer it this way, but it is important to recognise that when it is done the adviser ceases to be an adviser and becomes a pleader of a special cause.

Instructional developers and evaluators often fall into this trap. When one looks at the range of the products that they typically produce, one can only be surprised at the apparent lack of imagination. This often arises from a failure to consider the whole range of possible alternatives, and a too ready inclination to adopt a well-tried formula. Clients, therefore, are rarely involved with the decision, and are merely asked to go along with what the developer or evaluator suggests. Since the solution is largely being imposed upon the client organisation, the chances of it being rejected are thereby significantly increased. The 'not invented here' syndrome is too common a phenomenon for us to dismiss it lightly. The best augur or promise for success comes from client involvement and participation in every stage of the project, and from ensuring that it is the client who makes the decision as to which alternative should be adopted. This forms the very best basis on which to build a close and constructive relationship, and at the very least it ensures that each one has clear assumptions of the other's role in the decision-action process.

Assumptions underlying the relationship

All of us make assumptions of one kind or another, and these assumptions tend to determine, to a very large extent, the sorts of decisions we make. Unfortunately, people are not always aware of these assumptions, with the result that they can be dissatisfied with what is finally achieved or else they fail to realise the full potential of the situation with which they are presented. So it is with the delicate relationship between a developer or evaluator and his client. Indeed, a great deal of the success which can come from instructional development and evaluation depends, to a very important extent, on ensuring that both client and developer or evaluator deliberately and systematically determine the assumptions which underlie their particular perspective of the situation and its needs. If there are discrepancies between their two sets of assumptions, and almost inevitably there will be significant differences, then these must be brought out into the open and hopefully reconciled during the early part of their relationship.

Assumptions take many forms. Clients and developers or evaluators, for instance, can make quite different assumptions about the nature of man, the principles of behavioural science, the purposes of education, the nature and processes of instructional development and evaluation as well as a whole host of related topics. Even more immediately, they can make different assumptions as to their own expectations of each other. Some would view these discrepancies as irksome and bothersome, as something to be changed and altered so that everyone can start off — as it were — from the same common base. In the real world, however, this is rarely possible. The richness and diversity in basic assumptions need to be viewed as a resource, the potential of which can only be realised when the varying assumptions are brought out into the open and consciously faced. Rarely is it possible to make judgements; as Hamlet remarked 'for there is nothing either good or bad, but thinking makes it so.'

The relationship between a developer or evaluator and his client, of course, is rarely static; more typically it is constantly changing and dynamic in character. So it is with the assumptions that each may bring to the situation; these too develop and change as the situation changes and the relationship is able to develop and, hopefully, flourish. Despite this dynamic quality, however, it is possible and necessary to distinguish between three broad sets of possible assumptions. Any one of these (or sometimes even a combination of them) may underlie the relationship at any one time, although one will inevitably tend to characterise the relationship as a whole. One set of assumptions underlying the relationship can be labelled as product-orientated, the second as prescription-orientated, and the third as product-process-orientated. In each case, the character of the relationships and the related expectations are different in both quality and kind.

PRODUCT-ORIENTATED ASSUMPTIONS

Clients, developers and evaluators sometimes tend to think of their relationship as a professional one involving some kind of purchase model. In other words, the client recognises or perceives that he has a problem of one kind or another and engages or is offered the services of a developer or evaluator with the required professional technical skills. What is actually purchased, as it were, usually takes one or other of two forms: help or information. This distinction is a fundamental one as Tilles (1961) has pointed out, for the two processes are basically different. However, whatever the end-product may involve, what is ultimately 'purchased' normally takes the form of a package of materials with perhaps some associated hardware.

Implicit in this product-orientated view of the relationship are certain assumptions about the nature and distribution of the roles the participants are to play. The client tends to think of his role as similar to that of any customer. A need is perceived, a supplier chosen, an explanation is made as to what is needed, a final selection is made from a range of alternatives, and agreement is reached over cost and delivery. Responsibility for coming up with the desired end-product rests solely with the developer or evaluator; meanwhile the client continues to go about his normal, everyday activities. There is, of course, little or no guarantee that the client will actually recognise, like or even use the final product, for as with most commercial transactions how the product is ultimately used is almost always at the discretion of the customer.

PRESCRIPTION-ORIENTATED ASSUMPTIONS

The present tendency among developers and evaluators, although less so among clients, is to think of their relationship as a highly professional one involving something approaching a physician-patient model. The analogy, of course, is very appealing, particularly as — in a very real sense — it reverses the relative importance of the roles described under the product-orientated group of assumptions. Furthermore, the model introduces the useful concept of 'instructional health', emphasises the role of professional (and at times highly specialist) diagnosis, and suggests the need for regular checks so as to ensure that good health is being maintained. In a very real sense, the prescription-orientated set of assumptions suggests that what is obtained as a result of the relationship between the developer or evaluator and his client is less a product in the form of a package of materials, and more an ongoing, continuous and warm relationship aimed at maintaining a 'healthy' instructional state.

Implicit in this prescription-orientated view of the relationship are certain sets of assumptions about the nature and distribution of the roles to be played. In medicine, the patient usually visits his physician when *he* feels unwell or feels that something is amiss, and in effect he *asks* for professional help. Furthermore, the patient is normally willing to accept the diagnosis that is made and the treatment prescribed. This implies a very real relationship built upon confidence and trust, for the responsibility for the diagnosis is firmly in the hands of the physician. A similar relationship is perceived to exist between developer or evaluator and his clients. Something that is friendly and warm, confident and trusting; firmly founded on the idea that improvement is a matter of course provided that regular consultations are made and prescriptions followed.

PRODUCT-PROCESS-ORIENTATED ASSUMPTIONS

Both the product-orientated and the prescription-orientated models are widely prevalent, and represent important contributions to a theory of advice and action. Many instructional developers and evaluators often have a preference for the prescription model, and readily perceive their relationship with their client from that point of view. Not surprisingly, clients usually seem to prefer the product model, and accordingly view their relationship with developers and evaluators from that perspective. In an attempt to amalgamate the better features of both models, whilst overcoming some of the more obvious disadvantages, a third model of the relationship is becoming increasingly prevalent amongst clients and developers and evaluators. The most important advantage of this model lies in the enhanced possibility that all sides may set out with at least similar sets of assumptions, with the result that their expectations may be largely congruent. To a very great extent, the product-process model can be largely identified with what Tilles (1961) identified as a 'constructive relationship'.

The product-process orientated set of assumptions concern themselves with the view that the most efficient and effective relationship (see Davies, 1971) comes from considering it as *a process directed towards the achievement of some mutually agreed and valued instructional result in accord with the organisation's mission.* In other words, what is involved in the relationship is a system of decisions, reached by agreement, concerning what is expected in terms of both the results to be achieved and the changing roles to be exercised as advice is given and critically accepted. The relationship is essentially a dynamic one, as compared with the static relationships assumed in the two previous models, continuously changing until a final termination is achieved. The product-process view looks upon the relationship between the two parties as something to be *managed,* and above all a relationship that is managed by the client.

As Tilles (1961) points out, 'the logical way to start talking about the use of consultants is by raising the issue of desired results.' So it is with developers and evaluators, for the issue of the kind of desired results that are to be expected from the relationship determines the actual kind of help the client should seek as well as the range of roles that need to be exercised during the successive phases of the project. All too often, of course, it is difficult to get a client to think in such predetermined and concrete terms about the nature of the client developer/evaluator relationship. As a result, there is almost always a discrepancy between client and developer/evaluator assumptions and expectations, so that there is almost always bound to be some sort of disappointment even in the most successful of projects.

In considering the results that are to be achieved as a consequence of the relationship, six broad categories are possible. These can be arranged under the two headings of product and process:

1. Product-related results

    (a) *Improved student performance.* This will more typically take the form of a positive change in student learning, accomplishment and motivation. These three indicators, of course, form the more usual bases for measuring the success of the relationship.

    (b) *Improved allocation of resources.* This will hopefully take the form of a performance and cost conscious allocation and arrangement of both human and material resources.

2. Process-related results

(a) *Improved client skills in instructional development and evaluation.* Inevitably, the relationship between the client and the developer/evaluator has to be terminated at some point, and it is therefore of some importance for the client to develop a better understanding of the whole process of instructional development and evaluation. At the very least, the client should have learned enough from the relationship to be able to exercise a more responsible role in future projects. Hopefully, the client will be able to discern his development and evaluation needs more clearly and, at best, he should be able to exercise some of the skills himself.

(b) *Improved client-developer evaluator relationships.* At the start of any project, an evaluator or a developer is an outsider, but once he begins working within the organisation the relationship changes. Sentiments regarding the developer and evaluator become more precisely formulated, and the situation is reached when they are accepted, rejected or even ignored. Hopefully, relationships will prosper and flourish, so that the project's effectiveness can thereby be enhanced and the potential of the situation realised. Once the value of their contributions is seen, it is not unknown for the developer or evaluator to be directly recruited into the organisation on a more permanent basis.

(c) *Improved client relationships.* As a result of the efforts of the instructional developer and evaluator, the relationships within the more immediate client organisation will hopefully have been improved. The long discussions involving a determination of clear objectives, distribution of roles, allocation and arrangement of resources, etc can and should improve the quality of how the client's own staff relate to each other and to their other colleagues.

(d) *Improved developer and evaluator skills.* Hopefully, as a result of working on a specific problem with a client, developers and evaluators will acquire new and sharpen old skills. At the same time, they should gain new insights, awareness and increased sensitivity to the actual relationship processes involved in development and evaluation, so that they are better able to help manage similar situations in the future.

Since so many changes can take place as a result of the client developer/evaluator relationships, no one criterion for measuring the value of the changes brought about is possible. For this reason, the client must choose those criteria that are most appropriate to his purpose. Many clients are naturally tempted to take a short-term view of the results that have been achieved, yet it is very much in the developer and evaluator's interest to ensure that a long-term perspective is also taken. So many of the real and lasting benefits from instructional development and evaluation only emerge once the organisational system as a whole has had time finally to accommodate the changes that have been wrought.

Successive stages in the development of a relationship

Planned change of any kind involves a fairly definite sequence or cycle of activities. Typically this consists of four basic steps: diagnosis, planning action, implementing action and evaluation. So it is with such change-inducing activities as instructional development and evaluation. The actual number of steps, of course, can vary from one schema to another, but despite quite important variations the four basic steps are usually clearly discernible. These steps, however, describe the successive phases of the actual project or task itself and, as such, are descriptions of the duties and responsibilities performed.

Parallel with this cycle of task-orientated activities is another cycle involving the successive phases of development through which a developer-client, evaluator-client relationship passes. Seven activities, compared with the four typically used to describe task-orientated activities, seem to be apparent. These can be grouped under three broad headings:

1. *Entering into a relationship:*
   (a) initial contacts with the client system
   (b) negotiation of a formal relationship
2. *Maintaining an ongoing relationship:*
   (a) an analysis-orientated relationship
   (b) a decision-making-orientated relationship
   (c) an action-orientated relationship
3. *Terminating a relationship:*
   (a) evaluating the fruits of the relationship
   (b) reducing involvement and/or terminating the relationship.

These seven activities ordinarily overlap and interact. They are not easily defined; some of them seem to go on simultaneously, and some (like evaluation) seem to be going on all the time. To complicate matters even further, the task-orientated activity can be out of phase with the relationship-orientated activity. When this happens, and the task agenda fails to mesh with the relationship agenda, the results can be both disastrous and hilarious at one and the same time. The trick is to ensure that both task and relationships are *managed* in such a way that the two ongoing sets of activity are as compatible as possible. To state the paradox even further, in order to discover what you should be doing you should, in some way or another, already be doing it. Only in this way is it possible to balance, and evaluate the consequences of, each task and relationship-orientated activity.

ENTERING INTO A RELATIONSHIP

Entering into a relationship at the beginning of a new project is always a fairly exciting activity. Often the problem seems so pressing that there is a very natural tendency to want to get on with the job, rather than 'waste' time trying to establish the relationship and define roles in terms of what the client expects to be accomplished. Yet it is always good advice to enter into a project and a relationship very slowly, to feel the temperature of the water as it were, and to build a firm basis *before* attempting to plan how the project should be put underway.

Initial contacts with the client system

The initial contact with the client system is first made when someone from the client-organisation approaches an instructional developer or evaluator for advice on a particular problem. It is always worthwhile at this point to try and find out why you have been approached, for this will give an important insight into the client's reasoning. However, whatever the reason, great care should be taken to ensure that you listen and that you are encouraging, but that you are not preconditioned by what you are told. It is rarely possible, at this stage, even to guess at what the real problem may be, and any discussion should be avoided until a more formal exploratory meeting can be scheduled.

The all important exploratory meeting, which should be scheduled to last at least half-a-day, should have a slight degree of formality about it, and a fairly cut and dried agenda. Its purposes are to determine a little more precisely the characteristics of the problem, to assess whether or not a developer or evaluator is likely to be of any assistance, and finally to formulate what the next action steps should be. These purposes are usually best accomplished by having a fairly open-ended discussion, yet a constructive and helpful one in terms of the decisions that are to be made. An important part of the meeting, from the point of view of the developer or evaluator, will involve ascertaining with whom he will be immediately working, and who makes up the 'political' constituency of the actual client-organisation. The exploratory meeting will have been largely unsuccessful if a statement of real interest as well as a willingness to consider making some sort of resource commitment (financial or by freeing part of a faculty member's time) is not forthcoming from the constituency hierarchy.

Present at this exploratory meeting should be the specific client who first made contact with the developer or evaluator, the developer(s) and/or evaluator(s) themselves, and two or more representatives of the client system. These representatives should certainly include someone who is high enough in the organisation to be able to influence others if he is influenced, someone who is in tune with the idea of bringing in a developer or evaluator and who knows something of their skills, and finally someone who sees a range of specific problems that need to be worked upon. The important thing is to avoid hostile or sceptical people, for the aim of the exploratory meeting is not to argue the relative merits or demerits of the skills being offered; if this happens, the problem ceases to be explored, and the developer and evaluator are reduced to a selling rather than a consultant role.

Developers and evaluators should be as open and confronting as they possibly can at this meeting, partly to see how open the client is being and partly to make clear at the very outset how *they* define their role. This involves discussing such important, but seldom spoken about, concerns as what the developer's, evaluator's and client's payoffs may be. What is there in the project that makes it personally and professionally appealing and rewarding? A discussion that is open and authentic, that shows a client's genuine willingness to explore and that is carried on in a full spirit of inquiry is a very good indicator of a future relationship that will be both warm and constructive. If a client or client system wants mere reassurance for something that he has already begun, if he is looking for a quick solution to a superficial problem, if you are being used for 'political' purposes, if the client is unwilling to make some commitment of his resources to the project, or doubts the usefulness of your skills, then it is probably not worth pursuing the matter any further.

Negotiation of a formal relationship

This state is reached when a decision has been jointly taken that the project is worth pursuing, and a choice has been made as to the formal entry point into the client system. The choice of the formal entry point is particularly important, since the initial client contact can often be through one of the 'deviant' members of the organisation. Such people may well be willing to embrace change, but they are likely to have little or no real and lasting influence with the political constituency. If the formal entry point is *via* a deviant member, the project may well be highly successful in terms of immediate goals, but there is a low probability that it will ever be institutionalised.

Once the decision to proceed has been taken, the actual terms of the 'contract' can begin to be negotiated. Two contracts are in fact involved: one a *formal* contract, and the other a *psychological* contract. The formal contract involves reaching agreement over such things as what is to be done, how much time is to be devoted to the project, what client and consultant resources will be made available, the broad method of approach, how the level of involvement can be reduced and finally terminated, and the expected benefits for the client and the expected benefits for the developer and evaluator (see Frohman, 1970). The psychological contract is much shorter, and in a way more difficult to negotiate. Whilst the formal contract has been concerned with the actual values or objectives to be obtained and realised, the psychological contract is concerned with the expectations that each has of the other. It involves a willingness and commitment to diagnose and explore the issues surrounding the problem situation, to take time to find out rather than rush in hastily. It involves a willingness and commitment to spend real time on the project, not to drag one's feet or engage in veiled resistance, to listen to suggestions and a willingness to engage in the project with an open mind and a true spirit of inquiry.

As part of the formal and psychological contract, care should be taken to ensure that there is a real understanding of how the roles are being defined and allocated, and what each role involves. Three issues are particularly important here (Schein, 1969): selection of a setting in which to work, specification of a time schedule and method of working, and an allocation of duties and responsibilities. The latter is fairly straightforward, although some bargaining and negotiation may well be necessary with the political constituency. In selecting a setting in which to work, it is particularly important to engage in *focused processes* of observation and work, rather than in some broad, general type of exploration. Specifying a time schedule and method of working involves taking great care that the developer and evaluator's activities are congruent with the *values* of instructional development and evaluation. Steps should also be taken to ensure that it is understood that there are no 'pat' answers or standard solutions. The developer and evaluator should also be maximally available and visible at this stage, and busily engaged in setting up a network of relationships. Any project can only get under way when people understand what the project is really about, and the consultants involved are known and trusted.

MAINTAINING AN ONGOING RELATIONSHIP

In maintaining an ongoing relationship, three phases are involved: an analysis-orientated relationship, a decision-making-orientated relationship, and an action-orientated relationship. These relationship activities correspond to three task-orientated activities: diagnosis, planning action and implementing action. Although each of the activities is being treated separately, it is important to remember that they usually occur simultaneously, for every step in analysis embraces a decision and a corresponding action. Everything, in other words, involves an intervention into the client-system, so that each decision must take into account the probable consequences that are likely to stem from it in terms of both task and people.

Analysis-orientated relationship

During the stage of diagnosis, it is usual for close relationships to be developed. Obvious progress is being made on the project, and there is usually a feeling of involvement and participation in something rather exciting and worthwhile. The first step, of course, generally consists of gaining some broad overview of the total situation, followed by a fairly intensive stage of data-gathering for each of the concerns which can be identified. This usually involves direct observation, interviewing and the utilisation of questionnaires and similar instruments. Since some people may still feel somewhat threatened at this still early stage in the project, it is often better to begin with a series of interviews. The rather more depersonalised use of instruments for data-gathering should be left, as far as possible, towards the end, particularly if there is any reason to believe that some people may find them worrisome, burdensome or even menacing.

An essential part of diagnosis involves examining the client's felt or perceived problem. This, of course, may not be the real problem at all, but only a symptom of a much more general malaise. Inevitably more and more problems will be recognised as the analysis proceeds, and these will need to be sorted in some way or another. The client, assisted and advised by the developer or evaluator, should assign priorities for action, and by this activity it is often possible to lead him to a more sensitive awareness of the total situation as it really is. This will entail obtaining a full understanding of the goals both of the client-system and of the people who make up that system, together with their motivation and readiness for change and innovation.

Evidence also needs to be acquired of the system's and the people's *real* readiness for solving the problems which face them. Sometimes, a system is more able to live with a situation (and come to terms with it) than to try and change it. Slowly, as the analysis proceeds, the client-system and the client's actual motives will begin to emerge. Since these may well be different from what the client says or believes they are, a genuine understanding of the humaneness behind such discrepancies needs to be developed. What a client believes to be true, *is* true — at least for him — and will help control and shape his actual behaviour.

This means that, throughout the diagnosis stage, developer and evaluator need to develop an empathy for their client, as well as a full appreciation and understanding of his human foibles. Warmth, sincerity and tact are essential qualities in a consultant, as well as a ready recognition that he, too, may suffer from the same frailties so noticeable in his client. Developing such a close, warm and understanding relationship during the diagnosis stage of the project is a sound preparation for the rather more turbulent phase commonly associated with decision making.

A decision-making orientation

This stage in the project usually demands maximum participation and co-operation from both client and developer or evaluator. It is the time for choosing amongst possible alternative courses of action. Although the client, by the very nature of his role, must necessarily make the actual decisions, the developer and evaluator have an important, if not critical, part to play. They possess the specialist knowledge and skills which are essential resources to the situation, and yet this very expertise fits them for a decision-making role that they must in reality reject. At times, a client can feel that his advisers are failing by their refusal to make the decisions for him, that they are opting out of the situation and deserting him at a time of need. This, however, is the name of the game, for the responsibility is his and his alone. Nevertheless, instructional developers and evaluators must appreciate that an important part of their role at such times consists of encouraging, supporting and *actively* assisting their clients — perhaps in a way that extends beyond their function as advisers. It is a personal matter that involves some very careful thought, and a highly tuned sensitivity to both task and people needs.

The creation of a plan also involves some sort of simulation, in the sense that the consequences of each of the possible alternatives being considered can have quite different implications. There will be implications for the total system and political constituency, as well as for the information and management systems. There will be implications that affect the very bases of power, authority and influence, as well as the policy, culture and actual ecology of the programme. Finally, there will be very great implications for the task itself, as well as for the students involved. Each alternative must be viewed in the light of each set of implications, both positive and negative, in order to decide what type of intervention is likely to be optimal. In such circumstances, it is almost inevitable that the consultant and the client will disagree; indeed their disagreement should be viewed as a healthy response to a very difficult assignment. The danger lies in the disagreement either becoming so destructive that the relationship is irreparably damaged, or becoming so smoothed over by compromise that the ultimate plan is stunted or ill-formed. Disagreement and conflict must be *managed* by the client as an essential resource, but this can only be accomplished if the relationship is a strong and healthy one well able to withstand the trials of decision making.

In addition to the supporting role so far described, developer and evaluator have an additional task role in terms of the character of the interventions open to them. Very broadly, following Schein (1969) four types of intervention seem proper at this stage:

(a) *Agenda-setting interventions:* These are aimed at making the client-system and the client sensitive to their own processes, as well as generating some interest in the worth of analysing them.
(b) *Feedback of observations and other data.* These interventions are geared at making the client-system and the client orientated to what the issues may indeed be.
(c) *Teaching, coaching and counselling.* Almost inevitably, an adviser is forced into a teaching role whenever it is necessary for a client-system or a client to acquire a particular set of instructional development or evaluation skills.
(d) *Structural recommendations.* This kind of intervention, which violates some of the basic assumptions of advice, should be as rare as possible, for it is important for the client-system and the client to generate or at least to 'discover' their own solutions.

Involved in each one of these interventions is a basic question: 'Should an instructional developer or evaluator propose the actual solution to a problem?' Obviously, it is almost always better for the client if he learns to solve his own problems, and there are times when it is better for a consultant to withhold his expertise, particularly if it is likely to damage his role or the relationship. It is important to distinguish, however, the essential difference between helping a client-system or client to learn, and being an expert on the actual problem which the client is attempting to solve.

An action-orientated relationship

This is the stage when the best change strategy is implemented by the client-system. Developer and evaluator have a minimal role at this time, although it is sometimes very difficult to avoid feeling deeply involved, for the client needs to be able to feel that the resulting product is his and his alone. Success will depend, to a very large extent, on the quality of the diagnosis and the subsequent plan, but unanticipated hitches are almost inevitable.

Typically, these problems will be of two types, administrative or technical, but occasionally they can be traced back to still unresolved issues. These (see Kolb & Frohman, 1970) may be due to a failure to involve some key person or group, a failure to diagnose the situation adequately, or a failure to anticipate all the possible implications of the decisions taken. Whatever their character, the advisers must support and assist the client in such a way that the situation is rectified *before* blame is apportioned. It is more important, at this stage, for the change to be brought about as soon as possible than to engage in blame and self-recrimination. Post-mortems are more properly dealt with during the evaluation phase.

TERMINATING A RELATIONSHIP

So far we have been concerned with relationships within the context of the excitement of setting up a new project, and the general business involved with first planning and then implementing action. The last stage of any development or evaluation project has quite a different character and tends, in many ways, to be rather an anticlimax. This is not meant to suggest that this stage is, in any way, less important than its predecessors, but merely that it tends to have a rather different flavour in terms of the climate of interpersonal relationships.

Evaluating the fruits of the relationship

The ultimate goal of any change strategy, including instructional development and evaluation, is improved performance of one kind or another. This may take two general forms: improved effectiveness through the development of products or instruments, and improved effectiveness as a result of a change in the values and interpersonal skills of the people involved. In order to determine whether or not the venture has been successful, both formative and summative evaluation are essential. The former is a constant ongoing activity, usually, although not necessarily, carried out by the developers themselves, whilst the latter, in the interests of objectivity, is best carried out by an independent evaluator.

The very reasonableness of this approach, from the point of view of the developer or evaluator, is usually the first cause of misunderstanding. It is not unusual for the client to be either so certain that the project has been successful or so certain that it has been a waste of time, that he sees little or no point in carrying out a formal evaluation. Indeed, he may view it as nothing more than a piece of academic gamesmanship. The results, he feels, are either so obviously present or so obviously lacking that one is simply setting out to prove the obvious.

For this reason, the client needs to be very carefully prepared for this stage right from the initial set of meetings. Clients should be actively involved in the planning meetings when the dimensions on which the evaluation is to be carried out are decided. The potential bias created by this prior knowledge can be largely overcome by choosing objective evaluation indices that cannot be readily manipulated. Furthermore, in order gradually to wean the client from his dependency on developer and evaluator, the opportunity should be taken — if possible — to give the client an opportunity of gathering the information himself. The roles of developer and evaluator should be largely those of ensuring that the client invents all the ideas, acts as a facilitator, and serves as a resource. In any case, their actual physical involvement in the project will most likely have been gradually reduced by the time this stage has been reached.

Reducing involvement and terminating the relationship

Any developer or evaluator-client relationship is by its very nature temporary in character. Surprisingly, however, there is a tendency for people to *behave* as though the relationship is a permanent one, so that they are ill-prepared for the inevitable time of parting. For this reason, clients must be systematically prepared for the moment of termination, and the issue should certainly be discussed at the very first series of exploratory meetings. In other words, decisions about reducing involvement leading to the termination of the relationship should be taken as part of the business of entering *into* the relationship. Any decisions that are made, however, at this early stage as to the length of the engagement should always be subject to further negotiation according to the needs of the situation.

The decision to reduce the level of involvement and/or to terminate the relationship should, whenever possible, be a joint one, rather than a unilateral decision taken by just one of the parties. It is appropriate to make the decision when the evaluator, developer, client or all three feel that either nothing more can be immediately accomplished or the client is now able to work on his own. Often the client will wish to continue with the relationship, but it is as well to bear in mind that the character of his arguments for continuing is an indication of how much his confidence, skills and values have indeed changed. In any case, the level of developer or evaluator involvement should not be allowed to drop suddenly; instead there should be a gradual withdrawing from the scene. Reinvolvement is always possible, but only at the request of the client. Indeed, the very character of the relationships that have been developed over the project should always be regarded as a very precious human resource — a resource for future action that it would be foolish to waste or ignore.

Failure is far more common in development and evaluation projects than is generally recognised. Inevitably, there is a very human feeling that something ought to be saved, with the result that often desperate attempts are made to try and redeem the situation. Sometimes this is possible and well worthwhile, but the key as to whether it is feasible is to be found in the client's attitude. If the client is unwilling to continue to invest the necessary time and effort in the saving operation, it is best to terminate the relationship as quickly and as abruptly as possible. Mutual face-saving efforts are to be encouraged, although almost inevitably they will preclude anyone using the experience as a learning situation.

Some general factors contributing to effective relationships

Instructional development and evaluation are complex processes, and unless a client knows what he is looking for in the development/ evaluation relationship then he is likely to be disappointed with the results that are obtained. Many clients, of course, are not fully aware of the potential of instructional development and evaluation, and consequently misconceptions are likely to arise. For this reason, developers and evaluators have a responsibility to ensure that they help their clients develop a sensitivity to the process involved, so that they can make an informed decision as to what it is they actually want accomplished.

The fundamental value of the services offered by developers and evaluators lies in the contribution they make toward helping their clients increase *their* instructional effectiveness. In this sense, at least, the client is the more important party in determining the success of the relationship, for his attitude and expectations may preclude the organisation being helped, may prevent him from initiating a request for help and advice, may stop him from finding time to involve himself in the project, or may prompt him to ignore any of the advice offered. A developer or evaluator's effectiveness, therefore, will tend to multiply to the extent that he begins to realise his client's objectives. As these objectives begin to be realised, so the value of the contributions of the developer and evaluator will increase in the eyes of the client. As the objectives of the client remain unfulfilled, so the value of the developer and evaluator's efforts will diminish from the client's point of view. Nothing, in other words, succeeds like success.

SKILLS OF EFFECTIVENESS

In our consideration of the many factors that contribute to an effective relationship, two underlying threads are clearly discernible. Firstly, development and evaluation should never be imposed *upon* a client, and secondly, a client should always exercise an active decision-making role at every stage of the project. The importance of his contributions will, of course, vary with the particular phase the project has reached, but at no time should he feel that he is uninvolved. It is the client's project, not the developer's or evaluator's; their role is strictly one of advising him what the range of his options may be.

Experience suggests that this role is best preserved and enhanced when a particular set of factors is systematically borne in mind. The effectiveness of development and evaluation will be significantly increased when a client-organisation itself considers that some instructional change may be necessary, actively seeks help from a developer or evaluator to whom *they* ascribe expertise (rather than accepting an offer of help from a consultant), and does not place unreasonable constraints on his work. The quality of what is achieved will also be enhanced if the people making up the client-organisation are in general agreement as to the desirability of obtaining development and evaluation help, have participated in the discussions and decisions leading up to the arrangement to use developers and evaluators, and have themselves helped to choose their consultant from other possibilities available. Finally, the developer's and evaluator's work will have increased acceptability if they conduct a preliminary analysis so as to develop a proposed programme for their client's approval and acceptance, develop a range of alternatives on the basis of need rather than on the basis of standard solutions, continually report their progress, and finally work closely with members of the participating organisation within a co-operative rather than directive framework.

SYSTEM REQUIREMENTS

Outside the domain of the particular skills which contribute to the effectiveness of a development or evaluation project, there are also a number of important system requirements. These have long-term, rather than short-term, consequences. For this reason, developers and evaluators are often tempted to overlook their importance to their own survival, as well as to that of the instructional improvements they have hopefully helped bring about.

Whenever possible, and of course there are always those occasions when it is not possible, instructional development and evaluation should:

(a) *not be undertaken as isolated events:* consideration must always be given for the impact of the development or the evaluation on the client-organisation as a *total* system. Effective development and evaluation are best conceived as part of a total design for instructional improvement. In other words, the development or evaluation of a specific course is rarely as effective or meaningful as development and evaluation set within the broader framework of a subject or emphasis area plan for total renewal.

(b) *not be directed only at solving immediate problems:* helping to solve someone else's problems is always an attractive activity, but care has to be taken to ensure that it does not become an end in itself. Developers and evaluators should also aim at improving the ability of their client-organisation to anticipate and solve similar problems for itself in the future. In other words, they need to help the client-organisation increase its own collective wisdom.

In ensuring that instructional development and evaluation are conceived within the framework of these two requirements, the overall importance and impact of what is accomplished will more likely extend beyond the boundaries of the immediate project itself.

Conclusion

Instructional development and evaluation in a vacuum would be fairly simple and rather mundane processes. Fortunately, development and evaluation only make sense in the context of people, and yet — in an almost desperate attempt to realise the task — we sometimes tend to ignore the relationship side of the instructional situation. No matter how pert our development and evaluation procedures, no matter how sophisticated and scientifically based our techniques, little will be achieved if the quality of human relationships is overlooked or ignored. A project that is task orientated, without being also relationship orientated, thereby increases the probability of its own rejection.

In a very real sense, it would also seem that it is possible to distinguish between more rewarding and less rewarding relationships. The most important difference between:

(a) developers and evaluators who are skilful in their relationships with their clients, and
(b) clients who are skilful in their relationships with their developers and evaluators

121

would appear to be in the way that they *think* about the character of their relationship. In other words, the consequences of how the relationship is viewed or thought of has a significant impact upon the effectiveness of what is accomplished in both the long and short term.

Acknowledgements

The author wishes to acknowledge the invaluable assistance and advice of Mr Stephen J Guynn, an EDPA fellow in the DIST program at Indiana University, Bloomington, Indiana 47401.

References

Argyris, C (1961) Explorations in consultant-client relationships, *Human Organization* 20: 121-33

Bryson, L (1951) Notes on a theory of advice, *Political Science Quarterly* 66 3: 321-39

Daccord, J E (1967) *Management Consultants: A Study of the Relationship between Effectiveness and Several Personal Characteristics.* Unpublished Master's thesis, Sloan School of Management, MIT

Davies, I K (1971) Style and effectiveness in education and training: a model for organizing teaching and learning, *Instructional Science* 1 1: 45-85

Davies, I K (1973)|*Competency Based Learning: Management, Technology and Design.* New York : McGraw-Hill

Davies, I K and Schwen, T M (1972) *Toward a Definition of Instructional Development.* Washington, DC : Association for Educational Communications and Technology, Division of Instructional Development Monograph

Drucker, P F (1966) *The Effective Executive.* New York : Harper & Row

Frohman, M (1970) *Conceptualizing a Helping Relationship.* Ann Arbor : Institute for Social Research, Center for Research on the Utilization of Scientific Knowledge

Gardner, J W (1965) How to prevent organizational dry rot, *Harper's Magazine*, October, p20

Gombrowicz, W (1973) *A Kind of Testament.* London : Calder & Boyars

Kolb, D A and Frohman, A L (1970) An organization development approach to consulting, *Sloan Management Review:* 51-65

Lawrence, P R and Lorsch, J W (1969) *Developing Organizations: Diagnosis and Action.* Reading, Mass : Addison-Wesley

McGregor, D (1960) *Human Side of Enterprise.* New York : McGraw-Hill

Schein, E H (1969) *Process Consultation: its Role in Organization Development.* Reading, Mass : Addison-Wesley

Tilles, S (1961) Understanding the consultant's role, *Harvard Business Review* 39: 87-99

1.7 The Responsibilities of the Researcher

MARTEN D SHIPMAN

The responsibilities of the researcher are usually defined by reference to his integrity while engaged in research. This is not just to focus on technical issues, as there exist political and ethical responsibilities that form a code of respectable practice. However, there is a broader consideration for the researcher. This is derived from his relations with the audience for his work. Alongside the scrutiny of his work by professional colleagues there is a duty to those who read and act on the evidence produced.

The proliferation of users of psychology and sociology who are not within the scientific community but who selectively use the results from these areas of inquiry, makes a consideration of our responsibilities towards this audience a most topical subject. Within education this audience is not only the largest but, through the insistence on the professional training of teachers, the most captive. In addition there are administrators, inspectors, advisers and politicians, as well as teachers, who are influenced by research. The actual interpretation and use of the evidence may horrify the researcher who produced it, but the influence and the consequent responsibility this use carries remains.

The net impact of research evidence is not to provide solutions to problems. Only rarely and at a very mundane level can the researcher provide answers. Research takes too long and is too conditional to be of much direct use. But evidence from research can set the scene and influence the questions that are asked. The success of psychologists and sociologists concerned with education has been to puncture myths and explore the gap between reality and people's views of that reality. Whether we intend to be constructive or destructive we exert influence. This places on us a responsibility to consider the outcome of our research as well as to consider its reliability and validity.

The influence of the sociologists of education working in the UK in the 1950s and 1960s is a striking example. They contributed to the move towards comprehensive schooling and a move towards a more open system of higher education by revealing the gap between what was believed to be a competitive but fair education for all, and the unfair and systematic handicapping of working-class children. Even more important their work helped to change the theoretical basis for

123

streaming and selection by showing the frailty of tests as ways of classifying the young. The contemporary concentration on the curriculum will build on this to erase the more subtle way of producing sheep and goats through exposure to different curricular experiences.

The continuing responsibility

It may be unpleasant, but psychologists and sociologists engaged in teacher education, in research, and in writing books and articles, are an *élite*. They have a potential audience of half-a-million teachers, students, administrators and inspectors. They feed evidence into a variety of courses for which their subject matter acts as an academic crutch. This large audience is fed by few originators and disseminators. Taylor (1973) has estimated that there are one thousand five hundred sociologists in universities, two to three thousand in colleges of education, and five hundred in administration or inspection! This is roughly one per cent who are producing or wholesaling for the army of retailers.

The position of potential influence is occupied by radical and conservative research workers alike. Whether problems for study are taken or made, the audience should be considered. Indeed, making today's research issue ensures that it is taken tomorrow. Similarly, taking a problem for research is the most likely way of preparing the ground for the making of another. It may be unpleasant to be an *élite*, but it is the fate of the academic whose subject is the concern and livelihood of large numbers. Thus even the most trivial writing may be taken seriously by users outside the scientific community. There is no way of telling whether your work will be influential or merely support the roof of the university archive. The best seller in education is often the small-scale case study. There seems to be a law of inverse proportion between the size, control and reliability of research and the influence it exerts. The reason lies of course in the parallel law of decreasing certainty. As control increases, results become more conditional. Only the small-scale study confidently concludes. The large-scale study concludes that it all depends.

The new responsibility

The climate for social science has changed just as its audience has expanded. In the 1960s, sociologists struggled to secure a position within higher education. Researchers were suffering in a buyer's market. It was a hard life dominated by the conventional wisdom of inspectors, advisers and old guard educationalists which dominated official reports. Today sociology is established within academia, fortified by a queue of applicants for courses. Sociological and psychological research pads the appendices of official reports and social scientists have usurped chairs in education from which *ex cathedra* statements are expected to be made.

Obviously such a position should carry a responsibility to ensure the maximum reliability and validity in research. It calls for clear, honest, comprehensive reporting. But above all it calls for a recognition that there is a relation between the scientific community and those outside. This is even more important where a scientific community such as sociology is the reference for those working in a feeder subject such as education.

A scientific community regulates entry to a profession and controls standards through refereeing, external examining and editing. It excludes the amateur and admits those qualifying through degrees and diplomas. Unfortunately, the community, through its senior members, achieves this not only through the imposition of discipline in scientific work, but by sustaining the mystery of the craft. We may know the snags, the bias, the cranks and the comedians, but our students and readers do not. Every failure to communicate clearly, every failure to be honest about the status of evidence is a support for obscurantism or quackery. As teachers we are liable to compound this mystification. We add bits of unreliable evidence to personal impressions and near-fictions to produce plausible courses. In private we are sceptics, but we feed our students half-truths. We protect our position as scientists by suggesting that there is a consistent, reliable basis in research for a series of educational theories. Simultaneously we attack the positivism that remains the public's model of scientific inquiry. We cannot lose while we secure an audience by a claim to be scientific while we deny the worth of the scientific method that is the basis of the public's acknowledgement of our right to be heard.

The scientific community has another crucial job resting on the discipline of its members and the mysteries of the craft. Evidence is accepted, given the seal of legitimacy, not through any technical assessment against fixed standards of method or proof, but through agreement among established peers. This judgement is applied as the evidence is approved for publication, in its critical reception, in its inclusion in courses and in its use as a reference in later work. But social scientists are in a difficult position, as internecine strife produces not consensus over the validity of evidence, but a conflict over what is true and what is rubbish.

The result of this lack of agreement over the status of evidence is often a sociological nightmare. Swift (1973) has described a sequence from glib talk of a lack of brain power among children to glib talk of deprived home backgrounds as an explanation of unequal attainment in school. Tomorrow it is likely to be glib talk of inequality through exposure to different curricula. The nightmare remains the same at the core, regardless of its changing manifestations. Teachers who come to take our results uncritically come to perverse conclusions. Children who are seen as unteachable because of their social background or linguistic code are being handicapped as surely as their predecessors who were seen as lacking brains. Teachers can be confused by our devious way of concealing the lack of clarity in our work and the response is to simplify to a degree that seems to us a parody of the original intention. There are teachers who see reading as a way of indoctrinating children into capitalism, and the ability to calculate with a base of ten as a middle-class mathematical plot to emasculate working-class children. Social science has been liberating, but it can also be daft. But what we see as daft may be taken as self-evident truth by our students to the harm of their pupils.

Obviously I am exaggerating and being personal. My move from academia to a local authority has been unsettling, but it brought a recognition of the need for modest fact-gathering. This is tedious, but it is necessary if policy making is not to be based on guesswork. Here, evidence has to hold up against the views of very contrasting pressures. It is often necessary to find out not explain, to describe but not generalise, and report but not interpret. Ryan (1974) pointed out that it is useful to know that flat feet are disabling because this leads to remedial action. To show that falling arches are related to social class position is a bonus for the social scientist, but secondary for those responsible for easing the pain with limited resources.

It is probable that our major influence on the development of education has been on teachers rather than policy makers. Given the scope for grassroots innovation this is an important influence. Indeed it is the reason why we have to take responsibility for the quality of the package we peddle. But the irrelevance of social science to the policy maker is disappointing. We are in a different ball game. To those arguing over the future organisation of education the academic view is unimportant, mainly because those who decide see a different set of problems and describe them in a different language.

This problem is universal. Taylor (1973) has diagnosed it as resting in the role specificity of knowledge. Not only do professionals work within their own scientific frames of reference, they are socialised into exclusive modes of expression and understanding. Again the interplay of discipline and mystery that marks scientific communities can be used to exclude and to impress. The cost is in the sacrifice of influence where it matters most. In the present receptive climate within education we are in a precarious situation. Because the influence is at grassroots and not central, it is often invisible. Yet this increases the responsibility on us to be open, cautious and honest. Too many ideas in the social sciences turn out to have only passing popularity. We leave them behind and re-write our lecture notes. But our students and readers may have already converted the idea into practice and the harm done to children may linger on. Academic games can have serious practical consequences.

Conclusions

There is no point in being scathing about an inability to deliver reliable goods on time and on the open market. Further, the insertion of subversive ideas, however incomplete, is a traditional and legitimate activity of the social scientist. This is the way injustice is exposed and remedied. The social world is also unlikely to yield clear cut sequences and relations that are open to hypotheses that can be stated in a refutable form. The 'ifs' and 'buts' of the social scientist are annoying to the policy maker seeking a straight answer to an oversimplified question, but they do reflect reality.

There are, however, a few ways of narrowing the gap between

producer and consumer, whether to avoid the acceptance of hypotheses as facts by students or the rejection of reliable evidence by those who make crucial decisions. These are inevitably out of the Polonius stable and are a symptom of my own dotage, but beneath their obvious nature is a message that cannot be repeated too many times.

1. Modesty should be the rule even if this means sacrificing status.
2. Candour with those who do not have our inside knowledge is necessary even if this exposes our shortcomings.
3. Impressions should be clearly distinguished from evidence.
4. Science should not be simultaneously abused and used to bolster our own message.
5. A fair share of replication studies should be taken by everyone alongside the fresh starts that guarantee a more immediate recognition.
6. While the demolition job on positivism has been successful, the approach to refutable hypotheses and controlled investigation should be as close as possible.
7. Role specificity should be taken into account in reporting and communicating, even if this involves translating our own words. It is easier for us to read in the jargon than for outsiders to have to check it out.
8. Responsibility for the interpretation of evidence and its translation into action should be accepted by the producers. It is not sufficient to claim misrepresentation or misunderstanding after publication.
9. The microscopic and personal are fascinating but no substitute for the traditional sociological concern with institutions, power and change.

One consequence of a return to these central concerns will be to uncover the influence of social science in education. My own guess is that this influence has been underestimated because we have looked at the official, central level. The real success of social scientists seems to be bottom-up, not top-down. If this is true, the need for the exercise of responsibility increases, for the consumers are less sceptical and more receptive than are the policy makers who are usually assumed to be our audience.

References

Ryan, A (1974) The social sciences and their values, *New Society* 29 617: 280-83
Swift, D F (1973) Sociology and educational research. In W Taylor (ed) *Research Perspectives in Education.* London : Routledge & Kegan Paul
Taylor, W (1973) Knowledge and research. In W Taylor (ed) *Research Perspectives in Education.* London : Routledge & Kegan Paul

Part Two:
Procedural Techniques

Introduction

In the early days of programmed learning it seemed that constructing a
program was a fairly simple thing to do: objectives were defined, task
analyses were carried out, teaching sequences were determined,
programs were written, and then evaluated and revised. By the early
1970s, however, it was clear that things were not so simple. The aim of
Hartley's *Strategies for Programmed Instruction* (Butterworths, 1972)
was to show that there was a variety of procedures possible within each
of the major steps just listed. Since 1972 this development has
continued: each of the major steps has now become an area of research
and controversy in its own right. In this section of the text we present
papers which characterise each stage and which reflect this modern
diversity.

Defining objectives, or stating aims, has always been important for
educational technology. The original idea was that if aims could be
stated in a measurable way, then the achievement of these aims could
be measured. Once this was done then some sort of quality control
process was possible. The 'objectives movement' created great debate
and, eventually, this debate was seen to reflect the wider issues that
have ranged in educational circles for a very long time. Paper 2.1
introduces a section from the Introduction to Ivor Davies' *Objectives in
Curriculum Design* (McGraw-Hill, 1976). This Introduction discusses
first (a part omitted from this text) the notion that objectives contain
implicit value judgements and then it continues to discuss how
objectives fit into the process of planning within different value systems.
It is this part that we have included here. Davies' complete text
examines the history of the objectives movement, it presents many
examples of different approaches and it gives good practical advice to
people involved in this area of curriculum planning.

Paper 2.2 introduces a recent survey of techniques of task analysis
in an industrial context. It is indeed of interest to note that most of
the research debate on task analysis does take place within this
industrial/military framework. Educationalists, however, should not
be put off too much by this. If one reads between the lines, substitutes
'teacher' for 'trainer' and 'teaching' for 'training', much of value can be
drawn from Paper 2.2. (Trainers reading other papers can of course
reverse this procedure.) Despite the differences of vocabulary and

131

emotive connotations there is a great deal of generality in the literature of instruction. Paper 2.2 briefly updates a fuller paper (which is more directly related to a school context) provided by Duncan in 1972.

Paper 2.3 provides a tabular summary of a longer paper by George Posner and Kenneth Strike. The original paper argued that the debate about how content *should* be sequenced should first be prefaced by some discussion about how content *can* be sequenced. This paper thus lists the alternatives. In the early days of programmed learning it was stressed that teaching materials should be presented in a logical sequence (without really defining what that meant). Paper 2.3 provides a framework for discussing different ways of sequencing content and their implications.

It is a truism to say that learning involves the acquisition of new and related concepts and — in addition to the problem of knowing how best to sequence new material — it seems that little is known about how to teach concepts in the first place. In Paper 2.4 Susan Markle examines four areas from which one might expect to learn how to set about the task. These are current instructional situations, laboratory studies of concept acquisition, dictionary definitions, and Markle's own approach. Each (apart from the last, of course) is severely criticised in characteristic Markle style. Her castigations of 'muddy prose' and her comments on the importance of the visual layout of logical structures nicely introduce Paper 2.5.

Much time was spent discussing how to write instructional materials, particularly within the context of programmed learning. Thus there was a complete technology of 'frame-writing'. Today, however, the instructional text that learners might process within a program can vary enormously in complexity, difficulty and size. Paper 2.5 is introduced to indicate how research in the design of written materials is rapidly progressing. A more detailed presentation of the arguments of this paper (together with illustrations) is provided in Hartley's *Designing Instructional Text* (Kogan Page, 1978). It is perhaps worth restating here, however, that the guidelines presented in Paper 2.5 are just that — that is, they offer guides to solutions, but not the solutions themselves. General guidelines are helpful (that is, they are better than nothing), but each specific problem requires its own solution.

Paper 2.6 by Bernard Dodd and his colleagues is introduced at this point to reaffirm what was stated earlier. This is that instructional design is much more complex than it appears. Paper 2.6 shows that behind all the simplification (often enhanced by the use of flow-charts, or schematic diagrams) lies a wealth of hidden decision making. 'Stating objectives', 'analysing the task', 'presenting the materials' are catch-phrases which hide all of this. Dodd and his colleagues are interested in documenting this decision making so that data may be gathered in order to improve it.

In Part 1 we introduced the idea that new techniques of teaching required new techniques of evaluation and that social and political pressures were important features of curriculum evaluation. Paper 2.7 introduces a specific example of one new approach to evaluation — that of 'evaluation as illumination'. The aim of this approach is to take a wider look at what is going on — to illuminate the whole process — rather than simply to administer pre- and post-tests and assess knowledge gains. This paper is presented here shorn of its footnotes and thus perhaps it reads rather more dramatically than did the original. It should be remembered that many of Parlett and Hamilton's basic statements were qualified in their original version. One footnote, however, that we thought worth emphasising here was this one:

> This paper has focused on the evaluation of innovatory programs. There is an obvious need (not always acknowledged) for comparable studies to be made of traditional teaching. Illuminative evaluation need not be confined to innovation.

Evaluation is a tricky problem: it is difficult to assign numbers meaningfully to events and feelings. A lucid (but conventional) treatment may be found in Davies and Davis (1975). Parlett and Hamilton remind us that we need to look more widely at what goes on in curriculum change.

Finally we come to a crucial problem in educational technology: how do we establish and support it? This issue is raised in Papers 1.6 and 2.6. Here, in Paper 2.8, Richard Hooper looks at this problem in the context of establishing computer-assisted learning in the United Kingdom. This paper is a salutary one to read (particularly for academics) for it emphasises that assimilation and dissemination are a political process. Hooper argues that in order to get things going one should:

☐ avoid working within a few centres of excellence in universities;
☐ spread applications widely in those areas of instruction that have power — the mainstream teaching departments;
☐ appoint program directors who know their ways around the corridors of power;
☐ involve the institution accepting the innovation in paying half the cost right from the beginning;
☐ have a clear deadline when the institution is to decide whether or not it is to finance the innovation itself.

Hooper, too, introduces another consideration: one can only disseminate ideas about educational technology to those who are prepared to listen. Like researchers, the receivers of research have their own value judgements and these undoubtedly colour their assessment of the research.

Hooper's paper is written with characteristic wit and energy. His final report will be published shortly after this book goes to press. It should make interesting reading.

Suggested further reading

Davies, I K (1976) *Objectives in Curriculum Design.* London : McGraw-Hill
Davies, I K and Davis, R W (1975) Measurement and testing for developers and evaluators. Module 52 in Series 5, *Evaluation.* San Francisco : Educational Development and Evaluation Training Resources, Far West Regional Laboratory for Educational Research and Development

Duncan, K D (1972) Strategies for analysis of the task. In J Hartley (ed) *Strategies for Programmed Instruction.* London : Butterworths

Gagné, R M and Briggs, L J (1974) *Principles of Instructional Design.* New York : Holt, Rinehart & Winston

Hartley, J (1978) *Designing Instructional Text.* London : Kogan Page. New York : Nichols Publishing Co

Hooper, R and Toye, I (eds) (1975) *Computer Assisted Learning in the United Kingdom.* London : Council for Educational Technology

Hooper, R (1978) *The National Development Programme in Computer Assisted Learning: The Final Report of the Director.* London : Council for Educational Technology

2.1 Objectives in Curriculum Design

IVOR K DAVIES

Excerpts from Chapter 1 of I K Davies (1976) *Objectives in Curriculum Design.* London : McGraw-Hill.

How do objectives fit into the process of planning?

Objectives lie at the very heart of the planning process, whether one is planning a curriculum or a single classroom lesson. Creative yet careful and conscientious preparation or planning, of course, is one of the many traits of an experienced teacher, for it enables a teacher to command the future rather than be commanded by it. By planning ahead, it is possible to anticipate and hopefully avoid unforeseen classroom difficulties, as well as to ensure that the potential of the situation is more effectively realised. Thus, planning in teaching and learning is intimately concerned with wise and intelligent behaviour. As Russell Ackoff (1970) pointed out:

> Wisdom is the ability to see the long-run consequences of current actions, the willingness to sacrifice short-run gains for larger long-run benefits, and the ability to control what is controllable and not to fret over what is not.

The essence of planning, and thus the indispensable property of objectives, is concern for the future and for its fulfilment. Unlike the fortune teller who only attempts to predict the future, a wise teacher attempts to control it and realise its potential for the benefit of the children in his or her charge.

In a very real sense, planning is anticipatory decision making. It involves deciding what to do and how to do it before any concrete action is taken. It involves deciding, after due consideration, the nature of the relationship between the *ends* that you wish to accomplish and the *means* that you have available to use. When both ends and means are known and agreed, no real problem or difficulty exists. All that is required is a set of methods or procedures that will assist you to do what you have in mind. When the ends have not been determined, and the means available are unknown, teachers and curriculum developers are faced with a problem that demands resolution. It is under these circumstances that curriculum development and good teaching demand creative, careful and sensitive planning — not only in terms of the task to be accomplished, but also in terms of the learners involved. In the last resort, however, the real benefits of planning may arise less from the actual plan produced, and more from the learning that results from being involved in the process of producing them. So it is with the writing

135

of objectives, participation in the process of identifying them can be more important than the actual listings produced.

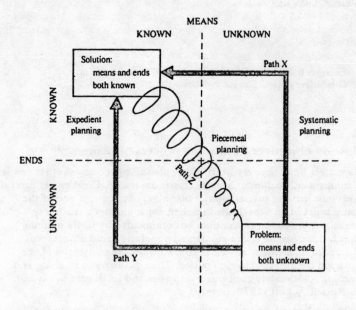

Figure 1. *A means-ends perspective of planning (Adapted from ideas from John Dewey, Karl Popper and Brian Lewis)*

The advice given to teachers and developers faced with this problem of undefined ends and means usually begins with the apparent truism that once the objectives have been defined everything else will follow. This advice, of course, outlines a systematic way of proceeding, but it is not the only way. Other alternatives are available, and need to be explored. The means-ends model, illustrated in Figure 1, is richer than at first appears. A number of paths are available, as will be seen in the diagram, and, basically, three types of planning can be recognised: systematic, expedient and piecemeal. An important discussion of the means-ends model will be found in Macdonald-Ross (1973), but the analysis that follows represents some important differences in point of view.

SYSTEMATIC PLANNING

Path X represents a systematic approach towards teaching and curriculum development. It involves first defining the ends or objectives to be achieved, and then selecting the means or procedures necessary for realising them. Such a seemingly 'rational' view assumes that you have a very clear idea of the future which you wish to command, for without such a blueprint it is impossible to define in any realistic way the objectives that you wish to reach. Since every step follows from their definition, success is ultimately dependent upon the accuracy of the predictions that are made. This so-called rational approach towards planning has been attacked by a number of philosophers, particularly Karl Popper (1966) and Michael Oakeshott (1962). Indeed, Popper regards the approach as 'utopian', convincing and attractive, and therefore the more misleading and dangerous.

A number of criticisms can be made against this particular view, which prides itself upon its scientific approach to facts and considerations. First, means and ends are isolated as successive steps in the process, rather than seen as heads and tails of the same situation. Furthermore, the ends are typically seen as unchanging, once their definition is complete; subject, certainly, to minor adjustments, but not to any radical redefinition as the project proceeds. Such a policy seems blatantly to ignore the fact that ideas and ideals commonly evolve during both the process of planning and its subsequent implementation. What seems desirable at one stage can be less convincing, necessary or even relevant at another. All too often a path X approach appears to argue for a static, rather than a dynamic, view of the world.

Even more worrying is the apparent assumption that not only is the project unchanging during the development or planning stages, but that sweeping changes must typically be initiated involving a radical reconstruction of the curriculum. All too often it is particularly difficult, if not impossible, to calculate the practical consequences of such a major reconstruction. Yet, path X proponents claim to plan 'rationally', when they often have neither the knowledge nor the means of determining whether they can make good their claims. Revolutionary claims were made for programmed learning some ten years ago, for de-schooling education five years ago, and for the integrated curriculum today, on the basis that the ideas and methodologies involved were the result of a 'rational' approach towards the solution of educational problems.

One further point is of particular concern. The rationality of the argument often seems to stop short of the real problem. Even if the means follow once the ends have been defined, how is the blueprint determined? In other words, the 'rational' approach often tends to overlook how ideal ends can be determined, and how the best means of realising these ends are likely to be identified. Values appear to be splendidly isolated from needs and wants, and from methods and procedures. Method is viewed as something detached from people taking ends to means.

Notwithstanding these difficulties, the path X approach does have a good deal to commend it in terms of its practical utility. Perhaps being aware of the assumptions and consequent dangers may be enough to guard against the worst excesses of such a systematic view. Indeed, the present movement towards what is increasingly being referred to as a 'competency-based' approach towards teaching and learning is little more than an application of this way of thinking. It is to be seen, for instance, in the recent development of competency-based programmes for reading and arithmetic skills to help overcome some of the perceived deficiencies in these areas, as well as in competency-based programmes for teacher training. A competency-based approach towards teacher certification is also being hotly debated.

The competency-based approach involves an explicit and detailed statement of both the competencies to be acquired (defined in terms of knowledge, attitudes and skills), and the criteria that will be used to determine whether or not the required standards of performance have been reached. In this way, it is argued, a person's progress through a course or programme can be determined on the basis of the competencies obtained, rather than by time or course completion. Teaching can be individualised on the basis of the objectives that need to be realised, learners can be held accountable for their own performance, and an entire course of training can be field-based as a practicum or internship if that is the most appropriate way of obtaining and practising the required skills. Although there is a great deal of resistance to such a seemingly mechanistic approach towards education, its impact is, for political reasons, likely to be very great indeed — particularly on existing schools, colleges and universities charged with preparing people for professional careers. Certification, for example, can be removed from successful completion of a course or programme of study, and opened to anyone, regardless of preparation and background, who can meet the so-called 'performance criteria'.

The Schools Council for the Curriculum and Examinations, founded in 1964 to find ways to organise the means of reviewing and reforming the school curricula of England and Wales, has also followed a systematic approach in some of its more successful development activities. Its Science 5/13 Project, for instance, broadly followed a path X approach in the first stages of its development. The formulation of a precise set of objectives, now almost *de rigueur* in curriculum matters, was one of the first priorities, and this analysis was subsequently reported by Ennever and Harlen (1969) in their important booklet *With Objectives in Mind*.

The objectives were selected to cover a science curriculum for children aged five to thirteen, and for this reason a developmental emphasis, based upon the work of Jean Piaget, was adopted. This emphasis is evidenced in the project by the increasing importance placed upon abstraction and generalisation, as more and more advanced materials for increasingly older age groups are presented. No attempt is made, however, to prescribe how this framework of objectives should be realised. The ends are defined, but not the means. Indeed, teachers are encouraged to decide for themselves as to how they wish to implement the curriculum — perhaps inviting the children to suggest what should be done. Teachers, however, may use the outline detailed in the materials, if they wish, as a precise guide for action, rather than as just an example of what may be done. In this way, Science 5/13 offers teachers not only a predetermined course of action, for those who want it, but also a more open-ended set of materials to be used in any manner appropriate to the situation.

EXPEDIENT PLANNING

Path Y, on the other hand, represents a more expedient approach towards teaching and curriculum development. Indeed, some people suggest that it comprises an irrational way of planning. At any rate, it involves first defining the means or procedures to be used, and then determining those objectives or ends that will best accommodate the limitations or constraints that you have imposed upon yourself. This path is very much closer to the traditional way of operating within the limits set by many educational situations and budgets, as circumscribed by the economic situation. It is also a responsible way of proceeding when the situation involves the development of values, attitudes or sentiments, for defining the ends to be achieved in these circumstances can contaminate the very values which you wish people to develop or reinforce for themselves. The Schools Council and Nuffield Foundation's Humanities Curriculum Project in England and the American National Instructional Television award winning series 'Inside out' are prime examples of this type of curriculum development, which deliberately avoids the notion of pre-stated objectives in terms of intentions to be realised. In both instances, an open-ended approach to curriculum development is prized above the realisation of specific values.

The general aim of the Humanities Project — and it is useful in this regard to see the use of an aim when they are rather out of fashion — is 'to develop understanding of the nature and structure of certain complex value issues of universal human concern' among adolescent pupils of average and below-average academic ability. These matters are identified by Lawrence Stenhouse and his colleagues at the University of East Anglia as including problems of war and peace, education, family, relationships between the sexes, people and work, poverty, living in cities, law and order, and race relations. Instead of starting with well-defined objectives, like the Science 5/13 Project, the developers began their work by gradually defining principles. These included ideas for developing inquiry-based discussion, the provision and handling of evidence, ways of coping with sensitive and controversial issues, and the procedures by which teachers could adopt a neutral role when leading such discussions in the classroom. For each of the nine issues identified, banks of illustrative study or resource materials were collected, including poems, newspaper articles and advertisements, extracts from books and plays, statistics and graphs, photographs and cartoons and paintings, audio tapes and records. It is envisaged that these would be drawn upon, added to, arranged and used as situations and needs arose.

At issue in the Project is the professional ethic of neutrality. In controversial situations, it is argued, learners should not be placed in a position where they are made to adopt attitudes or values which are not of their own making or choosing. The underlying aim is that a child should come to understand the nature and implications of his or her point of view, and grow to adult responsibility for adopting it and being willing to be held accountable for it. 'Whether or not a pupil changes his or her point of view', argues Stenhouse, 'is not significant for the attainment of understanding.' The teacher's task is to provide evidence relevant to the problem (evidence, incidentally, which is external to the teacher), as well as to chair discussions in a neutral and impartial manner.

The people involved in developing the Humanities Curriculum saw the main problem as:

> . . . not so much what ground to cover in the sense of what subjects to teach, but what information, ideas, experiences to grapple with, through what media, by what means. The problem is to give every man some access to a complex cultural inheritance, some hold on his personal life and on his relationships with the various communities to which he belongs, some extension of his understanding of, and sensitivity towards, other human beings . . . (Schools Council, 1965)

It is only fair to point out, however, that a number of educators, like Sally Wringe, voice important reservations about this way of developing a curriculum, and argue that this method fails to clarify the nature of achievement, what it entails, and what methodologies are consistent with these aims. A number of people have also spent a great deal of effort identifying objectives for the Humanities Project, despite the developers' continuing claim that they had none. But this, of course, is an almost inevitable consequence of a path Y approach.

PIECEMEAL PLANNING

While both path X and path Y represent two of the alternatives available to teachers and developers, the means-ends diagram (Figure 1) suggests that there is another major way of proceeding. This involves what Karl Popper calls a 'piecemeal' approach, which he recommends as being methodologically sound without the dangers often implicit in rational planning. Rather than defining either first the ends or the means in such a clear cut manner as in the other two paths, a cyclical, if not piecemeal, approach is adopted. This involves successive approximations or increments, for which no initial blueprint or master plan is necessary. Rather than adopting the reconstructionist or revolutionary approach implicit in paths X and Y, developers following this procedure will search for, and attempt to deal with, the greatest and most urgent evils rather than the greatest ultimate good. As Karl Popper (1966) points out in the context of society at large:

> It is the difference between a reasonable method of improving the lot of man, and a method which, if really tried, may really lead to an intolerable increase in human suffering. It is the difference between a method which can be applied at any moment, and a method whose advocacy may easily become a means of continually postponing action until a later date, when conditions are more favourable. And it is also the difference between the only method of improving matters which has so far been continuously successful, at any time, and in any place . . . and a method which, whenever it has been tried, has led only to the use of violence in place of reason, and if not to its own abandonment, at any rate to that of the original blueprint.

In other words, it is often better to forsake an ideal, which demands a complete reconstruction of the present without any guarantee that the future will be greatly improved, for the rather simpler approach of piecemeal development. At least, if anything goes awry, the damage will not be very great, and the situation is easily redeemable.

In following this approach in teaching and development work, one perhaps starts with some rough definition of the more important aims, before considering the resources needed. Then back to a more precise definition of objectives, before turning once again to the means available, etc. As a result of this constant turning and recycling backwards and forwards, as more and more information becomes available, a more realistic approach to development and teaching is sometimes possible. Education is really too complex an undertaking for it to be possible to start off with a complete and thorough definition of either objectives or resources, and certainly not as quite separate and divorced entities. These usually only become clear after creative, yet careful, thought and deliberation. For this reason, a path Z approach may be a more practical one for most classroom situations, for in it there is a merging and recycling of ends with means.

So much of curriculum development is seen as the responsibility of different people: philosophers sorting out values, curriculum technologists formulating the behavioural objectives and developing the materials, teachers teaching what they are given, students learning, and evaluators breathing down the necks of everyone. This might be a 'rational' way of organising things, but it is often a naive one. The advantages of the piecemeal approach is that it forces all the specialists into constant interaction with each other throughout the life of the project, and, above all, it places the teacher in a central position in development work. Sound development is most likely when teachers play an active role in every stage of the project. Emerson's dictum that 'the ends pre-exist in the means' only underlines the point that objectives, teachers and resources are intimately intermingled and interrelated with learners in the educational process. For this reason, if for no other, a sound and thorough understanding of the concept of objectives is an essential part of the craft of teaching.

What are the differences between aims, goals and objectives?

Historically, British educators have been much more interested in defining aims than in stating objectives, while American teachers have been willing to think in terms of rather more concrete objectives. Wood (1968) of the National Foundation for Educational Research in England and Wales, believes that this may largely be due to the:

> ... more or less continuing dialogue which occurs between psychologists and educationists in the USA. The effect of the American psychologists' penetration into education can be seen in the greater urge to analyse and quantify among educationalists, which may explain why in this country, where the dialogue has been relatively intermittent, and where in any case the psychologists have been more clinically-minded, there has been a reluctance to analyse aims to a point at which precise behaviours emerge.

More recently, however, with the advent of renewed interest in curriculum development, aims have unfortunately tended to become unfashionable, whether or not they have been broken down into rather more precise objectives.

Interest in objectives has also tended to confuse some of the terms that are now used. For this reason, it is important to distinguish carefully between 'aims', 'goals' and 'specific objectives', all of which are sometimes referred to under the more general term of 'objectives'. When considering these terms, we need to determine their relationship to each other, as well as their overall relationship to the means-ends model, bearing in mind that it is intentional *human* action that is being discussed. All too often in education, we speak as though education, history and mathematics had aims and objectives, rather than the people who are teaching these subjects. It is counter-productive, of course, to draw too sharp a categorical distinction between the terms when defining their essential character. As with the means-ends model, it is their interactive rather than discrete character that needs to be appreciated. So much confusion seems to exist over the terms, however, that it is important to consider some definitions.

AIMS

An aim can broadly be defined as a general statement, which attempts to give both shape and direction to a set of more detailed intentions for the future. Indeed, some philosophers like to think in terms of the *aims of activities* (or organisations), and the *objectives of participants*. This at least explains why it is necessary to talk about 'breaking down aims', 'translating them', 'analysing them' or even 'choosing objectives in the light of them'. Generality, at any rate, is part of their very nature, and this property should be seen as relating to their function, rather than as a basis for criticising their lack of precision. Aims are a starting point. They are an ideal, an aspiration, a direction in which to go. They are visionary in character, and, therefore, in a very real sense unreal. For this reason, they should be constantly redefined as they are clarified by subsequent action. Aims limit the choice of goals and specific objectives.

GOALS OR GENERAL OBJECTIVES

While an aim indicates the direction to take, a goal describes the actual destination itself. Rather than being visionary in character, it is the focus of activity. An aim is concerned with an ideal, and as such can be broken down into a set of goals or events — each of which represents a turning point. Some of these need to be accomplished early, some can be concurrent, while others can be left until later. For this reason, some sort of ordering is necessary, so that priorities can be determined and allocated. The aim, in this way, can then be broken down, and mapped into a series of goals or events in much the same way that a network is constructed as a tool for planning a complex project like putting on a play or getting to the moon.

It is not that goals are in any way better than aims, they simply have a different role and purpose. They convert the question 'Why is that curriculum or subject being taught?' into the related question 'What destination do you have in mind for the learner as far as that curriculum or subject is concerned?' In other words, general objectives represent an attempt to operationalise the thinking represented by an aim, to make it more practical and less ethereal.

SPECIFIC OBJECTIVES

While goals express something of the strategy observed, specific objectives are tactical in nature. They are highly explicit and operational in form, as well as time-bound and quantifiable. Specific objectives attempt to describe, in the clearest terms possible, exactly what a student will think, act or feel at the end of a learning experience. Just as goals describe destinations or *events,* so a specific objective describes an *activity* that learners will be able to do to demonstrate their mastery. This technique of describing activities in measurable and observable terms is usually associated with behaviourism, and such objectives, therefore, are often referred to as 'behavioural objectives'.

This behavioural connotation is unfortunate. Many curriculum developers and teachers who use this method of defining objectives, do so for the sake of clarity and precision, and not because they are necessarily behaviourists. Furthermore, this process of defining phenomena in terms of measurable and observable properties was the contribution of the 'new' physics in the 1920s. Behaviourists and non-behaviourists have capitalised, and sometimes possibly overcapitalised, upon its possibilities ever since. The advent of programmed learning in the early 1960s did much to 'popularise' behavioural objectives, since the development of programmed texts called for a level of detailed analysis far beyond that more usually attempted in education at that time.

In his decidedly practical book, Edward Furst (1957) lays down not only a set of rules for developing specific objectives, but also suggests the requirements that need to be observed when writing them. These include the advice that among the minimal properties of a good objective are details of the behaviour desired, the responses that will be accepted as adequate, and details of any limiting conditions under which the response will be observed. An example of this kind of analysis is shown in Figure 2 for a simple, and common, task in elementary chemistry. It will be noticed that the example is concerned with inquiry, and, therefore, involves asking questions and formulating hypotheses — rather than being concerned with the mere acquisition of information. All too often the movement for specific objectives, with its emphasis on what are fondly called 'intended outcomes', has been misinterpreted as being overly concerned with the acquisition of knowledge as a product, rather than with knowledge as a dynamic process involving inquiry, making or doing, and dialogue. This emphasis on the activity component of specific objectives is an important one. One way of thinking of the relationship between specific objectives and aims, and between specific objectives and general objectives, is to go back to the means-ends model. Aims, as we have seen, can be thought of as ends, and general objectives or goals the *means* of realising those ends. Similarly, goals can be thought of as ends (or events desired), and specific objectives the means (or activities) by which they can be realised.

General objectives

After completing this unit you will be:
1. Familiar with the following basic terms in chemistry: dissolve, reactions, range, mean and linear.
2. Familiar with the effect of temperature on the dissolving time of selected solids in water.
3. Familiar with the process of setting up and verifying simple hypotheses.

Specific objectives				
Behaviour	+	*Conditions*	+	*Criteria*
1. To determine		the dissolving time (in seconds) of a white tablet placed in water at 100°C, 50°C and 10°C		by observing within 3 seconds of mean time
2. To determine		the dissolving time (in seconds) of a pink tablet placed in water at 100°C, 50°C and 10°C		by observing within 3 seconds of mean time
3. To record		both experiments in laboratory book, plotting the data on a graph		using relevant vocabulary
4. To identify by setting up, and verifying, hypotheses		the two solids by name, given a table of the dissolving times at 100°C, 50°C and 10°C of ten substances		without error, using only data in lab books and tables of dissolving times

Figure 2. *An example of a set of both general and specific objectives for a basic task in chemistry*

How do you justify your objectives?

In defining objectives, we have, in fact, been discussing the problems of *mapping* the relationship between means and ends. Implicit in the whole discussion has been an underlying assumption that the activities, characterised by any set of aims, goals or specific objectives, can in themselves be justified from an educational point of view. This, however, needs to be demonstrated, and probably the major contribution of the objectives movement is to be found in the way that it enables the question of which activities are most worthwhile to be discussed in a relatively open manner. Objectives help to make many of the activities explicit, if not painfully clear. They can be used to emphasise the interactive relationship between means and ends, facilitate what Malcolm Skilbeck has called 'the progressive self-realisation of aims', and enable discussions between developers, teachers and learners on 'Why this is necessary rather than that?' to take place.

RELEVANCY

In discussing the issue of justification in terms of any specific set of objectives, two words are commonly employed: 'relevance' and 'worthwhileness'. Of the two, relevance is probably the easiest to deal with, since it is concerned with what is useful and important. Objectives are relevant if they can be demonstrated to be related to the real world, and to problems facing people. Abstract and isolated activities, unrelated to human concerns, are likely to be regarded as irrelevant, unless steps are taken to demonstrate their utility. Different people, of course, are likely to regard the relevancy of any set of objectives in different lights. For this reason, it is essential to ask not only for an explanation of how objectives are relevant, but also for an explanation of whom they are thought to be relevant for and at what time.

One of the advantages of making objectives explicit (whether in the form of aims, goals or specific objectives) is the clarification they give to *people's* intentions for a learning situation. Most of the things that are done in education are potentially controversial in one way or another, and objectives can be used to help 'tease' out controversy so that it can become public. Sometimes some of the difficulties implicit in discussions on relevancy are concerned with disagreements as to logic, but usually, however, they are concerned with differences of perception. People can look at a situation, as we know only too well, in quite different ways, and so conclude quite different things. One of the prime advantages of defining objectives is to help prevent such misconceptions from arising, or at least to contribute towards their solution.

WORTHWHILENESS

It is very easy to take for granted that certain activities have a greater potential than others, and are, therefore, more educationally justifiable. Nevertheless, it is particularly difficult for educators to reach any real agreement on the criteria that can be used to determine whether one activity is more worthwhile than another. Yet education, as we have seen earlier in this chapter, involves something of worth being passed on to the learner, so that curriculum developers and teachers have to face the responsibility that is implicit in their role. Any number of criteria have been suggested in order to justify certain activities. Thomas Hobbes, for instance, argued for 'that what a man desires', John Stuart Mill for the desirability of happiness, and David Hume weighed the case for objectivity. Words like 'good', 'ought to', 'obligation', and 'improvement' abound in these classical discussions on justification.

More recently educators have argued for 'awareness', 'meaning', 'wants and needs', 'pleasure and satisfaction', as well as 'growth and freedom'. Little, though, has been said as to how these generalities can be made into useful criteria for developers and teachers to use when faced with the problem of choosing between different sets of objectives. One of the few authors to take up this issue of 'Why specifically these activities, rather than those?' is Richard Peters (1974, chapters 3 and 5). An important critical review of Peters' ideas will be found in Robinson (1974).

In deciding why one activity is supposedly more worthwhile than another, Professor Peters believes that consideration needs to be given to the actual nature of the activity itself, as well as to its relationship to other activities within 'a coherent pattern of life'. Peters furthermore suggests that the question cannot be divorced from considerations of time and commitment, and on this basis he outlines three possible criteria which can be used when making decisions about particular curriculum activities. First, an activity must be capable of going on for some time. Activities which are too easily and quickly mastered, he argues, are likely to be less worthwhile. Some preference should be given to activities which hold a learner's attention, demand a certain amount of skill and discrimination, and provide a constant source of challenge, pleasure and satisfaction. Secondly, activities should be compatible, rather than competitive. In other words, 'balance' is important. Activities, for instance, that are too demanding or occupy too much time need to be reviewed within the context of overall harmony. Coherence is an essential trait of a well-conceived set of activities. Thirdly, worthwhile activities are likely to be serious rather than trivial, particularly in terms of the contribution that they make to real life. Watching certain games can be very enjoyable, but this activity has little to tell us outside itself. Activities that are worthwhile contribute in a substantial way, either to illuminating other areas of life, or at least to improving the overall quality of living.

There are a number of difficulties inherent in the criteria that Richard Peters suggests, and there are many people who dissent from his views. But perhaps what is important from the point of view of objectives is that the question 'Why these objectives, rather than those objectives?' needs to be asked, and the criteria justified in terms of some rationale. It is important that not only the assumptions, but also the criteria should be made public in some way, so that developers and teachers can justify what they are doing not only to others, but also to themselves. The criteria of worthwhileness are not to be found within the subject matter, but within the person making the decisions. Sometimes it is the ends that are viewed as important and that need to be justified. At other times, the ends may be relatively unimportant, and it is the activities or the means involved that are construed as worthwhile. At still other times, both means and ends are equally valuable. The important thing is to ask the question, open up the possibilities, and be ready to explain the objectives chosen. If, as Socrates would have us believe, 'the unexamined life is not worth living', then surely the unexamined objective is not worth realising.

What is the role of objectives within the context of discovery?

One of the issues that often comes up when curriculum developers and teachers discuss the problems of relevancy and worthwhileness is the role of objectives within the context of discovery. It is, of course, rarely helpful to think of learners as passive recipients of self-contained items of knowledge, nicely parcelled together by well written specific objectives. There is little point in writing beautifully written objectives, when the task they represent should not be done in the first place. Learners are active participants in a knowledge-getting and knowledge-extracting process. They are natural problem solvers, constantly struggling to construct hypotheses, which they tend to hold on to until new facts or more comfortable hypotheses cause their rejection. Discovery of one kind or another, in other words, is the very essence of learning. At the same time, the contribution of this discovery or change process to the *education* of the pupil is likely to be enhanced when it is part of a carefully designed experience, which contributes to the development of those intellectual skills appropriate to the learner's needs in terms of the stage of development and growth reached.

In order to ensure that these opportunities are provided, so that learners are challenged and involved, aims and goals, and sometimes specific objectives, need to be identified and carefully organised or the necessary procedures agreed if objectives are not considered to be appropriate. If this stage is not handled sensitively, the experience can be trivial, if not commonplace, compared with the sense of adventure and excitement implicit in the natural approach of most learners to the world. Sensitivity demands, on occasion, not only well-designed and conceived learning materials and experiences, but also what Bruner (1974) calls opportunities for 'self-conscious reflectiveness'. Bruner points out that he is puzzled as to why traditional education seems to emphasise extensiveness and coverage over intensiveness and depth. He points out that children usually see memorising as a high-priority task. Rarely do they appear to sense a need for redefining, reshaping or reordering things. Cultivating reflectiveness, so that these activities can occur, Bruner feels, is one of the important problems facing anyone developing new curricula.

Balancing and harmonising these two dimensions of extensiveness and coverage on the one hand, with intensiveness and depth on the other, requires great skill and sensitivity. It also demands a ready appreciation of the importance of identifying those sets of aims, goals and specific objectives (or at least the procedures to be employed), which are most likely to result in learning experiences designed to encourage and develop personal growth and fulfilment. But here lies a very real problem, which is to be seen in two controversies that centre around the whole concept of objectives in education.

On the one hand, there is the debate, still raging after some sixty years of experience with objectives, regarding their advantages and disadvantages in teaching-learning situations. On the other hand, there is the more subtle debate regarding the role of objectives within the context of learning by discovery. The more general debate is considered in more detail in the original text (from which this extract is taken) but the more specific controversy will be discussed here since it has so many implications.

Learning by discovery is a complex issue, which can easily be oversimplified. One key area in the debate, however, centres around 'How much guidance ought to be offered to learners?' Some people favour minimal teacher guidance, and maximum opportunities for children to engage in true exploration. Others favour 'guided' discovery, with careful sequencing of the learning experiences and associated materials. While the debate may seem academic to some, it has enormous consequences not only in terms of the preparation of curriculum materials, such as that undertaken by the Schools Council,

Knowledge as a process	Knowledge as a product
'. . . a theory of instruction seeks to take account of the fact that a curriculum reflects not only the specific capabilities — but also the nature of knowledge itself — the knowledge-getting process. It is the enterprise *par excellence* where the line between the subject matter and the method grows necessarily indistinct. A body of knowledge, enshrined in a university faculty, and embodied in a series of authoritative volumes is the result of much prior intellectual activity. To instruct someone in these disciplines is not a matter of getting him to commit results to mind; rather it is to teach him to participate in the process that makes possible the establishment of knowledge. We teach a subject, not to produce little living libraries from that subject, but rather to get a student to think mathematically for himself, to consider matters as a historian does, to take part in the process of knowledge-getting. Knowledge is a process, not a product.' *Jerome Bruner*	'Obviously strategies are important for problem solving, regardless of the content of the problem. The suggestion from some writings is that they are of overriding importance as a goal of education. After all, should not formal instruction in the school have the aim of teaching the student 'how to think'? If strategies were deliberately taught, would not this produce people who could then bring to bear superior problem-solving capabilities to any new situation? Although no one would disagree with the aims expressed, it is exceedingly doubtful that they can be brought about solely by teaching students 'strategies' or 'styles' of thinking. Even if these can be taught (and it is likely that they can) they do not provide the individual with the basic firmament of thought, which is a set of externally oriented intellectual skills. Strategies, after all, are rules that govern the individual's *approach* to listening, reading, storing information, retrieving information, or solving problems . . . Knowing strategies, then, is not all that is required for thinking; it is not even a substantial part of what is needed. To be an effective problem solver, the individual must somehow have acquired masses of organised intellectual skills.' (To which Gagné added in an earlier edition of his book 'Such knowledge is made up of content principles, not heuristic ones.') *Robert Gagné*

Figure 3. *Two contrasting views of the spirit of educational objectives. (Reproduced from Bruner, J S (1966) Towards a Theory of Instruction. Cambridge, Mass : Harvard University Press, p72, and Gagné, R M (1970) The Conditions of Learning (2nd ed). New York : Holt, Rinehart & Winston, pp232-3)*

but also in terms of how the materials are to be used in classroom situations.

Although there is a lack of agreement over the precise meaning of the term 'discovery', the two approaches adopted by Jerome Bruner and Robert Gagné give something of the flavour of the debate, as well as indications of the contrasting roles that are sometimes given to objectives. Bruner, who has been strongly influenced by Jean Piaget, is most closely identified with the learning-by-discovery school. He believes that learners need to find some sort of match between what they know and what they are presently doing or experiencing. Discovery, he points out, does not take place outside the learner, but involves some internal reorganisation so as to accommodate new thoughts and ideas.

Gagné, on the other hand, has many of the qualities of a behaviourist, and he is closely identified with the 'guided discovery' school. He looks upon a learning task as being composed of a network of building blocks, each level in the network serving as a prerequisite for the next higher level, and so on. Gagné believes that it is much more efficient so to structure learning materials, on the basis of this network, or 'learning hierarchy' as he calls it, that a learner is led or guided towards the inevitable and final act of discovery — provided, of course, that all the prerequisites have been met. In this sense, discovery is conceived as taking place outside the learner, but is internalised once the insight has been gained.

Not surprisingly, both Bruner and Gagné have quite different views concerning the role of objectives in learning. For Gagné, objectives are the ends or products of learning, what he calls the 'learned capabilities'. Bruner places his emphasis, not on the products, but on the processes of learning, and for him objectives define the means or processes rather than the final product learning. Figure 3 indicates something of the flavour of their two points of view. It will be seen that while Bruner sees the definition of objectives as a means of posing the problem to be solved (with no indication of how the objectives are to be realised), Gagné sees the identification of objectives as the initial act of definition, as well as the stepping-stones or supports to be used along the way. Perhaps there is room for both points of view.

A focus — what are the issues?

This introductory paper has raised a number of issues to which there are really no clear cut answers. *What is the best way to go?* It all depends on where you want to go and how you want to get there. *Must developers and teachers have well-defined aims?* Probably not, their methods and procedures can reveal what these aims are much better than any high-sounding statement could ever do. *Does planning have to begin with a clear statement of objectives?* Not necessarily, there are other ways of proceeding. *What are aims, goals and specific objectives anyway?* All of them are statements of human intent, but they are written at quite different levels of specificity. *Which objectives are the most worthwhile?* It all depends upon your assumptions and criteria of worthwhileness. Asking the question is the first step towards justifying what you wish to do. *Do objectives really have a role in curriculum development, teaching and learning?* Yes, but opinions vary enormously. Some people have very strong views in favour of objectives, others have equally strong views against them. There is room, however, for a well-considered, middle-of-the-road position. The purpose of *Objectives in Curriculum Design* is to examine, from a number of points of view, the *concept* of objectives, so that developers and teachers can make up their own minds as to their appropriateness as useful guides for action.

Suggestions for further reading

Socket, Hugh (1972) Curriculum aims and objectives: taking a means to an end, *Proceedings of the Philosophy of Education Society* 6 1: 30-61
Peters, Richard (1959) *Authority, Responsibility and Education.* London : Routledge & Kegan Paul, pp83-95
Stenhouse, Lawrence (1968) The humanistic curriculum project, *Journal of Curriculum Studies* 11: 26-33
Broudy, Harry (1970) The philosophical foundations of educational objectives, *Educational Theory* 20: 3-21

Bibliography

Ackoff, R L (1970) *A Concept of Corporate Planning.* New York : Wiley
Broudy, H S (1971) Can research escape the dogma of behavioural objectives? *School Review* 79: 43-56
Bruner, J S (1966) *Toward a Theory of Instruction.* Cambridge, Mass : Harvard University Press
Bruner, J S (1974) *Beyond the Information Given.* London : Allen & Unwin
Central Advisory Council for Education (England)(1967) *Children and their Primary Schools, Volume 1 (Plowden Report).* London : HMSO
Coleridge, S T (1818) A preliminary treatise on method. In A D Snyder (ed) (1934). *Coleridge's Treatise on Method.* London : Constable
Dearden, R F (1968) *The Philosophy of Primary Education.* London : Routledge & Kegan Paul
Dewey, J (1916) *Democracy and Education.* New York : Macmillan
Dewey, J (1938) *Experience and Education.* New York : Macmillan
Ennever, L F and Harlen, W (1969) *With Objectives in Mind. Schools Council 5/13 Project.* London : Macdonald Educational
Furst, E J (1957) *Constructing Evaluation Instruments.* London : Longmans, Green
Gagné, R M (1970) *The Conditions of Learning* (2nd ed). New York : Holt, Rinehart & Winston
Gagné, R M (1974) *Essentials of Learning for Instruction.* Hinsdale, Ill : Dryden Press
Incorporated Association of Assistant Masters in Secondary Schools (1957) *The Teaching of Mathematics.* Cambridge : Cambridge University Press
Kenny, A (1963) *Action, Emotion and Will.* London : Routledge & Kegan Paul
Komisar, B P and McClellan, J E (1961) The logic of slogans. In B O Smith and R H Ennis (eds) *Language and Concepts in Education.* Chicago : Rand McNally
Macdonald-Ross, M (1973) Behavioural objectives — a critical review, *Instructional Science* 2 1: 1-50
Oakeshott, M (1962) Rational conduct. In M Oakeshott. *Rationalism in Politics and Other Essays.* London : Methuen
Peters, R S (1959) *Authority, Responsibility and Education.* London : Allen & Unwin
Peters, R S (1974) *Ethics and Education.* London : Allen & Unwin
Popper, K R (1966) *The Open Society and its Enemies.* London : Routledge & Kegan Paul
Robinson, K E (1974) Worthwhile activities and the curriculum, *British Journal of Educational Studies*
Scheffler, I (1960) *The Language of Education.* Springfield, Ill : Thomas
Schools Council (1965) *Raising the School Leaving Age, Working Paper No 2.* London : HMSO
Smith, E R and Tyler, R W (1942) *Appraising and Recording Student Progress.* New York : Harper

Spencer, H (1860) What knowledge is the most worthwhile? In H Spencer (1910). *Education: Intellectual, Moral and Physical.* New York and London : Appleton

Taylor, P H and Walton, J (eds) (1973) *The Curriculum: Research, Innovation and Change.* London : Ward Lock Educational

Toffler, A (ed) (1974) *Learning for Tomorrow.* New York : Random House

Williams, R (1961) *The Long Revolution.* London : Penguin

Wood, R (1968) Objectives in the teaching of mathematics, *Educational Research* 10 2: 83-98

Wringe, S (1974) Some problems raised by the Schools Council Humanities Project, *Journal of Curriculum Studies* 6 1: 30-43

2.2 Analysis for Training

JOHN PATRICK AND ROBERT STAMMERS

Excerpt from Patrick, J and Stammers, R (1976) *The Psychology of Training*. London : Methuen. Reproduced with permission of the authors and the publishers.

The acquisition of skill can be viewed as a process of *synthesis* of lower level activities into an integrated hierarchy of skilled performance. Training therefore must endeavour to encourage such a synthesis. In order to do this the trainer must gain an understanding of the task to be performed. This understanding must be in terms of what the component activities of the task are, and what demands, psychologically, they will place on the trainee. In other words some *analysis* of the task needs to precede the design of training for it. The initial component is to 'define training objectives', ie to state what is the goal of performance of the task. From this first stage criterion measures can be devised to 'test' trained people. The content of the training programme is also derived from this. All of this activity can be subsumed under the general heading of *task analysis*. The aim is to ascertain what the objectives of the task are, how these objectives can be met, and what the nature of the information processing demands will be on the performer in the attainment of these objectives.

An examination of the training literature and discussions with people in the field reveal that genuine difficulties exist over terminology. This is perhaps most apparent in the case of the processes of analysing activities to derive the training content. The terms 'job', 'task' and 'skill analysis' might be used interchangeably or to represent different processes or even to refer to different stages within the same process. Fortunately these different terms typically refer to the same process, that of identifying the training needs and determining the training content. It should be recognised, however, that the term 'job analysis' does have wider connotations in occupational psychology, for example, for personnel selection and job evaluation. It is, of course, widely accepted that some examination of the tasks should be carried out in order to determine what should constitute an appropriate training course. It is also accepted that this involves a description and a breakdown of the tasks into elements of some kind. However no such general agreement exists as to how this should be accomplished as there are a number of very different approaches and techniques which may be adopted.

'Job analysis' is probably the most commonly used term in industry. Under this heading *one* method of analysis is often described. It is, however, also used as a generic term under which various methods are subsumed. The *Glossary of Training Terms* defines it as, 'The process of examining a job in detail in order to identify its component tasks. The detail and approach may vary according to the purpose for which the job is being analysed, eg training, equipment design, work lay-out.'

It can be seen that wider aspects of activity than that relevant to training are covered by this definition. Thus Singleton (1968) uses the term job to refer to 'the overall unified activities of the operator' indicating that it is 'an operator oriented term'. Similarly Annett *et al* (1971) state that

> Job is thus a person-oriented concept, it usually has a title and contractual implications. These and other personnel considerations, on the basis of which tasks are assigned to jobs, will not be our concern, rather we shall address ourselves to *tasks,* as such, and the problem of determining their training implications.

For training purposes therefore the more specific term of 'task analysis' is preferred. Task analysis in the *Glossary of Training Terms* is 'A systematic analysis of the behaviour required to carry out a task with a view to identifying areas of difficulty and the appropriate training techniques and learning aids necessary for successful instruction.'

Task analysis is seen therefore both as a process of collecting information on task behaviour, and as a method indicating the necessary training. Annett *et al* (1971) emphasise that such an analysis should be an all-embracing activity, the end product of which should not only be a description of behaviour, but also form the basis for the design of the training programme.

> The most general way of looking at task analysis is as the process of collecting information necessary to reach decisions about what to train, how to train, even how well to train, and perhaps how much to spend on training. In short task analysis should lead *directly* to a training design specifying not only what is usually called 'course content' but also the output or criterion performance and the method or methods of training by which this can be achieved. (Annett *et al,* 1971)

This approach to task analysis will be adopted and described in further detail in this paper.

The term 'skills analysis' is used in two ways. Firstly as a synonym for job or task analysis, and secondly for the specific *technique* or analysis which has been described by Seymour (1966). In the former case emphasis is placed, during analysis, on the perceptual-motor aspects of the tasks in question, often leading to recording in great detail. Seymour's technique is a development of this approach whereby actions are recorded, together with information on which limb is used, etc. Emphasis is placed, quite rightly, on the perceptual aspects of the task, ie the cues used by the operator, both for input and feedback. Such an approach is limited mostly to those tasks that may be called 'skilled' in that they are basically manual tasks. Later in this paper a task analysis technique which claims generality of application is described. This latter technique does not preclude the use of detailed skills analysis. A compromise therefore would be to see *jobs* as made up of *tasks.* The tasks may need to be performed with more or less *skill* depending on their context, and require analysis in more or less detail.

Taxonomies

The process of analysis can be aided by the use of classification schemes which enables the analyst to categorise the various activities that he isolates. The development of such a taxonomy has often been advocated as the key to understanding skilled performance. However the usefulness of any taxonomy clearly depends on its purpose or objectives. Different taxonomies may be constructed for different purposes, a fact which is not often adequately recognised. A review of taxonomies for training by Annett and Duncan (1967) emphasises that one criterion is that the categories must be mutually exclusive and exhaustive. The additional major criterion is that the categories should specify different training characteristics. The utility of any taxonomy is therefore totally dependent on the relevance and usefulness of the categories for the purpose of training rather than the elegance of the taxonomic scheme.

The history of such approaches began with work study techniques which classified elements of work such as 'grasp', 'locate', etc. Work study techniques do not analyse skill in a way relevant to training problems. What essentially are recorded are sequences of movements and their nature. These isolated elements can then be assigned predetermined time values. One point that is made with these methods is that if such an analysis is to be useful for training, additional information, such as 'job knowledge', is required. Even with this, work study would seem to have limited applicability to the majority of tasks. As Conrad (1951) has pointed out: 'relatively casual observation and use of instruments which reveal nothing but overt bodily movements are likely to lead to concepts of skill which are extremely vulnerable.' Thus we are in danger of leaving out essential considerations of perception, anticipation, decision making, etc. A system to complement work study is provided by Crossman (1956). This records decisions to be made, senses used, etc as well as the motions carried out. Unfortunately although the technique is well documented it seems mostly appropriate for repetitive manual tasks, and also little indication is given on how a training programme may be derived from such an analysis.

A taxonomy which does put emphasis on the psychological demands of tasks is that of R B Miller (1967). Miller asks, what functions would have to be built into a robot to make him behave like a human being performing a particular task? He lists the following categories:

Concept of purpose
A function which could be programmed so that sooner or later he could discriminate relevant from irrelevant cues, responses and feedback, and to enable him to be turned 'on' by inciting cues and turned 'off' by criterion-matching cues. Concepts of purpose may be single-valued (such as reeling off a programmed procedure to a predictable series of cues) or multiple-valued (such as in inductive decision making). This 'concept of purpose' function, by the way, is the most difficult to design into a box.

Scanning function
Active or passive search for exposing his perceptive apparatus to task-inciting cues in the environment, or to cues generated by himself.

Identification of relevant cues function
A function whereby he identifies or differentiates a pattern of cues as a pattern either from a background or noise or from other patterns of cues. A label or some other discriminatory action would be attached to the identifying operation.

Interpretation of cues
Interpretation according to the 'meaning' or implication apart from the physical nature of the cue itself.

Short-term memory
For holding together, during a task cycle, the fragments of information that will be acted upon later or combined into a clump. This function is much broader than apperception span, by the way. It operates as extensively and as elaborately as the continuation of my concept of purpose and my recall of what I have said during this presentation.

Long-term memory
The case of recallable associations between and among stimuli and responses. The associations may be automatic perceptual-motor, or they may be symbolic in cognitive awareness. In relatively simple form, long-term memory is seen in strict precedural performance. But memory may also consist of trains of symbolic associations, such as images of a map or a terrain.

Decision making and problem solving
Techniques which may be divergent and convergent, computational or strategic, and so on; a trade off against long-term memory (or 'table lookup'); response selection or formulation in the absence of a sufficiently dominant association between the cue pattern, the response pattern and the concept of purpose. Problem solving requires information provided by the functions already mentioned plus processing by strategy rules or concepts with symbolic response repertoires. Decision making and problem solving can be usefully divided into further categories.

Effector response
The outputs that do work on the environment, including symbolic work. (Miller, 1967)

This technique puts emphasis on the kinds of activity being performed and their demands on the human operator. Different types of activity will have different implications for training. So as the analysis proceeds, using such an approach, different training requirements will emerge. But Miller does not directly relate different training methods to each category. Rather, he uses them to suggest that training for different functions will proceed separately as training exercises.

A different kind of taxonomy has been developed by Gagné (1970) which distinguishes behaviour in terms of eight different categories of learning:

Type 1 Signal Learning. The individual learns to make a general, diffuse response to a signal. This is the classical conditioned response of Pavlov . . .

Type 2 Stimulus-Response Learning. The learner acquires a precise response to a discriminated stimulus. What is learned is a connection . . . or a discriminated operant . . . sometimes called an instrumental response . . .

Type 3 Chaining. What is acquired is a chain of two or more stimulus-response connections. The conditions for such learning have been described by Skinner . . .

Type 4 Verbal Association. Verbal association is the learning of chains that are verbal. Basically, the conditions resemble those for other (motor) chains. However, the presence of language in the human being makes this a special type because internal links may be selected from the individual's previously learned repertoire of language . . .

Type 5 Discrimination Learning. The individual learns to make *n* different identifying responses to as many different stimuli, which may resemble each other in physical appearance to a greater or lesser degree. Although the learning of each stimulus-response connection is a simple type 2 occurrence, the connections tend to interfere with each other's retention . . .

Type 6 Concept Learning. The learner acquires a capability of making a common response to a class of stimuli that may differ from each other widely in physical appearance. He is able to make a response that identifies an entire class of objects or events . . . Other concepts are acquired by *definition*, and consequently have the formal characteristics of rules.

Type 7 Rule Learning. In simplest terms, a rule is a chain of two or more concepts. It functions to control behaviour in the manner suggested by a verbalised rule of the form, 'if A, then B,' where A and B are previously learned concepts. However, it must be carefully distinguished from the mere verbal sequence, 'if A, then B,' which, of course, may also be learned as type 4.

Type 8 Problem Solving. Problem solving is a kind of learning that requires the internal events usually called thinking. Two or more previously acquired rules are somehow combined to produce a new capability that can be shown to depend on a 'higher-order' rule.
(Gagné, 1970, pp63-4)

Some of these categories clearly overlap with those in Miller's taxonomy. Gagné's scheme is novel since the categories are arranged hierarchically. For example, concept learning is most efficient if the necessary discrimination learning precedes it. This technique is a more sophisticated attempt to relate categories of behaviour to not only their learning requirements but also a sequence of learning.

Hierarchical task analysis

An analysis technique, which can be applied to a wide range of tasks, has been developed at the University of Hull. Hierarchical task analysis is probably its best name and the process is outlined by Annett and Duncan (1967). Tasks are broken down into 'operations' which are the units of analysis. These are similar to the TOTE units proposed by G A Miller *et al* (1960). Operations are defined as: 'any unit of behaviour, no matter how long or short its duration and no matter how simple or complex its structure, which can be defined in terms of its objective' (Annett *et al*, 1971). The key to this technique is the operation which is identified with a behavioural unit. This focuses attention on the objectives of the task rather than just the activity being performed. It also should free us from any prejudice about the number of levels of description required in any analysis. Operations can be broken down into sub-operations, and these can again be subdivided. With such a general unit as the operation, no assumptions need to be made at the initiation of any analysis of how many levels of breakdown are necessary. Thus inherent flexibility is its main advantage over some techniques which assume a simple level of analysis throughout, ie a technique which simply records 'elements', or else others which prescribe a fixed number of levels of analysis, eg tasks, activities and elements.

The concept of the operation can be applied to a wide variety of tasks, in order to develop hierarchical descriptions of them which will give more or less detail depending on the context of the analysis. Let us now examine aspects of hierarchical task analysis in more detail. In Figure 1, the three components of an operation and their relationship to the operator or person performing them are presented. During the analysis of each operation it is necessary to isolate:

Input: signals or cues in the environment which tell the person to perform the operation

Action: the appropriate behaviour which needs to be performed during the operation

Feedback: signals or cues which tell the operator how adequate his actions are, and if he has completed the operation.

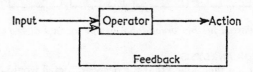

Figure 1. *An operation*

This entails a closer examination of tasks and their psychological demands. Whilst the description of the operation is simply a statement of its objectives, the analysis in terms of input, action and feedback begins to specify these demands. It should also record what is necessary in training for successful performance of the operation, ie preparing people to meet those demands.

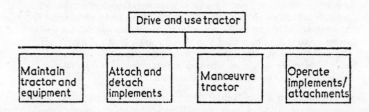

Figure 2. *First stage of a task analysis of tractor driving*

157

Analysis of a task in terms of operations should proceed hierarchically. The overall objectives of the task form the first operation. Let us use an example of the tractor driver. In Figure 2 the operation 'drive and use tractor' represents the overall objectives of a tractor driver. This operation can be broken down into four subordinate operations, which give more detail. Each of these can be analysed further, as in Figure 3, to give a more extensive hierarchical diagram of the task. Clearly such analysis could proceed to absurdly minute levels which would be of no consequence for training. The next problem is therefore to develop criteria which will specify how detailed any analysis should be.

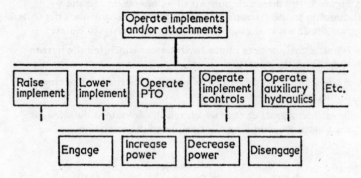

Figure 3. *Partial further breakdown of operation 4 of tractor driving*

CRITERIA FOR ANALYSIS

Previously it was mentioned that the degree of detail would depend very much on the context. Many techniques assume that analysts will use rules of thumb like, 'give more detail with critical tasks', or 'give attention to areas of special difficulty'. Whilst such rules may be useful, they are apt to be too vague and lacking in general applicability. In hierarchical analysis, Annett and Duncan (1967) suggest that as each operation is isolated two questions should be asked of it:

(i) what is the probability *without* training of inadequate performance?
(ii) what would be the costs to the system of inadequate performance?

If the best available estimates of these values, or rather their *product,* is unacceptable, then the performance in question is redescribed in more detail, ie broken down into subordinate operations and each of these is then submitted in turn to the same decision rule. In some cases it will be necessary to redescribe several times in increasing detail, in others not. The analysis ceases, either when the values specified in the rule are acceptable to the system, or when training requirements for adequate performance are clear. (Annett & Duncan, 1967)

The first question is directed at determining how likely, with a given trainee population, performance will be acceptable without training. In other words will a simple instruction suffice, or is more detail, ie further analysis, necessary? Using our tractor example, a specific piece of equipment is the power take-off (PTO), which is a means of powering equipment attached behind a tractor. From Figure 3 the statement 'operate PTO' is not sufficient detail for adequate performance, but subordinate to this, the statement 'increase power' will give sufficient information to the majority of trainees. This is a first step towards putting analysis and training into its context. The aspects considered here are the previous levels of training and the abilities and aptitudes of the trainees. If people are being recruited for a job which involves a new machine performing an old process, then the analyst will probably need to provide more detail for training school leavers for the tasks than for the operators of the old process. This estimate of the *probability* of failure for each operation is represented by P.

The second question places the operation into its costs context. Some operations need little or no training and some can be learned quickly in the job situation. Designing a training programme for some operations may cost more than it saves in lost production and inefficiency. On the other hand there may be very critical operations, which although simple may carry high financial penalties if performed inadequately. The *cost* value is represented by C.

The decision rule on redescription is then to combine P and C in a multiplicative fashion $(P \times C)$, and if the value is unacceptable to the system, then the operation can be further analysed. In this context the system refers to the environment in which the training specialist is working, the objectives he has been set, and the resources available to him. The multiplicative rule is used because if the value of either P or C is at or near zero, then their product also will be at or near zero. This therefore gives a quick indication of operations which are not critical or which present little learning difficulty. The $P \times C$ rule is applied to each operation in turn. Again if the value obtained is unacceptable, then that operation is further broken down, and the rule applied to each subordinate operation. This will most likely yield a large, irregular block diagram, but one in which only the essential operations will be represented.

RULES FOR SEQUENCING OPERATIONS

When an operation is broken down into subordinate operations the analyst must state how the subordinates are ordered. In other words he must state the rule governing the sequencing or selection of subordinates. Some operations are performed serially and follow very simple rules, such as, 'do A, then B, then C, etc'. Others involve performing two or more operations concurrently or in close temporal proximity. For example, the tractor driver often has both to 'manoeuvre tractor' and 'operate implements' at the same time. With other operations, on the other hand, no particular order may exist. For example, a traffic warden must be able to 'give parking tickets', 'direct traffic' and 'give directions to pedestrians', etc. There will be an order of priorities for these operations, but no actual predetermined sequence of them which is intrinsic to the job. In many tasks the sequence of operations is a branching one, one operation may lead to two or more alternatives. Figure 4 presents the sequence for locating

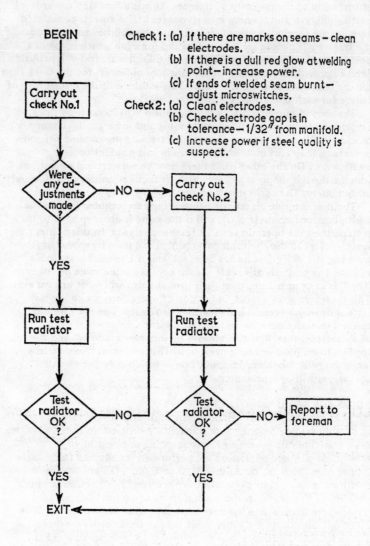

BEGIN

Check 1: (a) If there are marks on seams – clean electrodes.
(b) If there is a dull red glow at welding point – increase power.
(c) If ends of welded seam burnt – adjust microswitches.

Check 2: (a) Clean electrodes.
(b) Check electrode gap is in tolerance – 1/32″ from manifold.
(c) Increase power if steel quality is suspect.

Figure 4. *Decision tree for selecting sub-operations when leaking radiators are reported.* (From Annett *et al*, 1971)

No	Description of Operation and Training Notes	I/F	A	Redescribed
1	Fence with the sabre. Ⓡ Convention means an invariant order. 1,1 to 1,3. Score a hit on the target of the opponent without getting hit oneself within the rules. Must learn the convention – possibly fencing films.	-	x	1,1 - 1,3
1,1	Attack the opponent. Ⓡ Invariant order 1,1,1 to 1,1,3 although 1,1,1 (the grip) is maintained throughout the fight. The target is anywhere above the waist of the opponent including the arms. Once indicated this should be clear; may be helped by colouring the target area.	-	x	1,1,1 - 1,1,3
1,2	Defend an opponent's attack. Ⓡ Always 1,2,1 but defence may be by either evasion (1,2,2) or by parrying (1,2,3) Ⓘ The choice of alternative depends on the amount of pressure in the fight and upon the strengths and weaknesses of the opponent and is thus specific to each fight. Evasion should not be encouraged because it does not earn the right to attack.	x	x	1,2,1 - 1,2,3
1,3	Reply to opponent's attack. Ⓡ Operation 1,3,1 and 1,3,2 are wholly time shared but the type of hit (1,3,2) will vary from one riposte to another. All ripostes follow a parry by the rules of fencing.	-	x	1,3,1 - 1,3,2

I/F = presence (x) or not (-) of input/feedback difficulty.
A = presence (x) or not (-) of action difficulty.
Ⓡ Ⓘ = prefixes separating training comment from a description of the operation.
See text for fuller explanation.

Figure 5. *Extract from a task analysis table of fencing*

faults in the particular industrial process of radiator welding. A number of decisions have to be made, and particular sequences are dependent upon the outcome of each question. A decision tree or algorithm is a particularly useful way of recording this type of structure. The rule must be recorded when the operation is broken down. If any of the subordinate operations are further analysed then again *rules of sequence* or *selection* should be stated.

RECORDING THE ANALYSIS
We have progressed this far without discussing how exactly information can be recorded. This is because, whilst recording techniques are important, the general approach of the analyst is more important than the format of recording. Nevertheless some guidelines on recording can be given, although fuller expositions can be found in Annett *et al* (1971) and Duncan (1972). The hierarchical diagram is useful for showing the structure of the task, but limited in its capacity for recording detailed

information. It should be used in conjunction with a table, recording the name of the operation, or perhaps just assigning a reference number. The table consists of a number of columns, as shown in Figure 5, where the first stages of an analysis of fencing by J P Davies (1972) are presented. In the first column are the reference numbers to the diagram. The second and most important column contains a statement of the operation which is always in terms of an instruction to perform the operation. Also included in this column are the training comments, with suitable prefixes, which describe the rules for sequencing sub-operations Ⓡ, together with input Ⓘ, action (A) or feedback (F) difficulties. Any further training comment can also be made here, as well as possible training solutions (see next section). The final columns serve to indicate whether any difficulties exist in the operation, and if it is broken down, the numbers of sub-operations. At the conclusion of the analysis, the table will contain:

(a) a list of all operations, as instructions
(b) the rules for sequencing sub-operations (an additional decision tree may be useful here)
(c) notes on difficulties
(d) training comment.*

This will provide all the inputs for the next components in the training system, 'designing methods and media' and 'developing criterion measures'.

Training alternatives

The transition from task analysis to training design is not, however, a simple translation process. There will often be alternative methods of training and one training method may not be readily apparent at the time of analysis. All these alternatives, and ideas, no matter how vague, can be noted in the table at the time of analysis. They will have to be considered in the training design stage. The number and feasibility of these alternatives depend both on the level of development of the pertinent training research and the degree of familiarity of the task analyst with it. Nevertheless, such comments should be attempted, particularly when the real task situation is being viewed.

Another alternative which should be considered is whether to train or not to train. If lists of instructions or decision trees have been considered then they could be used not only for training, but also to supplant training, by supporting performance with what are called 'job aids' (Wulff & Berry, 1962). This is an important decision because very different kinds of performance may result. Even with the best designed training scheme occasional human errors may still occur. Job aids may be helpful in overcoming this problem. However their disadvantages need to be appreciated. They may function primarily as temporary crutches to performance and their removal or the transfer to

* Criticisms of this format and a suggested revision are given in Shepherd, A (1976) An improved tabular format for task analysis, *Journal of Occupational Psychology* 49: 93-104

a related task may reveal no underlying learning gains by the trainee. Such a decision, whether to train or use job aids, must depend on context and sometimes will depend on non-training considerations such as management preferences (see Duncan [1972] for further discussion of this area).

Sources of information

There are many methods of collecting task information and an analysis in any particular situation can utilise one or more of them.

Existing documentation. This can cover previous analyses, eg for work study. Operating manuals, maintenance guides, rules and previous training manuals can be useful. Accident reports may also point to critical operations.

Observation. Simple observations with note-taking can cover a multitude of situations. Photographic records, with the potential for fast or slow motion recording, extend observational power. Closed-circuit television is a very convenient form of visual recording, with a sound channel usually being available as well. The analyst can resort to practice of the task himself for further insight into the task demands. For some tasks continual observation may be necessary whilst for others activity sampling can be sufficient. Task performance can be accompanied by a verbal description of the process.

Interviews. Questions can be informally asked of the task performer during observation. Information may be spontaneously given, or it can be collected in a structured or unstructured interview situation. The *Critical Incident Technique,* outlined by Flanagan (1954), collects information on near accidents and critical or particularly difficult operations, which may be, or at least should be, very rare.

Simulation. In this context the word simulation represents any model of the real-life situation used for analysis purposes rather than training. Various kinds of simulation can be practised in order to both generate and validate information. These can range from full-scale simulations of systems to paper-and-pencil exercises. Simulations are necessary for a variety of reasons: (a) in the development of new systems where the tasks do not exist; (b) for the validation of information collected from operators. For example Duncan (1972) reports that even the most experienced operators did not use optimal strategies for fault detection in a chemical process. The optimal strategy was derived from a logical decision tree analysis of the task; (c) examination of some task situations may be dangerous. In a study of air traffic controllers Leplat and Bisseret (1966) presented simulated situations to them and studied the strategies adopted.

This brief overview of sources of information is not exhaustive. Our aim is to show that a range of approaches exists where the chief criterion must be utility, validity and reliability in collecting information about the task. Further details can be found in basic texts (eg Chapanis, 1959; Blum & Naylor, 1968).

Conclusion

The method of hierarchical task analysis has been advocated in this
paper, since it is general in its approach, and has been applied to a
range of tasks. However, there are a number of alternative methods
(see Annett & Duncan, 1967). The chief criterion for any analysis
method must be that it leads to positive training recommendations. In
addition it should be economic in its approach to data collection and
in harmony with current thinking in psychology on how human
performance is represented.

References

Annett, J and Duncan, K D (1967) Task analysis and training design, *Occupational
    Psychology* 41: 211-21
Annett, J *et al* (1971) *Task Analysis,* Training Information No 6. London : HMSO
Blum, M L and Naylor, J C (1968) *Industrial Psychology.* New York : Harper
    & Row
Chapanis, A (1959) *Research Techniques in Human Engineering.* Baltimore :
    Johns Hopkins Press
Conrad, R (1951) Study of skill by motion and time study and by psychological
    experiment, *Research* 4: 353-8
Crossman, E R F W (1956) Perceptual activities in manual work, *Research*
    9: 42-9
Davies, J P (1972) *Task Analysis and an Approach to Coaching in Sport.*
    Unpublished MSc dissertation, Applied Psychology Department, University
    of Aston in Birmingham
Duncan, K D (1972) Strategies for analysis of the task. In J Hartley (ed) *Strategies
    for Programmed Instruction: An Educational Technology.* London :
    Butterworths
Flanagan, J C (1954) The critical incident technique, *Psychological Bulletin*
    51: 327-58
Gagné, R M (1970) *The Conditions of Learning* (2nd ed). New York : Holt,
    Rinehart & Winston
Leplat, J and Bisseret, A (1966) Analysis of the processes involved in the treatment
    of information by the air traffic controller, *The Controller* 5: 13-22
Miller, G A *et al* (1960) *Plans and the Structure of Behavior.* New York : Holt,
    Rinehart & Winston
Miller, R B (1967) Task taxonomy: science or technology? *Ergonomics*
    10: 167-76
Seymour, W D (1966) *Industrial Skills.* London : Pitman
Singleton, W T (1968) Some recent experiments on learning and their training
    implications, *Ergonomics* 11: 53-9
Wulff, J J and Berry, P C (1962) Aids to job performance. In R M Gagné (ed)
    Psychological Principles in System Development. New York : Holt,
    Rinehart & Winston

2.3 Principles of Sequencing Content

GEORGE J POSNER AND KENNETH A STRIKE

This paper contains a summary of the main approaches to sequencing which are discussed by Posner, G J and Strike, K A (1976) A categorisation scheme for principles of sequencing content, *Review of Educational Research* 46: 685-90.

(The table which follows summarises the main points made in a lengthier article. The aim of the original paper was to spell out in detail different ways of sequencing content, to classify these ways, and to give examples. In this summary the exposition has been drastically curtailed and some of the examples have been modified. In the original article (see Acknowledgements), Posner and Strike distinguished between five sets of sequencing principles — word related, concept related, inquiry related, learning related and utilisation related — and discussed sub-categories within each set.)

Principles of sequencing content

Principles	Key ideas	Examples
1.0 *Word related*		
1.1 Space	Elements can be arranged in accord with their physical arrangements: eg closest-to-farthest, bottom-to-top, east-to-west.	Teach the names of the States in the USA according to geographical location. Teach the parts of a plant from the root to the stem to the leaves to the flower (or the reverse).
1.2 Time	Elements can be arranged in accord with the order of events in time.	Teach the names of the States in the USA in order of admission to the Union. Teach the major ideas of Marx before teaching about the Russian Revolution.
1.3 Physical attributes	Elements can be arranged in accord with physical characteristics (eg size, shape, complexity, etc).	Teach the names of the States in order of size. Teach the hardness scale for minerals from softest to hardest.

Principles	Key ideas	Examples

2.0 *Concept related*

Principles	Key ideas	Examples
2.1 Class relations	Elements which are instances of particular classes of things or events can be grouped together. One can teach the characteristics of a class before teaching about the members of it, or *vice versa.*	Teach about mammals before teaching about specific animals in that group. Define 'discrimination' before examining racial and sexual discrimination. Compare sound and light before teaching the concept of wave motion.
2.2 Propositional relations	Propositions are combinations of concepts that assert something. Of interest here is the sequencing of elements prior to establishing a proposition, and the relationship between propositions.	Teach the volume of gas at several temperatures before teaching Boyle's Law. Teach in deductive order the steps of a geometric proof. Teach an overview of the theory of natural selection before studying the adaptation of Darwin's finches.
2.3 Sophistication	Concepts and propositions can differ in their level of sophistication, complexity, abstractness, etc. (Bruner's 'spiral' curriculum, eg, returns periodically to deal with concepts at a higher level of sophistication.)	Teach real numbers before teaching about imaginary numbers. Teach what 'acceleration' means before teaching it as 'v/t'. Teach Newton's Law before Einstein's refinement of these laws in his Special Theory of Relativity.
2.4 Logical prerequisites	A concept or proposition is a logical prerequisite to another concept or proposition when it is logically necessary to understand the first concept or proposition in order to understand the second.	Teach what 'velocity' means before teaching that 'acceleration' is the change in velocity. Teach the concept of set before the concept of number.

3.0 *Inquiry related*

Principles	Key ideas	Examples
3.1 Logic of inquiry	Sequencing principles rooted in logic will reflect views of valid inference. Different logics will yield differing sequencing principles. Eg a view that considers discovery to be a	Discover ways to light a bulb with a battery, then generalise a rule. Explain how Galileo arrived at the hypothesis that the change in velocity per unit of time for a freely falling object is

Principles	Key ideas	Examples
	matter of generalising over numerous instances (ie induction) will provide instances prior to having the student discover the generalisations. A view that considers discovery to be a matter of testing bold conjectures will seek hypothesis-eliciting and then turn to a process of evidence collection.	a constant; then have pupils find that the acceleration of any object allowed to fall freely is 9.8/m/sec as long as air resistance is not a factor.
3.2 Empirics of inquiry	Some features of inquiry are rooted in descriptions of how successful scientists actually proceed or in the social or psychological conditions of fruitful inquiry. Suppose, for example, that successful inquirers were found to study a problem area before working on a specific problem. This might lead to sequencing content in such a way that it emphasised the need for a general survey of an area prior to a consideration of special problems.	Teach what other researchers have discovered about reinforcement schedules before teaching pupils to frame hypotheses about optimal reinforcement schedules.
4.0 *Learning related*		
4.1 Empirical prerequisites	If it can be determined empirically that the learning of one skill facilitates the learning of a subsequent skill, then the first skill can be termed an empirical prerequisite of the second. Empirical prerequisites contrast with logical prerequisites in that the latter are concerned with relations based on the logical properties of concepts and the former are concerned with empirically based relations regardless of their logical	Teach discrimination between initial consonants, and then teach the use of word attack skills, and then reading generally.

Principles	Key ideas	Examples
	necessity. (Naturally, what is logically necessary usually turns out to be empirically verifiable, but the converse does not always hold.)	
4.2 Familiarity	Familiarity refers to the frequency with which an individual has encountered an idea, object, or event — ie how commonplace it is to the individual. Sequences of this sub-type order elements from the most familiar to the most remote.	Teach about British schools before teaching about European schools before teaching about Arabic schools.
4.3 Difficulty	Factors affecting difficulty include (a) how fine a discrimination is required, (b) how fast a procedure must be carried out, and (c) how much 'mental capacity' is required for learning.	Teach long vowel sounds before short ones. Teach weaving slowly, then teach the pupil to speed up. Teach the spelling of short words before longer words. Teach rhymes before blank verse.
4.4 Interest	Elements that are interesting are commonly those about which the learner has some limited experience but they remain a challenge, retain the potential for surprise, or can arouse curiosity. Sequences of this type begin with those elements which are more likely to evoke pupil interest.	Teach pupils how to pick a lock before teaching them how a lock works. Teach pupils to dig out a local cellar before teaching archaeology.
4.5 Development	A human development category is not strictly speaking a sequencing category. However, much of the debate here centres on the importance of sequencing content in a way that reflects the manner in which children develop psychologically.	Teach mathematics first through concrete objects before dealing in abstractions. Teach pupils to base their concept of morality on authority, then on democratically accepted law, and finally on individual principles of conscience.
4.6 Internal-isation	If the educational intent of a sequence is to have the pupil internalise an attitude or value, then	Teach pupils to listen willingly to Christian ideas, then teach them to interpret voluntarily events in

Principles	Key ideas	Examples
	elements can be ordered in a manner that reflects an increasing degree of internalisation.	terms of a Christian ideology, then teach them to view the world based on a Christian value system. Teach pupils to recognise certain behaviours in others, then in themselves.

5.0 *Utilisation related*

5.1 Procedures	When a procedure or process is being taught in a training programme it is often appropriate for the sequence to reflect the order in which the steps will be carried out when the procedure is followed. Sometimes, however, one may start with the completion of the procedure, and work backwards — always completing the task at each stage.	In problem solving (i) analyse what is the problem; (ii) analyse its causes; (iii) decide how to eliminate or correct the factors causing the problem. Teach shoelace-tying by getting the child first of all to complete the last step (tying tight the two bows); then the next last (tying the second bow) and the last step (tying tight the two bows); then the third last step (wrapping the second lace around the first bow), the next last (tying the second bow) and then the last (tying tight the two bows); and so on.
5.2 Anticipated frequency of use	Some curriculum designs begin with the most important content, where the most important means that which the pupil is likely to encounter most often. In contrast with familiarity, anticipated frequency of use bases sequences not on past encounters but on predictions of future encounters.	Teach the use of means and standard deviations before analysis of variance. Teach compound interest before stock transactions. Teach a television repairman how to change a tube before teaching him how to change a resistor.

169

2.4 They Teach Concepts, Don't They?

SUSAN M MARKLE

To answer such a question, one could do for conceptual aspects of existing instructional materials what Anderson (1972) did in criticising the reporting of test construction procedures in educational research. To quote Anderson:

> The thesis of this paper is that educational research workers have not yet learned how to develop achievement tests that meet the primitive first requirement for a system of measurement, namely that there is a clear and consistent definition of the things being counted.

The same thesis is proposed for instructional materials, namely, that they do not meet the 'primitive first requirements' for instruction at the conceptual level. The 'they' in my title becomes a sample of the substitution set of producers who claim, either by specifically stated behavioural objectives or by simply naming a concept, that they teach the concept.

In specifying the 'primitive first requirements' for teaching concepts, I will overlook here a common prejudice that you would expect from an old-timer in programmed instruction, namely that the instruction will provide for meaningful student information-processing activities with feedback, and will restrict consideration to the purely formal surface requirements that sufficient information be there for the students to process as they will. When the students are literate, it is likely that a classification rule or identification algorithm will be provided — known in common English as a definition. The set of words which purports to be a definition should bear some clear relationship to the domain of the concept, where 'domain' means the range of examples that are to be included and the limits of the domain that separate examples from non-examples. Whether the stated definition communicates in the sense that students can operate with it is an empirical issue. The important point is that the definition must map clearly on to the domain. A second requirement is appropriate exemplification. Complex concepts require a complex set of examples, generated according to known rules. Conceptual instruction will dip into the non-example realm as well. If the subject matter is conceptually sound, these non-examples will usually be examples of co-ordinate concepts and the relationships between superordinate concepts and their sub-sets — the co-ordinates — will be made explicit. If the student is to demonstrate mastery of the concept, test items must follow certain rules: at the classification level, all the examples and non-examples the student is asked to process will be new and will bear a predictable relationship to the domain of the concept. Concepts can neither be taught nor tested by a single example. If the formal level of attainment is being evaluated, further requirements are imposed on the design of items. Asking a student to repeat or recognise the definition is totally inadequate: asking him to generate an example or two of his own does not satisfy the requirements of sampling the domain.

To determine whether a unit of instructional capital in any medium satisfies such formal requirements is not an easy task. Having already inspected quite a few instructional products in my career, I had already prejudged the results I would obtain from such a survey. What would we find? We would discover that the majority of so-called concept presentations consists of giving the learner a definition that does not define very well, if at all, accompanied in most cases by an example or two that in no sense exemplifies the broad domain to which the concept label is applied by subject-matter experts. Almost certain would be a total lack of non-examples or co-ordinate concepts. And, of course, the instruction will be capped in the testing situation, either in the student study guide or the instructor manual, by a test that in no way satisfies the conditions of learning and evaluation specified by Gagné (1965), Merrill (1971), Markle and Tiemann (1969), Englemann (1969), Anderson and Faust (1973), Klausmeier, Ghatala and Frayer (1974) and the host of others who have issued firm guidelines on what constitutes good instructional design at the conceptual level.

A preliminary attempt to launch such a survey by inspecting the non-random sample of instructional products in our field that are on my shelves, whether pure text, Kellerised, modularised, mediated, or programmed, produced rapid extinction of further investigatory behaviours along these lines. Most of our stated objectives are at the memory level; even when higher cognitive levels are included, the 'primitive requirements' are seldom met. As Coldeway (1974) found with one such package, being informed *via* behavioural objectives that you *will* generalise is not the same as being provided with sufficient information so that you *can* generalise. Chapters on conceptual learning may talk straight, but there are few signs that the authors are listening to themselves. Students in my Doctor of Arts course in instructional design do equivalent mini-surveys of materials in their own disciplines — math, chemistry, and biology — as a course project, with predictable results: the students get an A and the instructional materials an F. The deficit is not confined to psychology texts. In his recently translated book Landa (1974) provides similar examples from Russian textbooks. Of course there are exceptions, but it would hardly be news for me to inform you that 'they[1]', the instructional materials producers, rarely practise sound principles of instructional design in teaching concepts.

There are reasons for such deficits beyond the obvious one that some may lack knowledge of how to go about it. Among these are the politics of academic courses and the economic necessity to produce what will sell to the consumer-professor who adopts materials. Academics are content-coverage oriented; our encyclopaedic texts must cover everything in academically respectable fashion, and therefore we do not have the time to teach conceptually. If it is indeed a disaster area, who cares? Until we, the consumers, shift our buying habits, 'they$_1$' will continue to produce materials designed to be memorised and regurgitated.

Another substitution set of the variable 'they' in my title, 'they$_2$', could be those who have published the immense number of research reports in the Bruner (1956) model, the hundreds of laboratory studies of concept acquisition summarised not long ago by Clark (1971). For those of us in applied fields, looking for principles which can guide successful practice, it is all too easy to critique the standard laboratory situation. Its oversimplified too-rational universe of discourse, its all-too-obvious attributes of simple visual figures, and its game-like structure in which the learner — often a college sophomore — tries to discover which of a restricted set of classification rules the experimenter happens to have in mind — all these properties have been roasted by critics for their lack of relevance and generalisability to the real world of instruction (cf Markle & Tiemann, 1970; Anderson & Faust, 1973; Klausmeier *et al*, 1974). In the sense that one can easily tell a college sophomore that 'blue triangle' is the concept, with the result that he can classify with unerring accuracy thereafter, 'they$_2$' are not really in the concept teaching business.

Investigators in 'they$_2$' do not hold themselves accountable for teaching students anything at all, which is perfectly legitimate in basic research. However, their findings are often applicable, as Bruner himself predicted, to instruction in strategies or heuristics of information gathering, far more so than they are to the usual forms of teaching concepts in academic subject matters. Learners in this classic laboratory situation rarely exhibit ideal problem-solving strategies. That learners as young as six years old can be taught such efficient strategies was demonstated by Anderson (1965). Every year in my own classes, I confirm that even college sophomores can acquire them too. Landa (1974) has provided us with a model lesson for instructing sixth graders in the application of equivalent heuristics to the problem of unlocking the meaning of textbook definitions of concepts. Landa's term 'indicative features' is approximately synonymous with 'critical attributes'. The logical structures of these indicative features which students must identify in given definitions result in classification schemes similar to Bruner's conjunctive and disjunctive concepts. In another sense, these logical structures, hidden in prose definitions, resemble the distinction between critical attributes, the necessary properties in a conjunctive AND relationship, and variable attributes, the dimensions along which examples will vary in a disjunctive OR relationship. The reasoning methods that Landa teaches students to use in deciding whether a given specimen meets the logical properties of the definition are in a sense the mirror image of the ideal strategies taught by Anderson and others to learners who must discover the defining properties of a class from an array of examples and non-examples. Since the student who has a definition to be tested on a given specimen is engaging in the reverse process from a student who must determine defining properties from a set of examples, there should be common elements in the reasoning which must go on in each case.

Landa's work suggests that providing students with a supposedly clear statement of, say, three critical attributes does not guarantee that the student will process that information in a logical fashion. There is an intellectual skill here of the sort defined by Gagné (1970), and students are not born with this information applying skill any more than they are born with Bruner's ideal information-gathering strategies. When a student reads a definition that is meant to specify three critical properties in a conjunctive relationship, does he necessarily conclude that he must make three decisions about each and every specimen he inspects before he can determine whether it satisfies the conditions? Or does he jump to conclusions on finding that the most salient critical property is there? Jumping to conclusions on the basis of inadequate information is a common student error in the Bruner model as well. If the information-gathering skills required to solve the problems posed by 'they$_2$', the laboratory investigators, are as rare as the data seem to indicate they are, perhaps the skills required to learn from definitions are equally as rare.

Landa's heuristics clarify one unpublished result in a series of studies that Tiemann and I have been doing on the concept 'morpheme'. Given a complex definition presented, as it often is, as a single complex massively punctuated sentence, how does a student determine how many attributes are represented and that the relation between the attributes is indeed a conjunctive one? The verbal behaviour of definers, be they Russian or American, has not made this a simple task for students, a point I will return to later. We have found that the simple technique of arranging the three critical attributes on three separate lines produced significantly (p = 0.04) better classifying than did a linear prose presentation of the same words. Such techniques of visual layout of logical structures such as AND have been around a long time in sophisticated programmed instruction (Markle, 1969), but they are still all too rare in academic instructional materials.

One solution to the problem of poor instructional materials is better students, students trained with the intellectual skills necessary to unlock the secrets we hide from them in our muddy prose. Thus, while no college sophomore wants to or needs to learn the concept of 'blue triangle', there may be some benefits in 'they$_2$'s procedures for sophomore and sixth grader alike. It is unfortunate that few subjects who participate in these research studies leave the laboratory having acquired such transferable learning-how-to-learn skills.

Although research in the teaching of concepts by definition is not exactly new (cf Johnson & Stratton, 1966), a thundering herd of studies in this area has appeared in the last five years and the outlook is bullish for principles applicable to instructional design problems. The concerns of 'they$_3$' the third substitution set for my variable 'they', may be characterised as a search for the characteristics of the optimal mixture of information which will cause mastery of complex concepts. The findings range from one extreme, represented by Anderson and Kulhavy's demonstration of almost perfect acquisition resulting from

providing only a definition (1972), to the other extreme in which
Swanson found that providing a definition significantly *suppressed*
concept acquisition when compared to simple provision of examples
and non-examples (see Klausmeier *et al*, 1974). Obviously we are not
dealing with a simple unitary phenomenon.

The studies in this group have a distinct advantage over 'blue
triangle' studies — the concepts are real, academically respectable, ones.
To enumerate some of them for those unfamiliar with the literature,
Tiemann and I have been working with 'morpheme' (1974); Tennyson,
Woolley and Merrill with 'trochaic meter' (1972); Boutwell with
'RX$_2$ crystals' (1973); Shumway with 'commutativity' and
'associativity' (1974); Feldman with 'bilateral, rotational, and
translational symmetry' and Swanson with 'population', 'habitat' and
'community'. A veritable mini-rash of studies has appeared using
grammatical concepts such as 'noun' and 'adverb', although many are
marred by inadequate analysis and traditional *non*-definitions. A
blow-by-blow description of the findings of many of these studies can
be found in Klausmeier *et al* (1974). Briefly, with the exception of
Anderson and Kulhavy's study, a strong vote of confidence can be given
to the necessity for providing a full range of examples, what we
(Markle & Tiemann, 1969) have termed the minimum rational set of
examples. In direct contrast to the findings of 'they$_2$' (cf Clark, 1971)
non-examples have proved to have significant effects on correct
classification, especially those particular kinds of non-example defined
as close-in non-examples, specimens that lack only one of the set of
conjunctively related critical attributes. Because these concepts are real
ones and their examples complex, the treatment of what 'they$_2$' have
called 'irrelevant attributes' must of necessity differ. One cannot remove
these variable properties from an example of 'morpheme' or 'trochaic
meter' to make the presence of the critical attributes more salient to
the learner in the way that one can remove excess irrelevant properties
from a card with a blue triangle on it. The attributes vary from one
example to the next in a disjunctive OR fashion, but they are not
irrelevant in the sense that one can do away with them. We should
instead do away with the archaic term 'irrelevant'.

In these studies the method of testing concept acquisition at the
classification level is becoming increasingly more precise. Many of the
studies can now satisfy the kinds of criticism levelled by Anderson
(1972) at the measuring instruments in educational research. Given the
analysis and documentation of the critical and variable properties of
the domain of the concept, the rules for generating the testing
instrument can be specifically stated, to the point where numerous
equivalent tests could be generated. From this increased specificity,
we can also identify patterns of student errors more sophisticated than
simple mean number correct, patterns that result from manipulations
of the instructional variables. It was from the regularities emerging from
this group of studies that I drew the earlier prescriptions for evaluating
instructional materials to see if 'they$_1$' are doing the job they claim to
do.

In deference to our new emphasis on non-examples of concepts, let me eliminate from the ranks of 'they$_3$' a few standard teaching paradigms which lack a critical attribute or two. One is the illustration, found in almost all dictionaries and many texts, of objects with such limited variability that a single picture will cause most learners to identify correctly every instance of the object. Being visual is not the dimension at issue, as any of Boutwell's students would admit, since the concept of RX$_2$ crystal is picturable but difficult to learn. I do not mean to imply that no learning problems are involved here for certain age groups, as well covered in Klausmeier *et al* (1974). Indeed, when complex identities such as the classic Hullian Chinese ideographs are buried in complex environments, learning to recognise the next presentation of the same stimulus is a problem worthy of adult status. But, if recognition rather than classification is the response category, the instructional technique is a non-example of 'they$_3$'.

Another standard technique to be eliminated from concept teaching of 'they$_3$' type is definition by synonym. It would probably shock vocabulary instructors to be so summarily dismissed from the ranks of concept teachers, but I will throw the rascals out anyway. Much of the vocabulary instruction in one's own language boils down to acquiring a new, and usually longer and more prestigious, noise to be emitted in response to a category that one has already mastered. Thus, one learns that 'to circumvent a difficulty' means to 'get around a difficulty'. The new response will enable the learner to display his membership in the class of Latin- or Greek-derived multi-syllable speakers of the language. However, in the sense of having mastered a new classification scheme which was not previously in the repertoire, the learner has made no progress.

A more complicated variation on this theme is quite typical of high-school or college teaching. While 'Sesame Street' may teach quite a few basic geometric shapes and classes of animal to a high level of accuracy in classification, high-school mathematics and science courses will instil an extensive verbal repertoire about the geometric properties of shapes such as rectangles and triangles and the biological properties of animal classes such as reptiles and mammals. This type of learning goes beyond Klausmeier's 'formal level' in that mammals have many more properties — much more can be said about them — than would ever be required to formulate a foolproof classification rule. The difference between these verbal repertoires and concept learning is readily apparent in what would constitute a reasonable criterion test. You would hardly ask a high-school student to pick out the triangles from a set of geometric shapes; rather you ask him to talk at length about the properties of triangles. This then is not concept teaching of 'they$_3$' type, either. I did not intend, in my earlier criticisms of instructional materials, to denigrate this form of instruction. The criticisms of 'they$_1$' were levelled at instruction which aims at verbal repertoires empty of the underlying classification schemes which students do not yet have.

Are the research designs of this group of investigators models of good concept teaching? Do 'they$_3$' teach concepts? Anyone who has done any research, as distinguished from R&D work, ought to be able to answer that question. Since it is the habit of journals to reject studies in which no significant differences are found, and since significant differences will appear on tests of concept acquisition only if some students don't learn, it is obvious that these investigators cannot teach concepts to full mastery and survive in the publication world. For instance, group means under different treatments in our 'morpheme' studies range from 60 per cent to 80 per cent — below the level of mastery permitted in most mastery courses, and hardly sufficient to gain success as a practising lexicographer. The reason is not hard to discover. In all those cases where investigators have been kind enough to provide me with the actual instructional treatments used, and in our own studies, the standard instructional presentation is information *giving*, with research variables being the kinds and amounts of information given to the learner. We are in the learning-from-prose business, with classification rather than memory as the criterion. What seems to be required to assure mastery is a marriage of the variables investigated by 'they$_3$' with what in common educational parlance is called practice, what programmers call active responding, what mathemagenics investigators call question asking, what information-processing theorists call information processing (cf Rothkopf, 1972; Anderson & Biddle, 1975). Inadequate information is one problem and inadequate information processing is another. The cure for each of these inadequacies is different, but together they are equally applicable to powerful instructional designs.

If an investigator follows analytical strategies such as those suggested by Markle and Tiemann (1969) or by Englemann (1969) and documents the results of this activity in a form similar to that exemplified for 'morpheme' (Markle & Tiemann, 1974), then it is possible to be extremely clear about the make-up of the instructional set of examples and non-examples and to write a prescription for tests that cover the same domain in the fashion of domain-referenced testing procedures (Hively, 1974). It is not, however, quite so clear how one goes from the existing analysis to a replicable prescription for a definition. In parallel with the not-very-informative statements in research reports that 'students were given a test' which Anderson criticised (1972), there is a similarly not-very-informative statement in many of the research studies mentioned so far that 'students were given *a* definition.' It seems to me that the properties of the definition should be a factor in determining the relative significance of other parts of the instructional message.

Perhaps this is an area so creative that we can never determine all the variables involved, but I have been probing some of them by a haphazard reading of what dictionaries do and what rhetoric instructors say a definer ought to do. I will not dignify this activity with the title 'research' and certainly 'they$_4$', the authors of dictionary entries, do not promote themselves as teachers of concepts. However, we are squarely faced with the problem of specifying what it is we are doing to students when we present 'a definition' with greater precision than we do at present. There is, after all, no such thing as '*the* definition', the mimicry in our standard texts notwithstanding; if there were, we would have only one dictionary instead of the existing competition among the wordsmiths.

The advice from the field of rhetoric for generating a so-called 'conventional definition' (Martin & Ohmann, 1963) is to define by stating a class term, what I have been calling a superordinate set, and by listing what differentiates the item being defined from other members of this same set. Using as an example that all-time favourite of writers in the area of concept learning — the concept of 'dog' — ask yourself, what is the appropriate superordinate term for 'dog' in a useful definition? 'Dog' is a sub-set of a large number of superordinates, not all of which are hierarchically related to each other in neat ways. You could pick the immediate family — the *Canidae*. That will get you into instant trouble, as I have come to expect from advice on how to write anything. You must now attempt to put into words what differentiates 'dog' from wolves and foxes. No one, including all the psychologists who use this example, has ever defined what those differentiating attributes are. Dictionaries do not even try, although assuredly lexicographers must have the concept of 'dog' at the classification level. If *'Canidae'* is too severe a challenge, you could try 'mammal'. Or 'animal'. Or 'carnivore'. The relations between these superordinates resemble those in recent descriptions of the hierarchical organisation of memory and suggest that we might be able to agree on whether the superordinate term listed in an experimental definition is a close or a distant relation on the hierarchy to the concept being defined. At the very least, we can agree on the presence or absence of a superordinate term as a characteristic of a definition. Note that our rhetoric advisers differentiate between the class term — the superordinate — and a differentiating property. Names of superordinates are not defining properties.

Several other somewhat quantifiable variables appeared in my random walk, the least useful of which is probably the sheer number of words involved. However, some of the words in many definitions are irrelevant to the classifying task. For instance, *Webster's* tells us, under 'dog', that these were 'kept in domesticated state since prehistoric times', an interesting fact, perhaps, but without utility in the identification task. We could on this basis develop an irrelevancy count, a sort of signal-to-noise ratio from this kind of analysis, with the expectation that high noise would have effects on student processing. Irrelevant facts of this sort are not defining attributes either, but they occur in many definitions in texts, dictionaries, and research studies.

There are several sources which provide quantification of the frequency level or readability level of the words used in a definition. As an exercise in madness along that line, you might observe the definitions given in *Webster's III International Dictionary* of some of the prepositional concepts taught on 'Sesame Street'. 'Between', for instance, is defined as 'in an intermediate position in relation to two other objects', a reversal of the usual synonymising practice of providing simple words to indicate the meaning of difficult ones. A synonym is not a statement of the critical properties. Everyone has experienced the interminable run-around one can get into in dictionaries and glossaries, in which one technical term is defined in terms of another which is in turn defined in terms of the first. In any single definition, we can quantify the presence of a technical term, not only in relation to its readability, but also in terms of its meaningfulness to students, the latter empirically determinable.

Landa's (1974) work in applying predicate logic to definitions suggests a further area in which precision in specifying how our definitions define could be increased. Landa's immediate concern appears to be directed, not to the semantic horrors perpetrated in grammatical definitions, which may be truly unquantifiable, but solely to the logical horrors, which lend themselves to precise specification. As already mentioned, the ANDs in conjunctively related critical attributes and the ORs in disjunctive variable attributes can be buried in linear prose. Take a simple example such as 'a triangle is a three-sided closed figure.' Analytically, one can note that the superordinate, 'figure', is at the end of the sentence, and the three potential critical attributes which differentiate triangles from other figures are buried as modifiers, two of them hyphenated to each other. Surely there would be an effect on student information processing, of the sort I discussed earlier, if the properties of the concept rule were better laid out for student inspection. I believe this is a good explanation for the effects of attribute prompting in recent studies (see Klausmeier *et al*, 1974); by pointing out how an example exemplifies a property, the investigator is unlocking the AND structure of a murky definition. Attribute prompting is only one of several ways to do so. The defining process can be further improved by making certain that the logical connectives employed are the correct ones, rather than, as Landa found in some Russian sources and I have found in ours, using 'and' when the logical relation is really OR, and 'but' when the logical relation is AND. Creative definers might chafe at such restrictions on their self-expression, but reasonable care with these factors should improve definitions for instructional and research purposes.

In castigating 'they$_1$' early in this paper, I made a comment unsubstantiated at the time that most instructional products do a poor job of defining terms. The variables just described provide some of the standards for making such judgements — I was not operating as an art critic. Even more crucial is the frequent blatant omission of critical features of the concept, features which analysts find in surveying the full range of exemplification and the co-ordinates or non-examples, and which students require to classify correctly. If you think of a definition as a map on the domain, the pitfalls in faulty mapping should be apparent. Excess prose, technical or overly-literate terminology, and murky logical relations make the map difficult to read, but omitting features of the domain entirely is a more significant error. Students fall off the edge of a very flat world. Such faulty maps can be found in dictionaries, as we demonstrated by pitting our analysis-derived definition of 'morpheme' against the one in *Webster's III International*, producing a highly significant increase in classification skill by adding the missing critical feature (Markle & Tiemann, 1974). Now, I am certain that the prestigious lexicographers can easily negotiate the hazardous terrain, since morphemic analysis is basic to dictionary-making. But their attainment of the concept on the formal level left something to be desired!

I have applied some of these analytical procedures to the definitions used in several of the research studies of the 'they$_3$' group. While I do not choose to disclose the results, it appears that defining is a many-headed monster which we have not yet fully tamed. Experimental results are going to vary until we get a firm grip on it. Tennyson, Woolley and Merrill (1972), among others, advocate a technique they call 'instance probability analysis', in which the difficulty level of various specimens is calculated by having students attempt to classify on the basis of a definition alone. This suggests to me a potential method for testing the adequacy of the definition. Logically, such data could be used to indicate faults in the defining process rather than some hidden complexity in particular examples and non-examples. Perhaps there should be a prize offered by some lexicographer's charity to the first person who can bring students to mastery of the full domain of a complex concept such as 'morpheme' or 'trochaic meter' without ever resorting to examples and non-examples. It may just be possible, but as an instructional designer today, I will stick to the practices suggested by 'they$_3$'.

Meanwhile, we should take our existing definitions with a grain of salt. Undergraduate students in my psychology courses regularly struggle with the problems of locating the defining properties of concepts taught, perhaps intuitively but certainly well, on 'Sesame Street' by example and non-example only. Nowhere, least of all in dictionaries, are the classification rules available, although we all have these concepts firmly at the classification level. Students at both the graduate and undergraduate levels in particular disciplines participate in the same kind of exercise in fields in which textbook definitions and the classification rules that subject-matter experts obey are, to say the least, not congruent with each other. A graduate student, Linda Crnic, who really understood the concept of 'generalisation' at the classification level, located five critical attributes for that domain. I challenge you to find those attributes in any definition contained in any of our texts by whatever means of unlocking murky prose you choose to employ. I find that this analysis task requires the insights of both the research groups involved in concept acquisition. These students are applying the strategies basic to the research designs of 'they$_2$' to worlds not made up of blue triangles, in order to generate prescriptions applicable to the world of 'they$_3$', and ultimately to instruction, the world of 'they$_1$', where the need is great. In more cases than we like to think, many disciplines cannot demonstrate concepts at the level that Klausmeier and his colleagues define as 'formal'. The words used do not map on to the terrain the subject-matter experts can unerringly negotiate. Until we learn to communicate our results in definitions that will lead to student mastery of the domain, I will put my money on the prescriptions that can now be derived from the recent studies of concept acquisition using a master mix of definition and exemplification. With appropriate verification on learners, materials embodying these strategies could lead to mastery.

References

Anderson, R C (1965) Can first graders learn an advanced problem-solving skill ? *Journal of Educational Psychology* 56: 283-94

Anderson, R C (1972) How to construct achievement tests to assess comprehension, *Review of Educational Research* 42: 145-70

Anderson, R C and Biddle, W B (1975) On asking people questions about what they are reading. In G Bower (ed) *Psychology of Learning and Motivation (vol 9)*. New York : Academic Press

Anderson, R C and Faust, G W (1973) *Educational Psychology*. New York : Dodd, Mead

Anderson, R C and Kulhavy, R W (1972) Learning concepts from definitions, *American Educational Research Journal* 9: 385-90

Boutwell, R C (1973) Anxiety interaction with task difficulty, memory, support, and estimated task complexity in a concept identification task. Paper read at American Educational Research Association, New Orleans

Bruner, J S, Goodnow, J J and Austin, G A (1956) *A Study of Thinking*. New York : Wiley

Clark, D C (1971) Teaching concepts in the classroom: a set of teaching prescriptions derived from experimental research, *Journal of Educational Psychology* 62: 253-78

Coldeway, D O (1974) A comparison of a high and a low avoidance contingency used in a programed, instructor-paced course in psychology. Unpublished doctoral dissertation, University of Illinois, Chicago

Englemann, S (1969) *Conceptual Learning*. San Rafael, California : Dimensions Press

Gagné, R M (1965) *The Conditions of Learning*. New York : Holt, Rinehart & Winston

Gagné, R M (1970) *The Conditions of Learning* (2nd ed). New York : Holt, Rinehart & Winston

Hively, W (1974) Domain-referenced testing: basic ideas, *Educational Technology* 14: 5-10

Johnson, D M and Stratton, R P (1966) Evaluation of five methods of teaching concepts, *Journal of Educational Psychology* 57: 48-53

Klausmeier, H J, Ghatala, E S and Frayer, D A (1974) *Conceptual Learning and Development: A Cognitive View*. New York : Academic Press

Landa, L N (1974) *Algorithmization in Learning and Instruction*. Englewood Cliffs, New Jersey : Educational Technology Publications

Markle, S M (1964) *Good Frames and Bad* (2nd ed 1969). New York : Wiley

Markle, S M and Tiemann, P W (1969) *Really Understanding Concepts: or in Frumious Pursuit of the Jabberwock*. Champaign, Illinois : Stipes

Markle, S M and Tiemann, P W (1970) Conceptual learning and instructional design, *British Journal of Educational Technology* 1: 52-62. Reprinted in M David Merrill (ed) (1971) *Instructional Design: Readings*, pp284-96 Englewood Cliffs, New Jersey : Prentice-Hall

Markle, S M and Tiemann, P W (1974) Some principles of instructional design at higher cognitive levels. In R Ulrich, T Stachnik and J Mabry (eds) *Control of Human Behavior (vol III* pp312-23). Glenview, Illinois : Scott, Foresman

Martin, H C and Ohmann, R M (1963) *The Logic and Rhetoric of Exposition*. New York : Holt, Rinehart & Winston

Merrill, M D (1971) Necessary psychological conditions for defining instructional outcomes. In M D Merrill (ed) *Instructional Design: Readings*, pp173-84. Englewood Cliffs, New Jersey : Prentice-Hall

Rothkopf, E Z (1972) Structural text features and the control of processes in learning from written materials. In J B Carroll and R O Freedle (eds) *Language Comprehension and the Acquisition of Knowledge*, pp315-35. New York : Wiley

Shumway, R J (1974) Negative instances in mathematical concept acquisition: transfer effects between the concepts of commutativity and associativity, *Journal for Research in Mathematics Education* November, 5: 197-211

Tennyson, R D, Woolley, F R and Merrill, M D (1972) Exemplar and nonexemplar variables which produce correct classification behavior and specified classification errors, *Journal of Educational Psychology* 63: 144-52

Webster's Third New International Dictionary (1961). Springfield, Massachusetts : Merriam Co

2.5 Fifty Guidelines for Improving Instructional Text

JAMES HARTLEY AND PETER BURNHILL

This paper first appeared in *Programmed Learning and Educational Technology* (1977) 14: 65-73. It has been updated for this volume.

In this paper we have drawn together from the more technical literature a number of guidelines which we hope will be useful to people preparing instructional text. Such guidelines are of most use if examples can be provided to illustrate the points being made but this of course is not fully practicable in a paper of this length. However, we have tried to practise what we preach and we have listed authors who provide further examples. Comprehensive bibliographies on this topic have been provided elsewhere (Macdonald-Ross & Smith, 1973, 1977) and an excellent summary paper describing problems created by words is that of Chapanis (1965). Readers are reminded here, however, that guidelines are not dogma to be followed but rather ideas to think about when preparing instructional text. Guidelines make general statements which must be treated with caution when applied to specific problems.

We have divided the guidelines into three areas: prose materials and related features; the layout of tables and graphs; and typographical design.

1. Prose materials

A clear concise title at the beginning of an article orientates the reader and affects subsequent recall (Dooling & Lachman, 1971; Kozminsky, 1977).

There are a number of ways of asking readers to do things *before* they start to read an article which help their subsequent understanding of the material. Summaries, overviews, pre-tests and advance organisers are examples of such different pre-instructional strategies. The similarity of and the differences between these different approaches have been compared and suggestions provided concerning their use (Hartley & Davies, 1976; Hartley *et al*, 1978).

Headings and sub-headings (ranged from the left), together with a systematic use of space, convey more readily the structure of complex text (Hartley, 1978). Sub-headings, or summary statements, placed in the left-hand margin can help the reader to scan and to select relevant material (Hartley & Burnhill, 1976).

Readers usually remember more from discursive text when the headings and sub-headings are written in the form of questions rather than in the form of statements (Robinson, 1961). Questions encourage people to examine what they are reading and to look for related facts and ideas.

Questions influence the depth of processing. Specific questions help people to remember specific cases: higher-order questions lead to the recall of generalisations which include specific cases (Rickards & DiVesta, 1974).

A question put at the start of a discourse often leads to specific learning. Questions embedded in the text but given after the relevant content sometimes lead to more general learning (Anderson & Biddle, 1975).

It is best to ask questions about one thing at a time. Wright and Barnard (1975) reported that questions such as 'Are you over 21 and under 65?' caused difficulties for many people over 65 who answered each part of the question in turn.

Short sentences are easier to understand than long ones.
This self-evident proposition is often forgotten.

There are roughly four kinds of sentence. The *simple* sentence has one subject and one predicate ('Textbook design is difficult'). The *compound* sentence has two simple sentences joined by a conjunction ('Textbook design is difficult and it is not easy to do it well'). The *complex* sentence has one principle statement and one or more subordinate statements or clauses which modify the main statement ('Textbook design, which is a skill, is difficult'). The *compound-complex* sentence has all its statements modified by one or more modifying statements ('Textbook design, which is a skill, is difficult and it is not easy to do it well because artistry is also involved').

All these sentences are clear, but simple sentences are the easiest to understand. This is because they contain less information.
The implication of this is *not* that all the sentences in instructional text should be simple ones, but that a balance between sentence styles should be achieved.

Nonetheless, few sentences should contain more than one or two subordinate clauses. The more subordinate clauses or modifying statements there are, the more difficult it is to understand a sentence (Miller, 1964; Wright & Barnard, 1975).

Consider, for example, this examination rubric which appeared in a GCE examination paper in 1977: 'Alternative C: Answer four questions including at least one from at least two sections (1) - (5).'

183

Sentences are easier to understand when they are written in the active rather than in the passive voice. (*Compare:* The staff will hold a meeting next week *with:* A meeting will be held by the staff next week.)

Similarly it is easier to understand sentences which are positive and assertive than sentences which are negative and passive. Writers are more easily understood if they use positive terms (more than, heavier than, thicker than) rather than negative ones (less than, lighter than, thinner than) (Davies, 1972; Wright & Barnard, 1975).

Research suggests that it is usually best to avoid negatives — especially double or treble ones (Wason, 1965). (*Compare* this example given by Evans (1972): 'The figures provide no indication that costs would have not been lower if competition had not been restricted.' *with:* 'The figures provide no indication that competition would have produced higher costs.')

Negative qualifications *can* be used, however, for making a particular emphasis, and for correcting misconceptions. Double-negatives in imperatives (eg Do not . . . unless . . .) are actually easier to understand than single ones (Wright & Barnard, 1975). Negatives, however, are often confusing. We once saw, for example, a label fixed to a machine in a school workshop which read: 'This machine is dangerous: it is not to be used only by the teacher'!

Familiar words are more easy to understand than complex words or technical terms which mean the same thing. One author on style quotes a letter-writer in *The Times* newspaper who had asked a government department how to get hold of a book. He was 'authorised to acquire the work in question by purchase through the ordinary trade channels' — in other words to 'buy it'. Concrete words and phrases are shorter and clearer than abstract ones.

If new terms are essential, then it is helpful to print them in italic or bold type, or underline them (in typescript) when they are first introduced into the text. The research on underlining suggests, however, that this often has little effect unless the reader is told in advance why certain things have been underlined (Christensen & Stordhal, 1955; Rickards & August, 1975; Foster & Coles, 1977).

Ambiguities and abbreviations, particularly strings of capital letters, should be avoided. Readers easily forget what technical abbreviations stand for.

It is easier to follow a sequence of events in a sentence if the sequence corresponds to the temporal order. (*Compare:* The powder must be placed in the machine and the lid closed before it is switched on *with:* Before the machine is switched on, the lid must be closed and the powder placed in it.)

By and large footnotes should be avoided.[1] Excess material can be placed in an Appendix, although of course, it may not then be read. Footnotes cause irritation to typists and to printers, and many publishers expressly forbid them. Certainly footnotes are often irritating to the reader because they seem so irresistible.[2]

When presenting numerical data, prose descriptions often seem less off-putting than the actual numbers. Everyday words which act as rough quantifiers, eg 'nearly half the group', are adequate for most purposes and seem to be handled with reasonable consistency by most people.

Goodwin *et al* (1977) suggest phrases which can be used with confidence. These are as follows:

Numerical value to be conveyed	Suitable form of words
above 85%	almost all of . . .
60% - 75%	rather more than half of . . .
40% - 50%	nearly half of . . .
15% - 35%	a part of . . .
under 10%	a very small part of . . .

The effects of age and context may be important here, however. In tests of children's behaviour (eg 'take a few/lot of beads from this tray') effects were found which were due to age and to the total number of beads available (Cohen, 1960).

Similarly, verbal descriptions of probabilities are probably less off-putting for most people than are actual statements of probability. It is likely that people are less consistent in their interpretation of verbal descriptions of probability than they are in their interpretations of verbal descriptions of quantity (Cohen, 1960).

If precision is required then actual quantities may be given with the verbal quantifier. Eg one can say 'nearly half the group — 43 per cent — said . . .' or 'there was a distinct chance ($p < .06$) that . . .'

Complex instructions, legal documents, or 'government prose' are difficult to understand when set out in prose form. Flow charts or decision tables may be more effective, but the optimal format depends upon the topic and the conditions of use. It has been suggested that flow charts are perhaps best for sorting out complex information, but that linked statements are best if the material has to be remembered (Davies, 1972; Wright & Reid, 1973; Blaiwes, 1974). Of course the reader must know in advance how to read a flow chart or table. Many do not.

[1] As shown here footnotes cause an interruption in the main flow of the author's thought, and in the reader's perception of it.

[2] Caught you! (With apologies to Bob Mager.)

A systematic approach which emphasises the design and layout of instructional materials is called information mapping[tm]. Horn's (1976) text gives detailed illustrations.

2. Tables and graphs

Tables vary in complexity and function (eg from a calendar to a logarithm table). In the presentation of a complex table there must be a full and direct presentation of all the information a user will need. The reader should not have to work out an answer from the figures provided (Wright & Fox, 1972).

Tables can be designed to present information clearly without the need for printers' rules. Horizontal rules can be used to help group information, but they should be used sparingly (Hartley, 1978).

With complex tables it is helpful to have:
☐ items arranged so that they are scanned vertically rather than horizontally;
☐ appropriate spacing within and between columns (ie with related pairs closer than unrelated ones) (Wright, 1968; Wright & Fox, 1972).

If the columns in a table are lengthy then use regular line spacing (about every five items) as this helps retrieval (Wright, 1968; Wright & Fox, 1972).

Class Number	Subject	Day	Time	Room
66913	Arc Welding	Fri	7 − 9	W23
66923	Arc Welding (Advanced)	Mon	7 − 9	W23
66933	Oxy-Acetylene Welding	Tues	7 − 9	W23
66943	Oxy-Acetylene Welding (Advanced)	Thurs	7 − 9	W23
66953	Farm Welding	Wed	7 − 9	W23
66963	Welding for Agricultural Engineers	Wed	5 − 7	W23
66973	Welding for Agricultural Engineers	Thurs	5 − 7	W23
66983	Oxy-Acetylene Welding	Fri	5 − 7	W23

class	day	time	room	subject
67103	Fri	7 − 9	W23	Arc Welding
67113	Mon	7 − 9	W23	Arc Welding (Advanced)
67123	Tues	7 − 9	W23	Oxy-Acetylene Welding
67133	Thurs	7 − 9	W23	Oxy-Acetylene Welding (Advanced)
67143	Wed	7 − 9	W23	Farm Welding
67153	Wed	5 − 7	W23	Welding for Agricultural Engineers
67163	Thurs	5 − 7	W23	Welding for Agricultural Engineers
67173	Fri	5 − 7	W23	Oxy-Acetylene Welding

Figure 1. *The initial and the revised layout for timetables in a college prospectus. By repositioning the subject column to the right, the table takes less time (and is thus cheaper) to typeset.*

If the table is wide and contains many columns, then place row headings both to the left and to the right to help comprehension (Wright, 1968; Wright & Fox, 1972).

If there are many rows and columns, then number or letter headings. However, if possible avoid the use of numerous columns and rows and consequent footnotes (Wright, 1968; Wright & Fox, 1972).

Left-ranging tables (ie tables in which items are not centred over one another but range from the left-hand margin) are easier to construct and quicker to type and to typeset. Such tables are no less comprehensible than tables arranged in the centred style (Burnhill *et al*, 1975; Hartley *et al*, 1975a).

Tables separated from their associated textual reference may cause the reader to lose track of an argument. The same is probably true for graphs and illustrations. Text matter and related illustrations should be consistently positioned relative to one another rather than 'balanced' for aesthetic effect (Whalley & Fleming, 1975; Burnhill *et al*, 1976).

Graphs, like tables, have many different functions. It is often thought that the simplest kinds of graphs, and the easiest to understand, are line graphs, and bar charts (Schutz, 1961; Feliciano *et al*, 1963). This assumption may be true, but it depends upon the type of information being sought. Line graphs are probably better than bar charts for showing trends.

If the aim of a graph is to compare different conditions then several lines can be plotted on the same graph. However, a large number of lines can be confusing, and it is probably best to separate them by typographic cues (eg different symbols) or to use separate graphs (Schutz, 1961).

Bar charts can be subdivided (eg a total score can be shown as a composite of a number of different subscores) but such compound bar charts can be confusing (Croxton & Stryker, 1929; Hawkins *et al*, 1975).

Pie charts are said to be easy to understand but they can be misleading (Croxton & Stryker, 1929). It is difficult to judge proportions accurately when segments are small. It is also difficult to put in the lettering clearly. Pie charts give a general impression of quantitative relationships but, compared with bar charts, subtle differences are more difficult to detect. This is because bar charts are based on multiples of a square module or a regular unit of two-dimensional space so that quantitative differences are more easily seen. Pie charts are also difficult to understand if charts with different diameters are being compared (Hawkins *et al*, 1975). One possible reason for this is that in order to make a circle (or square) look twice as large as another, the large one has to be drawn almost four times the size of the small one.

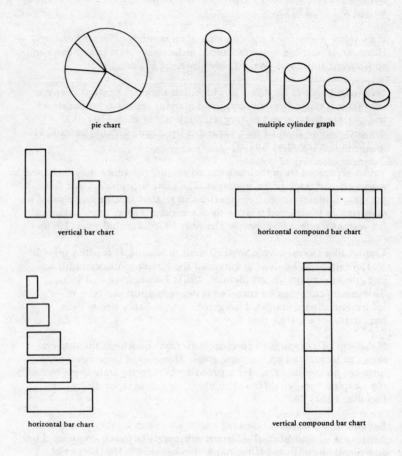

Figure 2. *Some different ways of presenting the same information*

For the same general reason, when the task of the reader is to estimate percentages and quantities, bar charts are a better method of presentation than are cross-sectional drawings of three-dimensional objects such as spheres, cubes, and blocks of columns (Dickinson, 1973; Hawkins *et al*, 1975).

Factors which inhibit the legibility of graphical aids are:
☐ reversed lettering (ie white letters on a black, or dark, background);
☐ show-through (ie the appearance on the page of the image of lines or drawings printed on the reverse side);
☐ words set at an angle to the horizontal;
☐ haphazardly arranged lines connecting labels to reference points;
☐ unprincipled variety of type-sizes and styles;
☐ functionless use of colour.

If the author knows in advance the page size of the final product, then this helps in the choice of suitably sized illustrations and graphic materials.

An excellent summary paper discussing the whole problem of presenting quantitative information in text is that by Macdonald-Ross (1977). This paper is particularly important because of the attention it gives to Otto Neurath's 'Isotype' system — a technique of graphic presentation not widely known (see Neurath, 1974).

3. Typographical design

The page size of text should conform to the sizes recommended jointly by the British Standards Institution and the International Organisation for Standardisation. Of these sizes, A4 (210 x 297 mm) and A5 (148 x 210 mm) are most commonly used.

The standard is rooted in the principle that a rectangle with sides in the ratio of 1 : 1.414 (1 : $\sqrt{2}$) may be halved or doubled without changing the ratio of width to depth. This ratio is also recommended for formats associated with overhead transparencies, slides and microfiche systems. In this way, the standard has implications not only for the economics of design, editing, specification, production, storage and use, but also for interchanging information between one method of presentation and another (Hartley, 1978).

The legibility of printed matter is a function not only of the clarity with which the characters are printed but also of the spacing of the material (see Figure 3). Word spacing should normally be no wider than the space required by a lower-case letter i; that is, about 0.25 of the type-size. Line spacing — the perpendicular distance from the base line of one line to the base line of the next line — should normally be greater than the specified type-size; say, 1.25 of the type-size. The relationship between word spacing and line spacing should be consistent throughout the text, otherwise the print will appear to be moving about on the paper (Hartley, 1978).

educational
educational

Figure 3. *Transfer lettering is frequently used in the preparation of artwork for instructional text. Although apparently easy to apply, great care needs to be used to ensure the proper spacing of character groups. The current fashion for very close character spacing does not aid legibility, especially when the information has to be taken in at a quick glance*

Legibility is impaired when the printer causes the word spacing to be changed from line to line in order to force out the lines to a fixed length ('justified' text). This practice is usually accompanied by the breaking and hyphenation of words at line ends in an attempt to minimise the spatial disorder brought about by the 'justification' of the lines. Erratic word spacing and the breaking of words at line ends is not only unnecessary but it also increases the cost of type-setting. Making corrections to justified text is much more costly. (Macdonald-Ross and Waller [1975], for example, estimate that authors' corrections to justified text in 1973 cost the Open University £22,000 or 6.3 per cent of the total print cost, and that this would be much reduced by the use of unjustified text.)

When text is required to be set unjustified, a fixed space (mid-space) should be specified for word spacing. This paper is set in unjustified text.

Another advantage of unjustified text is that the printer need not end a line with the first word of a new sentence. In short, the sense of the text can dominate line-length, rather than the size of the type.

It is difficult to recommend particular type-sizes without referring to specific type-faces because the different measurement systems used in typography conflict, and the designated type-size of a particular type-face does not specify the actual size of the printed image (Hartley, 1978). In general, however, a good all-purpose size is 10 point type on a 12 point line to line feed: 8 point on 10 point is possibly about as small as one would want to go in the design of instructional materials.

It is important to note that the larger the type-size the fewer the number of words per given line length. Large type-sizes (and/or short line lengths) can cause some problems — see Figure 4.

YOUR MANY ROLES IN LEADING DISCUSSIONS ...

Initiating	suggesting new ideas or new ways of looking at what you're discussing.
Seeking Information	asking for relevant facts or authoritative information on a subject.
Giving Information	supplying relevant facts or relating personal experiences.
Giving Opinions	stating an opinion about something the class is considering; perhaps challenging consensus or complacency.
Clarifying	restating something that someone has said. Translating a poorly worded statement into a clear one.
Elaborating	building on previous comments, giving examples.

YOUR MANY ROLES IN LEADING DISCUSSIONS ...

Initiating	suggesting new ideas or new ways of looking at what you're discussing.
Seeking Information	asking for relevant facts or authoritative information on a subject.
Giving Information	supplying relevant facts or relating personal experiences.
Giving Opinions	stating an opinion about something the class is considering; perhaps challenging consensus or complacency.
Clarifying	restating something that someone has said. Translating a poorly worded statement into a clear one.
Elaborating	building on previous comments, giving examples.

Figure 4. *A smaller type-size (but with the same line length) allows more words per line. This may be helpful when using narrow columns and complex text*

For this reason a two-column structure is probably better than a three-column structure for straightforward prose printed on an A4 page. In our opinion a three-column structure on A4 leads to line lengths which are too short.

A single-column structure on A4 is probably better than a two-column structure for text which is continually broken by tables, diagrams, graphs, etc, provided that paragraphs in the text are separated by a line space (Burnhill *et al*, 1976).

The underlying structure of the text is more readily seen when paragraphs are identified by the use of line space rather than indention of the first line. Indention especially impedes the recognition of structure when each paragraph contains no more than a line or two of text (Hartley, 1978). For the purpose of illustration, we have used consistent line spacing between paragraphs in this paper.

Capital letters should be reserved for the initial letter or letters of proper nouns and for the first letter of a sentence or a heading. Words are identified most rapidly when composed of lower-case characters. Capital letters occupy more lateral space than lower-case characters of the same type-size. For this reason lower-case letters (set in bold face if necessary) are better for headings and sub-headings than are long strings of capital or italic letters.

Using colour as a typographic cue is often unnecessary. The excessive use of colour can cause problems for the reader. Colour should be used sparingly and consistently, and its function explained to the learner. There is no need to use colour on every page simply because it is technically possible to do so. No colour has the contrast value of black on white.

Typographic style should be consistent throughout a text. Recommended practice is set out in detail in British Standard 5261; Parts 1 and 2, 1976, *Copy Preparation and Proof Correction*. The use of this standard should help to overcome the confusion caused by publishers and printers having differing house styles. Other relevant British Standards are listed at the end of this paper.

4. A concluding remark

There is one overall guideline which is applicable to *all* instructional text. This is that initial versions need to be tried out with samples of the target population for whom they are intended and revised on the basis of results obtained. This should be done before the material is finally committed to publication. One cannot assume just because one has, for example, constructed a graph, that the point being made is now automatically understood by the learner. The effectiveness of a graph — and anything else — needs to be tested. This article itself has been revised several times on the basis of readers' comments.

Acknowledgement

The paper was prepared with the financial assistance of the Social Science Research Council.

References

Anderson, R C and Biddle, W B (1975) On asking people questions about what they are reading. In G H Bower (ed) *The Psychology of Learning and Motivation* (Vol 9). New York : Academic Press, pp89-132

Blaiwes, A S (1974) Formats for presenting procedural instructions, *Journal of Applied Psychology* 59: 683-6

Burnhill, P, Hartley, J, Young, M and Fraser, S (1975) The typography of college prospectuses: a critique and a case history. In L Evans and J Leedham (eds) *Aspects of Educational Technology IX.* London : Kogan Page

Burnhill, P, Hartley, J and Young, M (1976) Tables in text, *Applied Ergonomics* 7 1: 13-18

Chapanis, A(1965) Words, words, words, *Human Factors* 7 1: 1-17

Christensen, C M and Stordahl, K E (1955) The effect of organisational aids on comprehension and retention, *Journal of Educational Psychology* 46 2: 65-74

Cohen, J (1960) *Chance, Skill and Luck.* Harmondsworth : Penguin

Croxton, F and Stryker, R E (1929) Barcharts versus circle diagrams, *Journal of the American Statistical Association* 22: 473-82

Davies, I K (1972) Presentation strategies. In J Hartley (ed) *Strategies for Programmed Instruction.* London : Butterworths

Dickinson, G C (1973) *Statistical Mapping and the Presentation of Statistics.* London : Arnold

Dooling, D J and Lachman, R (1971) Effects of comprehension on the retention of prose, *Journal of Experimental Psychology* 88: 216-22

Evans, H (ed) (1972) *Editing and Design* (Vol 1). London : Heinemann

Feliciano, G D, Powers, R D and Kearl, B E (1963) The presentation of statistical information, *Audio-Visual Communication Review* II 3: 32-9

Foster, J J and Coles, P (1977) An experimental study of typographic cueing in printed text, *Ergonomics* 20 1: 57-66

Goodwin, A R, Thomas, S K and Hartley, J (1977) Are some parts larger than others : quantifying Hammerton's qualifiers, *Applied Ergonomics* 8 2: 93-5

Hartley, J (1978) *Designing Instructional Text.* London : Kogan Page and New York : Nichols

Hartley, J and Burnhill, P (1976) Explorations in space, *Bulletin of the British Psychological Society* 29: 97-107

Hartley, J and Davies, I K (1976) Pre-instructional strategies: the role of pre-tests, behavioral objectives, overviews and advance organisers, *Review of Educational Research* 46 2: 239-65

Hartley, J, Goldie, M and Steen, L (1978) The role and position of summaries: some issues and data. (Paper available from the authors, Department of Psychology, University of Keele.)

Horn, R E (1976) *How to Write Information Mapping.* Lexington, Mass 02173 : Information Resources Inc, PO Box 417

Kozminsky, E (1977) Altering comprehension: the effect of biasing titles on text comprehension, *Memory and Cognition* 5 4: 482-90

Macdonald-Ross, M (1977) How numbers are shown: a review of the research on the presentation of quantitative data, *Audio-Visual Communication Review* 25 4: 359-409

Macdonald-Ross, M and Smith, E B (1973) *Bibliography for Textual Communication.* Institute of Educational Technology, Open University

Macdonald-Ross, M and Smith, E B (1977) *Graphics in Text: A Bibliography.*
Institute of Educational Technology, Open University
Macdonald-Ross, M and Waller, R (1975) *Open University Texts: Criticism and Alternatives.* Institute of Educational Technology, Open University
Miller, G A (1964) The psycholinguists, *Encounter* 23 1: 29-37
Neurath, M (1974) Isotype, *Instructional Science* 3 2: 127-50
Rickards, J P and August, G J (1975) Generative underlining strategies in prose recall, *Journal of Educational Psychology* 67 6: 860-5
Rickards, J P and DiVesta, F J (1974) Type and frequency of questions in processing textual material, *Journal of Educational Psychology* 66: 354-62
Robinson, F (1961) *Effective Study.* New York : Harper & Row
Schutz, H G (1961) An evaluation of formats for graphic trend displays, *Human Factors:* 99-107, 108-9
Wason, P (1965) The contexts of plausible denial, *Journal of Verbal Learning and Verbal Behaviour* 4: 7-11
Whalley, P and Fleming, R (1975) An experiment with a simple reading recorder, *Programmed Learning and Educational Technology* 12 2: 120-4
Wright, P (1968) Using tabulated information, *Ergonomics* 11: 331-43
Wright, P and Barnard, P (1975) Just fill in this form: a review for designers, *Applied Ergonomics* 6 4: 213-20
Wright, P and Fox, K (1972) Explicit and implicit tabulation formats, *Ergonomics* 15: 175-87
Wright, P and Reid, L (1973) Written information: some alternatives to prose for expressing the outcomes of complex contingencies, *Journal of Applied Psychology* 57 2: 160-6

Appendix

British Standard Documents

BS 1991 : 1964	Glossary of letterpress rotary printing terms
BS 3203 : 1964	Glossary of paper, stationery and allied terms
BS 2961 : 1967	Typeface nomenclature and classification
BS 4149 : 1967	Glossary of paper/ink terms for letterpress printing
BS 4189 : 1967	Conventional typographic character(s) for legibility tests
BS 1991 : 1967	Letter symbols, signs and abbreviations
BS 4160 : 1967	Inks for letterpress three — or four — colour printing
BS 4000 : 1968	Sizes of papers and boards
BS 4277 : 1968	Glossary of terms used in offset lithographic printing
BS 1413 : 1970	Specification for paper-sizes for books
BS 4786 : 1972	Specification for metric typographic measurement
BS 4187 : 1973	Parts 1 & 2. Specification for microfiche
BS 3700 : 1976	The preparation of indexes to books, periodicals and other publications
BS 5261 : 1976	Parts 1 & 2. Copy preparation and proof correction

2.6 Decision Making in Instructional Design

BERNARD T DODD, R J G LEHUNTE AND C SHEPPARD

Dodd, B T, LeHunte, R J G and Sheppard, C (1975) Decision making
in instructional design. In J P Baggaley *et al* (eds) *Aspects of
Educational Technology VIII.* London : Kogan Page. Reproduced
with permission of the authors, editors and publisher.

Introduction

A technology can be said to exist if there is an organised body of
knowledge which is useful to those who are engaged in some practical
endeavour in the fields of education and training. In instructional design
there is a large body of knowledge available, and there are a number of
established practices and techniques. However, we question whether
this knowledge constitutes a technology, since it provides hardly any
contribution to the decision-making structure in instructional design.

In their report *Programmed Instruction in the British Armed Forces*
(1966), Wallis, Duncan and Knight commented:

> The intensive research on PI, and its many fields of application, has given
> rise recently to the wider concept of a 'technology of training'. Some of
> the component tools of this technology are already well developed.
> Others are primitive by comparison. We have noted that an adequate
> realisation of the concept entails a taxonomy of training tasks or
> objectives, and a classification of training techniques, each of them
> founded upon an acceptable psychological basis. Neither exists at
> the present time, however, and their construction presents an
> immediate research requirement.

This paper describes a research project currently being undertaken by
the Admiralty Research Laboratory (Applied Psychology Unit) in
conjunction with Inbucon Learning Systems Limited. The aim of this
project is to define the relationships between analysis and instruction —
encompassing not only the selection of training techniques, but all
decisions made in the instructional design process. The basic premise of
the project is that the ability to design instructional systems (making
best use of human and other resources) is at root a rational activity, so
there must be at least one algorithm which expresses this.

In order to define a decision-making structure we have adopted the
following approach:

(1) define decisions made in instructional design;
(2) establish those criteria which influence decisions, including task
features, learner characteristics and practical constraints;
(3) develop rules to link input criteria with recommendations.

A system has been established providing recommendations for some fifty instructional design decisions. The scale and complexity of the decision-making structure has necessitated the use of a computer to process data.

A literature search has been carried out throughout the project. This has revealed that there are many systems of classification in existence for examining task features or ability requirements, and the American Institute for Research project on *The Development of a Taxonomy of Human Performance,* under Fleishman, provides a great deal of fundamental material towards this end. However, most such classification systems are 'open-ended', without following through to instructional design decisions. There are very few published papers which explicitly recommend algorithms for one or more instructional design decisions, although Davies (1969) and the ITRU publication on *CRAMP* provide processes for selecting instruction methods on the basis of the task to be learned.

Defining instructional design decisions

Many schematic diagrams of the instructional design process have been produced. Their common feature is to show the process as a series, or cycle of neat discrete stages, albeit with feedback between some of the stages. In practice the process consists of a succession of approximations, starting with a gross declaration of intent, and moving through to a precise definition of the instruction requirement.

One fundamental feature which the schematics do not illustrate is that there are a large number of decisions in instructional design. Consider, for the first two stages alone of a schematic, that there are over ten decisions to be made (Figure 1).

In all there are some fifty instructional design decisions. The majority of these decisions are made by the designer, but some may be made by the customer, the designer's supervisor or the instructor. For example, the decision on instructor:learner ratio is often predetermined to comply with administrative requirements, irrespective of what is desirable for a particular activity to be learned, or a particular type of learner.

Figure 2 shows the main categories of decisions, with illustrations. In each of the illustrations the designer has a number of choices. For example, the choice of instruction methods and materials can include:

Objectives with resource access
Demonstration and practice with learner question sheet
Demonstration and practice with instruction plan
Discussion with discussion pointer sheet
Self-study, information sheets
Self-study, programmed instruction
Coaching
Exposure
Controlled exposure
Graduated exercises
Lecture with guide notes
Objectives only (conduct of session left to instructor)

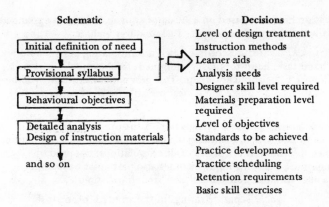

Figure 1

Decision category	Illustrations
Instruction output	What level of objective action should be achieved through instruction?
Design	What depth of design treatment should be undertaken?
Instruction	What instruction methods and materials best meet the need?
Practice	What types of practice should the learner carry out?
Installation and operation	What 'maintenance' actions are required to ensure continued effective operation of the instruction scheme?
Organisation	What is the preferred staff:learner ratio for this instruction?

Figure 2

This set of choices, together with the choice of practice methods and presentation media, gives a large number of possible permutations. In view of the large choice, and the fact that designers base most of their decisions on 'experience', there is a high risk of poor selection. This risk is compounded by the fact that the person commissioning or attempting to evaluate the instruction scheme may have no reliable yardsticks with which to assess the suitability of choice.

Criteria for decisions

Instructional design decisions are based on three types of input factor — task features, learner characteristics and practical constraints.

During the research project a set of those tasks features which contribute to design decisions has been developed. The initial

classification has been based on a study of seaman tasks, and expanded
to suit a wider range of task types. Task features include:

Nature of task: a short descriptive label, discriminating between body
action, hand task, hand tool task, equipment task, symbolic rote task,
symbolic task-rules application, etc. This group of descriptions will be
expanded to accommodate the widest possible range of activities to
be learned.

Shape of behaviour pattern: recognition of the predominant pattern of
behaviour to be learned, including the categories chain, discrimination,
chain with discriminations, series of discriminations, pyramid of
discriminations, etc. This input includes also particular behaviour
features like 'stimulus continuum' and 'undefined stimuli'.

Cueing and feedback: separate ratings of the strength of intrinsic
cueing and intrinsic feedback in the task.

Task size: an accurate count, or estimate of the number of separate
responses in chain behaviours, and different stimuli in discriminations.

Frequency: a measure of the frequency of occurrence of the task in the
'post-instruction' situation.

Situation constraints: recognition of any constraints on task
performance, such as variable quality of task stimuli, variable quality
of environmental stimuli, personal hazard.

Likely complex elements: definition, and difficulty rating, of individual
task elements which learners are likely to find difficult, such as high
work load, need for extraordinary use of senses, consequence
interaction of elements, competing behaviours. This list is still being
developed and there is a need to define typical difficult elements as
comparators for rating.

Family grouping: a cross-referencing activity between tasks under
scrutiny, and tasks previously learned, to show groupings of like tasks,
like sub-skills, like difficult elements, and like generalised behaviours.

At present, the breakdown of task features possibly includes too
much detail, since some of the inputs overlap. Also, some of these inputs
call for interpretation (eg shape of behaviour pattern) or assessment (eg
difficulty rating of complex elements). These inputs will be refined
when a data bank of processed tasks has been developed, and it will be
possible to complete the inputs at different levels of detail.

In addition to task features, input information of learner
characteristics and practical constraints will include the characteristics
shown in Figure 3.

For the instructional design practitioner it is the practical constraints
which usually prove to be the dominant influence in design decisions.
For example, the complexity of a particular task may point to a
design approach which includes detailed analysis, but this can be
overridden if there is a very tight time constraint on design time.

Learner characteristics	Learner motivation Pre-ability range Learning capability range Self-starting ability Responsibility Literacy
Practical constraints	Design time available Job facilities/funds available Numbers to be trained Stability of task Instructor skill level Learner availability Instructor motivation Instruction time available Skill of instructional designers Intended life of instruction scheme

Figure 3

DECISION-MAKING RATIONALE

A set of rules (translator) has been defined to link input information with decision outputs.

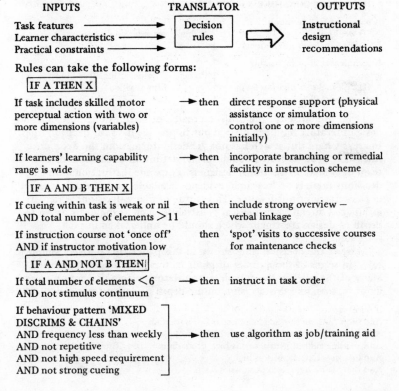

INPUTS	TRANSLATOR	OUTPUTS
Task features ⟶ Learner characteristics ⟶ Practical constraints ⟶	Decision rules ⟹	Instructional design recommendations

Rules can take the following forms:

IF A THEN X

If task includes skilled motor perceptual action with two or more dimensions (variables) → then direct response support (physical assistance or simulation to control one or more dimensions initially)

If learners' learning capability range is wide → then incorporate branching or remedial facility in instruction scheme

IF A AND B THEN X

If cueing within task is weak or nil AND total number of elements >11 → then include strong overview — verbal linkage

If instruction course not 'once off' AND if instructor motivation low then 'spot' visits to successive courses for maintenance checks

IF A AND NOT B THEN

If total number of elements <6 AND not stimulus continuum → then instruct in task order

If behaviour pattern 'MIXED DISCRIMS & CHAINS' AND frequency less than weekly AND not repetitive AND not high speed requirement AND not strong cueing → then use algorithm as job/training aid

---

ALWAYS X UNLESS A THEN Y

Always	⟶	instruct to task performance objective
Unless		
No job facilities/funds available AND no like facilities available	⟶ then	enabling ('knowing how to') objective
Member of family group of 3 or more like tasks	⟶ then	instruct to task performance objective and inter-task transfer level (ability to perform like tasks through transfer plus application
etc		of basic principles)

IF A THEN X OR Y

If learner responsibility high AND learner motivation low AND learner initiative low	⟶ then	apply status reward reinforcer or material reward reinforcer
If task member of family group (like task previously learned) AND no personal hazard AND no high level (>7) complex element	⟶ then	self-study, information sheets or exposure or controlled exposure

IF A THEN CONSIDER X

If nature of task 'symbolic rote' AND weak/nil cueing AND total number of elements >6	⟶ then	consider mediation
If technical skill of instructors is low AND task includes high/medium level motor skill	⟶ then	consider using closed loop film or video

From the outset of the project a search of instructional research and design literature has been carried out to provide data for decision rules. In areas where this search has not yielded information, the decision rules have been derived through formal definition of the actions of a team of skilled instructional designers. For some instructional design decisions there is no 'research' evidence available, and research is either not necessary or not feasible. This is true of many decisions which are influenced directly by practical constraints, such as the decision on the depth of design treatment which should be undertaken in each situation.

Most of the decision rules shown in this paper are relatively simple rules, in terms of the number of input factors affecting each decision. Many of the rules in the complete 'translator' system depend on several input factors, like this decision on the depth of design treatment:

If numbers to be instructed <30 And life of instruction scheme once off or uncertain And technical skill of instructors is high And training skill of instructors is high or medium And instructor availability is high And there is no high level personal hazard	Then first level instructional design only (training

And there are no high level complex elements And there is no high speed requirement And trainee availability is not a constraint	spec + plan, + objectives and exercises + control system)

Applying the decision rules

A system has been developed, using a computer, to enable instructional designers to apply the decision rules to tasks they are considering. The stages of operating the system are as follows:

COLLECT & CLASSIFY DATA   Information is collected about each task to be learned, the learners, and any practical constraints. An input form is completed for learner characteristics and constraints, while separate task input forms are completed for each task (or for one task out of each family group).

Some of the information is used in its 'raw' form, but certain factors require classification or assessment:

Nature of task	— selecting a label from a given list
Shape of behaviour pattern	— identifying the shape in accordance with given definitions
Likely complex elements	— assessing the difficulty of elements, using a 1 - 10 scale
Learner characteristics	— applying a 3-point scale to each characteristic, to show how pronounced it is
Practical constraints	— applying a 3-point scale to each constraint, to indicate its severity.

INPUT TO COMPUTER   The information on input forms is coded and fed into a computer terminal. The computer applies the decision rules, and prints out recommendations.

INTERPRET COMPUTER OUTPUT   The computer prints out a list, showing one or more recommendations under each decision. Figure 4 shows a typical print-out extract:

2.1 PRACTICE METHOD	
TASK PRACTICE	RULE 3
COVERT PRACTICE – MENTAL REHEARSAL	RULE 25
UNLESS LENGTHY PRACTICE TO PERFORMANCE STD	
2.2 PRACTICE DEVELOPMENT	
WHOLE TASK PRACTICE ONLY	RULE 32
	127
2.3 PRACTICE QUALITY STANDARDS	
END PERFORMANCE QUALITY STD THROUGHOUT	RULE 35

Figure 4

The print-out states:

Output recommendation: in this example the recommended form of practice is practice in the task itself, supported by mental rehearsal.

Recommendation riders: some recommendations may carry a qualifying statement, like the 'mental rehearsal' rider above. Riders are included wherever there is a limitation or exception in particular circumstances.

Rule references: each recommendation includes code references of the rules used, so that the instructional designer can check the rules if he wishes.

Future development plans

The system described in this paper is at an early stage of development. It is currently undergoing 'proving' trials, to assess the recommendations for a number of tasks and different training situations. Proposed future developments include:

1. Practical trials. In proving trials the system will be applied to tasks which selected instructional designers are currently considering (or for which instruction already exists). These trials have two aims:

(i) to build a 'data bank' of tasks, giving body to the system;
(ii) to assess the value and practicality of the system, identifying skills required to use the system and areas of training need for users.

2. Extending system capability. At present the system can accommodate motor perceptual activities and relatively low-level cognitive activities. It requires further development to provide complete sets of recommendations for the broadest possible range of tasks (and possibly for 'subject matters' as well).

3. Task classification development. Within the system classifications are used for:

nature of task
shape of behaviour pattern
likely complex elements.

These classifications require expansion and refinement in order to provide comprehensive coverage.

4. Producing a manual version of the system. A manual version of the decision-making system will be produced, either in full detail or in simplified form. Recommendations will be made for the use of this information in the training of instructional design staff and evaluators.

Bibliography

Many publications, and personal contributions through discussion, have acted as sources for the ideas which are now expressed by the rule set of TRANSLATOR 6 (current version of the system). The following list shows key sources and also indicates those which are currently influencing the development of the system.

* These items describe detailed sub-systems which will be built into TRANSLATOR where the need for finer analysis is established.

† These items indicate ways in which the general methodology may be further developed in future work.

Annett, J, Duncan, K D, Stammers, R B and Gray, M J (1971) *Task Analysis.* London : HMSO †

Bernstein, B R and Gonzalas, B K *Learning, Retention and Transfer.* Minneapolis : Honeywell Inc

Bloom, B S (ed) (1956) *Taxonomy of Educational Objectives.* New York : David McKay

Carden, G R (1970) *An Evaluation of the Effects of Repetition of Written Examples.* Texas : A & M Univ, Department of Industrial Training

Chambers, A N (1969) *Development of a Taxonomy of Human Performance — a Heuristic Model for the Development of Classification Systems.* Pittsburgh : AIR †

Chesler, D J (1972) *Application and Utilization of Training Aids and Devices.* San Diego, California : Naval Personnel and Training Research Laboratory

Clark, M C (1972) *Aspects of Transfer that Relate to the Development and Design of Instructional Materials.* Arizona State University, Instructional Resources Laboratory

Davies, I K (1969) Structure and strategy — instructional decision-making, *RAF School of Education Bulletin* Autumn, 6: 48-54

Dodd, B T (1965) *Teaching/Learning Strategies.* Sheffield University : Programmed Instruction Centre for Industry

Dunn, T G and Hansen, D (1972) *Learning by Graphics.* Florida : State University, CAI Center

Engel, J D (1970) An approach to standardizing human performance assessment, *HumRRO Professional Paper:* 26-70

Farina, A J and Wheaton, G R (1971) *Development of a Taxonomy of Human Performance — a Task Characteristics Approach to Performance Prediction.* Pittsburgh : AIR *

Foley, J F Jr (1969) *Job Performance Aids Research: Summary and Recommendations.* Wright-Patterson AFB : AF Human Resources Laboratory *

Gagné, R M (1965) *The Conditions of Learning.* New York : Holt, Rinehart & Winston

Gilbert, T F (1962) *Mathetics: The Technology of Education* (reissued). London : Longman

Holt, J (1964) *How Children Fail.* London : Pelican

Hunter, H G *et al* (1969) The process of developing and improving course content for military technical training, *HumRRO Technical Report:* 69-9

Jeantheau, G G (1971) *A Study of Training Device Support Materials.* Darien, Connecticut : Dunlap & Associates

Martin, E (1973) *Serial Learning Theory.* Michigan : Ann Arbor Human Performance Center †

Miller, E E (1963) *A Classification of Learning Tasks in Conventional Language.* Aerospace Medical Research Laboratories: TDR-63-74

Miller, R B (1971) *Development of a Taxonomy of Human Performance — a User-oriented Approach to the Development of Task Taxonomies.* Pittsburgh : AIR

Norman, D A and Lowes, A L (1972) *Adaptive Training of Manual Control.* Fort Worth, Texas : Naval Training Devices Center

Pearn, M, Belbin, M and Toye, M (1972) *CRAMP: A Guide to Training Decisions.* Cambridge : Industrial Training Research Unit

Resnick, L B and Wang, M C (1969) *Approaches to the Validation of Learning Hierarchies.* Pittsburgh University : Learning Research and Development Center †

Seidel *et al* (1968) *A General Systems Approach to the Development and Maintenance of Optimal Learning Conditions,* Professional Paper 1-68. George Washington University

Smith, R G (1966) The design of instructional systems, *HumRRO : Technical Report:* 66-18

Smith, R L *et al* (1972) *Job Behaviour Analysis Manual.* Los Angeles : Mentec Corporation *

Smode, A F (1971) *Human Factors Inputs to the Training Device Design Process.* Darien, Connecticut : Dunlap & Associates *

Stolurow, L M (1964) *A Taxonomy of Learning Task Characteristics.* Aerospace Medical Research Laboratories: TDR-64-2

Taylor, C L (1972) *Response Factors and Selective Attention in Learning from Instruction.* Arizona State University : AFHRL

Teichner, W H (1971) *Development of a Taxonomy of Human Performance — an Information-theoretic Approach.* Pittsburgh : AIR †

Wallis, D, Duncan, K D and Knight, M A G (1966) *Programmed Instruction in the British Armed Forces.* London : HMSO

Wheaton, G R and Mirabella, A (1972) *Effects of Task Index Variations on Training Effectiveness Criteria.* Orlando, Florida : Naval Training Equipment Center †

Yagi, K, Bialeck, H M, Taylor, J E and Garman, M (1971) The design and evaluation of vocational technical job analysis, *HumRRO : Technical Report:* 71-15 *

2.7 Evaluation as Illumination

MALCOLM PARLETT AND DAVID HAMILTON

Parlett, M and Hamilton, D (1972) Evaluation as illumination: a new approach to the study of innovatory programs. Occasional paper No 9, University of Edinburgh : Centre for Research in the Educational Sciences. Reproduced with permission of the authors.

Innovation is now a major educational priority. For nearly two decades it has expanded and proliferated. It absorbs increasing sums of public and private money. Its impact is felt throughout the world. Curricula are restructured, new devices introduced, forms of teaching permutated. But decisions to change are more than educational: questions of politics, ideology, fashion and finance also intervene.

More recently — to aid decision making — innovation has been joined by evaluation. Increasingly, committees and foundations fund evaluation studies as an integral part of innovation programmes. Like innovation itself, evaluation has rapidly developed a legitimacy and importance of its own: professional journals have been launched and research centres established. The 'evaluator' has emerged as a new and influential figure. In short, both innovation and evaluation have become 'big science'.

As a new field, programme evaluation has encountered a wide range of problems, both theoretical and methodological. Current concerns include the 'roles' of evaluation; the neutrality of the evaluator; the value of classroom observation; the function of 'formative' evaluation; the use of 'objectives'; and the value of long-term studies. Confusion is engendered as rival proposals, models and terminologies are voiced and then rapidly countered. As a developing field of study, evaluation proceeds in the absence of coherent or agreed frames of reference.

More generally within educational research two distinct paradigms can be discerned. Each has its own strategies, foci and assumptions. Dominant is the 'classical' or 'agricultural-botany' paradigm, which utilises a hypothetico-deductive methodology derived from the experimental and mental-testing traditions in psychology. Almost all evaluation studies have resided within this traditional paradigm.

More recently, a small number of empirical studies have been conceived outside the agricultural-botany framework, and relate instead to social anthropology, psychiatry, and participant observation research in sociology. Such research can be thought of as representing a second and contrasting paradigm, with a fundamentally different research style and methodology from that of mainstream educational research. We outline here an approach to evaluation that belongs to this alternative, or 'social anthropology' paradigm.

Traditional evaluation and the agricultural-botany paradigm

The most common form of agricultural-botany type evaluation is presented as an assessment of the effectiveness of an innovation by examining whether or not it has reached required standards on pre-specified criteria. Students — rather like plant crops — are given pre-tests (the seedlings are weighed or measured) and then submitted to different experiences (treatment conditions). Subsequently, after a period of time, their attainment (growth or yield) is measured to indicate the relative efficiency of the methods (fertilisers) used. Studies of this kind are designed to yield data of one particular type, ie 'objective' numerical data that permit statistical analyses. Isolated variables like IQ, social class, test scores, personality profiles and attitude ratings are codified and processed to indicate the efficiency of new curricula, media or methods.

Recently, however, there has been increasing resistance to evaluations of this type. The more notable shortcomings may be briefly summarised as follows:

1. Educational situations are characterised by numerous relevant parameters. Within the terms of the agricultural-botany paradigm these must be randomised using very large samples; or otherwise strictly controlled. The former approach entails a major data collection exercise and is expensive in time and resources. It also runs counter to the need, widely acknowledged, for evaluation before large-scale application rather than after it. The latter procedure — of strict control — is rarely followed. To attempt to simulate laboratory conditions by 'manipulating educational personnel' is not only dubious ethically, but also leads to gross administrative and personal inconvenience. Even if a situation could be so unnervingly controlled, its artificiality would render the exercise irrelevant; rarely can 'tidy' results be generalised to an 'untidy' reality. Whichever approach is used, there is a tendency for the investigator to think in terms of 'parameters' and 'factors' rather than 'individuals' and 'institutions'. Again, this divorces the study from the real world.

2. Before-and-after research designs assume that innovatory programmes undergo little or no change during the period of study. This built-in premise is rarely upheld in practice. Yet it remains fundamental to the design, constraining the researchers from adapting to the changed circumstances that so frequently arise. It may even have a deleterious effect on the programme itself, by discouraging new developments and redefinitions mid-stream. Longitudinal studies, for these reasons, rarely can serve an effective 'formative' or cybernetic function.

3. The methods used in traditional evaluations impose artificial and arbitrary restrictions on the scope of the study. For instance, the concentration on seeking quantitative information by objective means can lead to neglect of other data, perhaps more salient to the innovation, but disregarded as being 'subjective', 'anecdotal' or 'impressionistic'. However, the evaluator is likely to be

forced to utilise information of this sort if he is satisfactorily to explain his findings, weigh their importance and place them in context.

4. Research of this type, by employing large samples and seeking statistical generalisations, tends to be insensitive to local perturbations and unusual effects. Atypical results are seldom studied in detail. Despite their significance for the innovation, or possible importance to the individuals and institutions concerned, they are ironed out and lost to discussion.

5. Finally, this type of evaluation often fails to articulate the varied concerns and questions of participants, sponsors, and other interested parties. Since classical evaluators believe in an 'objective truth' equally relevant to all parties, their studies rarely acknowledge the diversity of questions posed by different interest-groups.

These points suggest that applying the agricultural-botany paradigm to the study of innovations is often a cumbersome and inadequate procedure. The evaluation falls short of its own tacit claims to be controlled, exact and unambiguous. Rarely, if ever, can educational programmes be subject to strict enough control to meet the design's requirements. Innovations, in particular, are vulnerable to manifold extraneous influences. Yet the traditional evaluator ignores these. He is restrained by the dictates of his paradigm to seek generalised findings along preordained lines. His definition of empirical reality is narrow. One effect of this is that it diverts attention away from questions of educational practice towards more centralised bureaucratic concerns.

Illuminative evaluation and the social-anthropology paradigm

Although traditional forms of evaluation have been criticised in this way, little attempt has been made to develop alternative models. The model described here, *illuminative evaluation*, takes account of the wider contexts in which educational programmes function. Its primary concern is with description and interpretation rather than measurement and prediction. It stands unambiguously within the alternative anthropological paradigm. The aims of illuminative evaluation are to study the innovatory programme: how it operates; how it is influenced by the various school situations in which it is applied; what those directly concerned regard as its advantages and disadvantages; and how students' intellectual tasks and academic experiences are most affected. It aims to discover and document what it is like to be participating in the scheme, whether as teacher or pupil; and, in addition, to discern and discuss the innovation's most significant features, recurring concomitants and critical processes. In short, it seeks to address and to illuminate a complex array of questions:

> Research on innovation can be enlightening to the innovator and to the whole academic community by clarifying the processes of education and by helping the innovator and other interested parties to identify those procedures, those elements in the educational effort, which seem to have had desirable results. (Trow, 1970)

The paradigm shift entailed in adopting illuminative evaluation requires more than an exchange of methodologies: it also involves new suppositions, concepts and terminology. Central to an understanding of illuminative evaluation are two concepts: the 'instructional system' and the 'learning milieu'.

THE INSTRUCTIONAL SYSTEM

Educational catalogues, prospectuses and reports characteristically contain a variety of formalised plans and statements which relate to particular teaching arrangements. Each of these summaries can be said to constitute or define an instructional system; and includes, say, a set of pedagogic assumptions, a new syllabus, and details of techniques and equipment. This 'catalogue description' is an idealised specification of the scheme, a set of elements arranged to a coherent plan. Despite their immense variation, the Dalton Plan, performance contracting, programmed learning, the integrated day, team teaching, 'Sesame Street' and 'Man: A Course of Study' can all be considered as instructional systems in these terms.

The traditional evaluator builds his study around innovations defined in this way. He examines the blueprint or formalised plan and extracts the programme's goals, objectives or desired outcomes. From these, in turn, he derives the tests and attitude inventories he will administer. His aim is to evaluate the instructional system by examining whether, for example, it has 'attained its objectives' or met its 'performance criteria'.

This technological approach fails to recognise the catalogue description for what it is. It ignores the fact that an instructional system, when adopted, undergoes modifications that are rarely trivial. The instructional system may remain as a shared idea, abstract model, slogan, or shorthand, but it assumes a different form in every situation. Its constituent elements are emphasised or de-emphasised, expanded or truncated, as teachers, administrators, technicians and students interpret and reinterpret the instructional system for their particular setting. In practice, objectives are commonly reordered, redefined, abandoned or forgotten. The original 'ideal' formulation ceases to be accurate, or indeed, of much relevance. Few in practice take catalogue descriptions and lists of objectives very seriously, save — it seems — for the traditional evaluator.

To switch from discussing the instructional system in abstract form to describing the details of its implementation is to cross into another realm. Here the second new concept is required.

THE LEARNING MILIEU

This is the social-psychological and material environment in which students and teachers work together. The learning milieu represents a network or *nexus* of cultural, social, institutional and psychological variables. These interact in complicated ways to produce, in each class or course, a unique pattern of circumstances, pressures, customs, opinions and work styles which suffuse the teaching and learning that occur there. The configuration of the learning milieu, in any particular classroom, depends on the interplay of numerous different factors. For instance, there are numerous constraints (legal, administrative, occupational, architectural and financial) on the organisation of teaching in schools; there are pervasive operating assumptions (about the arrangement of subjects, curricula, teaching methods and student evaluation) held by faculty: there are the individual teacher's characteristics (teaching style, experience, professional orientation and private goals); and there are student perspectives and preoccupations.

Acknowledging the diversity and complexity of learning milieux is an essential prerequisite for the serious study of educational programmes. The argument advanced here is that innovatory programmes, even for research purposes, cannot sensibly be separated from the learning milieux of which they become part. If an evaluation study hinges on the supposed perpetuation of the instructional system in more or less its original form, it makes an arbitrary and artificial distinction: it treats the innovation as a self-contained and independent system, which in practice it is manifestly not.

The introduction of an innovation sets off a chain of repercussions throughout the learning milieu. In turn these unintended consequences are likely to affect the innovation itself, changing its form and moderating its impact. For example, at the Massachusetts Institute of Technology, it was found that switching from 'distributed' to 'concentrated' study (a change from students taking several subjects concurrently to intensive full-time study of a single subject) was, in the event, far more than a rescheduling arrangement. It demanded new pedagogic forms (continuous lecturing would have led to 'overload'); it resulted in new role relationships between faculty and students (daily contact encouraged a degree of informality impossible with two meetings a week, of one hour each); and it changed peer relations between students (their working alongside the same students continuously led to much greater interaction than is usual in MIT sophomore classes). Such profound shifts in the learning milieu produced a further range of important secondary effects, apparently far removed from the innovation as such, but ultimately deriving from it.

To attempt to gauge the impact of the innovation (in this instance 'concentrated study') without paying attention to factors such as these, would clearly be absurd. In the above study it was possible to trace how each of these milieu effects had its corollary in the intellectual sphere: eg the informality encouraged normally silent students to ask questions; and although the range of different learning activities was regarded as excellent for achieving basic comprehension of the subject matter, it might have put the students at a disadvantage in a conventional exam.

Connecting changes in the learning milieu with intellectual experiences of students is one of the chief concerns for illuminative evaluation. Students do not confront 'knowledge' in naked form; it comes to them clothed in texts, lectures, tape-loops, etc. These form part of a wider set of arrangements for instructing, assessing and counselling which embody core assumptions about how knowledge and pedagogy should be organised. This 'management' framework, in turn, is embedded within wider departmental and institutional structures, each with its own set of procedures, and professional and societal allegiances. Although apparently far removed from the assimilation and schematisation of knowledge at the classroom level, these 'higher-order' aspects of the school or college environment cannot be ignored. To take an example: teaching and learning in a particular setting are profoundly influenced by the type of assessment procedures in use; by constraints of scheduling; by the size and diversity of classes; by the availability of teaching assistants, library, computing and copying facilities. These, in turn, are dependent on departmental priorities; on policies of faculty promotion; on institutional myths and traditions; and on local and national pressures.

The learning milieu concept is necessary for analysing the interdependence of learning and teaching, and for relating the organisation and practices of instruction with the immediate and long-term responses of students. For instance, students' intellectual development cannot be understood in isolation but only within a particular school or college milieu. Equally, there are phenomena of crucial educational significance (such as boredom, interest, concentration, 'floundering' and intellectual dependency) that make nonsense of the traditional psychological distinction between 'cognitive' and 'affective', and which customarily arise as responses to the total learning milieu, not to single components of it. Students do not respond merely to presented content and to tasks assigned. Rather, they adapt to and work within the learning milieu taken as an interrelated whole. They pay close attention to 'hidden' as well as 'visible' curricula. Besides acquiring particular habits of studying, reading and responding, they also assimilate the conventions, beliefs and models of reality that are constantly and inevitably transmitted through the total teaching process.

Organisation and methods of illuminative evaluation

Illuminative evaluations — like the innovations and learning milieux that they study — come in diverse forms. The size, aims, and techniques of the evaluation depend on many factors: the sponsors' preoccupations; the exact nature and stage of the innovation; the number of institutions, teachers and students involved; the level of co-operation and the degree of access to relevant information; the extent of the investigator's previous experience; the time available for data collection; the format of the required report; and, not least, the size of the evaluation budget.

Illuminative evaluation is not a standard methodological package but a general research strategy. It aims to be both adaptable and eclectic. The choice of research tactics follows not from research doctrine, but from decisions in each case as to the best available techniques; the problem defines the methods used, not *vice versa*. Equally, no method (with its own built-in limitations) is used exclusively or in isolation; different techniques are combined to throw light on a common problem. Besides viewing the problem from a number of angles, this 'triangulation' approach also facilitates the cross-checking of otherwise tentative findings.

At the outset, the researcher is concerned with familiarising himself thoroughly with the day-to-day reality of the setting or settings he is studying. In this, he is similar to social anthropologists or to natural historians. Like them he makes no attempt to manipulate, control or eliminate situational variables, but takes as given the complex scene he encounters. His chief task is to unravel it; isolate its significant features; delineate cycles of cause and effect; and comprehend relationships between beliefs and practices, and between organisational patterns and the responses of individuals. Since illuminative evaluation concentrates on examining the innovation as an integral part of the learning milieu, there is a definite emphasis both on observation at the classroom level and on interviewing participating instructors and students.

Characteristically in illuminative evaluation there are three stages: investigators observe, inquire further, and then seek to explain. Thus, in a study of a pilot project in independent learning in British secondary schools, early visits to the participating schools yielded a number of common incidents, recurring trends and issues frequently raised in discussion. These we either observed ourselves, or heard about from teachers and pupils. (For example, we noticed that teachers spoke in different ways about the independent learning materials provided for use with their classes. While some regarded the sets of materials as constituting, collectively, a course of study, others saw the same materials as having a supplementary or ancillary function, to be used simply as a collection of resources to draw upon as, when or if necessary.)

The second stage began with the selection of a number of such phenomena, occurrences or groups of opinions as topics for more sustained and intensive inquiry. A change of emphasis accompanied this development. During the first, exploratory stage, we had become 'knowledgeable' about the scheme. At the second stage this enabled our questioning to be more focused; communication to be more coherent and relaxed; and, in general, observation and inquiry to be more directed, systematic, and selective. (Thus — in our contacts with the teachers — we sought to find out more about the status they assigned to the independent learning materials, and the extent to which they integrated them with others.)

The third stage consisted of seeking general principles underlying the organisation of the programme; spotting patterns of cause and effect within its operation; and placing individual findings within a broader explanatory context. It began with our weighing alternative interpretations in the light of information obtained. Thus, why did teachers differ in their attitudes towards the materials? It seemed in general that teachers' views depended on the availability of related materials in the school; on their previous experience with similar methods; and — most critically — on whether or not they saw the material as 'displacing' or as 'supporting' the teacher. A number of other lines of investigation led to the same central issue: that of the changed role of the teacher in an independent learning setting.

Obviously the three stages overlap and functionally interrelate. The transition from stage to stage, as the investigation unfolds, occurs as problem areas become progressively clarified and redefined. The course of the study cannot be charted in advance. Beginning with an extensive data base, the researchers systematically reduce the breadth of their inquiry to give more concentrated attention to the emerging issues. This 'progressive focusing' permits unique and unpredicted phenomena to be given due weight. It reduces the problem of data overload; and prevents the accumulation of a mass of unanalysed material.

Within this three-stage framework, an information profile is assembled using data collected from four areas: observation; interviews; questionnaires and tests; documentary and background sources.

OBSERVATION

As noted above, the observation phase occupies a central place in illuminative evaluation. The investigator builds up a continuous record of ongoing events, transactions and informal remarks. At the same time he seeks to organise this data at source, adding interpretative comments on both manifest and latent features of the situation. In addition to observing and documenting day-to-day activities of the programme, the investigator may also be present at a wide variety of other events (eg faculty and student meetings, open days, examiners' meetings, etc).

Much of the on-site observation involves recording discussions with and between participants. These provide additional information that might not otherwise be apparent or forthcoming from more formal interviews. The language conventions, slang, jargon and metaphors that characterise conversation within each learning milieu can reveal tacit assumptions, interpersonal relationships and status differentials.

Finally, there is a place for codified observation, using schedules for recording patterns of attendance, seating, utilisation of time and facilities, teacher-pupil interaction, etc. The illuminative evaluator is cautious in the deployment of such techniques. In that they record only surface behaviour, they do not facilitate the uncovering of underlying, more meaningful features.

INTERVIEWS

Discovering the views of participants is crucial to assessing the impact of an innovation. Instructors and students are asked about their work, what they think of it, how it compares with previous experiences; and also to comment on the use and value of the innovation. Interviews vary as to the type of information or comment that is sought. While brief, structured interviews are convenient for obtaining biographical, historical or factual information, more open-ended and discursive forms are suitable for less straightforward topics (eg career ambitions and anxieties).

Though desirable, it is rarely possible to interview every participant, except in small innovatory programmes or with large research teams. Interviewees, therefore, must usually be selected randomly or by 'theoretical' sampling. This latter mode requires seeking out informants or particular groups who may have special insight or whose position makes their viewpoints noteworthy (eg students who have won prizes or failed altogether; marginal faculty members, who may have close knowledge of the innovation but have stayed outside it; young assistants teaching in their first semester, etc). Those interviewed can also include more distant but equally relevant figures: eg, at the college level, deans, administrators and student counsellors; and, beyond the college, curriculum developers and foundation officials from whom the innovation stemmed.

QUESTIONNAIRE AND TEST DATA

While concentrating on observation and interviews, the illuminative evaluator does not eschew paper-and-pencil techniques. Their advantage in larger-scale illuminative studies is especially evident. Also survey-type questionnaires used late in a study can sustain or qualify earlier tentative findings. Free and fixed response formats can be included to obtain both quantitative summary data and also qualitative open-ended (and perhaps new and unexpected) comment. If necessary, this qualitative data can be content analysed, to furnish further numerical results.

There are, of course, several valid objections to questionnaires, particularly if they are used in isolation. Unless most carefully prepared, questionnaires can lead to mindless accumulations of uninterpretable data. Expensive in time and resources, such careful preparation must be weighed against the benefits likely to accrue. A second drawback is that many recipients regard questionnaires as impersonal and intrusive. Others, keen to express their complicated views, find the questionnaire a frustrating, indeed trivialising, medium. From these dissatisfied groups, some do not reply; yet these non-respondents may be the most important in certain respects. For example, in an unpublished questionnaire study at MIT, non-response was found to be the best predictor of student drop-out.

Besides completing questionnaires, participants can also be asked to prepare written comments on the programme; to go through checklists; or to compile work diaries that record their activities over a specific period of time.

Finally there are published or custom-built tests of attitude, personality and achievement. Such tests enjoy no privileged status within the study. Test scores cannot be considered in isolation; they form merely one section of the data profile. Interest lies not so much in relating different test scores, but in accounting for them using the study's findings as a whole.

DOCUMENTARY AND BACKGROUND INFORMATION

Innovations do not arise unheralded. They are preceded by committee minutes, funding proposals, architectural plans and consultants' reports. Also other primary sources are obtainable: eg non-confidential data from registrars' offices; autobiographical and eye-witness accounts of the innovation; tape recordings of meetings; and examples of students' assignments.

The assembly of such information can serve a useful function. It can provide an historical perspective of how the innovation was regarded by different people before the evaluation began. The data may also indicate areas of inquiry (eg how representative were the students taking part?); may point to topics for intensive discussion (eg why were certain major features of the original proposal later abandoned?); or may expose aspects of the innovation that would otherwise be missed (eg why were subject requirements not fulfilled?).

Problems and possibilities of illuminative evaluation

First encounters with the radically different perspective of illuminative evaluation prompt a number of important questions. Foremost is usually concern over the 'subjective' nature of the approach. Can 'personal interpretation' be scientific? Is not collection, analysis, and reporting of data, sceptics ask, entirely at the discretion of the researchers themselves?

Behind such questions lies a basic but erroneous assumption: that forms of research exist which are immune to prejudice, experimenter bias and human error. This is not so. Any research study requires skilled human judgements and is thus vulnerable. Even in evaluation studies that handle automatically processed numerical data, judgement is necessary at every stage: in the choice of samples; in the construction or selection of tests; in deciding conditions of administration; in selecting the mode of statistical treatment (eg whether or not to use factor analysis); in the relative weight given to different results; and, particularly, in the selection and presentation of findings in reports.

Nevertheless, the extensive use of open-ended techniques, progressive focusing, and qualitative data in illuminative evaluation still raises the possibility of gross partiality on the part of the investigator. A number of precautionary tactics are possible. During the investigation different techniques can be used to cross-check the most important findings; open-ended material can be coded and checked by outside researchers; consultants to the evaluation can be charged with challenging preliminary interpretations and playing devil's advocate; and members of the research team can be commissioned to develop their own interpretations. At the report stage, in addition to the findings, critical research processes can also be documented: theoretical principles and methodological ground rules can be discussed and made explicit; criteria for selecting or rejecting areas of investigation can be spelled out; and evidence can be presented in such a way that others can judge its quality.

Even with such precautions, the subjective element remains. It is inevitable. When the investigator abandons the agricultural-botany paradigm his role is necessarily redefined. The use of interpretative human insight and skills is, indeed, encouraged rather than discouraged. The illuminative evaluator thus joins a diverse group of specialists (eg psychiatrists, social anthropologists and historians) where this is taken for granted. In each of these fields the research worker has to weigh and sift a complex array of human evidence and draw conclusions from it.

A further issue also focuses on the position of the investigator. Does not his presence have an effect on the conduct and progress of the innovatory scheme he is studying? Certainly it does; indeed, any form of data collection creates disturbance. Illuminative evaluators recognise this and attempt to be unobtrusive without being secretive; to be supportive without being collusive; and to be non-doctrinaire without appearing unsympathetic.

This leads to an important point: that research workers in this area need not only technical and intellectual capability, but also interpersonal skills. They seek co-operation but cannot demand it. There may be times when they encounter nervousness and even hostility. They are likely to be observing certain individuals at critical times in their lives (eg students about to leave, or instructors with a high personal investment in the innovation). The researchers need tact and a sense of responsibility similar to that pertaining in the medical profession. They seek and are given private opinions, often in confidence. They are likely to hear, in the course of a study, a great deal about personalities and institutional politics that others might be inquisitive to know. There are especially difficult decisions to make at the report stage: although full reporting is necessary, it is essential to safeguard individuals' privacy.

Such problems, confronting many research workers in the human sciences, are exacerbated in the case of close-up, intensive studies of the type outlined here. The price of achieving the richer, more informative data of illuminative evaluation is the greatly increased attention that must be paid to the evaluator's professional standards and behaviour. Although there can be no fixed rules, there are certain guidelines for the illuminative evaluator. For instance, to retain the viability and integrity of his research position and the trust of the participants in the programme, the investigator needs, from the outset, to clarify his role; to be open about the aims of his study; and to ensure that there is no misunderstanding or ambiguity about who, for example, will receive the report.

Besides concern with the investigator's special position, illuminative evaluation also prompts questions concerning the scope of the investigation. Is illuminative evaluation confined to small-scale innovations? Can it be applied to innovations that are being widely implemented? Detailed studies of specific learning milieux may be insightful and valid, but are the results and analyses generalisable to other situations? Is it possible to move from the particular to the universal?

Despite its basis in the close-up study of individual learning milieux, illuminative evaluation can also be applied on a wider scale. Suppose an innovatory programme had been adopted by many different schools. At the beginning of the evaluation a small sample of schools could be selected for intensive study. As the study progressed, and as it focused on selected salient issues arising in the different learning milieux, the number of schools studied could be expanded. The new investigations, now more selective, could be pursued more speedily, with concentration more on noting similarities and differences between situations, than on full documentation of each learning milieu. At the same time it is necessary to remain extremely flexible and to be open to new issues that arise in the later stages of a study. Finally, with this further information assimilated, short visits, or even — in the last resort — mailed questionnaires could be used for the remainder of the institutions.

The full progression — from small sample studies to larger-scale inquiries — is often only necessary in widely applied programmes. But there is another way in which perceptive and rigorous study of specific situations can yield more generally applicable insights with either large- or small-scale investigations. Learning milieux, despite their diversity, share many characteristics. Instruction is constrained by similar conventions, subject divisions and degrees of student involvement. Teachers encounter parallel sets of problems. Students' learning, participation, study habits and examination techniques are found to follow common lines; and innovations, as such, face habitual difficulties and provoke familiar reactions. There is a wide range of overlapping social and behavioural phenomena that accompany teaching, learning and innovating. This is widely acknowledged. However, few of these phenomena have been pinpointed, adequately described or defined accurately. Illuminative evaluation aims to contribute to this process. There is a need for abstracted summaries, for shared terminology and for insightful concepts. These can serve as aids to communication and facilitate theory-building. They have been conspicuously absent from most research in education. Yet, without this conceptual equipment, the universals of teaching will be cyclically discovered, described, forgotten, rediscovered, and described again.

Decision making, evaluation and illumination

The principal purpose of evaluation studies is to contribute to decision making. There are at least three separate but related groups of decision makers to whom the evaluator addresses his report: (i) the programme's participants; (ii) the programme's sponsors, supervisory committee or educational board; (iii) interested outsiders (such as other researchers, curriculum planners, etc).

Each group or constituency will look to the report for help in making different decisions. The participants, for example, will be anxious to correct deficiencies, make improvements and establish future priorities. The sponsors and board members will be concerned with pedagogic issues but will also want to know about the innovation's costs, use of resources and outside reputation. The outsiders will read the report to decide whether or not the scheme has 'worked', or to see whether it could be applied or adapted to their own situations.

Clearly, if the evaluator is to acknowledge the interests of all these groups, he cannot — even if requested — provide a simple 'yes' or 'no' on the innovation's future. A decision based on one group's evaluative criteria would, almost certainly, be disputed by other groups with different priorities. A 'mastery of fundamentals' for one group is for another a 'stifling of creativity'. The investigator does not make decisions. Indeed, in these terms he cannot — except as a representative or agent of one of the interest groups.

Illuminative evaluation thus concentrates on the information-gathering rather than the decision-making component of evaluation. The task is to provide a comprehensive understanding of the complex reality (or realities) surrounding the programme: in short, to 'illuminate'. In his report, therefore, the evaluator aims to sharpen discussion, disentangle complexities, isolate the significant from the trivial, and raise the level of sophistication of debate.

Summary

When an innovation ceases to be an abstract concept or plan, and becomes part of the teaching and learning in a school or college, it assumes a different form altogether. The theatre provides an analogy: to know whether a play 'works' one has to look not only at the manuscript but also at the performance; that is, at the interpretation of the play by the director and actors. It is this that is registered by the audience and appraised by the critics. Similarly, it is not an instructional system as such but its translation and enactment by teachers and students, that is of concern to the evaluator and other interested parties. There is no play that is 'director-proof'. Equally, there is no innovation that is 'teacher-proof' or 'student-proof'.

If this is acknowledged, it becomes imperative to study an innovation through the medium of its performance and to adopt a research style and methodology that is appropriate.

This involves the investigator leaving his office and computer print-out to spend substantial periods in the field. The crucial figures in the working of an innovation — learners and teachers — become his chief preoccupation. The evaluator concentrates on 'process' within the learning milieu, rather than on 'outcomes' derived from a specification of the instructional system. Observation, linked with discussion and background inquiry, enables him to develop an informed account of the innovation in operation.

Ideally, the output of his research will be regarded as useful, intelligible and revealing by those involved in the enterprise itself. Further, by addressing key educational issues it can also be seen as a recognisable reality by others outside the innovation. If the report is seen merely as an arcane or irrelevant addition to a research literature already ignored by practising educators, clearly the evaluator will have failed.

In attempting to document the teacher-student interactions, intellectual habits, institutional constraints, etc that characterise classroom life, the investigator contributes to a field that has received only minimal attention from social scientists. Until recently, perceptive accounts of learning milieux have, more often than not, been found in 'travellers' tales' or 'non-fiction' novels rather than in educational

217

research reports. The investigator has, therefore, not only short-term goals, but also the long-term goal of contributing to a developing and urgently required new field of study.

This approach does not cure all ills, nor can any one approach do so. Certainly, no simplified instant solutions to perennial educational questions will be delivered by such studies. Indeed, by discarding a spurious 'technological' simplification of reality, and by acknowledging the complexity of educational process, the illuminative evaluator is likely to increase rather than lessen the sense of uncertainty in education. On the other hand, unless studies such as these are vigorously pursued there is little hope of ever moving beyond helpless indecision or doctrinal assertion in the conduct of instructional affairs.

Reference

Trow, M A (1970) Methodological problems in the evaluation of innovation. In M C Wittrock and D E Wiley (eds). *The Evaluation of Instruction.* New York : Holt, Rinehart & Winston, p302

2.8 A Story of Assimilation and Dissemination

RICHARD HOOPER

Hooper, R (1977) A story of ASS and DISS. Paper presented to the
Educational Technology International Conference, University of Surrey,
March 1977. Reproduced with permission of the author and the Council
for Educational Technology.

In January 1973, a few days after the launching of the good ship
NDPCAL (National Development Programme in Computer Assisted
Learning) from the Government dry dock, on its five-year
£2.5-million odyssey, two aims — ASSimilation and DISSemination —
were pinned firmly to the masthead. These twin aims, assimilation
(NDPCAL jargon: 'institutionalisation') and dissemination
('transferability') are crucial to any understanding of the National
Programme's activities over the past five years. Now, in the closing
months of the five-year odyssey, it seems appropriate to review:

  (a) the reasons for choosing the aims of ASS and DISS;
  (b) the strategies adopted to achieve ASS and DISS; and
  (c) a tentative, brief evaluation of the success of the ASS and
      DISS policy.

Assimilation

The term 'assimilation' (which I will regard for the purposes of this
paper to be synonymous with NDPCAL's term 'institutionalisation') is
defined within the National Programme as the successful take-over of
an innovation on to local budgets on a permanent basis after the
period of external funding runs out. To use a medical metaphor,
assimilation is successful transplant without subsequent tissue rejection.

REASON FOR SELECTING ASS

The reason for selecting ASS as the main aim of the National Programme
is probably obvious — growing concern in the educational technology
community at the lack of success with the assimilation of innovation
over the past twenty years on both sides of the Atlantic. The
influential US Carnegie Commission on Higher Education wrote in its
1972 report, *The Fourth Revolution:*

> One of the great disappointments of the national effort to date is that for
> all the funds and effort thus far expended for the advancement of
> instructional technology, *penetration* of new learning materials and media
> into higher education has thus far been shallow. (Author's italics) (The
> Carnegie Commission Higher Education, 1972, p47)

Surprisingly, given the obviousness of this aim of assimilation, very few educational technology or curriculum development projects on either side of the Atlantic have adopted it explicitly. The large schools' curriculum development projects, funded in the UK and the USA, have tended to have as their aim the development of high quality teaching materials, based on appropriate definition of educational objectives, and a sound curriculum design. For example, the Schools Council History 13-16 project 'aims to help teachers of history by suggesting suitable objectives and by promoting the use of appropriate materials and ideas for their realisation' (Schools Council, 1974, p34). In higher education, many of the educational technology projects have had what I would describe as research aims — to demonstrate the value of, for example, computer-assisted learning (CAL), to identify its cost effectiveness, to elaborate its theoretical bases. A lot of the early work in CAI (computer-assisted instruction) in the USA was carried out by educational psychologists interested in using CAI systems to explore human learning, for example Patrick Suppes' work at Stanford University (Rothenberg & Morgan, 1975, p66).

Many of these schools and higher education projects have assumed, and on occasions claimed, that the existence of high quality teaching materials, positive research data or elegant theoretical explications, will ensure the assimilation of the particular innovation. History would suggest that such an assumption is quite unwarranted. Indeed, I believe that, in many cases, the research project syndrome ('Here today, gone tomorrow') clearly militates *against* successful assimilation. Educational decision making is, in fact, to the chagrin of those who inhabit the Age of Reason, 'incremental and disjointed . . . polycentral' and not all that rational (Kogan, 1976, p2). The independent educational evaluation team of the National Programme, UNCAL, has put it neatly:

> The belief that innovations succeed on their merits, a belief that sustained the rational optimism of the first generation of curriculum developers, has never been much in evidence at the centre of the National Programme . . . the citadel of established practice will seldom fall to the polite knock of a good idea. It may however yield to a long siege, a pre-emptive strike, a wooden horse or a cunning alliance. (UNCAL, 1975, p49)

Thus, within the National Programme, assimilation has been seen above all as a political process, involving a whole range of factors that go far beyond the existence of good software or positive research results. In the USA, it is still the conventional wisdom to say that lack of good, cost-effective software is the major obstacle to CAL's advance (Anastasio & Morgan, 1972; Bitzer, 1976). I believe this to be a misleading half-truth.

ASS STRATEGIES

NDPCAL's view of ASSimilation is best understood by examining the strategies adopted to pursue it. The main ASS strategies can be listed as follows:

(a) the choice of location of projects,

(b) organisational structure and the choice of project director,
(c) matched funding,
(d) critical mass,
(e) curriculum integration,
(f) 'riding the educational wave',
(g) closing the programme.

Location of projects: The first major strategic decision in pursuit of ASS concerned the choice of location of projects. The original National Council for Educational Technology reports of 1969, which led to the setting up of NDPCAL, recommended the development work to be carried out at a few research centres attached to universities (Hooper, 1974). Given ASS as an aim, this would have been, in my view, a totally unproductive strategy. For computer-assisted learning (CAL) or computer-managed learning (CML) to survive in the longer term future, projects had to be based close to the sources of institutional power, and that power in the British system of education is highly distributed. Two things followed from this. First, the Programme used its funds to encourage as many growth points across the UK (around eighty in 1975/6) as was compatible with money available and the requirements of critical mass. Secondly, the majority of higher education projects, for example, were located not in educational technology nor educational research departments which are, whether we like it or not, on the periphery of institutional power, but in the mainstream teaching departments — physics, chemistry, mathematics. At schools level, for the same reasons, projects (with one exception) have been located directly in local education authorities, and not in universities which has been the Schools Council pattern. Universities can have no continuing commitment to an innovation that is not for their own consumption.

Organisational structure: Following on from the location of projects, there were particular concerns about the choice of project director and the organisational structure in the project. To the radical innovator, or researcher, discussion of organisation may appear tedious and irrelevant. Yet it is crucial. In another context, the Open University, organisational changes, for example to do with the 'course team', have been central to making innovation happen. Who reports to whom, and who is on which committee, are highly relevant considerations for projects aiming at assimilation. The choice of project director is also crucial. Does the project director have academic credibility? Can he or she manage? Can he or she present results in a convincing way to colleagues and to decision makers? Does the director know the way around the corridors of power in the particular institution or local authority?

Matched funding: 'Matched funding' was a specific strategy used to strengthen the chances of future assimilation. Unlike many research funding agencies, the National Programme did not pay overheads to project institutions. On the contrary, project institutions were expected to contribute resources alongside NDPCAL funding. These resources were usually academic staff time, accommodation, and computing facilities. The existence of matched funding enabled

NDPCAL to evaluate, in a very practical way, the local political power of a potential project director. More importantly, it ensured the involvement of decision making at the project's inception, thus preparing the ground well in advance for the vital assimilation decisions later on. In the Hertfordshire schools computer-managed project, for example, officials from County Hall were involved, through matched funding, at the project negotiation stage in 1973. The same officials were to play a key role in the later (successful) negotiations for post-1977 assimilation. Another strength of 'matched funding' is that it softens the financial transition to assimilation at the end of external funding, since parts of the project are already being paid for locally.

Critical mass: The strategy of 'critical mass', called somewhat mischievously 'The Numbers Game' within the National Programme, is premised on the belief that an innovation which is in *widespread* use across an institution or authority will acquire the broad base of support and visibility that is difficult to stop. By contrast, the CAL research experiment with a handful of students on alternate Fridays can be closed down without much trouble. In one recent assimilation negotiation in one of our higher education projects, the project director pointed out to the university that if the CAL work were not continued, someone else would need to provide three thousand hours of student teaching from October 1977.

Curriculum integration: The strategy of curriculum integration tries to ensure that CAL or CML developments happen within a framework of broader curriculum and course redesign. This is to avoid the innovation remaining an optional extra, which can be discarded at a time of financial squeeze. At Imperial College, for example, a group of third-year courses in heat transfer and fluid flow has been totally redesigned around a computing core. If CAL were to be discarded, then the courses themselves would also have to go. At Imperial College, the computer programs are referred to in the final examination papers — hard evidence of assimilation. By contrast, much educational television teaching is not assessed in final exams and therefore is in danger of being neglected by students, and by teaching staff.

'Riding the educational wave': The penultimate ASS strategy can be termed, to continue the nautical metaphor, 'riding the educational wave'. This relates to the need to develop innovations that reinforce existing trends within the educational system. For example, drill and practice uses of the computer in maths have never found much favour in British schools because maths teaching has largely moved away from this pedagogy. Test-marking by computer, on the other hand, has quickly found favour because it has ridden in on top of the existing wave of objective testing and continuous assessment. But of course, as with surfing, choosing the right wave is important. Some waves look all right but are, in Australian surfing parlance, 'dumpers'.

Closing the programme: The final — in every sense of the word — ASS strategy was the decision taken to close the Programme down at the end of its five-year term. This concentrates the mind on assimilation wonderfully!

Dissemination

Turning from ASS to DISS, the seascape is immediately more familiar. Many educational technology and curriculum development projects have stressed the importance of dissemination. For the purpose of this paper I will regard the term 'dissemination' as synonymous with the NDPCAL term 'transferability'. Dissemination is defined here as the systematic attempt to promote the spread and adoption of new ideas or practices.

REASONS FOR SELECTING DISS

NDPCAL selected DISS as a twin aim alongside ASS for two reasons. First of all, dissemination was essential to spread the high costs of developing CAL and CML, in the accepted tradition of economies of scale. Secondly, dissemination was a useful mechanism for testing the resilience and worthwhileness of the innovation, and I shall return to this topic at the end of the paper.

Attitudes to dissemination changed during the course of the Programme. I myself started out thinking rather rigidly in terms of the dissemination of complete CAL packages or instructional systems. In one of our earliest transferability projects, at Cambridge University, I was taught the error of my ways. Dissemination of ideas and experience may be as valuable as the dissemination of teaching materials. The key to understanding and promoting dissemination is its valued diversity. 'Not only do the "products" to be transferred show considerable diversity, so do the environments from and to which the transfer is made' (NDPCAL, 1975, p2).

The 'ideological' approach to DISS, that gradually emerged within NDPCAL, needs to be identified. In essence, we came to question the conventional wisdom that 'the dissemination problem' is just a 'communication problem', and that dissemination failure can be attributed solely to failures of communication.

> The problem of communication is a product of the rhetoric of curriculum development rather than of the reality. The rhetoric is premised on an unexamined assumption: that all of us concerned with the education of pupils — teachers, administrators, advisers, researchers, theorists — basically share the same educational values and have overlapping visions of curriculum excellence. A confirmation of the argument is the proposition that if there are major discrepancies between the advocacies of the support groups and the behaviour of the practitioner groups ... then there is *prima facie* a problem of communication ... All this is not to say that there are no problems of transmission which can be accounted for in terms of poor presentation: of course there are. But curriculum innovators face a much more significant problem which needs to be distinguished from this but is often confused with it: the issue of whether people want to hear what they have to say. The answer does not necessarily lie in saying it more clearly. (MacDonald and Walker, 1976, p44)

DISS STRATEGIES

The following list of strategies to achieve DISSemination has been used by the National Programme:

(a) inter-institutional projects,
(b) personal contact,
(c) existing communications channels,
(d) presentational skills,
(e) technical portability,
(f) program exchange centres.

It is worth noting that the main Schools Council DISS strategy of commercial publication has barely been used at all by NDPCAL.

Inter-institutional projects: The first, and key, DISS strategy was the funding of inter-institutional projects. By contrast, most higher education research and development funding has tended to go to single institutions. Funding of inter-institutional projects encourages the idea of dissemination being seen as part of development, not an afterthought. In the design of teaching material, decisions of an educational and technical nature can take into account the differing requirements of a spectrum of potential users, thus making the end product more easy to disseminate. Inter-institutional funding is a departure from the tradition of 'centres of excellence', and 'centre-periphery' models of curriculum development. Inter-institutional projects multiply the number of participating teachers and therefore the likelihood of future assimilation *via* critical mass. Inter-institutional projects, designed as co-operative federal networks, grow organically as interest grows. They are based on the belief that teachers will more readily adopt an innovation if they have participated in its development. This reduces the power of the NIH (not invented here) syndrome. It also, finally, enables the conflicting, non-consensual values of the participants to be voiced early on, thus reducing the so-called 'communications problem'.

Personal contact: House, in his book *The Politics of Educational Innovation,* wrote:

> To control the flow of personal contact is to control innovation. As the flow of blood is essential to human life, so direct personal contact is essential to the propagation of innovation . . . Who knows whom and who talks to whom are powerful indicators of where and when an innovation is accepted, or if it is accepted at all. (House, 1974, p6)

Personal contact has been a central DISS strategy. By comparison with many research-funding agencies, NDPCAL has always, for example, been generous with travel and subsistence money. Inter-project visits, overseas visits, intra-project meetings, meetings with prospective adopters, conferences, have all been directly encouraged.

Professor Ayscough, the director of the large CALCHEM project, based at Leeds University and Sheffield Polytechnic, has summarised the NDPCAL view perfectly:

> We are, after all, trying to address ourselves to practising teachers who are not particularly interested in educational research as such . . . the CALCHEM project has expanded very satisfactorily without the support of weighty analysis and impressive publications. Our conclusion is that *those who have pursued their investigations of CAL to the point at which they have a reasonable grasp of what we are doing, recognise that the real evidence*

they seek can only be obtained by observing the system in action ...
dissemination of this particular innovation has occurred almost entirely
on a person-to-person basis and by direct observation, not by evangelical
contribution to seminars and journals. (Ayscough, 1976, p6)

Existing communications channels: Personal contact has been
strengthened by exploiting the existing communications channels used
by practising teachers, for example, the Chemical Society or the
Geographical Association. NDPCAL has worked directly with these
professional associations, setting up workshops, journal articles and
special publications, to accelerate dissemination. By and large in initial
encounters with CAL, chemistry teachers, for example, will listen to
other chemists and not to educational technologists or computing
specialists. There is one disadvantage of this subject discipline-based
strategy — it reduces opportunities for interdisciplinary work and
cross-disciplinary transfer.

Presentational skill: The presentational skill of project staff was
emphasised early on in the National Programme as an important, yet
often overlooked, component of dissemination strategy. Presentational
skill is *not* synonymous with slick, professional presentation. Indeed,
in educational circles, slick presentations can be counterproductive. In
the military training environment, by contrast, it is essential.

The educational evaluation team, UNCAL, alerted us to the need
to consider the varying requirements of different audiences. Choice of
language used is all-important. Computing and educational technology
jargon may put off the customer, whereas a few scrawled equations on
the blackboard may seduce him. In addition to the usual conferences,
various other mechanisms have been used to encourage projects to
pay attention to presentation. The mid-term evaluations of projects,
two-day site visits which lead to decisions to continue or suspend
further funding, have been particularly useful in this respect. In
addition, 'software fayres' have been and are being organised to
serve as opportunities for projects to present themselves to wider
audiences. NDPCAL is possibly unique as a funding agency in having
purchased exhibition stands and lighting equipment for its portfolio of
projects.

Technical portability: It is, I hope, clear from the DISS strategies
outlined so far that, within NDPCAL, the major problems surrounding
dissemination are seen to be human and psychological, rather than
technical. In the USA, the cultural tendency is to be concerned with
the technical considerations of CAL at the expense of human factors.
To stress human factors is, of course, not to deny the existence of a
number of significant technical obstacles. Because of the way that the
world computing industry has developed, the 'portability' of software
from one machine to another, even within the same manufacturer's
range, is often difficult. In brief, the main components of NDPCAL's
strategy in relation to technical portability concerned choice of
programming languages ('standardising' on BASIC, FORTRAN and COBOL),
emphasis on good documentation, and good program design (for
example, ease of modification and modularisation).

Program exchange centres: The final DISS strategy used by NDPCAL involved the funding of subject discipline-affiliated program exchange centres. Activities of these centres include the maintenance of a catalogue and library operation, 'standards' setting, teacher training, consultancy, salesmanship, the encouragement of new software development. The NDPCAL-funded geography package exchange (GAPE) operates under the auspices of the Geographical Association (see above).

Tensions between ASS and DISS

Before reviewing the success of the ASS and DISS strategies outlined, one further point about them needs to be made. When ASS and DISS were pinned to the masthead, it was not realised that, in some senses, the two aims are mutually incompatible. Within, for example, a university, the cultural and financial incentives tend to favour ASS at the expense of DISS. Unlike written textbooks with their accompanying royalties, there are still no real rewards for CAL dissemination (except in heaven). The parent institution, especially at times of economic stringency, will tend to question the extra resources that are necessary to make a product that is working well locally, transferable. In some of our projects, the tensions between ASS and DISS have not been satisfactorily resolved. In some others, success with DISS has been used by canny project directors to bolster a slightly shaky case for ASS. By and large it is our experience that ASS is a necessary precondition and launch platform for DISS, but DISS is not usually a necessary precondition for ASS. (DISS *within* an institution is likely to speed ASS, however.) As a result, DISS needs special attention from funding agencies both now and in the future, unless there is a radical change in reward structures for innovators. John Fielden, who has directed the independent financial evaluation of the National Programme, has shown that the benefits from DISS accrue most of all to the 'nation' in terms of lower total costs as expressed in costs per student hour, somewhat less to the importing institution, and barely at all to the originating institution (Fielden, 1977).

Evaluating the success of ASS and DISS

The ASS, and to a lesser extent the DISS, aims of the National Programme cannot, by their very nature, be properly evaluated until after NDPCAL has closed down. On the evidence to date, sprinkled with appropriate dashes of salt, it would seem likely that seventy per cent of the projects will achieve satisfactory levels of assimilation and dissemination. The presence of independent financial and educational evaluators in the National Programme will serve, I hope, to counterbalance any undue optimism on the part of myself and project staff now that the 'season of claims and mellow fruitfulness' is nigh.

In general, the ASS and DISS strategies adopted by NDPCAL have been more successful in the higher education and military training sectors, than in schools and in industrial training. In the higher education projects, for example, we may achieve close to a hundred per cent success rate with assimilation of CAL and CML activity.

Evidence to support the claims for ASS success are set out in detail in my final report (Hooper, 1978). A sample of that evidence would be the recent decision by the Senate of the University of Leeds to make three *tenured* appointments for the Computer Based Learning Project; the Computer Board's approval of a Prime computer and support staff at the University of Surrey dedicated to a university-wide CAL service (with a matched funding:NDPCAL funding ratio of 8:1); the purchase in 1976 of a dedicated CAL machine at the University of Glasgow for use in five teaching departments; the decision by Hertfordshire County Council to continue to support the schools computer-managed mathematics project after 1977; in military training, the recent purchase with Army funds of an ICL 1903 Educational System dedicated to CAMOL (Computer Assisted Management of Learning) at Catterick Camp. A Federal Committee in Canada on Computer Communications in Education has written about NDPCAL in a survey of international developments: '. . . initial results indicate a high probability of the Programme successfully achieving its objective of "assimilation of computer-assisted learning on a regular institutional basis at reasonable cost" ' (Dept of Communications, 1975, p13).

A sample of the evidence to support the claims for DISS success is as follows. The Engineering Sciences Project, for example, based at Queen Mary College, London, began in 1973/74 in five engineering departments in three institutions, grew to ten engineering departments in six institutions by September 1976, involving twenty-nine academic staff and some seven hundred and fifty students, and had transferred CAL packages to twenty-one other institutions in the UK and abroad. The CAMOL project, a joint development between NDPCAL and International Computers Ltd (ICL), involved by 1976/77 one university, two polytechnics, a grammar school, an FE college and the trade training school at Catterick. In addition, a large local authority was preparing to purchase CAMOL for use in its secondary schools, and a pilot operation with Open University students in Northern Ireland was starting. At Glasgow University, the 'content-free' computer software produced, and in use, for medical teaching, has been transferred successfully for use in the training of guidance counsellors, and in police training. At the London Business School, the CAL techniques for management training have been used in courses for managers from the nationalised industries, large private sector companies such as Unilever, and other educational institutions undertaking management training. Finally, the Physical Sciences Program Exchange, based at Wolverhampton Polytechnic, has grown from nineteen to sixty-two members (including twenty-one overseas institutions) since 1975. That same Canadian report commented:

> The high level of US federal funding which has been provided on a multidisciplinary basis has made possible major achievements in hardware, software and courseware for CAL. In contrast to the UK, however, federal funds have not generally been used to emphasize transferability, nor to promote the development and application of standards. Thus, in terms of national development of CAL, the US federal funding has not had the impact that it might otherwise have had. Many of the projects which did not

go beyond the experimental stage were undertaken on a local basis and might well have continued had they been undertaken as cooperative projects involving several institutions, with the results available to a larger 'market'. (Dept of Communications, 1975, p13)

ASS + DISS + evaluation

The story of ASS and DISS cannot end neatly here. Success in achieving ASS and DISS is a very useful, practical, credible criterion for measuring the worthwhileness of computer-assisted learning, but is not a sufficient criterion. Both ASS and DISS have been used within the National Programme as 'obstacle courses' to test the resilience of the various innovations, and the claims of project staff. The achievement of ASS by itself, particularly when money is tight, is indeed good evidence of the value of CAL or CML. The achievement of ASS + DISS by a project is better evidence still because it increases the size of the test-bed. The achievement of ASS + DISS + ASS (ie the innovation that has been assimilated in the originating institution is successfully imported and assimilated in a new institution) is better evidence still — but again not sufficient. We need evaluation — preferably independent evaluation — to enter and hold the ring, for one simple reason: unworthwhile ideas in education can and do get assimilated and disseminated. Only one example of this is needed (and we can all think of more than one) to make ASS and DISS indicative but never sufficient criteria for measuring worthwhileness.

The arrival of evaluation brings with it new tensions to the story of ASS and DISS, and new conflicts for the funding agency. Does the good ship NDPCAL, as it nears its final port of call, continue supporting a project which looks like achieving the assimilation of a poor computer application? On the other hand, when December 1977 comes, will the worthwhile and the imaginative computer application necessarily be assimilated and disseminated?

References

Anastasio, E J and Morgan, J S (1972) *Factors Inhibiting the Use of the Computer in Instruction.* EDUCOM, Interuniversity Communications Council Inc

Ayscough, P (1976) Academic reactions to educational innovation, *Studies in Higher Education* 1 1

Bitzer, D L (1976) Foreword. In Anastasia Wang (ed) *Index to Computer Based Learning.* Milwaukee : University of Wisconsin

Carnegie Commission on Higher Education (1972) *The Fourth Revolution,* A report and recommendations of the Carnegie Commission on Higher Education. New York : McGraw-Hill

Department of Communications (1975) *Federal Working Committee on Computer Communications in Education: Final Report.* Ottawa : Department of Communications, Educational Technology Branch

Fielden, J (1977) The financial evaluation of NDPCAL, *British Journal of Educational Technology* 8 3

Hooper, R (1974) The National Development Programme in Computer Assisted Learning — origins and starting point, *Programmed Learning* 11 2

Hooper, R (1978) *The National Development Programme in Computer Assisted Learning — final report of the Director.* London : Council for Educational Technology

House, E (1974) *The Politics of Educational Innovation.* Berkeley, California : McCutchan Publishing Corporation

Kogan, M (1976) *The Next Ten Years — A Speculative Essay on Educational Futures.* (Commissioned paper for NDPCAL future study on computers in education and training in the 1980s). London : National Development Programme in Computer Assisted Learning

MacDonald, B and Walker, R (1976) *Changing the Curriculum.* London : Open Books

NDPCAL (1975) *Transferability in Computer Assisted and Computer Managed Learning.* Working Paper No 3. London : National Development Programme in Computer Assisted Learning

Rothenberg, D and Morgan, R P (1975) *Case Studies of Innovation in the Educational Service Sector.* St Louis, Missouri : Washington University

UNCAL (1975) *The Programme at Two.* An UNCAL evaluation report on the NDPCAL. Centre for Applied Research in Education : University of East Anglia

Part Three: Applications

Introduction

In the early days of educational technology there seemed to be an emphasis on the machinery for Educational Technology One — as Davies called it. There seemed to be a tendency to think of things existing apart from what they actually did or accomplished. Thus one thought of the blackboard, the language laboratory, the television, the radio, the teaching machine and the teacher as things quite separate from each other and from the systems of which they were a part. Even today much research is carried out on different components of teaching and learning without reference to any total system.

However, in the examples which we have chosen for this section of the book, we have tried (by inference) to illustrate how this thinking is naive. In all of our examples wider considerations are given due attention. Our aim in this section, therefore, has not been to provide a paper on television, a paper on a tape-slide program, a paper on this and a paper on that, but to provide papers where different approaches are integrated — in different ways — to illustrate the many different perspectives held by educational technologists today. In a sense, these perspectives represent different aspects of the various philosophies introduced in the Prologue. In our selection, the first three papers represent a continuation of developments from the earlier field of programmed learning. The next four papers present diverging approaches to teaching and learning in higher education. Part three ends with two papers to illustrate military and industrial uses of educational technology.

We start with a rather specialised use of educational technology — that of its application to the mentally handicapped. Paper 3.1 by John Hegarty is an important review for several reasons. In particular, it highlights the role of the teacher in addition to that of the machine, and it emphasises the need for simple devices which teach rather than for complex devices which do not work. Other conclusions, too, can be drawn from Hegarty's paper: it seems that more complex machinery has been used with the more handicapped child and that simpler devices have been used with the less severely handicapped. If we turned this position round (ie gave more complex machinery to the less severely handicapped) there might be greater progress. Certainly, at present, it looks as though much ingenuity and effort have been wasted — although undoubtedly knowledge (of a negative sort) has been gained.

Paper 3.2 introduces a different aspect of programmed instruction — that of using it to encourage creativity in art-work. One of the common and recurring remarks made about programmed instruction since its inception is that it can only teach facts, and that it cannot teach people to think and to be creative. Such a challenge has proved irresistible. Robert Williams (Paper 3.2) surveys the research in this context and his paper is presented to illustrate typical research in this area. Williams' paper is important for two other reasons: (i) it demonstrates the complexity of the problem, and (ii) it shows the tenacity of researchers. (It took nearly seven years —without financial support — to carry out the work involved.) Williams' review of the literature, and his own experiment, indicates the various approaches that people have taken towards creativity and educational technology. The replies to people who argue that thinking and creativity cannot be encouraged by educational technology take several forms. Some people argue that if you can measure a thing, then you can teach it and assess your success (Williams' approach). Others argue that you can 'sharpen' latent creative abilities by instruction (see Covington and Crutchfield, cited by Williams). Others argue that students better taught will progress further, and thus they are likely to be more 'creative', or better problem solvers.

This latter view is that taken by Papert in Paper 3.3. Papert argues that children can be given 'unprecedented power to invent and carry out exciting projects by providing them with access to computers'. He maintains quite simply that we ought to teach children to learn, to think and to play, and that using computer-assisted technology is one way to do this well. In this paper we see a different perspective from that of early programmed learning: we see a more cognitive appraisal of the capacities of children. (A striking example of an application of this approach to autism has been provided by Weir and Emanuel, 1977.)

In Paper 3.4 we introduce the seminal paper 'Goodbye Teacher . . .' which describes the initial 'Keller plan'. Fred Keller's method of teaching has spread like wildfire — encompassing virtually all the subject matters taught in institutes of higher education. The success of the system (and variants on it) has been phenomenal. (One writer, for instance, estimated in 1977 that over one thousand articles had been published or presented on the method.) It seems clear that the factors that have contributed to the success of the method represent a combination of the principles of programmed learning and those from social learning theories. It is important to recognise, however, that despite its more modern name of 'personalised instruction', the Keller teaching method is still instructor dominated: the content, the tests, and the final method of assessment are all instructor controlled.

Paper 3.5 introduces a rather different approach to higher education — that of the Open University in the United Kingdom. This university has several features which differentiate it from other universities both in the United Kingdom and abroad. The Open University is primarily an instructor-controlled correspondence university which uses texts and (to a much smaller extent) broadcast materials. Courses are planned and prepared by course-teams rather than individuals. There are no formal entrance requirements and the students are mainly adults. Degrees are awarded following the accumulation of sufficient credits, and assessment is based fifty per cent on examinations and fifty per cent on course-work. The university is computer based and achieves much of its cost effectiveness through economies of scale. In 1977, for example, approximately sixty thousand students were enrolled.

Paper 3.5 by Brian Lewis is actually the fourth in a series of personal articles about the Open University written from the viewpoint of an educational technologist who works within it. The Open University is considered by many to be a classic example of the application of educational technology (vintage 1970) to specific problems in higher education. Lewis' paper is a salutary reminder that the best can always be improved. Readers particularly interested in the Open University can find several readable accounts now available, the most recent and the most detailed — at the time of writing — being that provided by the Vice-Chancellor, Walter Perry (1976).

Papers 3.6 and 3.7 present sharply contrasting approaches to medical training (and to the approaches advocated in Papers 3.4 and 3.5). Paper 3.6 introduces the notion of self-directed learning in medical education. It is assumed that the students are responsible and motivated adults, and that they can direct their own learning. Such a viewpoint seems somewhat startling in the context of medical education. Paper 3.7 illustrates just the opposite. Here flow-charts are used to guide instruction. The users of the charts do not have to be especially trained or even need to learn. These four papers (3.4 to 3.7) illustrate sharply how social, economic and political forces shape educational technology and *vice versa.*

Finally, in Papers 3.8 and 3.9, we turn to the application of educational technology in occupational and military spheres. Paper 3.8, especially written for this text, describes the use of computers in the training of British Airways staff. This paper illustrates an effective integration of computer-assisted learning and simulation on the one hand, with programmed learning on the other. The final paper, 'Computers in military training', is a survey of the use of computers for military training in the UK and the USA. The work carried out in the UK was supported by the National Programme on Computer Assisted Learning (described by Richard Hooper in Paper 2.8) In Paper 3.9 Roger Miles describes a variety of uses — simulations, computer-assisted learning, computer-managed learning — and contrasts the British style of research with that conducted in the USA. Distasteful as it may be to some, there is no doubt that the contributions of military-based research to educational technology have been enormous.

Suggested further reading

Barrows, H S (1976) Problem-based learning in medicine. In J Clarke and
  J Leedham (eds) *Aspects of Educational Technology X.* London : Kogan Page
Cleary, A, Mayes, T and Packham, D (1975) *Educational Technology and the
  Mentally Handicapped.* London : Wiley

Essex, B J (1977) *Diagnostic Pathways in Clinical Medicine.* Edinburgh : Churchill Livingstone

Ghiselin, B (ed) (1952) *The Creative Process.* New York : Mentor Books

Hooper, R (1978) *The National Development Programme in Computer Assisted Learning: The Final Report of the Director.* London : Council for Educational Technology

Hooper, R and Toye, I (eds) (1975) *Computer-Assisted Learning in the United Kingdom.* London : National Council for Educational Technology

Johnson, K R and Ruskin, R S (1977) *Behavioral Instruction: An Evaluative Review.* Washington : American Psychological Association

Perry, W (1976) *Open University.* Milton Keynes : Open University Press

Semb, G and McKnight, P C (1977) Future trends in PSI research, *Educational Technology XVIII* 9: 50-55

Tunstall, J (ed) (1974) *The Open University Opens.* London : Routledge & Kegan Paul

Vernon, P E (ed) (1970) *Creativity.* Harmondsworth : Penguin Books

Weir, S and Emanuel, R (1977) *Using LOGO to Catalise Communication in an Autistic Child.* Research Report No 15. Edinburgh University : Department of Artificial Intelligence

3.1 Teaching Machines for the Severely Retarded: A Review

JOHN R HEGARTY

Edited version of Hegarty, J R (1975) Teaching machines for the severely retarded: a review, *British Journal of Mental Subnormality* 21: 103-114. Reproduced with permission of the author and the editor.

Introduction

Skinner's arguments, put forward in the 1950s, stimulated the adoption of teaching machines in many areas of education, and the last two decades have seen an increase (as well as a decline) in machines, programmes and research in this field. As might be expected, one area of education which received particular attention was the teaching of the mildly retarded. During the 1960s at least five major reviews of the use of teaching machines with the mildly retarded appeared (Stolurow, 1960a, 1960b, 1961; Greene, 1966; Malpass, 1967). These reviews indicate that the main emphases of the studies were upon the teaching of reading, writing and arithmetic by simple, often manually-operated machines of traditional, Skinnerian design. Few clear conclusions emerge from these studies; as Greene (1966) noted, it is generally hard to conclude much about what particular programme and machine variables are important, whether children can properly operate the machines used, what are the effects of programmes for children of different IQs and so on. Nevertheless, the reviews suggest that mildly retarded children can respond to and learn from this type of approach.

Rather unexpectedly, this enthusiastic attempt to explore a new and promising technique in the field of mild retardation was not matched by workers in the field of severe mental handicap. Comparatively few studies of the use of teaching machines with the severely handicapped have appeared even to the present day. A shortage of appropriate hardware and an increasingly wide use of behaviour modification techniques have undoubtedly contributed to this lack of interest. Nevertheless, the main reason for the neglect may lie in the fact that research workers have found it genuinely difficult to find a role for teaching machines in the education of the severely handicapped. It is the aim of this review to consider critically the use of teaching machines with these people and to consider whether, after some twenty-one years of research in this field, their use in schools can still be advocated.

Review of relevant studies

It would seem strange to some workers in programmed instruction to call a combination of lever-manipulandum, reward-dispenser and ancillary programming equipment a 'teaching machine'. Neither were most of the studies which used such apparatus with the severely retarded described by their authors as studies of 'teaching machines'. Yet in such apparatus we have all the necessary conditions of a Skinnerian machine, namely, overt responses required of the subject, immediate positive reinforcement of correct responses, a permanent record of responses and provision for response shaping. It is, therefore, necessary to begin this review with a discussion of studies conducted with the severely retarded in which such free-operant devices were used.

Early studies of the free-operant behaviour of the severely retarded examined basic parameters of operant responding. Thus, House *et al* (1957), Ellis *et al* (1960), Orlando and Bijou (1960), Bijou and Orlando (1961) and Headrick (1963) studied the sensitivity of subjects to changes in reinforcement schedules: Orlando (1961), Barrett and Lindsley (1962) and Orlando and Bijou (1960) examined the development of stimulus control over responding. Later studies considered practical applications: Bricker and Bricker (1969) used a free-operant technique to carry out pure-tone audiometry. Watson *et al* (1968), wishing to know for how long operant responding could be maintained, attempted to gauge the long-term preferences of subjects for different kinds of reinforcement and Gardner (1971) used a ball-rolling apparatus to normalise stereotyped hand-waving.

Several criticisms of these studies can be made. The representativeness of the samples of subjects for the severely retarded population as a whole is not always clear, few of the studies consider the long-term use of free-operant apparatus, and little is said about the educational implications of the work for the severely retarded. On the other hand, the studies do provide otherwise unobtainable, basic data about the use of these elementary 'teaching machines'. They suggest that, in free-operant devices, we have apparatus with which at least some severely retarded adults will work to obtain cigarettes, sweets or exchangeable tokens as reinforcers. Moreover, sensitivity to different reinforcement schedules has been demonstrated as well as the possibility of teaching subjects basic discriminations (for example, to respond only in the presence of a particular stimulus, or to respond to one particular manipulandum). Finally, it may be argued that such apparatus fosters skills fundamental to the operation of more traditional and complex teaching machines.

Attempts to develop free-operant apparatus into a more explicitly teaching machine were made by Friedlander *et al* (1967). A flexible apparatus ('Playtest') was evolved which could be used by retarded children with mental ages of less than one year. This device was not intended to be a *single* teaching machine but one which could present a wide variety of visual and auditory stimuli and which could be operated by the subject in a variety of ways, according to his particular needs or handicaps.

The 'Playtest' apparatus is a convenient conceptual bridge leading from 'free-operant' devices — where the primary interest lies in response characteristics — to multiple-choice teaching machines where interest focuses upon the learner's visual discrimination performance.

The first landmark we reach after crossing this bridge is the work of Sidman and Stoddard, who hoped that by using the methodology of operant conditioning and programmed instruction they might achieve a means of effective non-verbal communication with the severely retarded. After initial work by Sidman with a severely retarded adult, Sidman and Stoddard (1966) developed teaching programmes which (a) taught children to discriminate a circle from an ellipse and (b) measured the children's circle-ellipse difference threshold. These programmes were presented on a multiple-choice device which required children to touch the odd stimulus in an array of eight. Correct choices were reinforced by a chime and a sweet. Incorrect choices caused stimuli to remain on display until a correct choice was made, when the previous frame was displayed. The programmes were constructed on principles of stimulus fading (cf Terrace, 1963a, b), the step-size of the frames of the programme being determined empirically in order to produce error-free performance.

Sidman and Stoddard's teaching machine required children to respond to the odd stimulus in an array. A more popular teaching machine format for the retarded has, however, been matching to sample, and it is with machines presenting stimuli in this format that we shall be concerned for the remainder of this review. In matching to sample, the learner has to select from an array of (say, three) choices the one which is the same — or matches — one displayed above or below the array.

The first teaching machine presenting programmes in the matching-to-sample format was that used by Hively (1960). Hively studied the responses of twenty-seven normal children (CA 3 to 5 years) to his machine, noting how keen they were to use it and how easily they worked through the matching to sample problems presented by the machine. Hively reports that twenty-five of the children worked with the machine for as many sessions as were offered but that only four children were consistently able to match to sample on the machine.

With a machine of different design Hively carried out further research (1962) to develop a programme which would teach children to match to sample. The outcome of this work was a series of 132 slides which taught children to match correctly four complex and abstract forms. As in the work of Sidman and Stoddard, 'fading' was used to lead children gradually from easy to hard discriminations.

Although Hively did not study the responses of retarded subjects to his machine his work is of relevance to this review in two ways. Firstly, because Skinner used Hively's machine as an illustration of his belief that only teaching machines could adequately teach young children to make discriminations and, secondly, because the commercially produced, British machine, the 'Touch Tutor' (see below) had a similar mode of operation.

Bijou (1968) developed a rather more sophisticated machine than the one used in Hively's second study. The apparatus was intended to exert close control over children's matching behaviour by requiring children to respond to (and hence, to attend to) the sample stimulus before the choice stimuli appeared on view and by presenting previous

239

slides after incorrect choices, after the manner of Sidman and Stoddard's device. Bijou developed a series of programmes for the machine which aimed to teach children increasingly difficult visual discriminations. Early items in the series required discriminations between simple shapes, while later ones introduced factors, firstly of rotation and, at the end of the series, of mirror-image reversal of shapes. Developing the programme on successive groups of normal children and using fading as a main principle of programme design, Bijou eventually devised a reasonably effective teaching programme. In a final evaluation with six normal children, using a test made up of slides from the programme, errors were made on approximately half of the slides before the programme and on about fifteen per cent after completion of the programme.

After developing the machine and programme with groups of normal children, Bijou studied the responses of eighty-nine retarded children (MA range 4 to 9 years, IQ 32 to 66). It appeared that the procedure was able to teach children to discriminate rotated forms but not to teach them to distinguish stimuli with mirror-image reversal as well as rotation. Bijou believed that the reason for this ineffectiveness lay in a combination of the reinforcing properties of the machine and the sequencing of the programme frames, and accordingly modified his procedure. The main modifications were to the apparatus which was altered to allow for more powerful reinforcement of correct first choices than for correct choices made after an error on a frame and elimination of the machine's presenting the previous slide after an error. In addition, the initial instructions to children in the use of the machine were made longer and more explicit. Unfortunately error-rate still remained high and Bijou concluded that his machine, procedures and programme were ineffective in teaching such difficult visual discriminations to these retarded children.

A W Staats' interest in matching-to-sample teaching machines seems to have originated in his ideas on the relationship of speech development to reading (eg Staats & Staats, 1962). Inspired by Skinner's analysis of language, Staats believed that speech and reading were analogous processes, both being acquired by the reinforcement of vocal responses to stimuli. Reading, however (in contrast to speech), was taught in too brief a period with poor conditions of reinforcement. As a first step towards improving the teaching of reading, Staats resolved to study, experimentally, relevant reinforcement variables. An initial experiment (Staats *et al*, 1962) demonstrated the value of such extrinsic reinforcement as toys or sweets during the learning of a sight vocabulary by normal four-year-old children, after which more elaborate apparatus was devised consisting of a matching-to-sample teaching machine, token reinforcement system and recording apparatus (Staats, 1964). Preliminary testing of this was done (Staats *et al*, 1964b) and a fuller evaluation of reinforcement variables was made (Staats *et al*, 1964a). These studies showed that pre-school children would maintain a high rate of correct responding on the apparatus with exchangeable tokens as reinforcement and that they would learn to make discriminations between letters and groups of letters.

Staats (1968) reported studies with six retarded children (MA 3 to 6 years, IQ 32 to 67) using programmes developed with young normal children. Additional frames or further instructions were given to the retarded children at points in the programmes at which difficulties were encountered, and Staats succeeded in getting all children to the same stage of discriminative performance as that reached by the normal children. Staats noted particular difficulties in the comprehension of verbal instructions. Whereas it had been possible to introduce variations in the task by verbal instructions to the normal children, non-verbal instructions had to be devised for the retarded children. This had been especially noticeable while initially teaching children to operate the machine — whereas normal children had required only two sessions to learn the chain of operations, even those retarded children with the highest MAs and IQs had needed five sessions.

Studies of multiple-choice teaching machines with the retarded received an impetus, notably in Britain, with the commercial introduction of the 'Touch Tutor' in 1968. The first published descriptions of this machine (which required the subject to match to sample, reinforcing him for matching correctly by 'speaking' the name of the sample stimulus) consisted of general accounts of the machine and brief descriptions of preliminary work with it (Cleary & Packham, 1968a, b; Mayes, 1968) in addition to a more technical account (Cleary & Packham, 1968c). Initial work with the machine carried out by its designers studied the responses of severely subnormal children and pre-school normal children to the machine (Harper et al, 1971; Huskisson et al, 1969). Children appeared to respond well to the machine in these studies, indicating the possible potential value of the device in the education of such children. The commercial production of the 'Touch Tutor' offered a unique opportunity for this potential to be explored and sales reflected some of the interest which the appearance of the machine generated. By March 1971 some twenty machines had been sold in Britain, mainly to schools or research bodies concerned with ESN and SSN children (Cleary & Packham, 1972).

Work with the 'Touch Tutor' during this time followed three broad paths. Firstly, studies were carried out to investigate the responses of severely subnormal children to the machine and to simple, easily discriminable stimulus material presented on it (Levinson, 1970a, b; Beasley & Hegarty, 1970; Hegarty, 1973). Secondly, work was directed at developing programmes for the 'Touch Tutor' which would be of immediate relevance to schools — for example, programmes aimed at teaching social competence (Moseley, 1970a). Thirdly, an attempt was made to use the 'Touch Tutor' for the diagnosis and remediation of perceptual deficits in severely subnormal children (Cunningham, 1970) — an application for teaching machines which was strongly advocated by Sidman and Stoddard (1966) and which is a recurrent theme in this literature. In addition, the originators of the 'Touch Tutor' were devising sophisticated, electronic amendments to the machine which would reduce, it was hoped, the number of incorrect responses made to programme materials (Cleary & Packham, 1972).

Unfortunately, few positive results emerged from these studies and work with the 'Touch Tutor' ceased. The machine itself suffered no better fate. Kapota (1970), on behalf of Behavioural Research and Development Ltd (the manufacturers of the 'Touch Tutor') noted: 'After four or five years the company has produced sixteen machines at a heavy loss . . . it is estimated that the sale of 200 machines over the next two years is necessary if we are to recover our losses.' This was not achieved and in 1971 the company went into liquidation, despite redesigning the 'Touch Tutor' for compatibility with modular, solid-state programming equipment marketed by the company. To the author's knowledge, the machine is still available to special order but is not being actively marketed.

Discussion

Implicit in the introduction to and use of teaching machines with the mentally handicapped is the belief that they offer something which educational techniques presently in use do not. Strangely, it has been rare for researchers to make explicit their expectations in this respect — a fact which makes evaluation of their work difficult. Since, however, most workers have followed Skinner in their techniques and methods, it will be helpful to consider his views on the advantages offered by teaching machines and to ask how far these have been realised. In doing so we shall need to pay particular attention to the everyday use of these devices in schools. For, whatever value they may appear to have in a research laboratory, the potential of teaching machines as a powerful educational technique will only be realised if they can be used widely.

Skinner (1961a) described a matching-to-sample teaching machine, believing that it would teach children to make discriminations far more effectively than would a human teacher:

> We call an effective person 'discriminating' . . . but . . . the number of reinforcements required to build discriminative behaviour in the population as a whole is far beyond the capacity of teachers. Too many teachers would be needed and many contingencies are too subtle to be mediated by even the most skilful.

If such machines were widely available in schools, he believed, they would have a profound educational effect: 'Our children would be far more skilful in dealing with their environments . . . They would lead more effective lives.' The reason was reiterated:

> In the light of what we know about differential contingencies of reinforcement, the world of the young child is shamefully impoverished. And only machines will remedy this, for the required frequency and subtlety of reinforcement cannot otherwise be arranged. (Skinner, 1961c)

As far as the author is aware these statements had little foundation. Skinner seems to have carried out no research himself with matching-to-sample teaching machines, although he apparently designed Hively's machines as well as a programme in matching-to-sample format to teach form discrimination to young children (cf Holland, 1960, 1962). Since no other research was then available, these claims were no more than an imaginative translation of the results of animal studies into the field of human education. Have they been justified by the results of subsequent research?

Crucial to this rationale is the belief that matching-to-sample machines will supply 'the required frequency and subtlety of reinforcement'. Unfortunately, while it is true that the machines described above provide frequent reinforcement, they have failed to provide subtle reinforcement. Hively (1960) noted the development of persistent patterns of incorrect responding (for example, pushing both choice windows of the machine simultaneously or the chaining of incorrect and correct responses) in 18 of the 27 children participating in the study. Hively attributed them to 'accidental contingencies of reinforcement' supplied by the machine. In his second study (1962) similar patterns of responding occurred despite more accurate stimulus programming, and the prospect of eliminating them entirely seemed bleak:

> No matter how carefully one designs a sequence of correlations between the *occurrence* of stimuli and the *availability* of reinforcement, the actual contingencies of reinforcement in a given case depend upon what the subject observes . . . From the experimenter's point of view it is a matter of chance.

Although others have noted the occurrence of error-patterns in the performance of young normal children, they appear to be particularly prevalent in the responses of retarded subjects to multiple-choice teaching machines. Sidman and Stoddard (1966) managed to reduce error-patterns by careful programme design while developing their circle-ellipse discrimination programme upon groups of normal children, but found them reappearing in the performances of retarded children (1967). Bijou (1968) found that reinforcement contingencies adequate for normal subjects failed to control the responding of retarded subjects. During the work of Edwards and Rosenberg, a buzzer had to be used to interrupt systematic error-patterns when these were detected by a watchful experimenter. In the author's own work, error-patterns were widespread in the responses of severely subnormal children to the 'Touch Tutor' (Hegarty, 1973). Barrett and Lindsley (1962) described idiosyncratic patterns of responding to two manipulanda in a free-operant task, regarding them as organismic variables which 'interfere with efficient differential response to immediate contingencies in a controlled environment'.

In the literature reviewed here error-patterns have been attributed typically to spurious reinforcement contingencies. While this may be so, these studies have had a conspicuous lack of success in eradicating error-patterns by the manipulation of machine and programme design, only human intervention appearing to be effective (cf Staats, 1968). Accordingly, one is forced to conclude that multiple-choice devices such as those described here are often unable to provide adequately *subtle* reinforcement for the teaching of discriminations. *Far from teachers being unable to mediate the subtle contingencies of reinforcement deemed important by Skinner for the teaching of discriminations to children, it seems that only they can do so.* Moreover, there is no evidence that more traditional teaching materials (such as the widely used sets of cards involving matching to sample) are less effective than machines for teaching discriminations. They may even be more effective and are considerably cheaper, easier to use and more flexible.

The teaching of discriminations was not the only advantage of teaching machines foreseen by Skinner. They also offered: student-paced instruction, liberation of the teacher from repetitive 'drill' work, frequent positive reinforcement during learning, and the opportunity of evaluating and revising teaching material (Skinner, 1954, 1958, 1961a). It is important to ask whether these advantages apply to the machines reviewed here when used with the retarded.

Of these four advantages the first two pertain mainly to features of machine design. Providing that pupils are able and willing to respond to a particular teaching machine without the close presence of a teacher, 'student-paced instruction' and 'liberation of the teacher from "drill" work' will follow automatically. In the studies reviewed here there appeared to be no obvious problem of severely retarded pupils being unable or unwilling to respond to free-operant or multiple-choice devices. Indeed, Bijou remarked on the willingness of retarded children to 'come to the laboratory for repeated sessions' which was in contrast to the 'reluctance' of normal children. Similarly, the present author found this not a major problem, even though some children would make no responses to the 'Touch Tutor' (Hegarty, 1973). However, it is necessary to remember that most of the devices used have been 'easy' to operate in that they required neither fine manual dexterity nor the ability to read. Problems could arise with machines demanding these skills.

The second two advantages are less easy to achieve. The first depends, if the machine cannot provide it, upon the availability of carefully designed, appropriate teaching programmes. These require the enthusiasm and ability of teachers to produce, test and revise teaching material. As may be seen in the previous section, efficient programmes for the machines reviewed here are difficult to create, even for experienced researchers with technical resources and time at their disposal. For teachers, hard-pressed with existing problems and without technical and financial assistance, the task of creating educationally valuable material for multiple-choice or free-operant devices would be impossible. It could be argued that these obstacles are not insurmountable. A central agency could be established to produce programmes in conjunction with teachers. Or special funds could be allocated to schools to appoint their own specialists in educational technology. Actually, experience of both solutions has been gained. With respect to the first, Cleary and Packham offered to produce programmes for the 'Touch Tutor' to specifications supplied to them. Unfortunately, little advantage was taken of this facility, mainly, no doubt, because few teachers had machines and funds at their disposal, but also (for those few who had) because of real difficulties in devising new programmes. In discussions with teachers who had had experience of the 'Touch Tutor', the author found not only a lack of psychological expertise which made concepts of discrimination learning, fading, etc foreign ones, but also a paucity of ideas for new programme material. In other words, they failed to see what the machine could be used to teach.

With respect to the second solution, Marshall (1969) and Morgan (1971), both head-teachers, used multiple-choice teaching machines widely in their schools for mildly subnormal children. Particularly relevant to this review is the work of Morgan who, disliking the 'Touch Tutor', devised his own multiple-choice, audio-visual machine, wrote a wide range of programmes for it and gave it a central position in his school's curriculum. In the author's opinion, Morgan's use of the machine in this way is, educationally, the highlight of this literature. The machine did not stand alone as a researcher's plaything but was part of the teaching fabric of a school. Its programmes were relevant to the children's other experiences in the school, they were encouraged to use it as a matter of course, and teachers recognised the need for devising supplementary material for it. Significantly, the researcher was a headmaster, not a visiting research psychologist, and perhaps this was the important feature. It does suggest, however, that a keen exponent of educational technology, in direct and influential contact with a school, could ensure a valuable and continuing place for teaching machines there.

Do teaching machines, therefore, offer something that conventional techniques do not? Having considered Skinner's arguments for these devices it would seem that they do not. They fail to offer the most important advantage — precise reinforcement of correct responses, and they pose extreme problems for the teacher in the design and analysis of programme material. Certainly, children are able to use them on their own, but this is true of most ordinary toys and educational apparatus.

Conclusions

Since the demise of the 'Touch Tutor', two companies have introduced matching-to-sample machines of similar format — one in the USA and one in Britain. Possibly there will be others. Underlying this review is the question of whether such machines can ever have any major, beneficial impact on the education of the severely mentally handicapped or whether they are doomed to a brief life in the open with a long death in some educational store-room. The author would like to argue that the value of expensive and sophisticated machines such as those described here is limited. Not only do they pose difficulties for the pupils using them, but they pose even greater ones for the teacher.

If this, then, is the conclusion of this review, one must finally ask whether it applies only to the sophisticated, free-operant and teaching machine devices we have discussed. Is there, despite our arguments, a place for automatic devices of a simpler kind — which require fewer financial and teaching resources but which nevertheless have some characteristics of the machines discussed so far. Beasley (1974) described an 'automated teaching aid' for the severely mentally handicapped. Consisting of an automatic slide projector and cassette tape recorder, housed in a box with a back-projection screen, this device presented pictures with an accompanying commentary — analogous to a child being told a story from a picture book. Since colour transparencies taken with any camera could be used for the pictures and the verbal commentary could be made easily, the aid was potentially usable in any school. Moreover, encouraging results were obtained in early studies with it. One other device recently described is a very simple version of the 'Touch Tutor' (Anon, 1975). It involves a frame in which a matching-to-sample problem drawn on pieces of card can be inserted. The teacher selects a switch at the rear of the apparatus according to the position of the correct choice stimulus, the student makes a choice by pressing a panel on the front of the machine and, if he is correct, a light is illuminated. If his choice is wrong, however, nothing happens. No studies with this machine have been reported, but one would imagine that it would have the appeal of the more sophisticated machine for mentally handicapped persons bored with endless matching cards with none of the heartache for the teacher of more sophisticated gadgets.

Finally, the reader is referred to the work of Newson, who has been responsible for creating a number of toys aimed at fostering the development of handicapped children. Parents of handicapped children are advised on toys suitable for developing particular skills in their children and are able to borrow them for use at home. The operation of this 'toy library' is described in a tape-slide presentation by Head and Mogford (1972) and the development of some of the toys in a tape by Newson (1972). Backed by research expertise as this toy library is, it seems to represent a valuable and efficient medium for designing simple devices for the handicapped and promoting their wider use.

This review has discussed some twenty-one years of research with young normal and handicapped people into the use of a number of gadgets with very similar features. The author would like to think that this period is long enough to have failed to demonstrate the value of complicated teaching devices for the mentally handicapped and that no more will be heard of them other than in restricted applications. Instead, research workers and equipment producers may perhaps with great value apply themselves to the production of small teaching aids and gadgets which are inexpensive enough to be used for individual children and detailed needs as well as to the establishment of toy libraries and resource centres for promoting them.

References

Anon (1975) A simple matching trainer, *Apex* 3 1: 24

Barrett, B H and Lindsley, O R (1962) Deficits in acquisition of operant discrimination and differentiation shown by institutionalised, retarded children, *Am J Ment Defic* 67: 424-36

Beasley, N A (1974) Teaching machines and the programmed approach in the education of the mentally handicapped. In H C Gunzburg (ed) *Experiments in the Rehabilitation of the Mentally Handicapped.* London : Butterworths

Beasley, N A and Hegarty, J R (1970) The use of the Touch Tutor with SSN children, *J Ment Subnorm* 16 2: 113-18

Bijou, S W (1968) Studies in the development of left-right concepts in retarded children using fading techniques. In N R Ellis (ed) *International Review of Research in Mental Retardation III.* New York : Academic Press

Bijou, S W and Orlando, R (1961) Rapid development of multiple schedule performances with retarded children, *J Exp Analysis Behav* 4: 7-16

Bricker, W A and Bricker, D D (1969) Four operant procedures for establishing auditory stimulus control with low-functioning children, *Am J Ment Defic* 73: 981-7

Cleary, A and Packham, D (1968a) Learning by touch, *New Education and Programmed Learning News* 4 5: 21-3

Cleary, A and Packham, D (1968b) A teaching system for visual discrimination skills. In W R Dunn and C Holroyd (eds) *Aspects of Educational Technology II.* London : Methuen

Cleary, A and Packham, D (1968c) A touch detecting machine with auditory reinforcement, *J Appl Behav Analysis* 1: 241-345

Cleary, A and Packham, D (1972) *Teaching Machine Project.* Final Report on Social Science Research Council Grant HR 256. National Lending Library

Cunningham, C C (1970) The use of programmed learning in the teaching of visual perceptual skills. In P J Mittler (ed) *The Work of the Hester Adrian Research Centre. Teaching and Training Mongr Supp* 8: 22-7

Ellis, N R, Barnett, C D and Pryer, M W (1960) Operant behaviour in mental defectives: exploratory studies, *J Exp Analysis Behav* 3: 63-9

Friedlander, B Z, McCarthy, J J and Soforenko, A Z (1967) Automated psychological evaluation with severely retarded, institutionalised infants, *Am J Ment Defic* 71: 909-19

Gardner, W I (1971) *Behaviour Modification in Mental Retardation.* Chicago : Aldine

Greene, F M (1966) Programmed instruction techniques for the mentally retarded. In N R Ellis (ed) *International Review of Research in Mental Retardation II.* New York : Academic Press

Harper, R, Cleary, A and Packham, D (1971) An automated technique for the training of retarded children, *Programmed Learning* 8 1: 1-9

Head, J and Mogford, K (1972) *Nottingham University Toy Library for Handicapped Children.* Chelmsford : Medical Recording Service Foundation. Tape 72-73

Headrick, M W (1963) Effects of instructions and initial reinforcement on fixed-interval behaviour in retardates, *Am J Ment Defic* 68: 425-32

Hegarty, J R (1973) Some experiments in the use of the Touch Tutor with severely subnormal children. Unpublished PhD thesis, University of Keele

Hively, W (1960) An exploratory investigation of an apparatus for studying and teaching visual discrimination using pre-school children. In A A Lumsdaine and R Glaser (eds) *Teaching Machines and Programmed Learning: A Source Book.* Washington, DC : National Education Association

Hively, W (1962) Programming stimuli in matching to sample, *J Exp Analysis Behav* 5: 279-98

Holland, J G (1960) Teaching machines: an application of principles from the laboratory, *J Exp Analysis Behav* 3: 275-87

Holland, J G (1962) New directions in teaching machine research. In J E Coulson (ed) *Programmed Learning and Computer-based Instruction.* New York : Wiley & Sons

House, B J, Zeaman, D and Fischer, W (1957) *Learning and Transfer in Mental Defectives.* Progress Report No 1, Research Grant M-1099. NIMH, quoted by Denny, M R (1964) Research in Learning and Performance. In H A Stevens, and R Heber (eds) *Mental Retardation.* University of Chicago Press

Huskisson, J, Packham, D and Cleary, A (1969) Pre-reading experiments with the Touch Tutor. In A P Mann and C K Brunstrom (eds) *Aspects of*

Educational Technology III. London : Pitman

Kapota, K J (1970) Report on behalf of Behavioural Research and Development Ltd. In Moseley (1970b)

Levinson, F (1970a) Summary of Touch Tutor studies at Harperbury Hospital. In Moseley (1970b)

Levinson, F (1970b) The use of Touch Tutors with severely subnormal children, *Behav Technol* 2: 10-11

Malpass, L F (1967) Programmed instruction for retarded children. In A A Baumeister (ed) *Mental Retardation: Appraisal, Education and Rehabilitation.* London : University of London Press

Marshall, A E (1969) *An Experiment in Programmed Learning with ESN children.* Oxford : Pergamon Press

Mayes, J T (1968) *The Touch Tutor: A Progress Report.* Xth International Automation and Instrumentation Conference, Milan

Morgan, J H (1971) DIY at Dinsdale Park School, *Special Education* 60 4: 21-3

Moseley, D (1970a) Touch Tutor Evaluation Programme. In Moseley (1970b)

Moseley, D (1970b) Papers arising from a meeting of Touch Tutor personnel, January 1970. Unpublished Report, National Society for Mentally Handicapped Children

McCarthy, J J, Stevens, H A and Billingsley, J F (1969) *Program Development for Severely Retarded, Institutionalized Children.* Report on project conducted at Central Wisconsin Colony and Training School, Wisconsin, USA

Newson, J (1972) *Playthings for the Handicapped Child.* Chelmsford : Medical Recording Service Foundation. Tape 72-21

Orlando, R (1961) The functional role of discriminative stimuli in free operant performance of developmentally retarded children, *Psychol Rec* 11: 153-61

Orlando, R and Bijou, S W (1960) Single and multiple schedules of reinforcement in developmentally retarded children, *J Exp Analysis Behav* 3: 339-48

Sidman, M and Stoddard, L T (1966) Programming perception and learning for retarded children. In N R Ellis (ed) *International Review of Research in Mental Retardation II.* New York : Academic Press

Sidman, M and Stoddard, L T (1967) The effectiveness of fading in programming a simultaneous form discrimination for retarded children, *J Exp Analysis Behav* 10: 3-15

Skinner, B F (1954) The science of learning and the art of teaching, *Harv Educ Rev* 24: 86-97

Skinner, B F (1958) Teaching machines, *Science* 128: 969-77

Skinner, B F (1961a) Why we need teaching machines, *Harv Educ Rev* 31: 377-98

Skinner, B F (1961b) Pigeons in a pelican. In Skinner (1961c)

Skinner, B F (1961c) *Cumulative Record.* London : Methuen

Staats, A W (1964) A case in and a strategy for the extension of learning principles to problems of human behavior. In A W Staats (ed) *Human Learning.* New York : Holt, Rinehart & Winston

Staats, A W (1968) *Learning, Language and Cognition.* London : Holt, Rinehart & Winston

Staats, A W, Finley, J R, Minke, K A and Wolf, M M (1964a) Reinforcement variables in the control of unit reading responses, *J Exp Analysis Behav* 7: 139-49

Staats, A W, Minke, K A, Finley, J R, Wolf, M M and Brooks, L O (1964b) A reinforcer system and experimental procedure for the laboratory study of reading acquisition, *Child Development* 35: 209-31

Staats, A W and Staats, C K (1962) A comparison of the development of speech and reading behaviour with implications for research, *Child Development* 33: 831-46

Staats, A W, Staats, C K, Schutz, R E and Wolf, M M (1962) The conditioning of textual responses using 'extrinsic' reinforcers, *J Exp Analysis Behav* 5: 33-40

Stolurow, L M (1960a) Automation in special education, *Except Child* 27: 78-83

Stolurow, L M (1960b) Teaching machines and special education, *Educ Psychol Measur* 20: 429-48

Stolurow, L M (1961) *Teaching by Machine.* Washington, DC : US Office of Education Co-operative Research Monograph No 6

Terrace, H S (1963a) Discrimination learning with and without 'errors', *J Exp Analysis Behav* 6: 1-27

Terrace, H S (1963b) Errorless transfer of a discrimination across two continua, *J Exp Analysis Behav* 6: 223-32

Watson, L S, Orser, R and Sanders, C (1968) Reinforcement preferences of severely mentally retarded children in a generalized reinforcement context, *Am J Ment Defic* 72: 748-56

3.2 Programmed Instruction for Creativity

ROBERT E WILLIAMS

Williams, R E (1977) Programmed instruction for creativity, *Programmed Learning and Educational Technology* 14: 50-64. Reproduced with permission of the author and the editor.

Introduction

During the last few decades there has been an increasing interest in creativity. It has been stated that this accelerated interest was due to the space race and, in particular, the fact that the USSR put a man into space before the USA did. There was no shortage of scientists who possessed knowledge, but there was a dearth of scientists who knew how to use that knowledge creatively. The need for creative ability has become apparent in many fields today.

Rogers (1954) stated, 'Not only individual maladjustment and group tensions, but international annihilation will be the price we pay for lack of creativity . . . investigations of the process of creativity, the conditions under which this process occurs, and the ways in which it may be facilitated, are of the utmost importance.' Similar conclusions were reached following studies in the field of creativity. Torrance (1967a) said, 'It was commonly thought that creative thinking, the production of new ideas, invention, and the like, had to be left to chance . . . I do not see how any well informed person can still hold this view.' The need for increasing creative ability, or developing an awareness of its importance, was considered the major problem area. The author's field of interest was in the area of visual creativity, but a general interest in the overall field of creativity was also involved.

Studies in the field of programmed instruction seem mainly to be concerned with learning in terms of acquiring knowledge of a factual nature, and many authorities have questioned the suitability of programmed instruction for purposes other than the acquisition of factual knowledge. Stolurow (1964), however, predicted 'Learning from auto-instructional programming will be shown to be capable of aiding persons to solve problems creatively.'

As a result of conclusions reached during studies in the areas of creativity and programmed instruction, it was decided to accept the obvious challenge. The research to be described in this paper was to ascertain whether or not it was possible to increase creativity by means of programmed instruction. The aim of the study was finally stated in the form of the question: 'Can programmed instruction be effective in increasing creativity, particularly in the visual field?' The decision was taken to develop a 'creativity programme' that would increase creativity as measured by chosen instruments.

Preparation

Preparation for the study involved two main areas:

(i) a review of the literature in the fields of creativity and programmed instruction (with particular reference to previous attempts to increase creative ability using programmed instruction), and

(ii) the selection and development of instruments for measuring creative ability.

REVIEW OF LITERATURE: CREATIVITY

Many definitions of the term 'creativity' were examined. Torrance (1962a) stated that creativity is a 'process of sensing gaps . . . forming ideas or hypotheses concerning them, testing these hypotheses and communicating the results'. Many researchers have stressed the importance of originality, eg Kneller (1965). Other definitions stress the elaboration of creative ideas. A distillation of aspects that define creativity is provided by MacKinnon (1967) who postulated that creativity must fulfil at least three conditions: '(1) a novel response, (2) that is adaptive to reality, and (3) is elaborated; the idea is developed to the full.' The bulk of the literature was reviewed in three areas: the creative person, the creative process and the creative product. For a full review and report of this research the reader is referred to Williams (1975); a brief summary is given here.

Creative person

The controversial relationship between creativity and intelligence, as investigated by Getzels and Jackson (1962), and Wallach and Kogan (1965), was considered. The tenets given by MacKinnon (1962) were accepted in this area, where he states, 'above a certain required minimum level of intelligence . . . being more intelligent does not guarantee a corresponding increase in creativeness.' Hudson (1966) reinforced these ideas when he said, 'the factors that determine an individual's creativeness are personal not intellectual.'

A number of traits that are common to creative personalities have been postulated. These were condensed under nine headings, which, with remarks made by researchers in the field, were listed as follows:

Adventurous: Cropley (1967) stated that 'Highly creative thinkers were significantly more willing to take intellectual risks.'

Contemplative: Torrance (1967b) said that a creative person 'may look like daydreaming when he's thinking'. The related concept of 'regression in the service of the ego' was discussed by Barron (1967). A critic of this concept is Ray (1967).

Individualist: McGuire (1967) stated that 'creatively intelligent independence, and a certain amount of self-discipline are essential elements of emotional learning.'

Questioning: Arnold (1962) remarked that the creative person is 'fired with a spirit of enquiry'.

Energetic: Barron (1967) said that creative persons had 'vigour, and an exceptional fund of psychic and physical energy'.

Humorous: Koestler (1964) has dealt extensively with this trait, which he linked with the associative, emotional and original aspects of creativity.

Emotional: Maslow (1962) found that young creatives were often 'undisciplined . . . called childish, irresponsible, wild, crazy, irregular, emotional'.

Versatile: This trait is based on concepts of 'divergency'. Hudson (1966) and Cropley (1966) have reported research in this area.

Persevering: A number of researchers have stressed involvement, commitment, a sense of destiny, and the ability to elaborate as associated with this trait, eg Guilford (1959) and Torrance (1966).

It does not follow that a person who exhibits all these traits is necessarily creative. Guilford (1967a) stated '. . . no one of them is a dependable sign, nor would all of them collectively be sufficient.' Some of the traits listed appear to be contradictory when compared. The literature on the creative person is often muddled and fragmentary; but creative persons can display all the above behaviour patterns at one stage or another in their creative activity. However, the underlying factors that make up the creative personality remain elusive.

Creative process

The creative process was examined using the four well-known stages proposed by Wallas (1926) as a basis; these are: preparation, incubation, illumination and verification. These stages overlap and interchange in the creative process, but they are distinguishable one from another.

Importance of preparation: The importance of preparation is recognised or implied by a number of researchers, eg Ghiselin (1952). Guilford (1967b) has been concerned with the recognition or sensing of the problem. Gathering knowledge from a variety of fields is also important, as pointed out by Simon (1964). The associative theory of creativity developed by Mednick and Mednick (1964) is based on similar concepts. A few of the most important activities in the preparatory stage may be summarised as follows: sensory collection, experimentation, skill development, general research, particular research, and recording of knowledge gained in these activities.

Incubation: More has been written concerning this stage than any other although the mental processes involved in creative work cannot easily be observed. Theories and models have been devised and tested, but our knowledge in this area is still limited. Theories range from psychoanalytic to behaviourist concepts; from subconscious *regression* to controlled S-R methods. No definitive theory of creativity in this incubatory stage has yet been formulated. Theories based on regression have been used by many investigators, eg Schiller and Freud (1938); and Barron (1967) who stated '. . . I believe the creative individual not only respects the irrational in himself, but courts it as the most promising source of novelty in his own thoughts.' Some terms that have been used to describe creative processes are: daydreaming, doodling, combining, building, serendipity, synthesis and association.

Illumination: Illumination is usually interpreted as the 'sudden flash', as the solution to the problem appears. Youtz (1962) considered that 'New solutions usually appear whole', and Hallman (1967) found an element of 'surprise. The shock of recognition which registers the novel experience.'

Verification: The term more commonly used to describe this stage is *evaluation.* This may lead to further creative thinking. Taylor (1967) proposed for this stage 'Deliberate effort, verify, elaborate, revise'. Verification may take place at a number of stages in the creative process before the solution is finally achieved. The *time* factor often complicates the verification stage. Ghiselin (1952) points out that the criteria for evaluation may not exist at the time of creation.

Creative product

The evaluation of productions as more creative or less creative is difficult. Brogden and Sprecher (1964) stated, 'Despite the fact that products lie at the heart of criterion problems, little work has been done with them.' Even in the field of art, where criteria for judgement have long been a major concern, this is still the case, as pointed out by Thomas (1964). In the visual arts early attempts at evaluation were concerned with aesthetics. Recently, such researchers as Lowenfield (1947), Arnheim (1954) and Brittain and Beittel (1960) have indicated criteria that are concerned with creativity in the visual arts. Burkhart (1960, 1962) has evolved concepts of deliberateness and spontaneity, and provided methods for judging them. The criteria of originality and relevance are important for evaluation, although Rogers (1954) has considered that the genuinely significant creation '. . . is most likely to be seen at first as erroneous, bad or foolish'. Some attempts must be made, however, to evolve criteria for the evaluation of creativity in products. Creativity is also concerned with the *improvement* of products, and this requires evaluation. Another criterion is concerned with the degree to which a product may change or add to the way of life.

Some criteria that may be useful in the evaluation of creativity are that a product should be: relevant, original, dynamic, complex, integrated, expressive of personality, capable of adding to or changing the way of life, and should show mastery of the media and subject areas. In visual artworks criteria concerned with asymmetry, spontaneity and utilisation of space are also relevant.

Identification of creative ability

Much recent research has been concerned with attempts to measure creative ability. Torrance (1964) reviewed attempts dating from 1900. A number of creativity tests have been based on visual art judgements, eg the Graves Design Judgement Test (1948) and the Barron Welsh Art Scale (1952). Projective tests, such as the Rorschach or Thematic Apperception Test, have also been used as tests of creativity.

The *paper-and-pencil* type of tests (eg Strong Vocational Interest Blank, Gough Adjective Checklist, MMPI, and Cattell's 16PF, HSPQ and CPQ) have also been used in measuring creativity, eg Cattell (1963), although they have not yet proved reliable. Tests of creativity itself have been devised, often based on work by Guilford in the 1950s, or Mednick (1962), whose Remote Association Test is well known. Torrance and his associates at Minnesota, eg Yamamoto (1964), developed tests of the Guilford type. The Torrance Tests of Creative Thinking (1966) represent a fully developed, tested measure of this nature.

Other researchers have developed or used similar instruments in their studies, eg Wallach and Kogan (1965) and Hudson (1966). Tests of creativity in the visual arts have been developed by Burkhart, and Brittain and Beittel (1960). Burkhart (1960, 1962) has developed measures of deliberateness and spontaneity.

Increasing creative ability

Most attempts to increase creativity have involved efforts to influence factors in the preparatory, incubatory and verification stages of the creative process. Some researchers have considered making the environment more conducive to creative activity, eg Arnold (1962) and Torrance (1962b). Kneller (1965) thought that there were two ways to increase creativity in education; either to modify the curriculum to draw upon creative potential in all subject matter, or to teach creativity in its own right.

The work of Lowenfield (1947) and Burkhart (1962) has been valuable in attempts to increase creativity in the visual field. Direct influences on the process factors have been successful. Many such attempts have involved the principle of 'deferred judgement'; the term often used in this context is that of 'brainstorming'. The work of Osborn (1953), Clark (1958) and Parnes (1962) has been influential in this area. The essence of brainstorming is that as many ideas as possible are conceived in a set time. During this time no criticism is allowed. The ideas produced, using techniques for combining, associating, etc during the session, often include original ways of solving the problem. Selection, elaboration and evaluation of the solution follow. Another development of brainstorming was the 'group ideation' method of 'synectics', popularised by Gordon (1961). Brainstorming methods have been used in industry, commerce, education and training.

Other methods for increasing fluency, flexibility, and originality in creative thinking have been devised. These also often involve processes that include association, building, combining, etc, for example, the work of Edward de Bono (1967) in lateral thinking is now well known. The work of Houston and Mednick (1963) in the field of operant behaviour — mainly concerned with the associative aspects of creative thinking — has also had some success.

REVIEW OF LITERATURE: PROGRAMMED INSTRUCTION

The literature of programmed instruction was reviewed with particular reference to the fact that most of the early basic principles have been challenged and all have undergone development. The work of the early programmed learning innovators, eg Pressey (1926, 1932) and Skinner (1954, 1961) was briefly reviewed. The work of Crowder (1960) in intrinsic programming, Mager (1964) in learner-based programming, and

Gilbert (1960, 1962) in mathetics was also considered.

Developing concepts were examined in the light of criticism of the primary principles:

Self-pacing: Concepts of self-pacing and individual instruction do not seem as mandatory as once supposed.

Immediate knowledge of results: The main value here appears to be in terms of the feedback of information rather than in reinforcement.

Active overt response: Overt responding is not always essential or effective, and much depends on the circumstances in which a response provides feedback.

Small steps: Conclusions reached from examination of various researches concerning frame size were:

(a) frames should be of optimum size for the learners and the material involved;
(b) the material should be challenging to the learner;
(c) a frame should elicit a response (covert or overt);
(d) a programme may involve frames of many different types.

Appropriate sequence of subject material: Numerous approaches have been devised. Skinner, Crowder, Mager and Gilbert, mentioned previously, have contributed valuable ideas. Task analyses, developed by Gagné (1965) and Davies (1971), have also proved useful. It is probable, however, that there is no one perfect approach to the problem of sequencing.

Evaluation: The work of Hartley (1963) has been valuable in the areas of internal and external evaluation. Comments on the uselessness of evaluation by *inspection* have been made by Rothkopf (1964). The classic method of assessment by means of pre-tests and post-tests appears to be the most satisfactory to date, although a programme may have effects that cannot be detected by the test instruments used. Recent developments in programmed instruction were reviewed, eg *adjunctive programming* advocated by Pressey (1964) and structural communication (Bennett, 1967). The value of decision trees, flow charts, algorithms, etc was also considered.

For useful information concerning researches on the developing nature of programmed instruction see Hartley (1974) and Mackie (1975).

Programmed instruction for creativity

A number of attempts to increase creativity by means of programmed instruction were reviewed; however, there were few of these.

The work of Crutchfield (1967) and the 'productive thinking program' developed by Covington, Crutchfield and Davies (1967) was interesting. This programme consisted of detective stories that involved the pupil in creative problem solving. Guides for 'good thinking' were of use in leading the learner to think creatively. As there were usually correct answers to the problems set, original answers to open-ended questions were not always possible. Studies by Covington and Crutchfield (1965) and Olton (1969), however, showed that the programme was effective.

Shackel and Lawrence (1969) developed an auto-instructional

programme that attempted to increase fluency, flexibility, originality and elaboration in essay writing. They found that the six programmed textbooks they devised were effective.

Torrance and Myers' (1964) 'idea books', and the 'imagi/craft' record programme by Cunnington and Torrance (1965) were also examined.

The Purdue creativity programme developed by Feldhusen *et al* (1970), consisting of audio tapes and printed exercises, has been reported as effective in studies by Bahlke (1967) and Feldhusen, Bahlke and Treffinger (1969).

Little has been found concerning programmed instruction in the area of the visual arts. It is apparent, however, that programmed instruction has been used successfully in attempts to increase some aspects of creativity.

SELECTION AND DEVELOPMENT OF INSTRUMENTS FOR MEASURING CREATIVE ABILITY

Following the examination of tests of creativity that could be used by pupils in the group situation, those chosen for use in the study were:

1. the Torrance Tests of Creative Thinking (figural forms A and B);
2. the CPQ and HSPQ second order factors for 'creativity' and 'exvia/invia';
3. four 'art judgement' instruments developed by the author. It was established, prior to the study to be reported, that there was a relationship between these tests and the Torrance tests and measures of creativity. The four tests were: a *gestalt* judgement where the work was awarded a score on the creativity it displayed; a *spontaneous* judgement where scores were awarded on a bipolar scale based on spontaneity and deliberateness; an *originality* judgement where a score was obtained by summing scores on seven factors (theme, use of work space, use of surface, variety, rhythm, use of media, and impact on judge — judged for the creativity displayed); and an *involvement* judgement where a score was obtained by summing scores on five factors (life, animation, emotion, media, and effect of media).

In a previous study a measure of interjudge reliability for these judgements was obtained: the average correlation (between two judges) was significant ($p \leq 0.005$).

For a more detailed review of the literature, and discussion of the various tests, etc the reader is referred to Williams (1975).

Development of the creativity programme

The programme was developed in three stages:

1. the selection of relevant factors concerned with creativity and programmed instruction;
2. considerations regarding objectives, subjects, conditions, etc; and
3. construction of the programme itself.

SELECTION OF RELEVANT FACTORS

Creativity

Relevant factors were chosen following a process of elimination and amalgamation. Factors were chosen from the areas: person, process and product.

Person: Traits considered socially unacceptable — being undisciplined, rebellious, crazy, etc — were rejected. Traits chosen as representative of the creative personality were: being questioning, adventurous, versatile, persevering, contemplative, individualistic, humorous, emotional and energetic. The need for a reasonably high level of intelligence was also included.

Process: Factors involved in the total process of creation, ie preparation, incubation, illumination, and verification, were chosen. Factors in the preparation stage considered useful were: mastering knowledge of subject and media, experimenting, using the senses, researching, developing skills, questioning, studying other creative work, and recording information. Factors related to the incubation stage included: association, combining, building, serendipity (doodling, daydreaming, luck in playing with ideas), and integration — factors related to the brainstorming method of creative thinking. The choice of *illumination* was to indicate the *point of solution* in the total process. Verification was more concerned with the product.

Product: The selection of factors involved in the verification or *evaluation* stage of production proved difficult. The bias of interest was towards evaluation in the visual field, although the factors finally chosen were considered to be suitable for the evaluation of other types of production. The final choice of criteria was that a creative product: should be fit for the purpose, be original, dynamic, complex, integrated, should reveal personality, mastery of subject, mastery of media, and should change or add to the environment.

Programmed instruction

In view of recent developments in programmed instruction, it was decided to adopt that type of programming which appeared to be appropriate at the various stages of the construction of the programme. Such factors as linear programming, branching and loops, frames, overt/covert response, learner-based programming, task analysis, adjunctive programming, etc were kept in mind. The method of presentation of the materials was also considered valuable from the motivational point of view.

OBJECTIVES, SUBJECTS AND CONDITIONS

The main objective of the creativity programme was to increase creative ability as measured by the chosen instruments. Whilst this was the objective in behavioural terms, it was hoped that the effect of the programme would extend beyond this. It is usual to set limits for the acceptance of scores on post-test instruments, eg ninety per cent or more of subjects achieve ninety per cent or more in the post-tests. In the present study, where the tests were open-ended, this type of limit was not considered practical. It was decided to limit decisions concerning attainment of the objective to observing whether statistical analyses of the data from the pre-tests and post-tests yielded significant differences between the means in an experimental situation.

The subjects for whom the programme was intended would be male and female pupils of secondary school age (thirteen to sixteen) of average ability. The pupils involved in the study itself were pupils at a rural secondary school in England. In this rural environment their attitude to life was practical, cultural interests were few, and visits to large towns or cities were rare. The pupils were of average or below average ability.

It was assumed that the pupils would have little knowledge of creativity itself, in terms of person, process or product, and that they would not consciously be able to use a deliberate creative process. It was assumed that the target population would be able to read, although problems often arise in this area. The aim was to produce a programme suitable for use in a normal English-speaking secondary school; it should be capable of being used within the normal school timetable and in the classroom situation in the usual double and single periods, thus avoiding disruption of the overall curriculum. The programme was to be considered as a part of the normal syllabus in art or creative studies departments.

CONSTRUCTION OF THE PROGRAMME

The programme was constructed in three stages:

- (a) the development of an overall strategy for attaining the objective;
- (b) the development of a suitable structure, including consideration of aims regarding the creative person, process and product, motivation and sequence, etc; and
- (c) the construction of the programme elements, units, illustrations, etc.

Strategy

Two main approaches were considered: indirect and direct. The indirect approach is concerned with attempts to alter the total environment to make it more conducive to creative activity. The direct approach is concerned with attempts to influence factors involved in the creative process itself; ie to increase fluency, flexibility, originality, elaboration, association, combining, building, etc. A number of authorities advocate the indirect approach, but modification of the whole curriculum was excluded by the conditions pertaining in the present case. Also, it was considered that the direct approach would be more suitable for programmed instruction methods. Therefore the strategy of the direct approach was chosen; creativity would be learned as a skill, with a final bias towards creative activity in the visual field.

It was decided that the programme should be written in such a way that it could be used by individuals or small groups.

Structure and sequence

It was realised that a consideration of a number of subsidiary objectives or aims would be instrumental in attaining the overall objective.

The major aim was that the pupils should learn to use a conscious creative process. The *deferred judgement* method of brainstorming appeared to be the most suitable method. A useful introduction to brainstorming appeared to be a brief outline of the four stages in the creative process. An interest in the area of *identification* was felt to be a possible motivating factor. It was decided that pupils should be able to identify creative persons as: questioning, adventurous, versatile, persevering, contemplative, individualistic, humorous, energetic, and emotional; intelligence would be included but not stressed.

Pupils should be able to evaluate products as more creative or less creative. The importance of this became apparent when the verification stage of the creative process was involved. Creation entails verification at various stages in the full development of a product; therefore, pupils should have some way of judging their own production. Pupils should be able to evaluate a product as: fit for purpose, original, dynamic, complex, integrated, revealing personality, possessing mastery of subject, possessing mastery of media, and changing or adding to the environment.

From the decisions reached it was apparent that the first part of the structure should involve the evaluation of products as creative or not, prior to judgement of the learner's own productions. The structural positions of the parts concerned with the creative person and creative process were next considered. It was decided that the section dealing with the creative personality should be the second part, and thus a 'light' section between the two 'heavier' parts, as far as the pupils were concerned. The section dealing with the creative process would follow, and lead into the use of the brainstorming method in the visual field.

The final structure arrived at was therefore:

(i) the evaluation of the creative product;
(ii) the identification of the creative person; and
(iii) the use of creative thinking processes.

Motivational considerations included the possibility that individuals wish to be creative in some way. Also considered were the motivational factors supposedly inherent in programmed instruction itself, ie the 'novelty' factor and 'knowledge of results'. Motivation was also expected from the format of the material, eg a *game* type of presentation. Also considered were the motivational aspects of the practical use of a creative process in the pupil's own life, the pupil's interest in the validity of concepts, the arousal of the pupil's interest through curiosity, his desire to become involved, and his liking for variety.

Construction of the programme

The construction of the programme followed the structure outlined above. It was divided into three *elements*. The first element was concerned with the evaluation of the creative product, identification of the creative person, and knowledge of some creative thinking processes. The second element involved the subjects in learning to use the brainstorming method of creative thinking, and the final element enabled the subjects to use this brainstorming process in the visual field.

The format was designed so that each part of the programme would fit into the normal double or single periods in a class timetable. This meant that the first two elements had to be subdivided into smaller units. The final format chosen for presentation was:

Element One:	Unit One	— product evaluation
	Unit Two	— identification of person
	Unit Three	— creative processes
Element Two:	Unit One	— the brainstorming process
	Unit Two	— using the brainstorming process
Element Three:	(one unit)	— brainstorming a visual product

The format for Element One: Unit One 'What is a creative product?' finally appeared as follows:

An envelope, with instructions for use, contained four items:
  (a) illustrations of ten products with information concerning them (eg as in Figure 1);

PRODUCT CARD No. 4

This product is intended to make it easy to carry liquids around, e.g. to carry water on a camp site.

The producer has studied the needs of people and the facts about carrying liquids.

He has considered the best and lightest materials and the best methods of making it simply and cheaply.

Nothing quite like this has been made before.

A 6 GALLON PLASTIC WATER CARRIER OR TRANSPORTER.

Figure 1. *Example of a product card*

  (b) a book, of the branching *recurring loop* type, to enable the learner to evaluate the product by making decisions. A page on the 'changes the environment' factor is given in Figure 2;
  (c) a score sheet on which the learner scored the products according to the decisions made and assessed the products as useless, useful, less creative, creative or very creative;
  (d) an example booklet, amplifying and explaining the more difficult factors; eg originality, integration, personality, and changes in the environment (Figure 3 shows the page for this factor).

CREATIVE FACTOR (8) CHANGES THE ENVIRONMENT

A product which CHANGES THE ENVIRONMENT changes or adds to the way that people live.

Such products as the wheel, the steam engine, the printing press, the telephone, radio, frozen foods, etc. have changed the way we live since the days of the cave man. Music, fashion in clothes, painting, plays, novels, games and sports, ornaments, hobbies, etc. have added to our way of life. Even products to do with war: bow and arrow, slings, guns, tanks, aircraft, battleships, etc. have changed the way we live. The invention of the atomic bomb and atomic power has changed, and is changing, the way we live now.

Look at page 6 in your example booklet D to help you decide if this product has changed or added to our way of living.

Does this product CHANGE THE ENVIRONMENT?

If your answer is YES, turn to page 26.
If your answer is NO, turn to page 27.

Figure 2. *Example of page from programme book B*

Following the completion of the score sheet the pupil was handed a master score sheet for comparison. It was pointed out that they might have disagreed with the master scores, and were free to do so. They should try and think why they differed however.

Element One: Unit Two 'Who is likely to be a creative person?' was a section in which the pupil was free to identify with various personality traits. In the first part of the unit chosen traits were illustrated humorously, eg the adventurous trait was illustrated as in Figure 4. The second part of the unit was composed of verbal sketches of six personalities, creative and non-creative. The pupils responded *overtly* on an answer sheet, judging the persons to be creative or non-creative and giving reasons for their choice. A master answer sheet enabled pupils to see if, and why, they were correct.

Element One: Unit Three 'What methods do creative persons use to produce creative products?' was a *covert* section of the programme, introducing the pupils to the stages of the creative process, and linking Element One to Element Two where creative thinking processes would be used. This booklet contained information and illustrations only. The preparation stage was stressed as a prerequisite to creative thinking.

Element Two: Unit One 'How to brainstorm' was also a *covert* section. It was intended to be a reference book for Unit Two. It introduced the concepts of the problem, preparing the mind, time

261

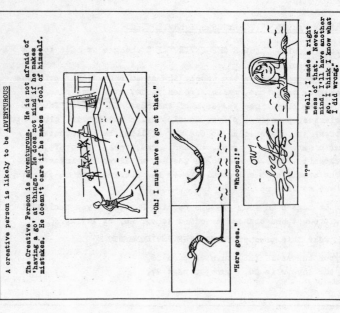

A creative person is likely to be ADVENTUROUS

The Creative Person is adventurous. He is not afraid of 'having a go' at things. He does not mind if he makes mistakes. He doesn't care if he makes a fool of himself.

"Oh! I must have a go at that."

"Here goes."

"Whoops!!"

"?"

"Well, I made a right mess of that. Never mind, I'll have another go. I think I know what I did wrong."

Figure 4. *Example of page from Element One: Unit Two 'Who is likely to be a creative person?'*

CREATIVE FACTOR (8) CHANGES THE ENVIRONMENT
Here are some examples of products that have CHANGED OUR WAY OF LIFE.

Television

Radio

Tractor

Car

The Wheel   Water Mill

Aircraft

Steam Engine

Atomic Power

Electricity   Theories and Ideas
****

Cooking

Ornamental products

Clothes (work, play, and fash)

Music

Poetry, Stories

Drama

Sculpture

Sports   and   Games

Here are examples of products that ADD TO OUR WAY OF LIFE. They make our life more interesting, enjoyable, comfortable, etc.
****

ALL THESE PRODUCTS CHANGE THE ENVIRONMENT IN SOME WAY. Products that do not do this rarely appear in large numbers.

Figure 3. *Page from example booklet D*

limits, the four basic rules of brainstorming (no criticisms, free-wheeling, quantity and combining ideas) and recording ideas. A method of selecting the best ideas, following the brainstorm session, was included.

Element Two: Unit Two 'You try some brainstorming' was the *overt* response section of this element. The learner could refer to Unit One when working through part one of this two-part unit. In both parts three problems were set (two verbal and one figural) and five minutes were allowed for each, followed by a period for the selection of the best ideas. A master brainstorm sheet was given for comparison on completion of part one, which was considered a practice section; for part two, no master sheet was available. As examples, a problem in part one was 'How many different ideas can you think of to make it "safer to live" at home?', and, in part two, 'How many ways can you think of to earn extra pocket money?' It was considered that the problems should not require any special preparation on the part of the learners.

At this point in the programme it was felt necessary that there should be some revision. A reminder leaflet was produced; this covered the basic areas dealt with, ie creative products, creative persons, and creative processes — including a condensed version of the brainstorming method. The pupils were able to keep this leaflet and use it when and where possible.

Element Three: (one unit) 'Brainstorm a painting' was the section that involved the visual area. Unlike the previous elements this was intended for use by the *individual* pupil (although it may be possible that small groups could work on this element).

The format involved the learner in work in four stages. The element itself was concerned with three of these stages, each one of twenty minutes' duration. The problem was to produce a painting that expressed an emotion. A choice of three emotions was given: misery, joy or fear. In the first stage the pupil made a list of words, ideas, etc that would express the chosen emotion. In the second stage the pupil experimented with media, and in the third stage the pupil chose those ideas, colours, etc that it was felt would most suitably express the emotion.

This work completed the actual unit. The pupils were then informed, in the last page of the booklet, that they would produce the actual painting on the chosen emotion in the next lesson.

On completion of the whole programme an appendix sheet was provided consisting of 'Hints for improving your creative power'. This was intended as a link between the work done in the programme and the possibilities for creative activity in general, outside the visual field.

The programme was physically produced by duplicating from typed and electronic stencils (where photographs were used).

Study to test the effectiveness of the creativity programme

EXPERIMENTAL PROCEDURE

The experimental design consisting of control and experimental groups, pre-tested and post-tested, was adopted. Two groups of subjects (two unstreamed forms, male and female pupils aged thirteen and fourteen, forty-one pupils in all) were subjected to similar conditions, except for the administration of the programme to the experimental group.

All pupils were given the pre-tests in year 1 (one form of the TTCT, the CPQ and two Art Works — 'the park' and 'own choice' — judged by the Art Work Judgement tests). In year 2 the experimental group worked through the first two elements of the programme in pairs, and worked as individuals for the final element. Following the treatment, the post-tests (equivalent forms of the TTCT, the HSPQ, and the two Art Works judged as previously) were administered to all pupils. The scoring methods for the tests were the same in both administrations and no major difficulties were experienced.

The data consisted of scores on the CPQ/HSPQ (creativity and exvia), the TTCT (scores for fluency, flexibility, originality and elaboration for the three activities and total — activity one was not scored for fluency and flexibility), and the two Art Works (scores for *gestalt*, spontaneity, originality, and involvement on each artwork): a total of twenty test items in all for year 1 and twenty-four for year 2.

The statistical analyses chosen to test the differences between the means of the two groups were: an overall analysis of variance (group x sex x year x tests — 2 x 2 x 2 x 24) for unequal Ns and repeated measures: analyses of variance (group x sex x year — 2 x 2 x 2) for the 24 test items and, in some cases, one-way analyses of variance and 't' tests. $p \leq 0.05$ was chosen as an acceptable level of significance.

The reliability of the artwork judgements was also retested at the time of the post-test administration — the average correlation obtained (on two judges) was significant at the $p \leq 0.005$ level.

RESULTS

The overall analysis of variance showed that the main differences between the means for the main effects and interactions reaching acceptable levels of significance were: sex, group x year, tests, sex x tests, and group x sex x year x tests (see Table I).

These effects and interactions were then examined using graphs for ease of interpretation. The group x sex x year x tests interaction was also examined for *direction of change* in scoring. Full details of the statistical procedures and results are provided in Williams (1975). The major findings from the analyses were:

Females scored higher than males overall and scored higher than males in the artwork judgements *gestalt*, originality and involvement. They were also more fluent and elaborate than males, although not necessarily more flexible or original as measured by the creativity test (TTCT). The creativity and extraversion factors of the personality test (CPQ/HSPQ) and the artwork spontaneity judgement did not distinguish between males and females.

As females scored higher than males it would be reasonable to conclude that, at age thirteen/fourteen, females are more creative than males, as measured by the tests. Whilst it would be unwise to generalise from these findings with a small sample of a particular population, there is evidence from other studies (eg MacKinnon, 1962) that creative persons tend toward femininity. The fact that, in the present study, the females were more creative than the males was, therefore, not surprising.

Source	SS	DF	MS	F	P
Between S's	17,917.19	40			
A	25.75	1	25.75	—	—
B	2,187.57	1	2,187.57	5.18	0.05
AB	198.40	1	198.40	—	—
swg	15,623.31	37	422.25	—	—
Within S's	602,735.10	1927			
C	226.05	1	226.05	2.29	—
AC	653.00	1	653.00	6.61	0.025
BC	15.33	1	15.33	—	—
ABC	357.61	1	357.61	3.62	0.10
C x swg	3,654.47	37	98.77	—	—
D	494,214.36	23	21,487.58	287.80	0.001
AD	955.21	23	41.53	—	—
BD	5,366.41	23	233.32	3.13	0.001
ABD	1,282.86	23	55.78	—	—
D x swg	63,536.15	851	74.66		
CD	1,592.08	23	69.22	2.78	0.001
ACD	1,279.25	23	55.62	2.23	0.001
BCD	743.18	23	32.31	1.30	—
ABCD	1,738.27	23	75.58	3.03	0.001
CD x swg	21,219.02	851	24.93		

Note: The ACD and CD interactions were found to be not significant when tested against the ABCD interaction. The ABC interaction ($p \geq 0.10$) is not considered significant.

Table I. *Analysis of variance:*
group (A) x sex (B) x year (C) x tests (D) (2 x 2 x 2 x 24)

The experimental group improved in scoring from pre-test to post-test administration in eighteen of the twenty-four test items, particularly in the originality measures, eg graph for artwork one, originality judgement (see Figure 5); whereas the control group did not significantly increase in scoring. In fact, overall, the scores for the control group decreased slightly from pre-test to post-test administration.

The fact that the experimental group increased the majority of its scores following the administration of the programme, whereas the control group did not do so, does not prove beyond doubt that the increase was solely due to the programme, but nonetheless the analyses of the data indicate that the null hypothesis — following the administration of a creativity programme, there will be no significant difference between the means of pre-test and post-test scores on creativity measures of male and female, control and experimental groups — should be rejected at a number of points. There is variance to explain, and there are grounds for supposing that the variance may be attributable to the creativity programme.

CONCLUSION

In view of this rejection of the null hypothesis it is felt that the original

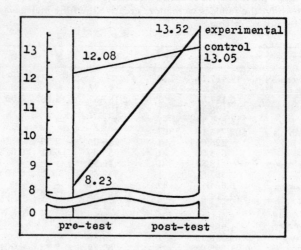

Figure 5. *Group x Year: Art Work 1 Originality factor.* $p \leq 0.05$

question, 'Can programmed instruction be effective in increasing creativity, particularly in the visual field?' may be answered 'Probably yes; there is sufficient evidence to warrant further design and development of programmed instruction for increasing creativity.'

References

Arnheim, R (1954) *Art and Visual Perception.* London : Faber & Faber

Arnold, J E (1962) Education for innovation. In S J Parnes and H F Harding (eds) *A Source Book for Creative Thinking.* New York : Charles Scribner & Sons

Bahlke, S J (1967), see Feldhusen *et al* (1970)

Barron, F (1967) The psychology of the creative writer. In R L Mooney and T A Razik (eds) *Explorations in Creativity.* New York : Harper & Row

Barron, F and Welsh, G S (1952) Artistic perception as a possible factor in personality style: its measurement by a figure preference test, *Journal of Psychology,* 33: 199-203

Bennett, J G (1967) Structural communication, *Systematics* 5 3: 185

de Bono, E (1967) *The Five-Day Course in Thinking.* Harmondsworth : Penguin Books

Brittain, W L and Beittel, K R (1960) Analyses of levels of creative performance in the visual arts, *Journal of Aesthetics and Art Criticism* 29 1: 83-90

Brogden, H E and Sprecher, T B (1964) Criteria of creativity. In C W Taylor (ed) *Creativity: Progress and Potential.* New York : McGraw-Hill

Burkhart, R C (1960) The creativity-personality continuum based on spontaneity and deliberateness in art, *Studies in Art Education,* National Art Education Association, 2 1: 43-65

Burkhart, R C (1962) *Spontaneous and Deliberate Ways of Learning.* Scranton, Pennsylvania : International Textbook Company

Cattell, R B (1963) High School Personality Questionnaire, Handbook (2nd ed); Children's Personality Questionnaire, Manual; Information Bulletin No 10.

Champaign, Illinois: Institute for Personality and Ability Testing

Clark, C H (1958) *Brainstorming*. New York : Doubleday & Co

Covington, M V and Crutchfield, R S (1965) Facilitation of creative problem solving. In I K Davies and J Hartley (eds) (1972) *Contributions to an Educational Technology*. London : Butterworths

Covington, M W, Crutchfield, R S and Davies, L B (1967) *The Productive Thinking Program*. Berkeley, California: Brazelton Printing Co

Cropley, A J (1966) Creativity and intelligence, *British Journal of Educational Psychology* 36: 259-66

Cropley, A J (1967) *Creativity*. London : Longmans, Green & Co

Crowder, N (1960) Automatic tutoring by intrinsic programming. In A A Lumsdaine and R Glaser (eds) *Teaching Machines and Programmed Learning: A Source Book*. Washington, DC : National Education Association of the United States

Crutchfield, R S (1967) Instructing the individual in creative thinking. In R L Mooney and T A Razik (eds) *Explorations in Creativity*. New York : Harper & Row

Cunnington, B F and Torrance, E P (1965) *Imagi/Craft*. Lexington : Ginn & Co

Davies, I K (1971) *The Management of Learning*. London : McGraw-Hill

Feldhusen, J F, Bahlke, S J and Treffinger, D J (1969), see Feldhusen *et al* (1970)

Feldhusen, J F, Treffinger, D J and Bahlke, S J (1970) Developing creative thinking: the Purdue creativity program, *Journal of Creative Behavior* 4 2: 85-90

Freud, S (1938) In A A Brill (ed) *The Basic Writings of Sigmund Freud*. New York : Random House

Gagné, R M (1965) The analysis of instructional objectives for the design of instruction. In R Glaser (ed) *Teaching Machines and Programmed Learning* (vol 2). Washington, DC : National Education Association

Getzels, J W and Jackson, P W (1962) *Creativity and Intelligence: Explorations with Gifted Students*. New York : John Wiley

Ghiselin, B (1952) *The Creative Process*. University of California Press

Gilbert, T J (1960) On the relevance of laboratory investigation of learning to self-instructional programming. In A A Lumsdaine and R Glaser (eds) *Teaching Machines and Programmed Learning: A Source Book*. Washington, DC : National Education Association

Gilbert, T F (1962) Mathetics: the technology of education, *Journal of Mathetics* 1 1: 7 and 1 2 : 7

Gordon, W J (1961) *Synectics*. New York : Harper Brothers

Graves, M (1948) *Decision Judgement Test: Manual*. New York : The Psychological Corporation

Guilford, J P (1959) Traits of creativity. In H H Anderson (ed) *Creativity and Its Cultivation*. New York : Harper & Row

Guilford, J P (1967a) Factors that aid and hinder creativity. In J C Gowans, G D Demos and E P Torrance (eds) *Creativity: Its Educational Implications*. New York : John Wiley

Guilford, J P (1967b) Intellectual factors in productive thinking. In R L Mooney and T A Razik (eds) *Explorations in Creativity*. New York : Harper & Row

Hallman, R J (1967) The necessary and sufficient conditions of creativity. In J C Gowans, G D Demos and E P Torrance (eds) *Creativity: Its Educational Implications*. New York : John Wiley

Hartley, J (1963) Some problems of internal and external evaluation of programs, *Programmed Instruction* 3 2: 5-7

Hartley, J (1974) Programmed instruction 1954-1974: a review, *Programmed Instruction and Educational Technology* 11 6: 278-91

Houston, J P and Mednick, S A (1963) Creativity and the need for novelty, *Journal of Abnormal Psychology* 66: 137-41

Hudson, L (1966) *Contrary Imaginations.* London : Methuen

Kneller, G F (1965) *The Art and Science of Creativity.* New York : Holt, Rinehart & Winston

Koestler, A (1964) *The Act of Creation.* London : Pan Books

Lowenfield, V (1947) *Creative and Mental Growth.* New York : Macmillan Co

Mackie, A (1975) Programmed learning — a developing technique, *Programmed Learning and Educational Technology* 12 4: 220-8

MacKinnon, D W (1962) The nature and nurture of creative talent, *American Psychologist* 17: 484-94

MacKinnon, D W (1967) Identifying creativity. In J C Gowans, G D Demos and E P Torrance (eds) *Creativity: Its Educational Implications.* New York : John Wiley

Mager, R F (1964) On the sequencing of instructional content. In J P DeCecco (ed) *Educational Technology.* New York : Holt, Rinehart & Winston

Maslow, A H (1962) Emotional blocks to creativity. In S J Parnes and H F Harding (eds) *A Source Book for Creative Thinking.* New York : Charles Scribner

McGuire, C (1967) Creativity and emotionality. In R L Mooney and R A Razik (eds) *Explorations in Creativity.* New York : Harper & Row

Mednick, S A (1962) The associative basis of the creative process, *Psychological Review* 69: 220-30

Mednick, S A and Mednick, M T (1964) Mechanisms of the creative process. In C W Taylor (ed) *Widening Horizons in Creativity.* New York : John Wiley

Myers, R E and Torrance, E P (1964) *Idea Books.* Lexington : Ginn

Olton, R M (1969) A self instructional program for developing productive thinking skills in 5th and 6th grade children, *Journal of Creative Behavior* 3 1: 16-25

Osborn, A F (1953) *Applied Imagination.* New York : Charles Scribner

Parnes, S J (1962) Can creativity be increased? In S J Parnes and H F Harding (eds) *A Source Book for Creative Thinking.* New York : Charles Scribner

Pressey, S L (1926) A simple apparatus which gives tests and scores — and teaches, *School and Society* 23 586: 373-6

Pressey, S L (1932) A third and fourth contribution toward the coming 'industrial revolution' in education, *School and Society* 36 934: 668-72

Pressey, S L (1964) Teaching machine (and learning theory) crisis. In J P DeCecco (ed) *Educational Technology.* New York : Holt, Rinehart & Winston

Ray, W S (1967) *The Experimental Psychology of Original Thinking.* New York : Macmillan Co

Rogers, C R (1954) Toward a theory of creativity. In H H Anderson (ed) (1959) *Creativity and Its Cultivation.* New York : Harper & Row

Rothkopf, E Z (1964) Some observations on predicting instructional effectiveness by simple inspection. In J P DeCecco (ed) *Educational Technology.* New York : Holt, Rinehart & Winston

Shackel, D S J and Lawrence, P J (1969) Improving creativity through programmed instruction, *New Zealand Journal of Educational Studies* 4 1: 41-56

Simon, H A (1964) Understanding creativity. In J C Gowans, G D Demos and E P Torrance (eds) *Creativity: Its Educational Implications.* New York : John Wiley

Skinner, B F (1954) The science of learning and the art of teaching, *Harvard Educational Review* 24: 86-97

Skinner, B F (1961) Teaching machines, *Scientific American,* 205 5: 90-102

Stolurow, L M (1964) Implications of current research and future trends. In J P DeCecco (ed) *Educational Technology.* New York : Holt, Rinehart & Winston

Taylor, C W (1967) Clues to creative thinking: the creative process and education. In J C Gowans, G D Demos and E P Torrance (eds) *Creativity: Its Educational Implications.* New York : John Wiley

Thomas, R M (1964) Art education, *Review of Educational Research* 34 2: 237-48

Torrance, E P (1962a) Measurement and development of the creative thinking abilities, *Year Book of Education* 125-42

Torrance, E P (1962b) Developing creative thinking through school experiences. In S J Parnes and H F Harding (eds) *A Source Book for Creative Thinking.* New York : Charles Scribner

Torrance, E P (1964) Education and creativity. In C W Taylor (ed) *Creativity: Progress and Potential.* New York : McGraw-Hill

Torrance, E P (1966) *Torrance Tests of Creative Thinking: Norms-Technical Manual.* Princeton, New Jersey : Personnel Press

Torrance, E P (1967a) Must creative development be left to chance? In J C Gowans, G D Demos and E P Torrance (eds) *Creativity: Its Educational Implications.* New York : John Wiley

Torrance E P (1967b) Non-test ways of identifying the creative gifted. In J C Gowans, G D Demos and E P Torrance (eds) *Creativity: Its Educational Implications.* New York : John Wiley

Wallach, M A and Kogan, N (1965) *Modes of Thinking in Young Children: A Study in the Creativity-Intelligence Distinction.* New York : Holt, Rinehart & Winston

Wallas, G (1926) *The Art of Thought.* New York : Harcourt, Brace

Williams, R E (1975) Programmed instruction for creativity. Unpublished doctoral thesis, University of Keele

Yamamoto, K (1964) *Experimental Scoring Manuals for the Minnesota Tests of Creative Thinking.* Ohio : Bureau of Educational Research, Kent State University

Youtz, R P (1962) Psychological foundations of applied imagination. In S J Parnes and H F Harding (eds) *A Source Book for Creative Thinking.* New York : Charles Scribner

3.3 Teaching Children Thinking

SEYMOUR PAPERT

Papert, S (1970) Teaching children thinking. Paper delivered to the IFID
Conference on Computer Education in Amsterdam, August 1970.
Reproduced with permission of the author.

Introduction

The phrase 'technology and education' usually means inventing new
gadgets to teach the same old stuff in a thinly disguised version of the
same old way. Moreover, if the gadgets are computers, the same old
teaching becomes incredibly more expensive and biased towards its
dullest parts, namely the kind of rote learning in which measurable
results can be obtained by treating the children like pigeons in a
Skinner box.

The purpose of this paper is to present a grander vision of an
educational system in which technology is used not in the form of
machines for processing children but as something the child himself
will learn to manipulate, to extend, to apply to projects, thereby
gaining a greater and more articulate mastery of the world, a sense of
the power of applied knowledge and a self-confidently realistic image of
himself as an intellectual agent. Stated more simply, I believe with
Dewey, Montessori and Piaget that children learn by doing and by
thinking about what they do. And so the fundamental ingredients of
educational innovation must be better things to do and better ways to
think about oneself doing these things.

I claim that computation is by far the richest known source of these
ingredients. We can give children unprecedented power to invent and
carry out exciting projects by providing them with access to computers,
with a suitably clear and intelligible programming language and with
peripheral devices capable of producing on-line real-time action.
Examples of such applications are spectacular displays on a colour scope,
battles between computer-controlled 'turtles', conversational programs
and game-playing heuristic programs. Programmers can extend the list
indefinitely.

Thus in its embodiment as the physical computer, computation
opens a vast universe of things to do. But the real magic comes when
this is combined with the conceptual power of theoretical ideas
associated with computation.

Computation has had a profound impact by concretising and
elucidating many previously subtle concepts in psychology, linguistics,
biology and the foundations of logic and mathematics. I shall try to
show how this elucidation can be projected back to the initial teaching

of these concepts. By so doing much of what has been most perplexing to children is turned to transparent simplicity; much of what seemed most abstract and distant from the real world turns into concrete instruments familiarly employed to achieve personal goals.

Mathematics is the most extreme example. Most children never see the point of the formal use of language. They certainly never have the experience of inventing original formalisms adapted to a particular task. Yet anyone who works with a computer does this all the time. We find that terminology and concepts properly designed to articulate this process are avidly seized by the children who really want to make the computer do things. And soon the children have become highly sophisticated and articulate in the art of setting up models and developing formal systems.

The most important (and surely controversial) component of this impact is on the child's ability to articulate the working of his own mind and particularly the interaction between himself and reality in the course of learning and thinking. This is the central theme of this paper, and I shall step back at this point to place it in the perspective of some general ideas about education. We shall return later to the use of computers.

The don't-think-about-thinking paradox

It is usually considered good practice to give people instruction in their occupational activities. Now, the occupational activities of children are learning, thinking, playing and the like. Yet, we tell them nothing about those things. Instead, we tell them about numbers, grammar and the French Revolution; somehow hoping that from this disorder the really important things will emerge all by themselves. And they sometimes do. But the alienation-dropout-drug complex is certainly not less frequent.

In this respect it is not a relevant innovation to teach children also about sets and linguistic productions and Eskimos. The paradox remains: why do we not teach them to think, to learn, to play? The excuses people give are as paradoxical as the fact itself. Basically there are two. Some people say: we know very little about cognitive psychology; we surely do not want to teach such half-baked theories in our school! And some people say: making the children self-conscious about learning will surely impede their learning. Asked for evidence they usually tell stories like the one about a millipede who was asked which foot he moved first when he walked. Apparently the attempt to verbalise the previously unconscious action prevented the poor beast from ever walking again.

The paradox is not in the flimsiness of the evidence for these excuses. There is nothing remarkable in that: all established doctrine about education has similarly folksy foundations. The deep paradox resides in the curious assumption that our choice is this: *either* teach the children half-baked cognitive theory *or* leave them in their original state of cognitive innocence. Nonsense. The child does not wait with a virginally empty mind until we are ready to stuff it with a statistically validated curriculum. He is constantly engaged in inventing theories about everything, including himself, schools and teachers. So the real choice is: *either* give the child the best ideas we can muster about cognitive processes *or* leave him at the mercy of the theories he invents or picks up in the gutter. The question is: who can do better, the child or us? Let us begin by looking more closely at how well the child does.

The pop-ed culture

One reads in Piaget's books about children re-inventing a kind of Democritean atomic theory to reconcile the disappearance of the dissolving sugar with their belief in the conservation of matter. They believe that vision is made possible by streams of particles sent out like machine gun bullets from the eyes and even, at a younger age, that the trees make the wind by flapping their branches. It is criminal to react (as some do) to Piaget's findings by proposing to teach the children 'the truth'. For they surely gain more in their intellectual growth by the act of inventing a theory than they can possibly lose by believing, for a while, whatever theory they invent. Since they are not in the business of making the weather, there is no reason for concern about their meteorological unorthodoxy. But they are in the business of making minds — notably their own — and we should consequently pay attention to their opinions about how minds work and grow.

There exists amongst children, and in the culture at large, a set of popular ideas about education and the mind. These seem to be sufficiently widespread, uniform and dangerous to deserve a name, and I propose 'the Pop-Ed Culture'. The following examples of Pop-Ed are taken from real children. My samples are too small for me to guess at their prevalence. But I am sure very similar trends must exist very widely and that identifying and finding methods to neutralise the effects of Pop-Ed culture will become one of the central themes of research on education. Examples of Pop-Ed thinking are:

(a) *Blank-mind theories.* Asked how one sets about thinking a child said: 'make your mind a blank and wait for an idea to come.' This is related to the common prescription for memorising: 'keep your mind a blank and say it over and over.' There is a high correlation, in my small sample, between expressing something of this sort and complaining of inability to remember poetry!

(b) *Getting-it theories.* Many children who have trouble understanding mathematics also have a hopelessly deficient model of what mathematical understanding is like. Particularly bad are models which expect understanding to come in a flash, all at once, ready made. This binary model is expressed by the fact that the child will admit the existence of only two states of knowledge often expressed by 'I get it' and 'I don't get it.' They lack — and even resist — a model of understanding something through a process of additions, refinements, debugging and so on. These children's way of thinking about learning is clearly disastrously antithetical to learning any concept that cannot be acquired in one bite.

(c) *Faculty theories.* Most children seem to have, and extensively use, an elaborate classification of mental abilities: 'he is a brain', 'he is a retard', 'he is dumb', 'I am not mathematical-minded.' The disastrous consequence is the habit of reacting to failure by *classifying* the problem as too hard, or oneself as not having the required aptitude, rather than by *diagnosing the specific deficiency* of knowledge or skill.

Computer science as a school subject

Talking to children about all these bad theories is almost certainly inadequate as an effective antidote. In common with all the greatest thinkers in the philosophy of education I believe that the child's intellectual growth must be rooted in his experience. So I propose creating an environment in which the child will become highly involved in experiences of a kind to provide rich soil for the growth of intuitions and concepts for dealing with thinking, learning, playing, and so on. An example of such an experience is writing simple heuristic programs that play games of strategy or try to outguess a child playing tag with a computer controlled 'turtle'. Another, related example, which appeals enormously to some children with whom we have worked is writing teaching programs. These are like traditional CAI programs but conceived, written, developed and even tested (on other children) by the children themselves.

Incidentally, this is surely the proper use for the concept of drill-and-practice programs. Writing such programs is an ideal project for the second term of an elementary school course of the sort I shall describe in a moment. It is said that the best way to learn something is to teach it. Perhaps writing a teaching program is better still in its insistence on forcing one to consider all possible misunderstandings and mistakes. I have seen children for whom *doing* arithmetic would have been utterly boring and alienated become passionately involved in writing programs to teach arithmetic and in the pros and cons of criticisms of one another's programs like: 'Don't just tell him the right answer if he's wrong, give him useful advice.' And discussing 'what kind of advice is useful' leads deep into understanding both the concept being taught and the processes of teaching and learning.

Can children do all this? In a moment I shall show some elements of a programming language called LOGO, which we have used to teach children of most ages and levels of academic performance how to use the computer. The language is always used 'on-line', that is to say the user sits at a console, gives instructions to the machine and immediately gets a reaction. People who know languages can think of it as 'baby LISP', though this is misleading in that LOGO is a fully-fledged universal language. Its babyish feature is the existence of self-contained sub-sets that can be used to achieve some results after ten minutes of instruction. Our most extensive teaching experiment was with a class of seventh-grade children (twelve-year-olds) chosen near the average in previous academic record. Within three months these children could write programs to play games like the simple form of NIM in which players take one, two or three matches from a pile; soon after that they worked on programs to generate random sentences — like what is sometimes called concrete poetry — and went on from there to make conversational and teaching programs. So the empirical evidence is very strong that we can do it, and next year we shall be conducting a more extensive experiment with fifth-grade children. The next sections will show some of the elementary exercises we shall use in the first weeks of the course. They will also indicate another important aspect of having children do their work with a computer: the possibility of working on projects with enough duration for the child to become personally — intellectually and emotionally — involved. The final section will indicate a facet of how more advanced projects are handled and how we see the effects of the kind of sophistication developed by the children.

You can take the child to Euclid but you can't make him think

Let us go back to Dewey for a moment. Intellectual growth, he often told us, must be rooted in the child's experience. But surely one of the fundamental problems of the school is how to extend or use the child's experience. It must be understood that 'experience' does not mean more busy work: two children who are made to measure the areas to two triangles do not necessarily undergo the same experience. One might have been highly *involved* (eg anticipating the outcome, being surprised, guessing at a general law) while the other was quite *alienated* (the opposite). What can be done to involve the mathematically alienated child? It is absurd to think this can be done by using the geometry to survey the school grounds instead of doing it on paper. Most children will enjoy running about in the bright sun. But most alienated children will remain alienated. One reason I want to emphasise here is that surveying the school grounds is not a good research project on which one can work for a long enough time to accumulate results and become involved in their development. There is a simple trick, which the child sees or does not see. If he sees it he succeeds in measuring the grounds and goes back to class the next day to work on something quite different.

Contrast this situation with a different context in which a child might learn geometry. The child uses a time-shared computer equipped with a CRT. He programs on-line in a version of the programming language LOGO, which will be described in more detail below.

On the tube is a cursor point with an arrow indicating a direction. The instruction

FORWARD 100

causes the point to move in the direction of the arrow through 100 units of distance. The instruction

LEFT 90

causes the arrow to rotate 90° without changing its position. The child knows enough from previous experience to write the following almost self-explanatory program:

```
TO CIRCLE
FORWARD 1
LEFT 1
CIRCLE
END
```

The word 'TO' indicates that a new procedure is to be defined, and it will be called 'CIRCLE'.

Typing

```
CIRCLE
```

will now cause the steps in the procedure to be executed one at a time. Thus:

First step: FORWARD 1	The point creeps ahead 1 unit.	
Second step: LEFT 1	The arrow rotates $1°$.	
Third step: CIRCLE	This is a recursive call; naturally it has the same effect as the command CIRCLE typed by the child. That is to say, it initiates the same process.	
First step: FORWARD 1	The point creeps on, but in the new slightly different direction.	
Second step: LEFT 1	The arrow now makes an angle of $2°$ with its initial direction.	
Third step: CIRCLE	This initiates the same process all over again. And so on, forever.	

It is left as a problem for the reader to discover why this point will describe a circle rather than, say, a spiral. He will find that it involves some real geometry of a sort he may not yet have encountered. The more immediately relevant point is that the child's work has resulted in a certain happening, namely a circle has appeared. It occurs to the child to make the circle roll!

How can this be done? A plan is easy to make:

Let the point go round the circle once.
Then FORWARD 1.
Then repeat.

But there is a serious problem! The program as written causes the point to go round forever. To make it go just once round we need to give the procedure an *input* (in more usual jargon: a variable).

This input will be used by the procedure to remember how far round it has gone. Let us call it 'DEGREES' and let it represent the number of degrees still to go, so it starts off being 360 and ends up 0. The way this is written in LOGO is:

TO CIRCLE :DEGREES	:DEGREES means: the thing whose name is DEGREES
IF :DEGREES = 0 STOP	
FORWARD 1	
LEFT 1	
CIRCLE :DEGREES − 1	Each time round the number by degrees remaining is reduced by 1

Now we can use this as a sub-procedure for ROLL:

```
TO ROLL
CIRCLE 360
FORWARD 10
ROLL
END
```

Or, to make it roll a fixed distance:

```
TO ROLL :DISTANCE
IF :DISTANCE = 0 STOP
CIRCLE 360
FORWARD 10
ROLL :DISTANCE − 1
END
```

Or we can make the circle roll around a circle:

```
TO FUNNY ROLL
CIRCLE 360
FORWARD 10
LEFT 10
FUNNY ROLL
```

These examples will, if worked on with a good dose of imagination, indicate the sense in which there are endless possibilities of creating even more, but gradually more, complex and occasionally spectacularly beautiful effects. Even an adult can get caught up in it! Not every child will. But if he does, the result is very likely to be a true extension of his experience in Dewey's sense. And evidence is accumulating for the thesis that there is scarcely any child who cannot be involved in some computational project.

More examples of turtle geometry

Another direction of varying the procedure CIRCLE is to give it inputs to specify at will the size of the forward step and the right rotation. The procedure thus obtained is called POLY in our classes:

```
TO POLY :STEP :ANGLE
FORWARD :STEP
RIGHT :ANGLE
POLY :STEP :ANGLE.
```

Now (POLY 11) is exactly the same as CIRCLE. But other inputs produce a spectacularly varied set of figures (as shown in Figure 1):

Changing a single line of the procedure can open up vast new possibilities. For example, let us replace the last line by POLY :STEP + 10 :ANGLE. Then each round of the program will take a bigger step forward! But before trying the procedure we should rename it.

```
TO POLYSPI :STEP :ANGLE
FORWARD :STEP
RIGHT :ANGLE
POLYSPI :STEP+10 :ANGLE
```

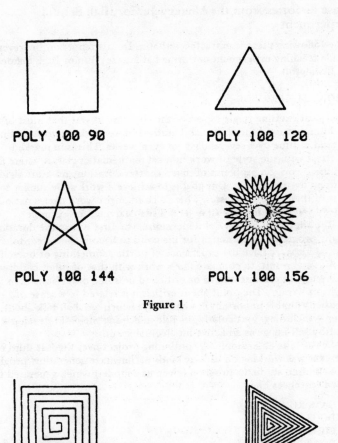

POLY 100 90

POLY 100 120

POLY 100 144

POLY 100 156

Figure 1

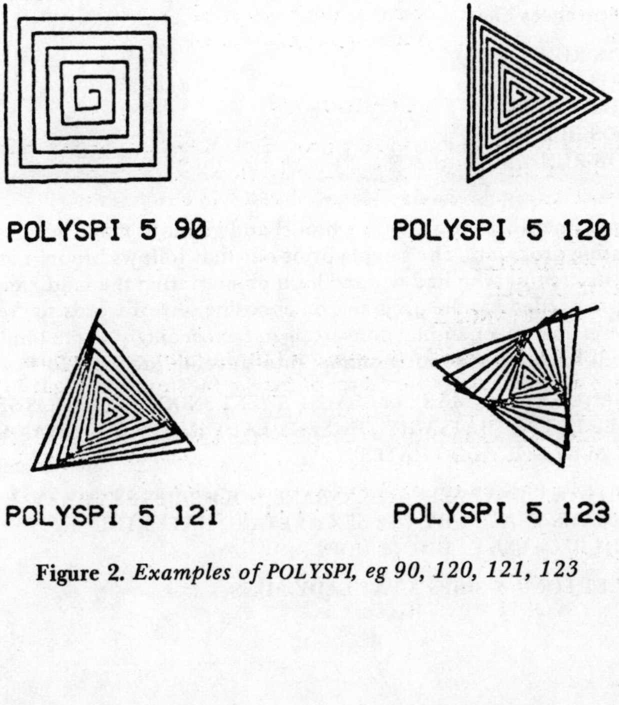

POLYSPI 5 90

POLYSPI 5 120

POLYSPI 5 121

POLYSPI 5 123

Figure 2. *Examples of POLYSPI, eg 90, 120, 121, 123*

Case histories from the Muzzey Junior High School experiment

The following piece is extracted verbatim from a report on the seventh-grade teaching experiment performed at Muzzey Junior High School at Lexington.

PROBLEM *V* PROJECT

The most exciting single aspect of the experiment was that most of the children acquired the ability and motivation to work on *projects* that extend in time over several days, or even weeks. This is in marked contrast with the style of work in most mathematics classes where the children work on problems of much shorter duration and more rigidly defined by the teacher. Our goal is to achieve a work style similar to that of the better art classes, where a child might work over a period of several weeks on making an object: a soap carving, for example.

The similarity has several dimensions. The first is that the duration of the process is long enough for the child to become *involved*, to try several ideas, to have the experience of putting something of oneself in the final result, to compare one's work with that of other children, to discuss, to criticise and to be criticised on some other basis than 'right or wrong'. The point about criticism is related to a sense of creativity that is important in many ways which we shall talk about later — including, particularly, its role in helping the child develop a healthy self-image as an active intellectual agent.

Let us take an example. A continuing project over the last third of the year was working on various kinds of 'language generating' programs. The children studied a program (given as a model) which generated two word sentences like:

CATS RUN
DOGS SHOUT
CHILDREN BITE
DOGS RUN
CATS RUN
etc

The assignment was to study the model and go on to make more interesting programs. The sample print-out that follows brought great joy to its creator who had worked hard on mastering the mathematical concepts needed for the program, on choosing sets of words to create an interesting effect and on converting her exceedingly vague (and unloved) knowledge about grammar into a useful, practical form.

INSANE RETARD MAKES BECAUSE SWEET SNOOPY SCREAMS SEXY
WOLF LOVES THATS WHY THE SEXY LADY HATES UGLY MAN LOVES
BECAUSE UGLY DOG HATES

MAD WOLF HATES BECAUSE INSANE WOLF SKIPS SEXY RETARD
SCREAMS THATS WHY THE SEXY RETARD HATES THIN SNOOPY
RUNS BECAUSE FAT WOLF HOPS

SWEET FOGINY SKIPS A FAT LADY RUNS

The next class assignment was to generate mathematical sentences which were later used in 'teaching programs'. For example:

8*BOX + 6 = 48
WHAT IS BOX?

Finally, in the last weeks, someone in the class said she wanted to make a French sentence generator . . . for which she spurned advice and went to work. In the course of time other children liked the idea and followed suit — evoking from the first girl prideful complaints like 'why do they all have to take my idea?' The interesting feature was that although they took her idea, they imprinted it strongly with their own personalities, as shown by the following case studies:

KM, the girl who initiated the project. Thoughtful, serious about matters that are important to her, often disruptive in class. Her approach to the French project was to begin by writing procedures to conjugate all the regular verbs and some irregular ones. The end of the school year fell before she had made a whole sentence generator. But she did make a program with competence at conjugating — eg given VOUS and FINIR as inputs it would reply: VOUS FINISSEZ.

MR, a gay exuberant girl, who made the 'SEXY COMPUTER' program quoted above. Only half seriously she declared her intention of making the first operational French sentence generator. In a sense she did — but with cavalier disregard for the Academy's rules of spelling and grammar!

JC, a clear mind with a balanced sense of proportion. Deliberately decided to avoid the trap of getting so involved with conjugation that no sentence would ever be generated. Too serious to allow his program to make mistakes. Found a compromise: he would make a program that knew only the third person — but was still non-trivial because it did know the difference between singular and plural as well as the genders: thus it would say, LE BON CHIEN MANGE but LES BONNES FILLES MANGENT.

A DETAIL FROM A CHILD'S MATHEMATICAL RESEARCH PROJECT

The fine texture of the work on projects of this sort can only be shown by case studies. The following vignette needs very little reference to LOGO — thus illustrating how the projects are more than programming.

J is the author of the last French program mentioned. A little earlier he is working on generating equations as part of a project to make 'a program to teach eighth-grade algebra'. He has perfected a program to generate equations with coefficients in the range of 0—9 using a 'random' number generator. His present problem is to obtain larger coefficients.

First solution: Almost everyone tries this: get bigger numbers by adding smaller ones obtained from the old procedure. Amongst other considerations, this looks like a good technique that has often paid well: use old functions to define new ones.

Consequences: J chooses his equation generator but soon finds some annoying features:

> The new coefficients are in the range of 0—18, which is unnatural and not very big.
> There is a preference for some numbers, eg 9 comes up ten times as often as 18!

Comment: The first problem can be alleviated by adding more numbers. One can even add a random number of random numbers.

But this aggravates the second problem. J understands this qualitatively but does not see a way out. It is interesting that children and adults often have a resistance to making numbers by 'non-numerical' operations.

In this case the solution is to concatenate the single digit random numbers instead of adding them. LOGO has a simple way to express this and J is quite accustomed to making non-numerical strings by concatenation. In fact, this is how he makes the equation!
Nevertheless he resists.

The problem is discussed in a class meeting and after some prompting everyone suddenly 'discovers' the solution.
New solution: J changes his program, now making numbers up to 99 by concatenation; he does some crude check of uniformity of distribution and tries his program.
Disaster: For a while it seems to go well. But in the course of playing with the 'teaching program' a user types 5 and is surprised to get a reply like:

> You knucklehead; you took 11 seconds and your answer is wrong. The answer is 05. Here is some advice . . . etc.

Comment: Poor J will get the sympathy of every mathematician who must at some stage have tried to generalise a result by extending the domain of an innocent looking function only to find that the extended function violates some obscure but essential condition. He is also in the heart of the problem of representation. Is '05' a good representation? Yes, no . . . have your choice, but face the consequences and be consistent. J's problem is that his procedures accept '05' for arithmetic operations but not for the test of identity!
Solution: Change the identity test or peel off the leading zero. J chose the latter. His program worked for a while and was used, in ways that we shall see, to great effect.
New step: Later J was urged to allow negative numbers. He found a good way: use the one digit random number generator to make a binary decision:

> If less than 5, positive; otherwise, negative.

That problem again: J had a program working perfectly with negatives. Then one day he decided to make it more symmetrical by using +5 and −5 for positive and negative. This brought him back to the old problems raised by differences between the machine's representation and that of the human user. At this point the year ended with J's program not quite as effective as it had been at its peak.

Further reading

Papert, S and Solomon, C (1972) Twenty things to do with a computer, *Educational Technology,* April

Papert, S (1972) Teaching children to be mathematicians v teaching about mathematics, *International Journal of Mathematical Education in Science and Technology* 3 3, July-Sept

LOGO memos, a continuing series of papers. Cambridge, Mass : Artificial Intelligence Laboratory, MIT

Minsky, M and Papert, S (eds) *New Educational Technology.* (Includes above and other related papers.) Cambridge, Mass 02138 : Turtle Publication, PO Box 33, Harvard Square Post Office

3.4 'Goodbye Teacher...'

FRED S KELLER

Excerpts from Keller, F S (1968) 'Goodbye teacher . . .', *Journal of Applied Behavioral Analysis* 1: 79-89. Reproduced with permission of the author and the editor.

When I was a boy, and school 'let out' for the summer, we used to celebrate our freedom from educational control by chanting:

Goodbye scholars, goodbye school;
Goodbye teacher, darned old fool!

We really didn't think of our teacher as deficient in judgement, or as a clown or jester. We were simply escaping from restraint, dinner pail in one hand and shoes in the other, with all the delights of summer before us. At that moment, we might even have been well disposed toward our teacher and might have felt a touch of compassion as we completed the rhyme.

'Teacher' was usually a woman, not always young and not always pretty. She was frequently demanding and sometimes sharp of tongue, ever ready to pounce when we got out of line. But, occasionally, if one did especially well in homework or in recitation, one could detect a flicker of approval or affection that made the hour in class worthwhile. At such times, we loved our teacher and felt that school was fun.

It was not fun enough, however, to keep me there when I grew older. Then I turned to another kind of education, in which the reinforcements were sometimes just as scarce as in the schoolroom. I became a Western Union messenger boy and, between deliveries of telegrams, I learned Morse code by memorising dots and dashes from a sheet of paper and listening to a relay on the wall. As I look back on those days, I conclude that I am the only living reinforcement theorist who ever learned Morse code in the absence of reinforcement.

It was a long, frustrating job. It taught me that drop-out learning could be just as difficult as in-school learning and it led me to wonder about easier possible ways of mastering a skill. Years later, after returning to school and finishing my formal education, I came back to this classical learning problem, with the aim of making International Morse code less painful for beginners than American Morse had been for me (Keller, 1943).

During World War II, with the aid of a number of students and colleagues, I tried to apply the principle of immediate reinforcement to the early training of Signal Corps personnel in the reception of Morse-code signals. At the same time, I had a chance to observe, at close hand

and for many months, the operation of a military training centre.
I learned something from both experiences, but I should have learned
more. I should have seen many things that I didn't see at all, or saw
very dimly.

I could have noted, for example, that instruction in such a centre
was highly individualised, in spite of large classes, sometimes permitting
students to advance at their own speed throughout a course of study.
I could have seen the clear specification of terminal skills for each
course, together with the carefully graded steps leading to this end.
I could have seen the demand for perfection at every level of training
and for every student; the employment of classroom instructors who
were little more than the successful graduates of earlier classes; the
minimising of the lecture as a teaching device and the maximising of
student participation. I could have seen, especially, an interesting
division of labour in the educational process, wherein the non-
commissioned, classroom teacher was restricted to duties of guiding,
clarifying, demonstrating, testing, grading, and the like, while the
commissioned teacher, the training officer, dealt with matters of course
logistics, the interpretation of training manuals, the construction of
lesson plans and guides, the evaluation of student progress, the selection
of non-commissioned cadre, and the writing of reports for his
superiors.

I did see these things, of course, in a sense, but they were embedded
deeply within a special context, one of 'training' rather than 'education'.
I did not then appreciate that a set of reinforcement contingencies
which were useful in building simple skills like those of the radio
operator might also be useful in developing the verbal repertoires,
the conceptual behaviours, and the laboratory techniques of university
education. It was not until a long time later, by a very different route,
that I came to such a realisation.

The story began in 1962, with the attempt on the part of two
Brazilian and two North American psychologists, to establish a
Department of Psychology at the University of Brasilia. The question of
teaching method arose from the very practical problem of getting a
first course ready by a certain date for a certain number of students in
the new university. We had almost complete freedom of action; we
were dissatisfied with the conventional approaches; and we knew
something about programmed instruction. We were also of the same
theoretical persuasion. It was quite natural, I suppose, that we should
look for fresh applications of reinforcement thinking to the teaching
process (Keller, 1966).

The method that resulted from this collaborative effort was first used in
a short-term laboratory course at Columbia University in the winter of 1963,
and the basic procedure of this pilot study was employed at Brasilia
during the following year, by Professors Rodolfo Azzi and Carolina
Martuscelli Bori, with fifty students in a one-term introductory course.
Professor Azzi's report on this, at the 1965 meeting of the American
Psychological Association and in personal correspondence, indicated a
highly satisfactory outcome. The new procedure was received
enthusiastically by the students and by the university administration.

Mastery of the course material was judged excellent for all who completed the course. Objections were minor, centring around the relative absence of opportunity for discussion between students and staff.

Unfortunately, the Brasilia venture came to an abrupt end during the second semester of its operation, due to a general upheaval within the university that involved the resignation or dismissal of more than two hundred teachers. Members of the original psychology staff have since taken positions elsewhere, and have reportedly begun to use the new method again, but I am unable at this time to report in detail on their efforts.

Concurrently with the early Brazilian development, Professor J G Sherman and I, in the spring of 1965, began a series of more or less independent applications of the same general method at Arizona State University. With various minor changes, this work has now been tried through five semesters with an increasing number of students per term (Keller, undated and 1967; Sherman, 1967). The results have been more gratifying with each successive class, and there has been as yet no thought of a return to more conventional procedures. In addition, we have had the satisfaction of seeing our system used by a few other colleagues, in other courses and at other institutions.

In describing this method to you, I will start with a quotation (Keller, 1967). It is from a hand-out given to all the students enrolled in the first-semester course in general psychology (one of two introductions offered at Arizona State University) during the past year, and it describes the teaching method to which they will be exposed unless they elect to withdraw from the course.

> This is a course through which you may move, from start to finish, at your own pace. You will not be held back by other students or forced to go ahead until you are ready. At best, you may meet all the course requirements in less than one semester; at worst, you may not complete the job within that time. How fast you go is up to you.
>
> The work of this course will be divided into 30 units of content, which correspond roughly to a series of home-work assignments and laboratory exercises. These units will come in a definite numerical order, and you must show your mastery of each unit (by passing a 'readiness' test or carrying out an experiment) before moving on to the next.
>
> A good share of your reading for this course may be done in the classroom, at those times when no lectures, demonstrations, or other activities are taking place. Your classroom, that is, will sometimes be a study hall.
>
> The lectures and demonstrations in this course will have a different relation to the rest of your work than is usually the rule. They will be provided only when you have demonstrated your readiness to appreciate them; no examination will be based upon them; and you need not attend them if you do not wish. When a certain percentage of the class has reached a certain point in the course, a lecture or demonstration will be available at a stated time, but it will not be compulsory.
>
> The teaching staff of your course will include proctors, assistants, and an instructor. A proctor is an undergraduate who has been chosen

for his mastery of the course content and orientation, for his maturity of judgement, for his understanding of the special problems that confront you as a beginner, and for his willingness to assist. He will provide you with all your study materials except your textbooks. He will pass upon your readiness tests as satisfactory or unsatisfactory. His judgement will ordinarily be law, but if he is ever in serious doubt, he can appeal to the classroom assistant, or even the instructor, for a ruling. Failure to pass a test on the first try, the second, the third, or even later, will not be held against you. It is better that you get too much testing than not enough, if your final success in the course is to be assured.

Your work in the laboratory will be carried out under the direct supervision of a graduate laboratory assistant, whose detailed duties cannot be listed here . . . There will also be a graduate classroom assistant, upon whom your proctor will depend for various course materials (assignments, study questions, special readings, and so on), and who will keep up to date all progress records for course members. The classroom assistant will confer with the instructor daily, aid the proctors on occasion, and act in a variety of ways to further the smooth operation of the course machinery.

The instructor will have as his principal responsibilities: (a) the selection of all study material used in the course; (b) the organisation and the mode of presenting this material; (c) the construction of tests and examinations; and (d) the final evaluation of each student's progress. It will be his duty, also, to provide lectures, demonstrations, and discussion opportunities for all students who have earned the privilege; to act as a clearing-house for requests and complaints; and to arbitrate in any case of disagreement between students and proctors or assistants . . .

All students in the course are expected to take a final examination, in which the entire term's work will be represented. With certain exceptions, this examination will come at the same time for all students, at the end of the term . . . The examination will consist of questions which, in large part, you have already answered on your readiness tests. Twenty-five per cent of your course grade will be based on this examination; the remaining 75% will be based on the number of units of reading and laboratory work that you have successfully completed during the term.

(In my own sections of the course, these percentages were altered, during the last term, to a 30 per cent weighting of the final examination, a 20 per cent weighting of the ten laboratory exercises, and a 50 per cent weighting of the reading units.)

A picture of the way this method operates can best be obtained, perhaps, by sampling the activities of a hypothetical average student as he moves through the course. John Pilgrim is a freshman, drawn from the upper seventy-five per cent of his high-school class. He has enrolled in PY 112 for unknown reasons and has been assigned to a section of about a hundred students, men and women, most of whom are also in their beginning year. The class is scheduled to meet on Tuesdays and Thursdays, from 9.15 to 10.30 am, with a laboratory session to be arranged.

Together with the description from which I quoted a moment ago, John receives a few mimeographed instructions and some words of advice from his professor. He is told that he should cover two units of laboratory work or reading per week in order to be sure of taking an A-grade into his final examination; that he should withdraw from the course if he does not pass at least one readiness test within the first two weeks; and that a grade of Incomplete will not be given except in special cases. He is also advised that, in addition to the regular classroom hours on Tuesday and Thursday, readiness tests may be taken on Saturday forenoons and Wednesday afternoons of each week — periods in which he can catch up with, or move ahead of, the rest of the class.

He then receives his first assignment: an introductory chapter from a standard textbook and two 'sets' from a programmed version of similar material. With this assignment, he receives a mimeographed list of 'study questions', about thirty in number. He is told to seek out the answers to these questions in his reading, so as to prepare himself for the questions he will be asked in his readiness tests. He is free to study wherever he pleases, but he is strongly encouraged to use the study hall for at least part of the time. Conditions for work are optimal there, with other students doing the same thing and with an assistant or proctor on hand to clarify a confusing passage or a difficult concept.

This is on Tuesday. On Thursday, John comes to class again, having gone through the sets of programmed material and having decided to finish his study in the classroom, where he cannot but feel that the instructor really expects him. An assistant is in charge, about half the class is there, and some late registrants are reading the course description. John tries to study his regular text, but finds it difficult to concentrate and ends by deciding to work in his room. The assistant pays no attention when he leaves.

On the following Tuesday, he appears in study hall again, ready for testing, but anxious, since a whole week of the course has passed. He reports to the assistant, who sends him across the hall, without his books and notes, to the testing room, where the proctor in charge gives him a blue-book and one of the test forms for Unit 1. He takes a seat among about twenty other students and starts work. The test is composed of ten fill-in questions and one short-answer essay question. It does not seem particularly difficult and, in about ten minutes, John returns his question sheet and is sent, with his blue-book, to the proctor's room for grading.

In the proctor's room, in one of ten small cubicles, John finds his special proctor, Anne Merit. Anne is a psychology major who passed the same course earlier with a grade of A. She receives two points of credit for about four hours of proctoring per week, two hours of required attendance at a weekly proctors' meeting, and occasional extra duty in the study hall or test room. She has nine other students besides John to look after, so she will not as a rule be able to spend much more than five or ten minutes of class time with each.

Anne runs through John's answers quickly, checking two of them as incorrect and placing a question mark after his answer to the essay question. Then she asks him why he answered these three as he did. His replies show two misinterpretations of the question and one failure in written expression. A restatement of the fill-in questions and some probing with respect to the essay leads Anne to write an OK alongside each challenged answer. She congratulates John upon his performance and warns him that later units may be a little harder to master than the first.

John's success is then recorded on the wall-chart in the proctors' room, he is given his next assignment and set of study questions, and sent happily on his way. The blue-book remains with Anne, to be given later to the assistant or the instructor for inspection, and used again when John is ready for testing on Unit 2. As he leaves the room, John notices the announcement of a twenty-minute lecture by his instructor, for all students who have passed Unit 3 by the following Friday, and he resolves that he will be there.

If John had failed in the defence of one or two of his answers, he would have been sent back for a minimal period of thirty minutes for further study, with advice as to material most needing attention. If he had made more than four errors on his test, the answers would not have been considered individually; he would simply have been told that he was not ready for examination. And, if he had made no errors at all, he would probably have been asked to explain one or two of his correct answers, as a way of getting acquainted and to make sure that he was the one who had really done the work.

John did fail his first test on Unit 2, and his first two tests on Unit 4 (which gave trouble to nearly everyone). He missed the first lecture, too, but qualified for the second. (There were seven such 'shows' during the term, each attended by perhaps half of the students entitled to be there.) After getting through his first five units, he failed on one review test before earning the right to move on to Unit 6. On the average, for the remainder of the course, he required nearly two readiness tests per unit. Failing a test, of course, was not an unmixed evil, since it permitted more discussion with the proctor and often served to sharpen the concepts involved.

In spite of more than a week's absence from school, John was able, by using the Wednesday and Saturday testing sessions, to complete his course units successfully about a week before the final examination. Because of his cramming for other courses during this last week, he did not review for his psychology and received only a B on his final examination. His A for the course was not affected by this, but his pride was hurt.

Sometime before the term ended, John was asked to comment on certain aspects of the course, without revealing his identity. (Remember, John is a mythical figure.) Among other things, he said that, in comparison with courses taught more conventionally, this one demanded a much greater mastery of the work assignments, it required greater memorisation of detail and much greater understanding of basic concepts, it generated a greater feeling of achievement, it gave much greater recognition of the student as a person, and it was enjoyed to a much greater extent (Keller, undated).

He mentioned also that his study habits had improved during the term, that his attitude towards testing had become more positive, that his worry about final grades had diminished, and that there had been an increase in his desire to hear lectures (this in spite of the fact that he attended only half of those for which he was qualified). When asked specifically about the use of proctors, he said that the discussions with his proctors had been very helpful, that the proctor's non-academic, personal relation was also important to him, and that the use of proctors generally in grading and discussing tests was highly desirable.

Anne Merit, when asked to comment on her own reactions to the system, had many things to say, mostly positive. She referred especially to the satisfaction of having the respect of her proctees, of seeing them do well, and of cementing the material of the course for herself. She noted that the method was one of 'mutual reinforcement' for student, proctor, assistant and instructor. She suggested that it ought to be used in other courses and at other levels of instruction. She wondered why it would not be possible for a student to enrol in a second course immediately upon completion of the first, if it were taught by the same method. She also listed several changes that might improve the efficiency of the course machinery, especially in the area of testing and grading, where delay may sometimes occur.

In an earlier account of this teaching method (Keller, 1967), I summarised those features which seem to distinguish it most clearly from conventional teaching procedures. They include the following:

(1) *The go-at-your-own-pace feature,* which permits a student to move through the course at a speed commensurate with his ability and other demands upon his time.
(2) *The unit-perfection requirement for advance,* which lets the student go ahead to new material only after demonstrating mastery of that which preceded.
(3) *The use of lectures and demonstrations as vehicles of motivation,* rather than sources of critical information.
(4) The related *stress upon the written word* in teacher-student communication; and, finally:
(5) The *use of proctors,* which permits repeated testing, immediate scoring, almost unavoidable tutoring, and a marked enhancement of the personal-social aspect of the educational process.

The similarity of our learning paradigm to that provided in the field of programmed instruction is obvious. There is the same stress upon analysis of the task, the same concern with terminal performance, the same opportunity for individualised progression, and so on. But the sphere of action here is different. The principal steps of advance are not 'frames' in a 'set', but are more like the conventional homework assignment or laboratory exercise.

The 'response' is not simply the completion of a prepared statement through the insertion of a word or phrase. Rather, it may be thought of as the resultant of many such responses, better described as the understanding of a principle, a formula, or a concept, or the ability to use an experimental technique. Advance within the program depends on something more than the appearance of a confirming word or the presentation of a new frame; it involves a personal interaction between a student and his peer, or his better, in what may be a lively verbal interchange, of interest and importance to each participant. The use of a programmed text, a teaching machine, or some sort of computer aid within such a course is entirely possible and may be quite desirable, but it is not to be equated with the course itself. (Keller, 1967)

Failure to recognise that our teaching units are not as simple as the response words in a programmed text, or the letter reactions to Morse-code signals, or other comparable atoms of behaviour, can lead to confusion concerning our procedure. A well-known critic of education in America, after reading an account of our method, sent me a note confessing to 'a grave apprehension about the effect of breaking up the subject matter into little packages' . . . 'I should suppose', he wrote, 'it would prevent all but the strongest minds from ever possessing a synoptic view of a field, and I imagine that the coaching, and testing, and passing in bits would amount to efficient training rather than effectual teaching.'

Our 'little packages' or 'bits' are no smaller than the basic conceptions of a science of behaviour and cannot be delivered all at once in one large synoptic parcel. As for the teaching-training distinction, one needs only to note that it is always the instructor who decides what is to be taught, and to what degree, thus determining whether he will be called a trainer or a teacher. The method he uses, the basic reinforcement contingencies he employs, may be turned to either purpose.

Many things occur, some of them rather strange, when a student is taught by a method such as ours. With respect to everyday student behaviour, even a casual visit to a class will provide some novel items. For example, all the students seated in the study hall may be seen studying, undistracted by the presence or movements of others. In the test room, a student will rarely be seen chewing on his pencil, looking at a neighbour's blue-book, or staring out of the window. In the crowded proctors' room, ten pairs of students can be found concurrently engaged in academic interaction, with no couple bothered by the conversation of another, no matter how close by. Upon passing his assistant or instructor, in the corridors or elsewhere, a student will typically be seen to react in a friendly and respectful manner — enough to excite a mild alarm.

More interesting than this is the fact that a student may be tested forty or fifty times in the course of one semester, often standing in line for the privilege, without a complaint. In one extreme instance, a student required nearly two terms to complete the work of one (after which he applied for, and got, permission to serve as a proctor for the following year).

Another unusual feature of our testing and grading is the opportunity given to defend an 'incorrect' answer. This defence, as I noted earlier, may sometimes produce changes in the proctor's evaluation, changes that are regularly checked by the assistant or the instructor. Occasionally, a proctor's OK will be rejected, compelling the student to take another test, and sensitising the proctor to the dangers of leniency; more often, it produces a note of warning, a correction, or a query written by the instructor in the student's blue-book; but always it provides the instructor with feedback on the adequacy of the question he has constructed.

Especially important, in a course taught by such a method, is the fact that any differences in social, economic, cultural, and ethnic background are completely and repeatedly subordinated to a friendly intellectual relationship between two human beings throughout a period of fifteen weeks or more. Also, in such a course, a lonesome, ill-favoured underprivileged, badly schooled, or otherwise handicapped boy or girl can be assured at least a modicum of individual attention, approval, encouragement, and a chance to succeed. The only prerequisite for such treatment is a well defined amount and quality of academic achievement.

Another oddity of the system is the production of a grade distribution that is upside down. In Figure 1 are the results from a class of 208 students at Arizona State University during the past semester. Note the diminishing relative frequency as one moves from A to D. The category of E, indicating failure, is swollen by the presence of eighteen students who failed to take up their option of W (withdrawal from the course). Grades of C and D were due to the failure of students to complete all the units of reading or laboratory before going into the final examination.

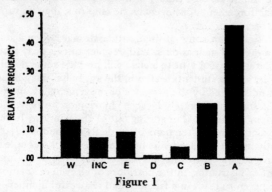

Figure 1

Figure 2 shows data from the class one year earlier. Essentially the same distribution holds, except for the category of Incomplete, which was then too easily obtainable. Discouraging the use of the Incomplete, together with the provision of more testing hours, apparently has the effect of regularising study habits and equalising the number of tests taken per week throughout the term.

In Figure 3 (filled bars), the grade distribution is for a section of twenty-five students in an introductory course at Queens College (NY) during the second semester of the past school year. The same method of teaching was employed as at Arizona State, but the work requirement was somewhat greater in amount. The distinctive feature here is the relative infrequency of low grades. Only four students received less than a B rating. Professor John Farmer, who provided me with these data, reports that the two students receiving F had dropped out of the course, for unknown reasons, after seven and eight units respectively.

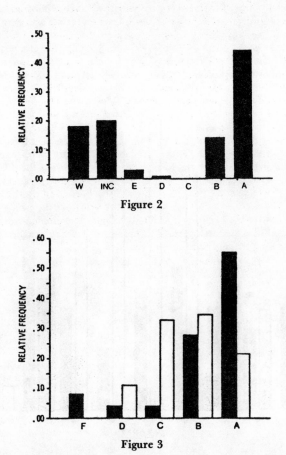

Figure 2

Figure 3

With this teaching method, students who are presumably inferior may show up better upon examination than presumably superior students taught by more conventional procedures. Figure 4 shows two distributions of grades on a mid-term examination. The empty bars represent the achievement of 161 students of an Ivy League College, mainly sophomores, in the first semester of a one-year lecture-and-laboratory course in elementary psychology. The filled bars represent the achievement of 66 Arizona State University students, mainly freshmen, on an unannounced mid-term quiz prepared by the Ivy League instructor and from which thirteen per cent of the questions had to be eliminated on the grounds of differential course coverage.

Relevant to this comparison is that pictured in Figure 3. The grade distribution obtained by Professor Farmer (and his associate, Brett Cole) is here compared with one obtained from a section of forty-six students in the same course, taught in the conventional manner by a

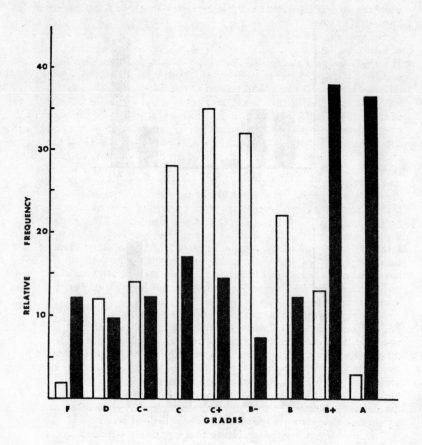

Figure 4

colleague who is described as 'a very good instructor'. The filled bars show the Farmer-Cole results: the empty ones are those from Professor Brandex.

Such comparisons are of some interest but they raise many questions of interpretation, and their importance should not be over-emphasised. The kind of change needed in education today is not one that will be evaluated in terms of the percentage of As in a grade distribution or of differences at the 0.01 (or 0.001) level of confidence. It is one that will produce a reinforcing state of affairs for everyone involved — a state of affairs that has heretofore been reached so rarely as to be the subject of eulogy in the world's literature, and which, unfortunately, has led to the mystique of the 'great teacher' rather than a sober analysis of the critical contingencies in operation.

Our method has not yet required a grant-in-aid to keep it going. On one occasion we tried to get such help, in order to pay for mimeograph paper, the services of a clerk, and one or two additional assistants. Our request was rejected, quite properly, on the grounds that our project was 'purely operational'. Almost any member of a present-day fund-granting agency can recognise 'research' when he sees it. I do think, however, that one should be freed, as I was, from other university demands while introducing a system like ours. And one should not be asked to teach more than two such courses regularly, each serving a hundred students or less, unless one has highly qualified assistants upon whom one can depend.

Neither does the method require equipment and supplies that are not already available to almost every teacher in the country. Teaching machines, tape recorders, and computers could readily be fitted into the picture. Moving pictures and television could also be used in one or two ways without detriment to the basic educational process. But these are luxuries, based on only partial recognition of our problem, and they could divert us from more important considerations. (Proctors, like computers, may go wrong or break down, but they can often be repaired and they are easily replaced, at very little expense.)

The need for individualised instruction is widely recognised, and the most commonly suggested way of filling this need is automation. I think that this solution is incomplete, especially when applied to the young; and I would like to mention a personal experience that bears upon the matter.

In the summer of 1966, I made numerous visits to a centre for the care and treatment of autistic children. One day, as I stood at the door of a classroom, I saw a boy get up from his chair at the end of a class period and give a soft pat to the object on the desk in front of him. At the same time, he said with a slight smile, 'Goodbye, Teaching Machine'!

This pseudo-social behaviour in this fundamentally asocial child amused me at the time. It reminded me of Professor Moore's description of the three-year-old who became irritated when his 'talking typewriter' made a mistake, called the device a 'big bambam', requested its name, and ended by asking, 'Who is your mother?' Today, however, I am not so sure that this is funny. It does suggest that affection may be generated within a child for an electro-mechanical instrument that has been essential to educational reinforcement. Unfortunately, such a machine, in its present form, is unlikely to generalise with human beings in the boy's world, giving to them a highly desirable reinforcing property. In fact, the growth of this type of student-machine relation, if it were the only one, would be a poor substitute for a directly social interaction.

In an earlier report upon our method, I mentioned that it had been anticipated, partially or *in toto*, in earlier studies and I described one of these in some detail. As for current developments by other workers in our field, I have not made any systematic attempt to examine the offerings, even those that deal with college or university instruction. However, I have been impressed by several of them which seem to have points in common with ours, which have met with some success, and which will probably be increasingly heard from in the future.

I started this paper on a personal note and I would like to end it on one. Twenty-odd years ago, when white rats were first used as laboratory subjects in the introductory course, a student would sometimes complain about his animal's behaviour. The beast could not learn, he was asleep, he was not hungry, he was sick, and so forth. With a little time and a handful of pellets, we could usually show that this was wrong. All that one needed to do was follow the rules. 'The rat', we used to say, 'is always right.'

My days of teaching are over. After what I have said about efficiency, I cannot lay claim to any great success, but my schedule of rewards was enough to maintain my behaviour, and I learned one very important thing: *the student is always right.* He is not asleep, not unmotivated, not sick, and he can learn a great deal if we provide the right contingencies of reinforcement. But if we do not provide them, and provide them soon, he too may be inspired to say 'Goodbye!' to formal education.

References

Ferster, C B and Perrott, M C (1968) *Behavior Principles.* New York : Appleton-Century-Crofts p542

Finger, F W (1962) Psychologists in colleges and universities. In W B Webb (ed) *The Profession of Psychology.* New York : Holt, Rinehart & Winston, pp 50-73

Keller, F S (1943) Studies in international morse code: 1. a new method of teaching code reception, *Journal of Applied Psychology* 27: 407-15

Keller, F S (1966) A personal course in psychology. In R Ulrich, T Stachnik and J Mabry (eds) *The Control of Behavior.* Glenview, Ill : Scott, Foresman, pp91-3

Keller, F S (1967) Neglected rewards in the educational process, *Proceedings of the 23rd American Conference of Academic Deans,* Los Angeles, January, pp 9-22

Keller, F S New reinforcement contingencies in the classroom. In *Programmiertes lernen,* Wissenschaftliche Buchgesellschaft, Darmstadt

Keller, F S (1967) Engineering personalized instruction in the classroom, *Rev Interamer de Psicol* 1: 189-97

Keller, F S and Schoenfeld, W N (1949) The psychology curriculum at Columbia College, *American Psychologist* 4: 165-72

Mahan, H C (1967) The use of Socratic type programmed instruction in college courses in psychology. Paper read at West Psychol Ass, San Francisco, May

Postlethwait, S N and Novak, J D The use of 8-mm loop films in individualized instruction, *Annals NY Acad Sci* 142 Art 2: 464-70

Sherman, J G (1967) Application of reinforcement principles to a college course. Paper read at American Educational Research Association, New York, February

3.5 Educational Technology at the Open University: An Approach to the Problem of Quality

BRIAN N LEWIS

Lewis, B N (1973) Educational technology at the Open University: an approach to the problem of quality, *British Journal of Educational Technology* 4: 188-204. Reproduced with permission of the author and Councils and Education Press.

In earlier papers in this series (Lewis, 1971a-c), an account was given of some of the more distinctive features of the Open University's multi-media teaching-at-a-distance system of adult education. The teaching arrangements of the Open University (OU) were described in some detail, and brief descriptions were also given of some of the more conspicuous *organisational* problems that arise when assorted groups of professionals (university lecturers, television and radio producers, graphics experts, educational technologists, editors, and many more) are brought together to produce multi-media teaching materials under conditions of acute time pressure.

In paper IV (Lewis, 1972) attention was switched to one of the many *educational* problems that the OU is being forced to confront. The problem that was singled out for special consideration was the problem of how to assess student learning in a teaching system which is obliged to assess, as well as teach, at a distance. The present paper begins with a brief review and reminder of the many additional problems (economic and social and humanitarian, as well as organisational and educational) that the OU is currently having to face. It then proceeds to describe some recent thinking on an educational problem of central importance to the whole enterprise — namely, the problem of ensuring that the OU's teaching materials have that hard-to-define something called 'quality'.

The present position

For the reasons given in the earlier papers, the Open University is an ambitious project. Its declared aim is to bring higher education within the reach of many thousands of adults who are able to study only on a part-time basis, and in their own homes. Moreover, it is striving to do this for adults who have *none* of the usual entry qualifications. And it is relying for its success on the novel deployment of a wide range of educational and mass media resources.

As indicated in papers I - III, the primary teaching resources are the home study (correspondence) materials, the nationwide television and radio broadcasts, the local study centres, and the short residential summer schools. The home study materials and the television and radio programmes convey the 'core' content of the courses. The local study centres provide opportunities for students to study and to discuss their problems either (a) among themselves, or (b) with visiting tutors or counsellors. The short residential summer schools, which are usually held in host universities, enable students to get together in larger numbers and for more ambitious purposes. A variety of additional teaching aids — such as home experimental kits, computer terminals, self-administered comprehension tests, homework and fieldwork assignments, tutor-marked and computer-marked feedback on homework, and assorted audio-visual aids — all help the student to consolidate his learning and to monitor his progress in an accurate way.

For a fairly comprehensive account of the OU's teaching system, the reader is referred to the papers (I - III) already cited. The teaching system is clearly one of considerable novelty and complexity. When it first started to operate, in January 1971, there was nothing quite like it anywhere else in the world. As might be expected, it had its teething troubles. In retrospect, it is rather astonishing that it ran as smoothly as it did. The fact remains that it weathered the early storms and, at the time of writing this particular paper, its public image is gratifyingly high. It has just conducted (June 1973) its first graduation ceremony. The student population stands at around 40,000. And over 35,000 applications have already been received in respect of courses due to commence in January 1974. The prevailing mood within the Open University is one of cautious self-congratulation. Everybody recognises that the system is still far from perfect. But the political decision to give it a chance appears to have been well vindicated.

Some major implications

If the Open University continues to be successful, it can hardly fail to exert a powerful influence on the future development, in this country, of higher education.

Consider, for example, the *economic* implications of the venture. If correspondence materials and television and radio broadcasts can be put to really effective use, it could be at least two to three times cheaper (as well as being more convenient) to teach degree courses in this way. The relative cheapness derives partly from the 'mass' nature of the teaching system, and partly from the fact that the average OU student is likely to be fully employed during the day (and, in consequence, no burden at all on the overall economy). Additional savings in cost arise from the fact that the OU does not require any expensive halls of residence for its students. Finally, there is a distinct possibility — currently being explored by the OU's marketing division — of securing a substantial income from the sale, in this country and abroad, of well-validated teaching materials. In these respects, the Open University appears to offer a highly cost-effective way of extending higher education in accordance with social and economic needs.

Next, consider the *social and humanitarian* implications of the OU system. Even if the OU served no economic purpose at all, there might still be thousands of people who come to see its courses as a means of self-fulfilment. The social value of alleviating frustrations and boredom in the home should not be underestimated. An essential feature of any 'ideal' society is that it should provide people, throughout the whole of their lives, with continuing opportunities to extend and change their interests and abilities. If the OU succeeds, it could play a central role in providing the kinds of opportunity that many people need.

Thirdly, consider the *educational* implications of the Open University. In this connection, it is worth drawing attention to the significance of offering, on a nationwide scale, a wide variety of undergraduate courses in the general areas of mathematics, science, technology, social science, education, and the arts. It is also worth pondering the significance of offering, also on a nationwide scale, short professional courses of a retraining or updating or socially important kind. A different form of significance derives from the fact that, unlike what happens in other universities, the OU's instructional materials are open to widespread public scrutiny. Whether they are good or bad, they are likely to provoke a great deal of valuable thought and discussion. Since many *non*-students are presumably inspecting some of the correspondence materials, and tuning in to some of the television and radio broadcasts, there may also be significant booster effects on the educational standards and sensitivities of the community as a whole.

Some recurring doubts

The miscellany of comments that have been made so far have all tended to represent the Open University in a highly favourable light. By drawing attention to some of the more striking economic and social and humanitarian and educational virtues of the OU system, an impression has been conveyed of a teaching system that might well turn out to be *preferable* to other (more conventional) systems.

There is of course a darker side to the picture. As many OU students have learned to their cost, studying with the Open University is by no means a 'soft option'. At the social and humanitarian level of argument, it can be argued that the provision of home study facilities is a doubtful blessing if the demands made on the student's spare time are unduly heavy or prolonged. For every OU student deriving unqualified benefit from our courses, there could be several whose marriage and family and social relationships are undergoing serious strain as a result of the study commitments that they have entered into. Home study facilities may also be quite unsuitable for younger students (in their late teens and early twenties) who, in their search for identity, need to get away from the homes in which they were brought up.

These are telling criticisms. But it would be quite misleading to suggest that they are the most important or the most uncomfortable criticisms. Of far greater consequence is the criticism that the Open University cannot possibly provide its home study students with an educational experience that matches, *in quality*, the educational experiences offered by full-time colleges of higher education.

In support of this criticism, it has been claimed (for example) that the average OU student is obliged to study in an educationally impoverished environment. The OU student typically has no access to first-class library and laboratory facilities. He has far fewer opportunities to talk with teachers and other students. He has much less time, overall, to devote to his studies. And he has almost no chance whatever of savouring, at first hand, the Great Minds that are said to inhabit the more distinguished colleges of higher education. For reasons such as this, some critics regard it as self-evident that the educational experience offered by the OU *must* be of sub-standard quality.

It is not the intention of this paper to discuss such allegations in detail. But it is worth remarking that they are less convincing than might appear at first sight. For example, it is by no means certain that extensive library and laboratory facilities are necessary (or even desirable) components of an effective system of higher education. A multiplicity of books, each written from a different perspective, can confuse as well as help. The existence of a well-stocked library can also induce academics to take rather less care with their lectures. It is all too easy for an academic to give his students a lightweight chat, and then invite them to go away and look up certain references. If this is done, and if (as so often happens) the academic then vanishes down the nearest bunny hole, the full-time student is left floundering in exactly the kind of 'independent learning' situation that critics of the Open University deplore.

At the risk of sounding unduly cynical, it is worth adding that in most full-time colleges of higher education, Great Minds are *not* in abundant supply. If there are any at all, they tend (with only a few distinguished exceptions) to be largely inaccessible to the average undergraduate. The Open University, with its nationwide system of television and radio broadcasts, is in a comparatively strong position to bring before its students Great Minds that happen to be especially relevant to the courses it is running. Moreover, its television programmes are able to offer dynamic visual materials of a kind which no other university has the resources to produce. Finally, it must not be overlooked that the average OU student is likely, on balance, to be more mature and more motivated to learn than the average teenage student at a conventional university. There is consequently much more to arguments about quality than meets the eye.

On taking quality seriously

The kind of discussion exhibited in the last section is in many respects deeply unsatisfactory. In the first place, it is incurably inconclusive. In the absence of any clear-cut agreement about what quality is, or might be, no decisive comparisons can possibly be made between the OU and other universities. Since the Open University is strikingly different from other universities, common sense suggests that it will probably be better in some respects and worse in others. If it could be shown that the OU is better in respects that do not really matter, and is worse in respects that matter a great deal, the allegation of 'overall inferiority' would be rehabilitated. But the case needs to be argued in a systematic way. It is not enough simply to make a string of bright-looking debating points.

This all poses a very considerable challenge to the educational technologist. The challenge is partly conceptual, partly empirical, and partly prescriptive. At the conceptual level, the educational technologist is being challenged to say what, in his opinion, quality in higher education *is*. At the empirical level, the challenge is to devise objective tests and measures of whatever he takes quality to be. At the prescriptive level, the challenge is to specify design procedures which will help to build his conception of quality into tomorrow's teaching materials.

In attempting to meet these challenges, the educational technologist must further decide whether he wants to function as a neutral reporter and synthesiser (of what other people have to say), or whether he wants to function as an independent theoretician. In the former capacity, he will simply try to discover and report what recognised authorities have to say about the nature of quality in higher education. In the latter capacity, his views on quality will be largely determined by the theory and/or value system that he happens to subscribe to concerning the essence of 'good' education. Between these two extremes, there are several compromise positions. For example, it might be possible to compile a comprehensive descriptive account of what certain well-known experts have to say, and to refrain from invoking one's own (possibly idiosyncratic) theories unless the opinions collected have irremediable defects or inconsistencies. In any event, the stance of the educational technologist clearly poses a whole cluster of additional problems. Attempts to say what quality is, and how it should be measured etc will inevitably be shot through with theoretical notions and value judgements which ideally need to be made explicit.

It need hardly be said that an exercise of this kind cannot easily be accomplished overnight. The work involved is surely no less than that involved in elucidating the notion of, say, *critical thinking*.

If we pause to look at the way in which educational theorists and philosophers have tackled the notion of critical thinking, we find exactly the kind of multiple (three-strand) inquiry that we have just been advocating in respect of the notion of quality. On the conceptual side, numerous papers have been written on what critical thinking is. On the empirical side, attempts have also been made to devise operationally useful indices and tests and measures of the ability to think critically. On the prescriptive side, substantial efforts have been made to prescribe ways of inducing and enhancing critical thinking in children and adults of all ages and abilities. Underlying all these efforts are various theoretical stances (concerning, for example, the relationship between critical thinking and formal logic), and various value judgements (concerning, for example, the desirability of being able to challenge certain kinds of assertion).

A recent monograph by D'Angelo (1971) reviews the literature on critical thinking, and cites over two hundred references stretching back over a period of thirty years or so. It is clear from the D'Angelo monograph that the whole area of inquiry is still in a rather unsatisfactory state. But it is nevertheless true that the overall effort has greatly enriched and deepened our understanding of what critical thinking is, and how it can be potentiated. When conceptual and empirical and prescriptive inquiries go hand in hand, worthwhile progress is almost certain to occur.

The suggestion now being made is that we should try to do for the notion of quality what educational theorists and philosophers have tried to do for the notion of critical thinking. Fortunately, a massively relevant literature already exists and, for this reason, we might safely expect to make good progress within just a few years.

The literature in question can mostly be classified under the general headings of educational technology, educational psychology, educational philosophy, educational sociology, and educational politics. In the field of educational technology, almost everything that has been written has had *something* to say, by implication at least, about the problem of quality. In the field of educational psychology, research findings in respect of topics such as learning theory and personality theory also have much to say. In the field of educational philosophy, discussions on the nature of education itself, and on the way in which it differs from (say) industrial training, provide orientations of a different but no less valid kind. In the field of educational sociology, insightful analyses can be found of such problems as where educational objectives come from, and why some kinds of knowledge are more highly valued by society than others. In the field of educational politics, tomorrow's aspiring (and self-selected) leaders — the anti-schoolers and the pro-schoolers, and the authors of white papers and red papers and black papers — show how one person's approach to quality education is another person's road to hell.

As usual, the pertinent issues are all scrambled together and confused and opaque. However, it should not be beyond the capacity of a good analytic mind to exteriorise and (thus) render explicit the structure of the underlying controversies — eg by showing how different views about quality (and, in particular, quality in higher education) stem from different theoretical standpoints and value systems. Even a cursory examination of the kind of literature cited in the last paragraph should be enough to convince the reader of the superficiality of the comments (on the quality of the OU educational experience) that were made in the previous section of this paper. If we are genuinely concerned about the quality of higher education, it is surely worth conducting the kinds of conceptual and empirical and prescriptive inquiry that have been carried out in respect of critical thinking. The material for the conceptual inquiry already exists in the literature just mentioned. If we did no more than probe this literature in a systematic fashion, we would be well on the way toward straightening out our ideas on the subject.

In view of the importance of this particular problem, the Open University's Institute of Educational Technology (IET) decided at an early date to devote some research effort to it. The original impetus for this effort came from a deliberately provocative and somewhat notorious memorandum that I circulated, in 1970, on the need for quality control at the Open University. The memorandum suggested, among other things, that the OU might do well to institute procedures of quality control to check on the quality of the educational materials that its academic staff were producing. For the reasons given in paper II (Lewis, 1971b), most academic members of staff responded to this suggestion with a mixture of derision and outraged incredulity.

As an unrepentant advocate of the need to take the problem of quality seriously, I continued to hold intermittent discussions and seminars on the subject until, by the middle of 1972, I felt I was able to make a first rough-and-ready attempt at devising a comprehensive conceptual framework. The result was a paper which tried to capture, in an operationally tractable manner, what I took to be the key ingredients of 'quality' in higher education. The paper was written in the form of a *research proposal*, because it was manifestly speculative and needed to be carefully checked against the reality provided by actual educational texts. After going through several drafts, it was submitted to the Ford Foundation in the form of a three-year research proposal, and the Ford Foundation generously funded it in full (at around $120,000) as from January 1973.

The remainder of this paper accordingly follows the pattern of paper IV (Lewis, 1972) by reproducing, in only lightly edited form, the substantive content of the three-year research proposal. It seemed appropriate to retain the original wording as much as possible, in order to provide the most authentic account of the way in which the project came into existence. At the time of writing this paper, the main ideas contained in the proposal appear to be standing up rather well. The perceptive reader will hardly fail to notice that very few educational experiences (either inside or outside the OU) come anywhere near to meeting the more stringent criteria that I propose. In this respect, the proposal accurately reflects my personal views on the current state of higher education. I happen to think that the quality of the OU's educational materials compares quite favourably with that of other universities. But I also happen to think that this is faint praise indeed.

Indices of quality in higher education: some tentative proposals

> During a counterpoint class at U.C.L.A., Schoenberg sent everybody to the blackboard. We were to solve a particular problem he had given and to turn around, when finished, so that he could check on the correctness of the solution. I did as directed. He said, 'That's good. Now find another solution'. I did. He said, 'Another'. Again I found one. Again he said, 'Another'. And so on. Finally I said, 'There are no more solutions'. He said, 'What is the principle underlying all of the solutions . . ?'
> John Cage, *Silence,* MIT Press, 1961

The story quoted above captures, in a fairly succinct way, the general import and intention of this proposal. Briefly, we would like to secure a scientifically tractable characterisation of what constitutes quality in education (and especially in *higher* education). At the present time, the word 'quality' tends to refer to that indefinable something which some educational materials have got and which others have not got. This is an unsatisfactory state of affairs. If we cannot say more clearly what quality *is*, we can hardly offer cogent positive advice on how to build it into our educational materials (and, hence, into the thinking of our students).

A large number of researchers have tried, of course, to sharpen and operationalise the notion of quality. Under the general rubric of 'Educational Technology', there are Bloom-type taxonomies for educational objectives, Tyler-type prescriptions for curriculum design, system-theoretical prescriptions for the design of teaching systems in general (eg Searles, 1967), and numerous heuristics and recommendations (eg for subject-matter analysis and behaviour control) which are all aimed, in general terms, at improving the quality and effectiveness of educational materials. In addition, there are numerous related inquiries — eg into classroom interaction, and the relationship between teaching styles and learning styles — which are seeking to improve the affective and human-relations aspects of teaching.

This rather massive research activity has undoubtedly generated large numbers of useful insights into different facets of the teaching and learning process. And nothing that is said in this proposal is intended to disparage the very real contributions that other researchers have made. The brute fact remains, however, that there is still a great deal of low-quality education around. And there is an increasing feeling that there is more to 'quality' — especially in the field of higher education — than has become apparent from the vast amount of educational research conducted so far.

Another way of expressing the point made in the last sentence would be to say that previous research has identified *some* of the essential ingredients of quality, *but not all.* There is more to quality, in higher education, than meets the eye. And this proposal offers a way of looking at the problem which, in our opinion, could usefully supplement and illuminate research work that is going on elsewhere.

THE PROBLEM OF QUALITY

Rightly or wrongly, most experienced educators believe that they can recognise quality in educational materials — just as most experienced artists believe that they can recognise quality (and even greatness) in works of visual and musical and dramatic art. The fact that these people cannot say, in clear-cut analytic terms, what constitutes 'quality' does not in any way deter them from believing very strongly that they can recognise it when they see it. As Kotarbinski (1966) once put it, it is not necessary to be able to define a sparrow, in order to recognise it.

In the field of art, the non-definability of quality and greatness can be intellectually disquieting, but it is otherwise not too serious. In the field of higher education, the non-definability of quality is less acceptable. The reason for this is the one mentioned earlier — namely, that there is still a great deal of low-quality education around. And, interestingly enough, the application of the best insights of educational research does not always seem to improve matters very much.

In the hey-day of programmed learning, there were many theorists who seemed to think that educational quality could be virtually *guaranteed* simply by adopting Skinner-type principles of behaviour control. According to this view, poor quality teaching has two main sources:

1. teachers are not sufficiently clear about what they want their students to achieve; and
2. even when they are clear, they commonly fail to simplify and order the content of their teaching in a sufficiently intelligible way.

Point 1 leads, of course, to the well-known requirement that teachers should pre-specify 'behaviourally-defined objectives'. And point 2 leads to the requirement that subject matters should be broken down into well-sequenced, easy-to-assimilate, bits of information. There is no doubt that teaching can be made much more effective by assiduously attending to requirements 1 and 2 above. But it does not take much perception to see that these requirements are not, by themselves, sufficient to *guarantee* a high-quality product. To see this, we need to look no further than the numerous low-grade programmed texts which devote hundreds of 'frames' simply to establishing the rudimentary beginnings of some well-defined subject matter. It is no accident that programmed texts are usually *introductory* texts. Their very format prevents them from conveying a depth understanding of conceptually-rich subject matters — and this is one reason why there are almost no programmed texts to cover advanced-level subject matters in higher education.

BEYOND BEHAVIOURAL OBJECTIVES

As a result of over three years' intensive experience of course production at the Open University — during which time considerable efforts were made to make the behavioural objectives approach work — we can now say, quite categorically, that there are severe limitations to what this particular approach can achieve in the field of higher education. It would take too long to defend this dogmatic statement in detail. So we will simply say that we have become increasingly convinced of the need to go beyond the behavioural objectives approach and to specify (in addition to behavioural objectives) the *structure of the subject matter* that each teacher is trying to convey.

To justify this last assertion, perhaps it is sufficient to notice that students (like everyone else) can be right for the wrong reasons. This simple fact is, by itself, enough to establish a distinction between (a) what students say and do, and (b) the knowledge that underlies and informs what these same students say and do. Ideally, we need to specify both — the former being specifications of *behaviour,* and the latter being specifications of *knowledge.* At the same time, we need to elucidate the (extremely subtle) relationships between (a)-type and (b)-type specifications.

If we do this, we discover that it becomes possible to talk in a sensible way about explanation and understanding and (most important of all) *depth* understanding. These are expressions which are not easily treated by behaviouristic approaches, for the obvious reason that statements about explanation and understanding etc are statements about the nature and quality of the knowledge that lies *behind* observable behaviour.

At the present time, a small group of us are working on ways of representing knowledge by means of concept-relation diagrams and matrices. This is proving to be a most illuminating inquiry because it raises deep questions about the interrelatedness of key concepts and topics (ie concept-clusters) in particular subject-matter areas. It also gives considerable insight into what would, and would not, count as a 'depth understanding' of such subject matters. The construction of concept-relation diagrams also brings other advantages. For example, it is possible to define different teaching strategies on the diagrams, and it is possible to differentiate key (kernel) concepts from ancillary (supporting) concepts. The basic distinction between behavioural specifications and knowledge specifications also has important implications for the theory and practice of *assessment*. For example, it is possible to maintain clear-cut distinctions between assessment procedures which inquire what students can say and do, and assessment procedures which inquire what students know and understand.

Once again, it is beyond the scope of this proposal to elaborate on the somewhat tantalising remarks thrown out in the last few paragraphs. We have tried to say only as much as is necessary to convince the reader that we are operating within a theoretical framework which *is* different from that of other researchers in the field. Perhaps we should add that our theoretical framework has been developed, over three years, as a response to hard practical problems of course design at the Open University. We accordingly expect the fruits of our inquiries to take the form of practical prescriptions for the *design* (as opposed to the *intuiting*) of better quality courses.

QUALITY REVISITED

One way of approaching the problem of quality is to list the distinguishing characteristics of acknowledged experts or 'master performers' in the subject matter or discipline being taught. To some extent, a comprehensive list of *possible* characteristics has already been gathered together by Bloom and his associates. However, our own particular framework suggests a somewhat different approach. Instead of collecting, in the manner of Bloom *et al*, large numbers of indeterminately-related abilities, we prefer to think in terms of just three distinguishable abilities applicable to just three different problem-solving domains.

Very briefly, the three distinguishable abilities are:

(a) the ability to recognise and recall, and
(b) the ability to explain, and
(c) the ability to justify the explanations one gives.

The three different problem-solving domains are:

(i) the domain of individual *problems* which arise within the discipline being taught, and which are characteristic of that discipline;

(ii) the domain of *problem-solving procedures* which are used to solve the problems of (i) above;

(iii) the domain of *higher-order problem-solving procedures* which are implied in the use of (ii) above, and which can be applied to seemingly different problems in seemingly different disciplines.

Underlying the first classification scheme [(a)-(c)] is the belief that, for every subject matter whatever, it should be possible for the quality student to state all the essential facts, $F_1, F_2, \ldots F_n$ of that subject matter — along with an explanation of why/how $F_1, F_2, \ldots F_n$ happen to be the case. In addition, it should be possible for the student to justify/support/explain the why/how explanations that he gives.

The second classification scheme [(i)-(iii)] reminds us that the 'facts' $F_1, F_2, \ldots F_n$ can refer either to problems within this discipline, or to the problem-solving procedures that enable such problems to be solved, or to the higher-order problem-solving procedures which help the student to transfer his problem-solving capability from one discipline to another.

If our educational materials self-consciously seek to induce each of the three abilities (a)-(c), over each of the problem-solving domains (i)-(iii), they constitute a teaching instrument which operates at nine distinguishable levels — each level being slightly more 'abstract' than the level before. In our opinion, this is a promising and tractable way of looking at 'levels of tuition' — because each level is operationally distinguishable and capable of correspondingly distinct methods of *assessment*. In further support of this claim, the next part of this research proposal comments on these nine levels in somewhat greater detail.

LEVELS OF TUITION AND UNDERSTANDING

Level 1 tuition is primarily concerned with imparting what teachers consider to be the 'basic introductory facts' of a particular discipline or sub-discipline. In level 1 tuition, the student typically takes a passive (spectator, as opposed to participant) role. He is 'hearing about' the subject matter, rather than doing it. For this reason, the student's comprehension of level 1 tuition can usually be tested by recourse to simple tests of recognition and recall. The teacher talks about the subject matter, and the student's task is to try to make sense of (and, hence, to remember) what the teacher has to say.

It need hardly be said that some subjects (eg mathematics) do not lend themselves at all well to pure level 1 treatment. And it can be argued that *all* level 1 tuition is defective insofar as it fails to involve the student in actively doing things (eg laboratory work, or pencil-and-paper exercises) or in challenging what the teacher is saying. Nevertheless, a great deal of level 1 tuition goes on in higher education — especially in the humanities and behavioural sciences. The standard undergraduate textbook — unaccompanied by work manuals or student exercises etc — is the most ubiquitous mediator of level 1 tuition.

Much of the Open University's Foundation Course materials have a level 1 flavour. The student is first of all shown, in general terms, how a particular discipline is divided up into loosely-related and overlapping topics. And he is then shown how particular topics and sub-topics get handled by various experts in the field. In other words, he is shown some of the commoner tricks — argumentative and/or experimental — that workers in the field get up to. And this is intended to pave the way for deeper treatment (of the same topics) in subsequent courses.

It is necessary to insist that the coverage in such courses is essentially lightweight. Topic headings are named, but the relationships existing among the various topics are not well defined. Also, the relationships existing among concepts *within* a topic are usually not well defined. More often than not, this kind of course is little more than a mention list. Various facts and phenomena and procedures are mentioned to the student who, at the end-of-course examination, is simply expected to mention them back to the examiner.

Level 2 tuition goes beyond level 1 insofar as it enables the student to offer *explanations* of the various ideas and phenomena that level 1 tuition introduces.

Within any discipline, there are certain things that happen (or can be made to happen), and there are certain propositions that are held to be true. These are the so-called 'facts of the case' — and the aim of level 1 tuition is to try to fix these in the student's mind. At level 2, however, the student is expected to be able to explain *how it is* that certain things happen (or can be made to happen), and *why it is* that certain propositions hold true.

The difference between level 1 and level 2 can therefore be re-phrased as follows. As a result of level 1 tuition, the student should know that, within the discipline under consideration, certain facts, $F_1, F_2, \ldots F_n$ *are* the case. As a result of level 2 tuition, he should further know *why* (or *how*) facts $F_1, F_2, \ldots F_n$ are the case.

Explanations can of course take a variety of forms. We can explain how things get done by specifying some rule of procedure or a set of heuristics. We can explain how concepts are related to one another. We can explain how observations are related to theories. And so on. It is beyond the scope of this proposal (and it would anticipate some of the results that we hope to secure in our research program) to elaborate on this particular issue. But it is appropriate to say that we hope to construct a *unified framework* for talking about (and, hence evaluating) different forms of explanation. Presumably it is at least obvious that, in introducing the requirement that students be able to offer explanations, we have indeed moved up to a higher level of cognitive functioning. And this requires a correspondingly higher level of tuition.

Two further points are worth making:

(a) by requiring the student to give explanations, we automatically shift him from the passive spectator role (permitted by level 1 tuition) to the active participant role. At level 2, the student is immersing himself in the subject matter, rather than simply looking at it from a distance;

(b) the ability to give correct explanations is commonly regarded as good evidence that the student *understands* the subject matter. For the reasons discussed in the next section, we take the slightly different view that the ability to explain is a necessary but *not* a sufficient index of understanding.

Level 3. In addition to requiring a student to offer an explanation of some fact or phenomenon, we might require him to *justify* the explanation that he gives. In calling for a justification we are, in effect, calling for an explanation of his (earlier) explanation. Another way of putting the point would be to say that we are asking the student to show how his explanation can be derived from other (and preferably deeper) considerations.

There are several reasons for being interested in the student's ability to justify the explanations that he gives:

(a) In the first place, many explanations are simple enough to be rote-memorised — perhaps with the aid of arbitrary mnemonics. In such cases, the student can offer the required explanation without having the faintest idea why it has the form that it does have. In the limiting case, he may have no idea how the explanation might be backed up or supported. Indeed, he might not even be aware that a rationale (for his explanation) is within his intellectual reach. For example, many readers of this proposal may well be able to recall the somewhat mysterious procedure, in arithmetic, for calculating the 'square root' of a number — by pairing off digits from the decimal point, etc. We can explain from memory how the trick is done. But how many of us could explain why our explained procedure works?

(b) By contrast, some students can do very much more than offer bare explanations. In addition to being able to explain, they have a conceptual framework (in their minds) which is powerful enough to enable them to *deduce* the required explanation. This additional ability — the ability to back up one's explanation with a convincing exposition of why the explanation works — brings us nearer to what is commonly called 'understanding'. In brief, we might say that understanding is indexed by a dual capability — the ability to explain, coupled with the ability to justify one's explanation.

(c) A further reason for being interested in justification is that many explanations can be justified in different, but equally valid, ways. Moreover, many explanations can be justified in quite inappropriate ways. To obtain a student's justification is to gain useful insights into the way in which he sees the pertinent subject matter.

Level 4. By way of recapitulation, let us remind ourselves that level 1 tuition is mainly concerned with conveying certain facts $F_1, F_2, \ldots F_n$ about the discipline under consideration. Level 2 tuition is mainly concerned with explaining why/how $F_1, F_2, \ldots F_n$ happen to be the case. And level 3 tuition is concerned with providing a conceptual framework within which it is possible to justify/deduce the explanations offered at level 2.

At level 4, we direct our attention to the desirability of showing *flexibility of approach* to the various problems posed within the discipline. What we have in mind is the fact that, within a particular discipline, there is usually more than one way of tackling the problems that can occur. If the discipline is indeed characterised by a varied repertoire of problem-solving methods, the quality student might be expected to show special sensitivity concerning the choice (of method) that he makes on any given occasion. In effect, we might expect such a student to have a set of recognition procedures which enables him to say, 'this problem can best be tackled in this way, and that problem can best be tackled in that way.'

Once more, there is a great deal that might be said in elaboration of the ideas mooted in the previous paragraph. For example, we might distinguish between specific problem-solving procedures and generalised problem-solving procedures. And we might distinguish between disciplines that contain different-but-compatible ways of tackling the same problems, and disciplines that contain different-but-incompatible ways of tackling the same problems. Consider, for example, the various problem-solving procedures available in social survey work — obtrusive *v* unobtrusive observation, questionnaires *v* personal interviews, semantic differential scales *v* Kelly Grids, and so on. Level 4 tuition, as we understand it, would be self-consciously directed at telling the students what kinds of problem-solving procedures are best suited for what kinds of problem.

Levels 5 and 6. The ability to switch from one problem-solving method to another, as different circumstances arise, can be based either on blind rule-of-thumb pattern recognition or on informed insight. In other words, flexibility of perspectives/approach/problem solving ideally needs to be coupled with the ability to *explain* why the switching occurs, along with a further ability to *justify* the explanation that is given. Levels 5 and 6 accordingly deal with these two additional abilities. Thus level 5 tuition should enable the student to offer coherent explanations concerning the way in which he switches from one problem-solving procedure to another. And level 6 tuition should enable the student to justify the explanations that he acquired at level 5. In this respect, levels 5 - 6 are roughly analogous (but at a higher level of abstraction) to levels 2 - 3 respectively.

In case the point is not obvious, levels 1 - 3 can be construed as dealing mainly with the efficiency with which students handle *individual* problems in the discipline under consideration. Levels 4 - 6 can be construed as dealing mainly with the efficiency with which students handle whole sequences of problems which, as a matter of *fact*, are amenable to a variety of treatments. It follows that levels 4 - 6 require assessment procedures in which measurements are taken over whole sequences of test items.

Finally, it is worth adding that levels 5 and 6 are indeed essential additions to level 4. To see this, it may be enough to remind ourselves that most politicians are very good at switching their approach (eg from a moral to a legal to an economic standpoint) as circumstances change.

Whether or not these politicians could explain the grounds on which they switch, and whether or not they could additionally justify the explanations that they offer, is another matter. Presumably they could offer weak explanations ('This is the best way of putting my case . . .') and weak justifications ('The end justifies the means . . .'). But, in the very act of offering such explanations and justifications, they would reveal the impoverished structure of their thinking. The important point to notice is that the ability to explain and justify successful flexibility calls for considerable penetration into the conceptual structure of the subject matter. If there is no elaborate conceptual structure present, the task is easy. But this is the exception rather than the rule and, even in politics, it is not at all easy to switch *successfully* from one stance to another. If a person can successfully switch from one mode of explanation to another as different problems arise, and if he can explain and justify what he is doing at every stage, there are good grounds for crediting him with having a 'depth understanding' of the subject matter.

Levels 7 - 9. It can be argued that the kinds of argumentative manoeuvres that go on inside one discipline are very similar to the kinds of argumentative manoeuvres that go on inside other disciplines. In every case, there are experts and general practitioners who bring to bear (on the discipline) certain *presuppositions* which inform — and also, perhaps, bias — the way in which they gather and interpret what they take to be 'the evidence'. Within most disciplines, it is possible for different schools of thought, based on different presuppositional schemes, to co-exist side by side. In such cases, the different presuppositions will also determine, to a large extent, the nature and quality of the interaction that takes place between the members of different schools — and, in particular, the kinds of dismissive strategies that each adopts towards the other.

People who are impressed by similarities rather than differences may well think that the way in which historians argue is very similar to the way in which literary critics argue and the way in which theologians and politicians and trade unions (and, for that matter, husbands and wives) argue. The possibility therefore arises of looking at changes of problem-solving behaviour *across* seemingly different (but actually similar) areas of human endeavour. In other words, the possibility exists of repeating levels 4 - 6 across disciplines — rather than within a single discipline — in order to elucidate the conditions under which people need to change their mode of functioning when shifting from one discipline or 'activity' or 'situation' to another.

This, in general terms, is what levels 7 - 9 aim to do. By examining the structure and dimensionality of problems across disciplines, rather than within disciplines, tuition at levels 7 - 9 makes a positive contribution to the need for *generalist* education. This has several noteworthy implications:

(a) First of all, there is the kind of student who gets his intellectual satisfaction from interrelating a variety of different disciplines — rather than probing just one in great depth. Society *needs* this kind of person (the generalist, rather than the specialist), but the present system of higher education does not make adequate provision for him.

(b) Secondly, the establishing of similarities and differences (of technique and argumentation) across disciplines opens up the way for a sensible discussion of *career choice*. If we can show that the intellectual and/or 'skill' content of discipline A is very similar to that of discipline B, then the student who has mastered A will know that, with only minor modifications of cognitive functioning, he can switch to B.

(c) Another way of putting the point is to say that by mastering what is common to disparate disciplines, and by seeing clearly what is not common, a student (together with the educational system) can discern what potential he has for moving from one area of activity to another. This is tantamount to saying that he acquires 'learning sets' — ie in addition to learning the specific content of specific disciplines, he *learns how to learn*.

CONCLUDING REMARKS

The ideas exhibited in this proposal constitute, in rather sketchy form, the emerging fruits of three years' thinking about the practical and theoretical problems of producing quality courses and quality students. To avoid making this proposal inordinately long, we have not gone into the fine details of the theoretical framework. And we have not expounded any of our ideas on the subject of special-purpose assessment procedures.

To the expert reader, some of the implications of our approach (for the problem of assessment) will no doubt be obvious. For example, it is generally impossible to test at levels 3, 6 and 9 by means of multiple-choice questions alone. If we wish to test a student's ability to justify the explanations that he gives, we must minimally adjoin a 'short-answer' facility to our multiple-choice questions. In other words, certain test items will invite the student to select what he considers to be the best/correct answer, and *then* to say, in his own words, why he chose that particular answer.

The perceptive reader might also have realised that levels 4, 5 and 6 call for measures over *sequences* of test items, rather than measures over individual test items. And certain kinds of understanding (eg those at levels 8 and 9) may call for a special kind of *conversational* testing. These are matters that cannot be gone into here. We mention them only to indicate the kinds of thinking and development work involved in the research programme that we have in mind.

To what extent do our nine levels succeed in capturing what is normally meant by 'quality' in students? Well, it is often said that the quality student should be able to challenge and extend and even *transform* the knowledge he is given. At first glance, it might be thought that our framework does not allow for this kind of creative ability in the quality student. But it turns out that creative ability is in fact directly implied by our requirement that the student should be able to justify the explanation that he gives. A student who has a conceptual framework strong enough to enable him to *deduce* particular explanations undoubtedly has the ability to generate novel explanations also. In addition, it should not be overlooked that levels 7 - 9 can be powerful *potentiators* of creative thinking — because they are centrally concerned with helping the student to see analogies between one discipline and another. For reasons such as these, we believe that our approach, when fully developed, *will* capture everything that needs to be said about quality — at least at the cognitive level.

References

Bloom, B S (ed) (1956) *Taxonomy of Educational Objectives: The Classification of Educational Goals. Handbook* 1. *Cognitive Domain.* New York : McKay

Bloom, B S, Hastings, J T and Madaus, G F (1971) *Handbook of Formative and Summative Evaluation of Student Learning.* New York : McGraw-Hill

D'Angelo, E (1971) *The Teaching of Critical Thinking.* Amsterdam : B R Gruner

Kotarbinski, T (1966) *Gnosiology.* London : Pergamon

Lewis, B N (1971a) Course production at the Open University I: some basic problems, *British Journal of Educational Technology* 2 1

Lewis, B N (1971b) Course production at the Open University II: activities and activity networks, *British Journal of Educational Technology* 2 2

Lewis, B N (1971c) Course production at the Open University III: planning and scheduling, *British Journal of Educational Technology* 2 3

Lewis, B N (1972) Course production at the Open University IV: the problem of assessment, *British Journal of Educational Technology* 3 2

Searles, J E (1967) *A System for Instruction.* Pennsylvania : International Textbook Co

Tyler, R W (1950) *Basic Principles of Curriculum and Instruction.* Chicago : University of Chicago Press

3.6 The 'McMaster Philosophy': An Approach to Medical Education

VICTOR NEUFELD AND HOWARD S BARROWS

Neufeld, V and Barrows, H S (1974) The 'McMaster philosophy': an approach to medical education, *Journal of Medical Education* 49 11: 1040-50. Reproduced with permission of the authors and the editor.

In 1966 the 'founding fathers' of the Faculty of Medicine at McMaster University conceptualised an approach to medical education. Now, eight years later and with the fifth class having been admitted in 1973, these original concepts are often referred to as the 'McMaster philosophy'. It is a tribute to the clarity of the original vision that, to a large extent, its various components have been expressed, maintained and expanded in the actual programme. While various aspects of the programme have been described elsewhere, the authors propose here, in a single statement, to describe the fundamental concepts as they are currently practised.

The goals of the MD programme focus on the individual student-physician. The emphasis is placed on specific capabilities and characteristics rather than a store of knowledge. The faculty recognises the fact that the body of factual knowledge in the programme is inevitably both incomplete and redundant; because of this, a high value is placed on the student's ability to manipulate data, to recognise and define problems, and to evaluate their solutions. Rather than a commitment to 'streaming' (that is, to prepare students for specified careers), the programme prepares 'undifferentiated' physicians who, at graduation, will be able to select more specific postgraduate training programmes. Despite this, there is sufficient flexibility in the programmes so that the student can shape his studies toward developing career goals.

The general goals of the programme stated in terms of outcomes for the student, are as follows:

1. To identify and define health problems and to search for information in order to resolve or manage these problems.
2. Given a health problem, to examine the underlying physical or behavioural mechanisms. A spectrum of phenomena might be included, from molecular events to those involving the patient's family and community.
3. To recognise, maintain, and develop personal characteristics and attitudes required for professional life.
4. To develop the clinical skills and to learn the methods required to define and manage the health problems of patients, including their physical, emotional, and social aspects.

5. To become a self-directed learner, recognising personal educational needs, selecting appropriate learning resources, and evaluating progress.
6. To be able to assess critically professional activity related to patient care, health care delivery and medical research.
7. To be able to function as a productive member of a small group which is engaged in learning, research or health care.
8. To be aware of and be able to work in a variety of health care settings.

The three-year programme consists of four phases: the first two are ten weeks each, and the last two are one year each. Phase I is an introduction to the community, its facilities and people; to the learning strategies of problem solving, independent study and small-group tutorials; to universal concepts in structure, function, and behaviour; and to basic clinical skills. Phase II concentrates on the body's response to stimuli, using pathophysiologic models such as ischemia, inflammation and reactive depression. Phase III consists of four ten-week combined organ system units, using more specific disease entities in a problem-based approach. The clinical clerkship, Phase IV, comprises three major blocks: hospital-based, ambulatory and elective. Throughout the programme there are additional extensive elective opportunities, both concurrent with ongoing phases and in two blocks between phases.

The following components of the educational programme, while stated separately, are interrelated. None of these ideas is entirely novel in education. What is perhaps more unusual is the combination of these ideas into a single and unified approach and the creation of an administrative arrangement which allows these ideas to flourish.

Self-directed learning

If physicians are to be life-long learners and able to assess changing health care needs, to keep up with changing concepts and new knowledge, and to adapt their own performance accordingly, they must develop the requisite skills during the formative years of medical school training. Therefore, in the McMaster programme, the student is assumed to be a responsible and motivated adult. He is encouraged, with appropriate guidance, to define his own learning goals, to select appropriate experiences to achieve these goals, and to be responsible for assessing his own learning progress. In defining his learning goals, the student is encouraged to review his previous experiences in academic training, his future career plans, and the current learning opportunities at McMaster. The student is helped by a tutor or an adviser in defining these personal goals and in seeing their relationship to the goals of the tutorial group as well as to the overall programme goals. It is important that these personal objectives are clear, assessable and realistic.

The student is responsible for the design of his own programme, bearing in mind his responsibilities to the tutorial group. The schedule facilitates this independence, with a maximum of one optional classwide event per day. A large range of learning resources is available to the student to help him achieve his objectives. Self-directed learning also involves the learning of methods for managing information; included are such basic abilities as efficient reading and the effective use of practical personal information retrieval (filing) systems, study outlines and notes, medical journals and texts, and the medical library.

Approximately twenty-five weeks in the three-year programme are designated for 'electives'. Elective time in the McMaster programme means individual time when the student does not need to consider concurrent responsibilities to the tutorial group. Most students use these periods for pursuing individual interests, shoring up areas of deficiency, or studying in other centres.

Just as the determination of goals and the selection of learning experiences are the student's responsibility, so self-evaluation is a component of self-directed learning. The prerequisites for this are a willingness to do it, an understanding of what the goals are and some idea of performance criteria (that is, the desired or expected level of performance or learning). How does this self-evaluation actually happen? It is a constant and informal process. The student has feedback about his own performance and makes value judgements about it in discussions with his peers, in tutorial discussions, and more formally in reviewing a write-up of a problem with his tutor or engaging in self-assessment exercises of various kinds. At the end of each unit he also reviews his progress comprehensively with his tutor.

Problem-based learning

Learning based on problems represents an alternative to studying blocks of classified knowledge in a strictly organised sequence. In problem-based learning, the learner focuses on a problem which he has identified and which involves genuine intellectual effort. The learner brings to the problem all of his previous information and expertise as well as his ability to think rationally about it. As he begins to ask questions, certain issues become defined which will require a further information search. After assembling the appropriate information, he synthesises a problem solution. The student learns to recognise that few problems in medicine are totally 'solved' and that wrestling with any one problem opens up many other questions which can be pursued either at that time or at some future date.

Since the problems encountered in medicine are primarily those of individual patients, most problem situations presented to the student relate to an individual clinical case. In this way the learning is highly relevant and similar to the method by which many health professionals learn in real life. There are many advantages in this kind of learning: it contributes to the student's motivation; it encourages active intellectual processes at the higher cognitive levels; it probably enhances the retention and transfer of information; it can be modified to meet individual student needs; and it encourages curiosity and systematic thinking.

Problem-based learning can occur in both individual and in small-group learning situations. In the tutorial group critical thinking can be encouraged and arguments developed; one idea can be constructively built on another; information can be pooled and strategies laid out for obtaining information from external sources as required.

A form of problem-based learning frequently utilised at McMaster is called 'biomedical problem solving'. It has been defined in the following terms. Given a description of a patient or other clinical situation, the tutorial group or individual student should carry out the following sequence of activities: a series of questions, which may be stated in lay terms, will be listed as they arise from the biomedical problem; these questions will be translated into issues in structure, function, behaviour and response to stimuli; acting singly or in a group, students will identify and study in depth educational resources which provide information relevant to issues previously identified; the students will then synthesise this information into a cogent explanation of the clinical situation, either during a group tutorial session or individually; the development of additional questions, suggestions and hypotheses for further steps in the evaluation and/or management of the clinical situation follows logically from this synthesis, and emphasises the fact that biomedical problems can be pursued in a number of directions and tend to be open-ended; the tutorial group will complete the process by evaluating individual and group performances, the biomedical problem itself, and the related learning resources.

The assumption of sequential learning is challenged by this approach. Sequences are based on arbitrary decisions which are frequently unrelated to real-life situations. It is commonly assumed that normal structure and function should be learned prior to the abnormal, and yet only by comparing the abnormal with the normal can the range of normal become clear to the student.

The sequence myth includes the idea that basic science must be learned prior to clinical science. In the McMaster programme, basic science and clinical science are interwoven. The central focus is on the series of biomedical problems. When tackling a clinical problem, the student asks questions about basic mechanisms, both physical and behavioural. Over time, the student spirals through the same content area several times in the programme, each time at a more sophisticated or broadly applied level. For example, he has an introduction to 'puffing and pumping' in Phase I, studies the model of myocardial ischemia in Phase II, delves more deeply into mechanisms of cardiac and respiratory dysfunction in Phase III, and learns directly from patients with heart and lung problems in Phase IV.

Also challenged is the assumption that information is required before problem solving can begin. In general, we tend to forget the fact that students bring a wide variety of expertise to the programme; that, to some extent, they can think logically (based on many years of problem-solving experiences in their personal lives and possibly in their schooling); and that, at the very least, they possess an intelligent 'lay public' baseline of information. Thus, with the recognition of an appropriate level of activity, problem-based learning can start at the beginning of the programme.

Is problem solving a legitimate goal in itself, or is it a vehicle to 'get at the content'? The acquiring of a problem-solving approach is a stated goal of the school. It is useless to have a stockpile of information without a method of handling it. On the other hand, given a good approach to problem solving, students will be able to define the information they require to handle encountered problems, not only during their medical school experience but also in medical practice. There is some evidence that the information learned in this way will be retained longer. Implicit in this philosophy is the recognition that no attempt will be made to 'cover' particular content areas — instead the student samples them in relevant problem situations. Rather than knowledge acquisition *per se*, it is the use of information in the solution of problems that is encouraged.

When problems are used effectively by a tutorial group or individual student, not only are the 'process goals' reinforced but also specific 'content goals' are tackled. The content focus is determined in the selection of the problem and in the specific issues defined while discussing it.

Problem-based learning includes more than simply learning around clinical problems. It represents a fundamental intellectual process which can be applied to physiologic problems in a research laboratory, to a problem of family dysfunction, or to problems of health care in the community.

Small-group learning

The small-group tutorial represents a laboratory of learning about human interaction where a student can develop interpersonal skills and become aware of his own emotional reactions. It is an opportunity to learn how to listen, to receive criticism, and in turn to offer constructive criticism. It is a forum for group problem solving, where the pooled resources of the group members, in terms of academic training, experience, personality, and perspective, are more effective than the sum of individual abilities. A small-group tutorial provides an opportunity for self-evaluation by which a student can compare informally his own learning progress with that of his peers. The small-group tutorial setting also facilitates the processes of peer evaluation. Many groups develop a sense of responsibility for the learning progress of each member, and students learn how to give accurate and candid feedback to each other. This process is often difficult because it represents a stark contrast to previous competitive educational systems from which some students have come. In addition, students learn about educational planning because they are free to design their own group programme within the general framework of a larger learning unit.

The faculty tutor has a key role in this learning group. Although he will be an 'expert' or content-area specialist in some branch of medical science, his role as a tutor is primarily that of a generalist and a facilitator. The tutor must understand the general goals and methods of the programme. He must be skilled in managing small-group interaction. While a participating member of the group, he must help the group become gradually more responsible for its own activity and more mature as a learning resource. He must co-ordinate effective and meaningful evaluation. He should himself be an example of self-directed learning and problem solving.

The tutorial role is relatively new for most faculty persons who come to McMaster. Particular concerns are the tutor's role as an evaluator and the tutor's 'non-expertise' in an integrated curriculum. The facilitator role is difficult for the faculty to learn and for the students to appreciate ('Why won't he just tell me?'). Using the facilitating approach, as contrasted with the didactic, the tutor attempts to assist the student in his learning progress. This includes encouraging, reinforcing, shaping and hinting, and may involve the use of parallel examples, of schema, of diagrams and of logical approaches. The facilitator utilises the principle of 'guided discovery', allowing the student to learn from his own mistakes but not letting him become totally frustrated by lack of progress. There is an obvious need for an adequate orientation to the tutor role for both students and faculty. Increasing efforts are being made toward tutorial orientation both before and during a unit.

While the need for defining the tutor role is recognised, each tutor brings his own individual approach to the tutorial. The group must recognise and use this individuality to the optimum, just as the individuality of each student member can be used for the benefit of the group. The tutor role definition need not cramp the style of any individual tutor — rather it should help to clarify relationships within the tutorial group and allow the group to function better.

Just as tutors evaluate students as colleagues, so students are asked to assess the contribution of faculty tutors to their learning. This process, when successful, helps to prevent faculty members from developing grand images of themselves. It is admittedly difficult for students and tutors to shape a learning climate where reciprocal assessments are offered and received in a constructive fashion. But with growing experience, the assessments of tutor contributions by students are becoming more useful.

Many tutors find that by functioning as non-expert tutors, they can update their knowledge in an area while working with students, thus maintaining an appropriate perspective on problems in the health field and on new knowledge which is available. Furthermore, they can share the excitement of exploring and discovering new ideas.

Learning resources

The discriminating and effective use of learning resources is itself a learning objective, particularly in Phase I in which a student may be confronting a wide range of resources for the first time. The student is expected to learn which are most appropriate for his particular need and his individual learning style. As he moves through the programme, the student will learn which resources are most useful for specific purposes. He has the opportunity, for example, of developing a personal library of notes, outlines, diagrams, reprints, handouts, card files and textbooks — all 'extensions' of his memory, readily available, familiar and adaptable for his continuing learning in the future. This personal library will be used in conjunction with additional resources in the main library or in designated study areas.

Two broad categories of learning resources are provided in the programme. There are learning resources which are designed to stimulate problem solving. These include actual patients, simulated patients (healthy individuals who have been specifically trained to mimic the history and physical signs of an actual patient), some computer-based physiologic models, and 'problem boxes'. A problem box is a McMaster term for a patient who has been 'captured' in an appropriate audio-visual format. For example, if the medical history is an important feature of the case, an audio tape of an actual or simulated patient is provided. If certain external physical features are important, these are provided in colour photographs or slides. If there is a movement disorder, appropriate film cassettes or video-tapes are made of the patient and are included in the box. Rather than describing certain laboratory investigations or x-rays, the actual x-rays in reduced size or actual blood films or pathology slides are included in the box as well. All of these bits of information about the patient are available in the box, and the student works through the case, following a guidebook.

A second type of learning resource provides information; such resources usually include selected readings, various audio-visual aids (particularly the carousel-tape show) and resource people. There are specialists or experts in a field who are available at the call of a tutorial group or individual student, much like a consultant specialist in medical practice is available to another practitioner when a particular problem arises.

Diagnostic evaluation

Diagnostic or 'formative' evaluation refers to frequent assessments with feedback made during the course of a learning experience. The term implies that each assessment provides the opportunity for modifying or 'forming' the student's learning progress. This evaluation is conceived of as a constructive and integral component of the learning process rather than a detached, anxiety-provoking activity. The purpose of such an evaluation system is primarily to facilitate student learning and to modify the learning programme. The main evaluator is the student himself, and this is consistent with the emphasis on self-directed learning. Participating with him are his peers and his tutor. The student or his tutor may request additional help in this evaluation process from resource people or from appropriate self-assessment sources of various kinds. It should be noted that individual student learning progress is not the responsibility of the unit planner but remains in the hands of the student and his tutor.

At the beginning of a unit a student and tutor commonly work out the objectives most appropriate for that student. They have available to them the overall goals of the phase and programme and the unit-specific goals suggested by the Unit Planning Committee. More specific personal objectives should then be defined by the student; and, based on these, decisions are made about appropriate learning experiences. This occurs both in individual discussions and in the small-group tutorial setting. During such discussions, the student(s) and tutor can decide on the methods of progress assessment, make judgements about actual progress, and modify the student's programme accordingly.

Toward the end of the unit, the student and tutor meet to summarise the progress achieved, as this relates to the student's statement of objectives and the general goals of the unit. The methods of assessment are selected to match the objectives. Critical thinking (problem-solving) ability can be observed in tutorial or individual discussions and in 'problem write-ups'. Included in the various self-assessment methods which are available to help the student determine whether the knowledge he has acquired is accurate are multiple-choice exercises, criterion problem write-ups, and some computer-based programs. Clinical skills are assessed by direct observation. These and other methods are used during a learning unit; there are no end-of-course examinations.

How is agreement achieved in this rather open system of evaluation? Several approaches have been used, the first of which is the continuous effort to clarify learning goals. Discussions involving both students and faculty occur in many places: in open discussions with the faculty, in the unit planning group meetings, in orientation sessions for tutors, in group tutorials and in individual discussions between the student and tutor.

It is often the case that once agreement about objectives has been reached, the choice of methods of assessment becomes fairly obvious and few major disagreements occur in the actual observations of the student's progress.

At the end of a unit, a summary statement prepared by the tutor includes a satisfactory or unsatisfactory progress report. Hopefully, indications about unsatisfactory progress will have been detected early in the unit and appropriate modifications in the student's programme made. Precise definitions of criteria for satisfactory or unsatisfactory levels of performance of all students have not been stressed. Although there are methods for specifying acceptable performance levels with respect to knowledge objectives, and to some extent to problem-solving and clinical skills, establishing performance criteria for learning objectives other than these is more difficult. Rather, the emphasis has been on a descriptive profile of strong and weak aspects of learning achievement, with the identification of learning problems to be resolved in the next unit.

Integrated learning

Integration occurs at various levels. At the planning level, faculty members from a broad range of disciplines, along with students, form planning committees and are responsible for each learning unit. An educational programme is, therefore, not a department-based responsibility, and members of the planning group are not specifically representatives of their departments or disciplines. They are, however, selected because of their educational planning ability.

This method of programme responsibility exemplifies the 'matrix management' approach which is being used within the Faculty of Health Sciences. In this system departmental administrators are responsible for manpower deployment, career development of each faculty member, and logistics (for example, salary and administrative personnel). Programmes are the responsibility of functional groups made up of individuals from many departments. A programme group is responsible for determining goals, requesting and managing resources, and evaluating programme activity. Also, programmes are individually budgeted.

On another level, each student is responsible for integrating his own learning. He has an opportunity at every point to look at a problem from all points of view, from the molecular to the social. In addition to exploring several areas within a single problem situation, a student also has an opportunity to develop an overview of a single discipline, organ system or mechanism. It can be seen that by such an integrated approach, certain concepts are encountered repeatedly in the student's learning experience.

Faculty responsibilities

When a full-time faculty member joins the McMaster adventure, there is an explicit commitment of a minimum of twenty per cent of his time to be devoted to educational activity; and the undergraduate MD programme is considered to have a first priority in this commitment.

There are several specific roles which any single faculty member can play in the education programme. One of these, the faculty tutor role, has already been described. Four other roles will be described briefly.

1. The function of a resource person is primarily to facilitate in-depth learning in a specific discipline. In terms of providing information, he is the 'last in the line' of resources utilised, following the student's individual thinking and reading, discussion in a tutorial group, and the exploration of audio-visual material. The resource person is warned against the 'nickelodeon effect', where a coin is plugged in and information spouts out. He is advised to adopt a facilitating approach in the same way as the tutor but within a particular content area. His contribution might include referring the student to an appropriate review article, producing a learning resource such as a paper handout or a slide-tape show or problem box. It may also involve evaluating the learning achievement of a student or of a tutorial group at the request of the tutor, the group or a student. Resource persons should be no less aware of the general goals of the programme and the approaches used than a faculty tutor. The resource person can also help a student become a more critical thinker. He can explore his specific frontier area of research with a student group,

demonstrating how certain broad issues become defined and how scientific exploration occurs. Clinicians can be viewed as resource persons as well, their contribution being to provide access to patients and to help students in the acquisition of clinical skills.

2. The unit planner is the person administratively responsible for a learning unit; he co-ordinates the efforts of the students and faculty members who are members of his planning group. The unit planner is usually an experienced tutor and resource person and should understand that such functions as programme evaluation and tutorial monitoring are also the responsibilities of the planning group. Unit planners are responsible for presenting a preview of a unit to the MD Education Committee (this committee is responsible for planning, implementing and evaluating the undergraduate MD education programme and is accountable through the associate dean (education) to the Faculty Council), as well as a detailed post-unit evaluation review, with clear suggestions for the subsequent modification of the particular unit.

3. The role of the faculty adviser is that of an advocate, career counsellor and sounding board over the course of a three-year association with the student. He receives student-learning progress reports as they become available. Of crucial importance is his awareness of learning problems which arise in more than one evaluation statement, and it is his responsibility to discuss such issues with the student. He also helps the student to decide on individual elective experiences. In addition he is responsible for letters of reference which may be required.

4. Discipline consultants from several specialities contribute to the programme in various ways: by preparing documents for unit planners which outline the important concepts in their disciplines, by participating as members of the unit planning groups, and by developing learning resources for student use. The intent in the MD programme is to consider principles from all disciplines relevant to the practice of medicine. These include physical (biological), behavioural, social, ethical, epidemiologic and clinical areas — all of which are considered to be basic to the understanding of problems of human health and disease.

An unusual feature of the McMaster system is the assessment of faculty, not only for their contributions in research and service but also for their contributions to education. The quality of the contribution of each individual serves as a basis for recommendations of salary increases, promotion or tenure. In the educational area the sources of information are the faculty member himself and the perceptions of students and faculty peers with whom the individual is associated. These considerations are undertaken on an institutional and programme basis rather than departmentally.

Selection of students

It is the overall goal of the Admissions Committee to select students who are most likely to fulfil all of the goals of the programme and who will thrive in a relatively unstructured learning environment. Two general policies apply to this process. The first is the principle of heterogeneity: given that applicants have the basic qualifications of a three-year university experience and a 'B' average minimum, students are then selected from a wide variety of academic backgrounds. Close to half of the students have undergraduate specialisation in fields other than the biologic sciences.

The second policy involves the selection of students not only on the basis of academic credentials but also on the basis of personal characteristics and abilities. Included are demonstrated abilities for independent learning, for imaginative problem solving, and for productive contributions to various small groups. Additionally, the committee members look for emotional stability, responsibility, motivation for a medical career and the capacity for self-appraisal. These academic and personal characteristics are then weighed in a series of decision-making steps leading to an offer of a place in the programme.

A review of the selection process in 1973-74 will illustrate some of the specific features. All the 2,352 applicants who met the basic requirements were initially assessed using two methods: an academic assessment of grade-point averages which resulted in a rank-ordered list and an assessment of an autobiographical letter with a biographical sketch, which included a listing of extra-academic activities. Each letter was reviewed by a team of three readers, one each from the faculty, the student body and the community. The specific items which were rated emphasised those personal characteristics which are reflected in the goals of the programme. A training programme preceded this review process. By including three 'control' letters in each batch and by computerising the data, it was possible to conduct such analyses as inter-rater agreement. Applicants scoring high on the autobiographical letter were also rank-ordered.

Using reference letters and a geographical region formula, 430 applicants (an equal number from both lists, with some double qualifiers) were invited to a set of interviews. Two methods were employed. A 45-minute interview with each applicant was conducted by a team of three interviewers, the team again consisting of one faculty member, one student and one community person. Each team had attended an interview training workshop in which 'simulated applicants' were used. Again, items rated reflected the goals of the MD programme. Interview teams were monitored through one-way glass audio systems by experienced interviewers, as one method of quality control. A second method was the simulated tutorial, in which groups of six applicants were observed through one-way glass discussing standard health problems. Applicants were assessed primarily for group skills and contributions to group problem solving.

Finally, all the information in the files of the 160 applicants ranking highest on a composite interview score were thoroughly reviewed by a collating committee, leading to the offer of places to 80 applicants, 40 each from the rank-order lists.

Conclusion

The experiment in medical education described here, now in its fifth
year of operation, is characterised by a clear statement of general goals
and methods. This central set of ideas is a cornerstone for all aspects
of the programme, the selection process, the objectives of component
parts of the programme, the evaluation system and the learning events
and resources. The overall emphasis is on the learner and the
facilitation of learning rather than on teaching. There is a climate
of enthusiasm and commitment and a willingness to risk and to learn
from mistakes. And there is a steadily increasing understanding of and
confidence in the foundational concepts which continue to attract
faculty and students to participate in this adventure.

3.7 An Approach to Rapid Problem Solving in Clinical Medicine

BRIAN J ESSEX

Essex, B J (1975) An approach to rapid problem solving in clinical medicine, *British Medical Journal* 3: 34-6. Reproduced with permission of the author and the editor.

Introduction

Most medical care in developing countries is provided in outpatient clinics, where large numbers of patients are seen in a short time. Most of this work is done by paramedical staff who undergo a three-year training programme which is almost exclusively hospital based. They are taught the skills of history taking and examination on patients admitted to health centres or hospitals. Conventional methods of teaching these skills are important but time consuming. Moreover, after such teaching students often find that they are unable to diagnose the problems of all 150 to 200 patients seen each morning, which leads to frustration and cynicism about the use of much of their training and results in the symptomatic treatment of most illnesses with little attempt at differential diagnosis. A new technique has therefore been developed to teach the special diagnostic skills needed to practise effective outpatient medicine.

Objectives and method

A project was undertaken in Tanzania to develop, test, and evaluate a method of diagnosis which would

(a) be problem orientated;
(b) have an acceptable level of accuracy;
(c) be based on history taking and clinical examination alone;
(d) enable a diagnosis to be reached in under three minutes;
(e) be suitable for teaching paramedical and medical students; and
(f) have a high level of repeatability.

It should also lead to a standardised pattern of referral to health centre or hospital. The technique was developed in the following four stages:

Identification of symptoms: A simple classification was developed to record the frequency of symptoms in children aged up to four years, and from five to fifteen years and adults. This was used to record all symptoms in all patients attending the dispensary and health centre clinics during two periods in the wet and dry seasons. Altogether 3,897 symptoms were identified in 2,962 patients; 34 different symptoms were recorded.

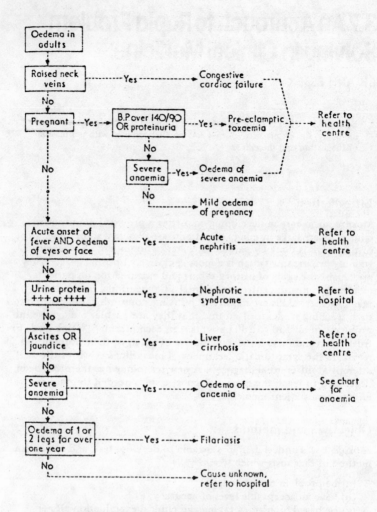

Figure 1. *Flow chart for swelling of legs in adults*

Differential diagnosis: The differential diagnosis for each symptom was obtained by studying children and adults in hospital and outpatient clinics over a three-month period in the coastal region of Tanzania.

Selection of diagnostic discriminants: The most discriminating symptoms and signs for rapid differential diagnosis were identified.

Construction of diagnostic pathway: The way in which the discriminating symptoms and signs were used to develop a diagnostic pathway is shown in the flow chart for swelling of the legs in adults (Figure 1). Fifty-two such charts were designed, covering a total of 34 symptoms and 18 physical signs in children and adults. The charts incorporate 130 common diseases and health problems seen in Tanzania but do not include rare diseases.

EVALUATION

The flow charts were used by a third-year medical student who had done no practical clinical training. He used a chart for each symptom and recorded the diagnosis and time taken to use each chart. The student's diagnosis was then compared with that of an experienced doctor using conventional history taking and examination. The time taken by both methods was also compared.

PATIENTS

All patients admitted to the general medical wards of the Muhimbili National Teaching Hospital in Tanzania over a seven-week period were included in the study, as were patients admitted to the obstetric, paediatric and gynaecology wards and those seen in the obstetric, gynaecology and ophthalmic outpatient clinics. Altogether, 1,249 patients were seen and the charts were used on a total of 2,030 occasions.

Results

ACCURACY

The closeness of agreement between the experienced doctors' diagnoses and those of the student using the flow charts is shown in Table I. Some symptoms and signs are subdivided according to the age of the patient or the presence of an associated symptom, and for these more than one chart is used — for example, the four charts for severe abdominal pain relate to adults with fever, adults without fever, children with fever, and children without fever. Seven charts are excluded from Table I because there were too few patients for proper evaluation.

On 1,904 (94 per cent) of the 2,030 occasions on which the charts were used the doctors agreed with the diagnosis. Of the 126 wrong diagnoses made with use of the charts, 58 would have resulted in the patient being given the same treatment or being referred; 36 in the patient being given unnecessary treatment or being referred; and 32 in the patient having substantially different management, which represented 1.6 per cent of all cases in the study.

Examination of the use of the charts for swelling of the legs in adults (Table II) and vaginal bleeding (Table III) showed agreement with the doctors' diagnoses in 99 per cent (71 out of 72 cases) and 82 per cent (111 out of 136 cases) of the cases, respectively, with the chart correctly diagnosing the most important causes of oedema (Table II).

Out of the 136 occasions on which the chart for vaginal bleeding (Table III) was used five cases of incomplete abortion were diagnosed as threatened abortion, and 13 cases of threatened abortion as incomplete abortion. Patients with an incomplete abortion who had little bleeding tended to be wrongly diagnosed as cases of threatened abortion. The doctor diagnosed an incomplete abortion on the basis of a vaginal examination, but the chart does not include this. Post-partum

% Agreement	Chart
100	Vomiting in adult Body weakness Weight loss in child Joint pain in adult Joint pain in child* Dysphagia* Incontinence* Fits in adult* Skin rash in child Unconscious adult Swelling of legs in child
Over 90	Diarrhoea in child Fever in adult Fever in child Headache Swelling of legs in adult Mild abdominal pain Red eye Dysmenorrhoea Dyspnoea in adult Dyspnoea in child Cough in child Anaemia in adult Fits in child (2 charts)
Over 80	Abdominal swelling (2 charts) Mental confusion Pruritus (2 charts) Weight loss in adult Severe abdominal pain (4 charts) Chest pain Haematuria* Vaginal bleeding Cough in adult Anaemia in child Jaundice in child (2 charts)
Below 80	Backache (50%)* Vaginal discharge (75%)

* Fewer than 15 cases.

Table I. *Percentage agreement between charts' and doctors' diagnoses (1,249 patients)*

Diseases	Cases diagnosed by doctor	Chart diagnosis	
		Agree	Disagree
Cardiac failure	45	45	
Cirrhosis	6	5	1
Nephrotic syndrome	5	5	
Severe anaemia	7	7	
Filariasis	6	6	
Unknown	2	2	
Acute nephritis	1	1	

Table II. *Swelling of legs in adults*

Diseases	Cases diagnosed by doctor	Chart diagnosis	
		Agree	Disagree
Post-partum haemorrhage	4		4
Incomplete abortion	62	57	5
Threatened abortion	31	17	14
Ante-partum haemorrhage	1		1
Menorrhagia	10	10	
Ectopic pregnancy	7	7	
Fibroids	17	17	
Cancer	3	3	
Ovarian cyst	1		1

Table III. *Vaginal bleeding*

haemorrhage was not included on the original chart for vaginal bleeding, and four cases were wrongly diagnosed as incomplete abortions. The chart now includes this diagnosis. Ante-partum haemorrhage is on the charts for severe abdominal pain and the chart for shock but it was not on the early chart for vaginal bleeding, and one patient with this condition was diagnosed as a case of ectopic pregnancy. It is now included on the chart for vaginal bleeding. With use of the original chart for vaginal bleeding the wrong diagnosis would have resulted in the same management in five cases, unnecessary referral in fourteen cases, and serious mismanagement in five cases. As a result of this evaluation the chart was redesigned to improve its diagnostic accuracy.

TIME TAKEN TO REACH DIAGNOSIS

The time taken by the student and doctors to diagnose 658 general medical cases is shown in Table IV.

Chart time		Doctors' time	
Total	Average per patient	Total	Average per patient
23.1 hours	1.9 minutes	150 hours	13.7 minutes

Table IV. *Time taken to diagnose 658 general medical cases in wards*

REPEATABILITY OF CHARTS

In a study to test the repeatability of the charts all the third-year rural medical-aid students in Kibaha Training School were divided at random into two groups, with ten students in each group. The ten students who came in the top half of the class in the examinations were equally distributed between the groups. Each day, one or two newly admitted patients who had not been seen by the students were selected for the study. On one day each student in group A diagnosed the patients by using the conventional method of history taking and examination, and students in group B diagnosed the patients by using the charts. Next day group A used the charts and group B the conventional method. The diagnoses made by the students were compared with the diagnoses made by the medical officer in charge of the health centre. With the aid of the charts 98 per cent of the diagnoses were made correctly, compared with only 70 per cent of those made using the conventional method.

The charts were used a total of 193 times, and there was close agreement between all the students who used them. When a chart was used by different students for the same patient they made the correct diagnosis more often than the group without the charts. When the charts were used by the students who had made the wrong diagnosis using the conventional method all made the correct diagnosis.

Conclusions

This problem-orientated method of diagnosis has been shown to have acceptable levels of accuracy, repeatability and rapidity. With practice, the student learns the pattern of sequences on the charts and soon develops confidence and skill in rapid problem solving without using them. Because of the high level of repeatability the method is of value in improving the performance of all students in a class.

For each diagnosis the charts indicate whether treatment can be given in a dispensary or at a health centre or hospital. This attempt to standardise referral patterns may lead to an improved quality of medical care. The charts are region-specific, and the epidemiological patterns of disease should be studied before they are used outside the African region. A complete account of this work has now been published in book form (Essex, 1977).

Reference

Essex, B J (1977) *Diagnostic Pathways in Clinical Medicine.* Edinburgh : Churchill Livingstone

Editors' footnote: Dr Essex has now developed charts for use in all developing countries, not just Tanzania. Interested readers should contact him directly.

3.8 Computer-assisted Instruction in British Airways

HARRY BUTCHER AND GERRY MOULT

1.0 Introduction

1.1 The paper describes how 'classical' programmed instruction techniques were applied and modified to construct a computer-assisted instruction (CAI) course in airline reservations.

1.2 In respect of the size of its target population, the geographical spread of its users and its coverage of the subject matter, the course is one of the most comprehensive ever produced by an airline or similar commercial organisation.

1.3 We shall discuss briefly the characteristics of the job and of the trainees, the environmental factors and the training resources which all determined the design of the course. We shall then show how the course as a whole and each individual section were designed to satisfy a large range of different requirements at the same time.

2.0 The background

2.1 British Airways, in common with all large international airlines, has a real-time computer system which is used (among other things) to control the inventory of seats and cargo capacity on each flight, to record reservations, and to exchange messages with other airlines relating to inventory and reservations.

2.2 All the world's airlines have adopted a common coding system for messages, called AIRIMP. Although it was originally developed to reduce TELEX communication costs, the universal acceptance of AIRIMP codings now enables airline computers to generate and exchange messages between each other automatically, using the worldwide data communication networks dedicated to airline use.

2.3 The computer terminal has therefore become an essential tool for airline salespeople, making available to them immediate and authoritative information about schedules and seat availability, enabling them to sell directly from inventory, and enabling them to exchange messages with other airlines requesting or confirming airline seats or other services.

2.4 The British Airways real-time computer network is called BABS. There are some three thousand BABS terminals in current use for reservations work, at over one hundred locations in all five continents, and they are used by about five thousand staff. Each terminal comprises a visual display unit (VDU) and a keyboard.

3.0 The training problem

3.1 Our trainees are not 'computer operators' nor 'technical' people in any sense, but salespeople who use the resources of the computer as an aid to selling and to communications.

3.2 They have to input data into the system in a highly encoded form. The system checks every entry in the following ways:

☐ does it conform to acceptable formats?
☐ if so, is it intelligible? (eg does a flight number correspond to a real flight?)
☐ is the complete set of entries logically consistent? (eg do the number of booked seats match the number of passenger names?)

Each of the above acceptance criteria generates a different kind of error response. Sales agents must be able to interpret every error response and take corrective action.

3.3 They must translate highly encoded system displays into terms which are intelligible to the customer, who may be face-to-face, as in a sales shop, or who may be at the other end of a telephone.

3.4 The complete range of BABS facilities is available to any sales person who has access to a terminal. However, they do not all need to be able to use all the facilities. For example, very large reservations offices may create specialist sections, and staff at some airport ticket desks may not be required to sell the full range of airline products bookable in the system, like hotel accommodation or holidays.

3.5 At the end of their 'technical' training we want our students to be sufficiently confident in their use of the BABS system to be able to treat it as servant rather than master. They will then be free to apply their mental energy to the more important and more skilful activity of establishing the customer's need and providing him with the product which best satisfies it.

4.0 The resources

4.1 A highly skilled central training department which had already established its credentials in the areas of programmed instruction and CAI. A consequent readiness on the part of British Airways supervisory and managerial staff all over the world to accept and use on-site training materials prepared by the central training department.

4.2   The resources of the BABS system itself. Apart from its obvious use as a communications network, and the appropriateness of using the BABS terminals as the medium for training staff to use BABS terminals, there are two specific facilities in the system which are designed for training purposes.

4.2.1   TRAINING AGENT MODE

Every 'agent' must sign in to the BABS system before it will accept any substantive inputs from him. That is, at the start of his work period he must identify himself to the system by entering a code which is matched against a table of duty codes stored in the computer. If an agent signs in using one of the codes that have been designated for 'training agents' then the system will respond to him in 'training agent mode'. This means that the system will respond to all his inputs with complete realism, using 'live' data as though he were a proper sales agent. The only difference is that when he enters 'End transaction' (which would normally be the signal for the computer to file away any records he has created, to update the relevant inventories and initiate the relevant messages) the computer simply forgets everything that has been done, and all the records and inventories remain in their previous condition.

'Training agent mode' therefore represents a complete simulation of the 'live' BABS system; in a sense, it *is* the live system. So, when it is used as a training medium, the training agent mode has all the familiar limitations of a simulator.

☐ It gives the student no guidance on what to do and when; so the 'motive power' has to be provided from outside the system.

☐ It responds automatically rather than analytically to the student's input. That is, it has no prior knowledge of what the student ought to have entered so it responds only to his actual entry. If he has made an error he will get an error response based on the system's own logic (see 3.2 above) and will need already to have sufficient knowledge of the system to interpret the response.

☐ The student needs to have recourse to a trainer or supervisor to help him out of any situation which he has not previously been trained to tackle.

The prime uses of training agent mode are therefore: practical exercises to follow up a training session, checking students' confidence in using the 'live' system, and illustrating system error responses as part of larger role-play exercises involving telephone selling.

4.2.2 COMPUTER-ASSISTED INSTRUCTION

The CAI system which is available in BABS is called UTS; for 'universal training simulator'. The name is unfortunate because, for the reasons discussed above, training agent mode is the true 'simulator' and UTS is both more and less than a simulator.

It is more than a simulator in that it can be used to train any task for which the stimulus and response can be represented on a VDU screen. It also controls the student's learning in the way that a live instructor might control it; namely, by telling the student what to do (stimulus), presenting him with the information he needs (prompt), comparing his response with the correct response (or with a set of possible correct responses), verifying his response if it is correct (reinforcement) and progressing to the next stage, or analysing his response if it is not correct, and offering feedback (remedial responses) to guide him towards the correct answer. It can be used for linear or branching programmes and for testing and marking students.

The reason that UTS behaves after the fashion of a human instructor is because every prompt stimulus, reinforcement and remedial response has been planned, laid out, written and entered in the computer by a human instructor. When the student is working on UTS *everything* that he sees has been prepared in advance by a human hand, nothing is generated spontaneously by the logic of the computer system as it is in training agent mode.

If we consider teaching and simulation as two styles along the same continuum; at one end of the continuum we could have 'pure teaching', which might be defined as maximum guidance and intervention from the teacher. At the other end of the continuum we could have complete simulation with no intervention from the teacher, and the student experiencing only the 'natural' consequences of his actions. Most training would be somewhere in the space between these extremes, and we would expect a complete course, even a complete lesson, to progress from the teaching end towards the simulation end. This is another way of expressing T F Gilbert's paradigm for a lesson sequence of 'demonstrate-prompt-release'.

It is one of the characteristics of UTS, in common with most CAI systems, that it can operate over almost the complete range of the continuum, but it is most comfortable at the teaching end. As it approaches the simulation end the amount of work required to produce a single frame increases at an accelerating rate. To achieve the effect of 'release', ie giving the student a chance to test his own grasp of a concept, the course writer is more likely to withdraw prompts and use 'unhelpful' remedial responses than he is to attempt a systematic simulation. The student achieves his true release in training agent mode.

The reason for this is that the course writer had to anticipate the student's input in order to plan his own branching, reinforcement and remedial responses. Suppose he has anticipated N possible student responses to a particular stimulus; for each of these responses there will be a specified action. The action may be simply to take the student on to the next frame in the teaching sequence, or to take him to any other specified frame in the course, or to display a remedial response which requires him to amend his existing response. However, if the student's response is not one of the N anticipated responses then the system cannot take an appropriate action.

This dilemma is resolved, in practice, by putting a 'safety net' error response in every frame which says, in effect, 'We don't know what your response was; we only know that it was not within the range of expected responses. Amend your response so that it falls within the range.'

To illustrate this principle suppose that N equals 1, then if the student did not make the correct response he would simply be told what the correct response was and asked to make it. If N equals 2, as in a choice of YES or NO, then if the student's response was XXX he would be told to answer YES or NO, he would not be told which was correct. Obviously the course becomes more adaptive as N increases, but the inherent limitations of the system will always remain.

It can never be a complete simulator, because this would theoretically require N to be infinitely large.

It can never be as adaptive as a live trainer who can interrogate the student to find out WHY he made a particular response.

It follows from this that the trainer who is preparing a course in UTS will need to possess all the familiar skills required to analyse the task, identify the characteristics of the target population, and plan a logical sequence for the training; but on top of all this he will need to exercise continuous judgement on where to place his training along the teaching/ simulation continuum, and he will also need to possess an unusual degree of insight into the students' perceptions so that he can anticipate their responses with a high degree of probability. Research and systematic testing of hypotheses obviously help in this task, but for a course of the size that we are describing it would never be possible to establish everything you need to know by research.

In what follows we shall describe how the BABS Reservations course was developed in UTS, looking first at the overall course design and then examining the detailed structure. It should be borne in mind throughout that the grand design and the detailed design remain covert to the individual student who sees only what he needs to see to meet his particular training need.

5.0   The target population

The important characteristics of the target population, from the point of view of course design, are as follows:

- ☐ reservations and sales functions may comprise the whole of their job, or may be only part of a wider set of duties;
- ☐ they are probably new recruits to the corporation without any previous experience of the airline or the travel trade;
- ☐ they have no experience of operating computer terminals, and probably no experience of keyboard operation;
- ☐ they may not be native English speakers. All British Airways staff who have contact with the public must be able to speak English. However, the general standards vary considerably from one country to another, and in many individual cases the speaking and reading abilities diverge;
- ☐ the target population is large and continuous; firstly, because there is a steady flow of staff through the relevant grades, and secondly, because the BABS network is continually expanding into new locations;
- ☐ new staff may join at any time and need to be trained immediately because, in most locations, they cannot do a productive job unless they can operate the BABS system;
- ☐ they are usually above average intelligence.

6.0   Task analysis

The course writers possessed, from the outset, a comprehensive formal description of the reservations agent's job. This comprehensive description came in two forms. Firstly, the BABS functional specifications which described in complete detail the kind of inputs which were acceptable to the system, how they were processed and what responses they evoked. (Any doubts about the precise meaning of a functional specification could always be resolved by trial and error on the system itself.) Secondly, the BABS *Operating Manual* which prescribed the procedures, ie the way in which the staff were expected to use the system.

The aim of the task analysis was to define how the system was actually used in practice. Which entries were used most frequently? If there was a choice of different ways of attaining the same end, which was chosen, and why? How much variation was there between different locations in the way they used the system? The answers to these questions led, almost inevitably, to the design described below.

7.0 Course design

7.1 One consideration which threatened to override the outcome of the task analysis is that the work content cannot easily be controlled by a supervisor. In most offices it is difficult to protect an inexperienced staff member and ensure that he has only the easy jobs. This is because every sales agent is in direct contact with the customer. The very first customer he meets may want to go round the world with his dog, with ten changes of direction and fifteen hotel bookings. Unless we can be sure that the new sales agent can always refer complicated tasks of this kind to a more experienced person we shall have to train him to tackle the complicated tasks himself. Therefore, so the argument runs, we ought to train new staff to deal with the full range of possible transactions which the customer may require.

7.2 The argument for a monolithic course would carry more weight if the training budget was unlimited. But we have to balance the study time of the course (ie the cost of studying the course) against the probable benefit of being able to meet every contingency. Furthermore we must take into account the probable attitudes of staff towards such a course, when it is used for on-site training. If they have no option but to study the course in its entirety from beginning to end or not study it at all, and if they feel that large parts of it are not relevant to their local needs, then they will tend to dismiss the whole of it and develop a makeshift alternative of their own.

7.3 The complete BABS Reservations course at present comprises over five thousand frames and takes an average of over seventy-five hours to complete. However, the 'complete course' is only a concept; the actual course which any individual student follows is related to the local requirement and his own personal abilities. This adaptability is achieved by using a modular system of course design which we have called the STRATIFIED BLOCK system.

7.4 The basic module of the course is a BLOCK. This is a self-contained unit of 15 to 40 frames (10 to 30 minutes study time) covering a single concept or transaction. The scope and boundaries of each block were defined *a priori* from a study of the logic of the subject matter. They were then matched against the results of our task analysis to locate each block in time and space; ie to define which groups of staff used the particular concept/transaction, when they used it, and how. In this way we were able to separate the blocks into STRATA.

7.5 So as not to complicate the structure we defined only three strata, which we called BASIC, ADVANCED and AIRPORT.

Figure 1 illustrates this structure in simplified form. In reality the total number of blocks in all three strata is over 150.

The Basic stratum is a complete course in itself, comprising the most probable and frequent transactions. It aims to train staff to be able to meet the requirements of ninety per cent of all customers without assistance. Many offices regard this as sufficient for new staff and are satisfied to progress from that point on the basis of on-the-job experience. This stratum (course) contains 2,000 frames and requires 30 to 35 hours of study time.

The Advanced stratum assumes a knowledge of the Basic. It aims to train the student to handle all normal customer requirements without assistance. It is about the same size as the Basic course and requires about the same study time; which neatly illustrates the relationship of diminishing returns between training and productivity. However, we would be failing in our obligations to the public if we did not have at least some staff at each location who were able to deal with all contingencies.

The Airport stratum covers those transactions which are peculiar to reservations and ticket desks at airports, for example, how to display and interpret lists of passengers who have arranged to collect their tickets at the departure airport. This stratum assumes a knowledge of some, but not all, of the Basic course.

7.6   It should be noted that the terms Basic and Advanced do not refer to difficulty or complexity but to frequency and probability. Many of the blocks in the Advanced stratum are very simple, while some of the blocks in the Basic are relatively difficult. A student who went straight through the Basic and Advanced strata might gain an impression of increasing complexity, but that would be as a result of the accumulation of detail rather than of any intrinsic difficulty in the subject matter.

7.7   We have defined the blocks as self-contained units, modules, and yet we have arranged them sequentially within our strata. In what sense, then, are they self-contained?

Firstly, it is in the logic of the subject matter that some blocks precede others. For example, before you can alter an existing reservations record you must be able to retrieve it from the computer's store. The blocks relating to retrieval therefore precede the blocks relating to amendment. However, while the amendment blocks *assume* that you have a prior knowledge of retrieval, they do not test for this knowledge or make it a condition of successful completion; still less do they require any knowledge of the specific contents of preceding blocks. If a student does not happen to have the prerequisite knowledge for a particular block it is possible for him to acquire it by entering speculative responses and learning from

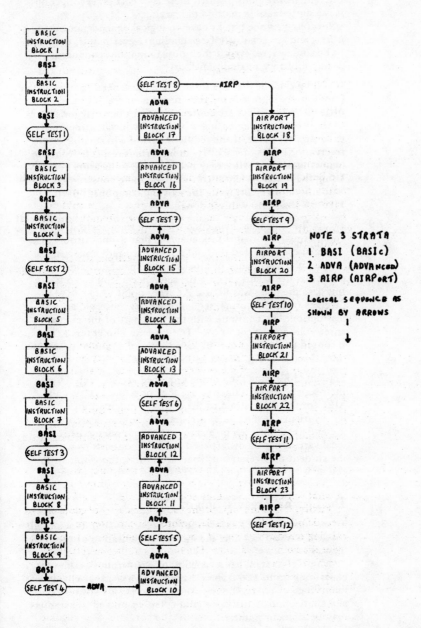

Figure 1

the remedial responses which these evoke. It takes longer but it is a quite feasible method of learning.

Secondly, some blocks have no logical dependence on any others and are genuinely free-standing. Nevertheless, they have to be somewhere, even if their position in the sequence is purely arbitrary or traditional.

7.8   It will be evident that the three strata are generalisations which only loosely represent the requirements of real jobs and real offices. Many offices are content to accept our categorisation of the work, supplementing it perhaps by locally prepared exercises. However, if the requirements of a particular reservations sales office differ in important respects from the mainstream, that office may need a made-to-measure course. Using the block system such a course can be constructed with minimum effort using the existing component parts. Figure 2 shows how this is done.

7.9   Figure 2 shows what happened when we were advised, after completing our original task analysis, that Rome Airport had a special training need that did not fit our ready-made strata. We planned a sequence of blocks which matched Rome's particular need, and we gave the sequence a 'course code'. In this case the code was ROMA. At every point where ROMA diverges from the normal sequence we have inserted an instruction: 'To continue with the next part of the course enter your course code now.' The student who enters ROMA is routed to the next part of *his* course; other students are routed according to their particular entry.

7.10   Students following the normal sequence are instructed by their supervisor or trainer to use the codes BASI, ADVA and AIRP for the three strata of the course. Students following local variants of the course are similarly told which code to use and need not even be aware that other codes exist. Every local variant has its own special index of contents to which the student may refer, but, apart from that, the whole of the course is a permutation of blocks shared with other courses.

8.0   The internal organisation of UTS

8.1   To explain how the flexibility of the block system is achieved we shall have to examine the internal organisation of the UTS 'library'.

The UTS system has a capacity of 676 'groups', each containing up to 126 frames. Each frame has a four-character identifier, eg AZ36. The first two characters are always alphabetic, and identify the group. The second two characters may be alpha or numeric.

Here is a listing of a typical group as it may be displayed on a VDU by a course writer.

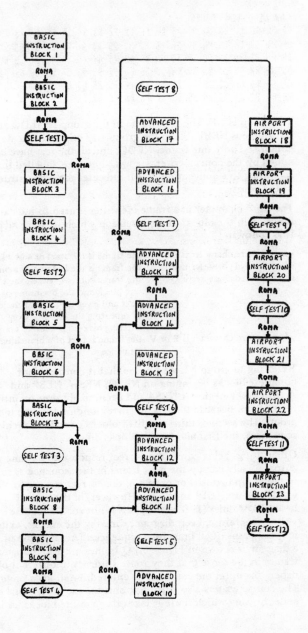

Figure 2

```
GR NE - 114 FRAMES
00 01 02 S0 05 06 07 08 09 10 11 12 13 14 15 16 17 18 19 L0
01 SW BJ BK BL WM BN 20 26 27 28 29 30 31 L1 02 S2 35 36 BF
BG WH BI 38 39 BO BP BQ WR BS 42 43 44 45 46 47 BT BU WV BW
50 51 BX BY WZ VR 54 1A 55 56 L2 03 S3 57 58 59 60 61 62 63
64 65 66 67 68 69 70 71 72 73 74 75 76 L3 04 S4 VB VC WD VE
79 80 81 82 83 84 85 86 87 BA BB BC BD BE
```

The group is NE. The first frame in the group is NE∅∅ and the last frame is NEBE. When the group was originally created it comprised only one frame, NE∅∅, and all the rest have been added by the course writer. He has, therefore, labelled them according to a convention which indicates the block structure of the course.

8.2   The third character in a frame identifier is used to indicate its function in the block. The convention which we have adapted is as follows:

when the 3rd character is S	the frame is the *start* of a block
when the 3rd character is L	the frame is the *last* one of a block
when the 3rd character is Q	the frame comes between the end of one block and the beginning of the next and gives the student the option of repeating the last block or entering his *course code* to continue
when the 3rd character is B or V	the frame is part of a branching sequence

Referring to group NE we can see that it contains four complete blocks beginning on NES∅, NESW, NES2 and NES3. A fifth block begins at NES4 and presumably runs on into the next group, because there is no corresponding L frame in this group. The second, third and fifth blocks contain branching sequences, the first and fourth blocks do not.

8.3   Other things being equal, the correct response to a frame will automatically call up the next frame in the sequence as shown in the group listing. For example, the correct answer to NE∅9 would call up NE1∅ and so on. However, in the case of branching frames (B, V and Q) this is not so. The course writers, therefore, keep diagrams showing the entries, exits and internal paths of all branching sequences. (An example of such a diagram is shown in Figure 3.) Q frames are also branching frames in the sense that they route students to different blocks depending upon the course code entered, BASI, ROMA, etc. . . The course writers also keep diagrams for each individual course code showing which route it takes through the blocks, as in Figure 2.

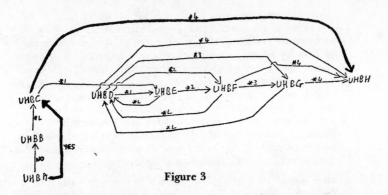

Figure 3

8.4 Here are examples of an S frame and a Q frame as they appear to the student

NES3

```
  **              ***BABS INDUCTION COURSE - BASIC***
                  **USING END ITEM KEY**


WHEN YOU ENTER THE 5 MANDATORY ITEMS IN A BASIC PNR - NEED YOU
ENTER THEM ALL SEPARATELY  --------  ANSWER YES OR NO
)
```

NEQ4

```
    GOOD - YOU HAVE NOW COME TO THE END OF-
                                          USING END ITEM KEY

  IF YOU WANT TO REPEAT THIS PART OF THE COURSE - ENTER  **  AND
  YOU WILL BE TAKEN BACK .......

  ..IF YOU WANT TO CONTINUE - ENTER YOUR ...COURSE CODE NOW...
  )
```

The titles on the S frame make it clear to the student that it is the beginning of new block. The two asterisks ** in the top left tell him and his supervisor that the block will probably take about thirty minutes to complete (about fifteen minutes per asterisk).

On the Q frame, if the student enters BASI, indicating that he is following the Basic course, he will be taken to NES4 which is the start frame of the next block. If he enters any other code he may be routed elsewhere.

8.5 The UTS system also has the facility to test the student. The test may take two forms: a 'self-test' which is overt and enables the student to check his own progress, a 'diagnostic' test which is covert and is used to determine the student's path

343

through the course.

On the first frame of a test sequence the course writer will instruct the system to start an error-count. An error is defined as an entry which does not progress the student on to the next frame, ie an entry which does not match the anticipated set of correct answers. On the last frame of a test sequence the course writer instructs the system to check the error count against the maximum permitted number of errors which he has entered. If the course writer has specified a maximum permitted error count of nine and the student has nine or less he will be routed to a 'pass' frame. If the student has more than nine errors he will be routed to a 'fail' frame.

8.6 Here is the listing of a group, VI, which contains a self-test. Once again we use the third character of the frame identifier to indicate the function of the frame. The test starts at VICO, (C for *count* the errors), and ends up at VITO, (T for *test*) which is followed by a *fail* frame VIFQ and a *pass* frame VIPO.

```
GR VI - 94 FRAMES
00 01 02 03 04 05 06 07 BR BB BC BD BE BF BG BH BI BJ BK BL
BM LO 00 C0 24 25 26 27 28 29 30 31 32 33 34 BN B1 B2 B3 B4
B5 B6 B7 B0 BP BQ BR BS BT BU BV BW BX BY BZ 55 56 57 58 59
T0 F0 P0 S1 64 N5 66 VA VB VC VD VE VF VG VH VI 76 77 H8 79
80 91 92 83 84 85 N6 87 88 89 90 ST 91 92
```

8.7 This is how these individual frames appear to the student. VICO, the first frame of the test.

```
                    ***COMPLETING THE BASIC FNK - PART 2***
                    **SELF TEST ON NAME CHANGE ENTRIES**



        NOW TRY A SELF TEST ON NAME ENTRIES ...REMEMBER TO...
                    ....CHECK YOUR ENTRY....
                    ..BEFORE.. PRESSING ENTER KEY.
        )


        NOW PRESS THE ENTER KEY FOR THE FIRST QUESTION.
```

VITO, when the student presses the 'Enter' key his error count will be automatically assessed against the standard specified by the course writer.

```
YOU HAVE NOW COMPLETED THE:-
                    SELF TEST ON NAME CHANGE ENTRIES

                TELL YOUR SUPERVISOR NOW

                HAVE YOU PASSED OR FAILED

                PRESS ENTER KEY TO FIND OUT
```

If the error count is greater than the standard he will be taken to VIFQ.

```
     BAD LUCK - YOU HAVE FAILED THE SELF TEST ON:-
                              NAME CHANGE ENTRIES


WE STRONGLY SUGGEST YOU TRY THE TEST AGAIN - ENTER  **  AND YOU
WILL BE TAKEN BACK.
)


PRESS THE ENTER KEY IF YOU WANT TO CONTINUE WITH THE NEXT PART
OF THE COURSE ON:-    COMPLETING THE BASIC PNR - PART 2
                      AVAILABILITY REQUEST ENTRIES.
```

If his error count is within the standard he will be taken to VIPO.

```
     GOOD - YOU HAVE PASSED THE SELF TEST ON:-


                         COMPLETING THE BASIC PNR - PART 2
                         NAME CHANGE ENTRIES

WELL DONE - THE TEST WAS NOT AN EASY ONE TO PASS...
)

WHEN YOU FEEL YOU ARE READY - PRESS ENTER KEY TO CONTINUE WITH
THE NEXT PART OF THE COURSE ON:-
                         COMPLETING THE BASIC PNR - PART 2
                         AVAILABILITY REQUEST ENTRIES
```

8.8 The procedure for covert, diagnostic tests is essentially the same except that the C frame will not tell the student it is a test, the T frame will not tell him that the test is finished, the P frame will look like any other teaching frame, and the F frame will be the first of a series of remedial exercises at the end of which he will rejoin the mainstream at the P frame.

8.9 The remedial exercises are presented only to those students who need them. Similarly, wherever there are branching sequences in the course the bright students are more likely to find the most economical path through the sequence, while the students who make mistakes will be given extra guidance. Finally, the students themselves may choose to repeat a block if they feel they need more practice. The cumulative effect of these three factors makes the course very much shorter for the bright student than it is for the less able student.

   To show how much difference this can make, let us suppose that two students were working systematically through the whole of the BABS Reservations course which comprises

5,000 frames. The bright student might complete the course having accessed only 4,000 frames, while the not-very-bright student may access as many as 6,000 frames, having voluntarily and involuntarily repeated a substantial part of the course. The second student needed more training than the first, and in this case he received fifty per cent more. Unless they were continuously monitoring each other's VDUs, neither of them would be aware of the size of the discrepancy between their two courses.

9.0 The anatomy of a frame

9.1 In this section we shall examine the structure of the individual frame in the course. We shall begin with a linear sequence showing how it appears to a student who makes the correct responses at first attempt. We shall then take one frame from the sequence and show what the student would see if he made a series of wrong responses. Using the same frame we shall see how the course writer prepared it. Finally we shall examine one critical frame within a branching sequence, as it appears to the student and as the course writer wrote it.

9.2 Figure 4 shows a linear sequence of six frames (VJ34 - VJ39). Except for VJ39 we show each frame twice; first, as it appears on the screen to the student; second, with the student's correct entry. This particular sequence is taken from a block on how to book an aircraft seat from a display of seat availability. It is not necessary to understand the technical contents of the frames to appreciate the following points.

9.2.1 In frames VJ34 - 37 the prompt (the first seven lines) is an exact replica of an availability display as it might appear in a 'live' situation. However, it has been designed to combine a number of features which would probably not all appear on the same display in real life.

9.2.2 The prompt remains the same while a series of different questions are posed about it. The entry which the student has to make is the same as he would make in real life, but the reinforcement which he receives is different, ie 'good', 'right again', 'correct'. Not until VJ38 is he shown the response which the live system would produce for his entry. If the 'live' response had been introduced earlier it would have constituted a distraction from the main teaching point.

9.2.3 The responses required of the student in frames VJ38 and 39 are not entries which he would ever be required to make on the live system. These are pure 'teaching' frames which do not attempt, even partly, to simulate the live system. Their function is, (a) to make the student form a mental connection with what has gone before, and (b) to make him examine closely the system response.

9.3   Figure 5 shows what happens on one of the frames, VJ36, when
        the student makes a wrong entry. The correct entry is N2F2.
        When the student presses the 'Enter' key on his keyboard his
        entry is scanned from left to right to see if it matches the
        correct answer. In this instance the correct answer has been
        analysed into four 'fields', so there are four separate error
        responses. As soon as the system has found an error (a
        mismatch) it scans no further but displays the relevant error
        response. Error responses are therefore displayed one at a time.
            In the top example the scan has found an error in the first
        field, ie his answer does not begin with N. It therefore displays
        the error response associated with this field. Notice that the
        error response is phrased in rather 'neutral' terms. This is
        because we do not know what the student's entry is, we only
        know what it is not; but, more importantly, it is because this
        particular error has a rather low probability and the likeliest
        reason is simply carelessness or mistyping.
            The second example shows what happens when the student
        has corrected his first error and re-enters his answer. The scan
        now picks up the error in the second field. Similarly in the
        third example.
            In the fourth example the style of the error response has
        changed. Although we still cannot be certain why the student
        has made the error, because we do not know exactly what he
        has entered, we do know that one reason is much more
        probable than all others. He has probably selected the flight
        on line 3, because it arrives at 1200, but has not noticed that
        there are no first-class seats available. The prompt was
        designed to illustrate this point, and our error response is
        phrased accordingly, although the error response still remains
        valid even if the student did not enter 3 instead of 2.

9.4   Figure 6 shows the same frame, VJ36, as the trainer wrote it.
        The student initially sees only that part which we have ringed.
        Below that, items 3A1 to 3D1 show the correct answer, N2F2,
        analysed into four 'check fields'. Finally in 4A1 to 4D2 we
        have the four error responses associated with the four check
        fields.
            This is a relatively simple example. The UTS system allows
        for a maximum of sixteen check fields, 3A to 30, with a
        maximum of sixteen alternative 'right answers' within each
        check field. And all of this is created by the course writer
        starting with an empty frame which looks like this:

```
    1 X RECID-T000
    ? 1 THIS GROUP IS BEING SET UP - CHECK WITH YOUR SUPERVISOR
3A1 SKIPTO
    4A1 USE SKIPTO
    )
```

V337

```
2FEB
1 LHR ORY 0900 1000 1000 F4Y0 BA 006 TRI   0
2 LHR CDG 1000 1055 F3Y4 BA 042 TRI   0
3 LHR ORY 1100 1200 FOY7 BA 012 TRI   0
4 LHR ORY 1200 1300 Y7  BA 014 TRI   0
5 LHR ORY 1300 1400 Y4  BA 016 TRI   0
6 LHR CDG 1400 1455 F5Y6 BA 044 TRI   0
>
GOOD - NOW MAKE ENTRY TO BOOK 2 Y CLASS SEATS DEP TIME 1300
```

V338

```
2FEB
1 LHR ORY 0900 1000 F4Y0 BA 006 TRI   0
2 LHR CDG 1000 1055 F3Y4 BA 042 TRI   0
3 LHR ORY 1100 1200 FOY7 BA 012 TRI   0
4 LHR ORY 1200 1300 Y7  BA 014 TRI   0
5 LHR ORY 1300 1400 Y4  BA 016 TRI   0
6 LHR CDG 1400 1455 F5Y6 BA 044 TRI   0
>N2Y5
GOOD - NOW MAKE ENTRY TO BOOK 2 Y CLASS SEATS DEP TIME 1300
```

```
1 BA 016 Y 2FEB LHRORY HS2    1300 1400

NOTE THE RESPONSE FROM THE SYSTEM WHEN YOU BOOK FROM AN
AVAILABILITY DISPLAY.
E)
IS THIS RESPONSE THE SAME AS THE RESPONSE YOU GET IF YOU BOOK
```

V334

```
2FEB
1 LHR ORY 0900 1000 1000 F4Y0 BA 006 TRI   0
2 LHR CDG 1000 1055 F3Y4 BA 042 TRI   0
3 LHR ORY 1100 1200 FOY7 BA 012 TRI   0
4 LHR ORY 1200 1300 Y7  BA 014 TRI   0
5 LHR ORY 1300 1400 Y4  BA 016 TRI   0
6 LHR CDG 1400 1455 F5Y0 BA 044 TRI   0
>
GOOD - NOW MAKE THE ENTRY TO BOOK 3
Y CLASS SEATS ON A FLT - ARR TIME AT CDG NEAREST TO 1100
```

V335

```
2FEB
1 LHR ORY 0900 1000 1000 F4Y0 BA 006 TRI   0
2 LHR CDG 1000 1055 F3Y4 BA 042 TRI   0
3 LHR ORY 1100 1200 FOY7 BA 012 TRI   0
4 LHR ORY 1200 1300 Y7  BA 014 TRI   0
5 LHR ORY 1300 1400 Y4  BA 016 TRI   0
6 LHR CDG 1400 1455 F5Y0 BA 044 TRI   0
>N3Y2
GOOD - NOW MAKE THE ENTRY TO BOOK 3
Y CLASS SEATS ON A FLT - ARR TIME AT CDG NEAREST TO 1100
```

```
2FEB
1 LHR ORY 0900 1000 F4Y0 BA 006 TRI   0
2 LHR CDG 1000 1055 F3Y4 BA 042 TRI   0
3 LHR ORY 1100 1200 FOY7 BA 012 TRI   0
4 LHR ORY 1200 1300 Y7  BA 014 TRI   0
5 LHR ORY 1300 1400 Y4  BA 016 TRI   0
6 LHR CDG 1400 1455 F5Y0 BA 044 TRI   0
>
RIGHT AGAIN - NOW MAKE THE ENTRY TO
BOOK 4 Y CLASS SEATS NEAREST TO ARR TIME 1000
```

1 BA 016 Y   2FEB LHRORY HS2   1300 1400

VJ39

NOTE THE RESPONSE FROM THE SYSTEM WHEN YOU BOOK FROM AN
AVAILABILITY DISPLAY.
>YES

IS THIS RESPONSE THE SAME AS THE RESPONSE YOU GET IF YOU BOOK
BY A DIRECT SEGMENT ENTRY ---------- ANSWER YES OR NO

---

1 BA 016 Y   2FEB LHRORY HS2   1300 1400

YES - THE SYSTEM RESPONSE IS THE SAME WHEN YOU BOOK FROM
AVAILABILITY - OR BY A DIRECT SEGMENT ENTRY.
>

NOW TYPE IN THE STATUS AND NUMBER OF SEATS BOOKED -3 CHARACTERS-
AS SHOWN IN THE ABOVE SEGMENT.

Figure 4

VJ36

2FEB
1 LHR OPY 0900 1000 F4Y0 BA 006 TRI   0
2 LHR CDG 1030 1055 F3Y4 BA 042 TRI   0
3 LHR OPY 1100 1200 F0Y7 BA 012 TRI   0
4 LHR OPY 1240 1300 Y7   BA 014 TRI   0
5 LHR OPY 1300 1400 Y4   BA 016 TRI   0
6 LHR CDG 1400 1455 FSY0 BA 044 TRI   0
>NXY2

RIGHT AGAIN - NOW MAKE THE ENTRY TO
BOOK 2 Y CLASS SEATS NEAREST TO DEP TIME 0900

2FEB
1 LHR OPY 0900 1000 F4Y0 BA 006 TRI   0
2 LHR CDG 1000 1055 F3Y4 BA 042 TRI   0
3 LHR OPY 1100 1200 F0Y7 BA 012 TRI   0
4 LHR OPY 1240 1300 Y7   BA 014 TRI   0
5 LHR OPY 1300 1400 Y4   BA 016 TRI   0
6 LHR CDG 1400 1455 FSY0 BA 044 TRI   0
>
CORRECT - NOW MAKE THE ENTRY TO BOOK 2 F CLASS SEATS NEAREST TO
ARR TIME IN PARIS AT 1200

2FEB
1 LHR OPY 0900 1000 F4Y0 BA 006 TRI   0
2 LHR CDG 1000 1055 F3Y4 BA 042 TRI   0
3 LHR OPY 1100 1200 F0Y7 BA 012 TRI   0
4 LHR OPY 1240 1300 Y7   BA 014 TRI   0
5 LHR OPY 1300 1400 Y4   BA 016 TRI   0
6 LHR CDG 1400 1455 FSY0 BA 044 TRI   0
>NXF2

CORRECT - NOW MAKE THE ENTRY TO BOOK 2 F CLASS SEATS NEAREST TO
ARR TIME IN PARIS AT 1200

VJ36

```
2FEB
1 LHR ORY 0900 1000  F4Y0  BA 006 TRI    0
2 LHR CDG 1000 1055  F3Y4  BA 042 TRI    0
3 LHR ORY 1100 1200  F0Y7  BA 012 TRI    0
4 LHR ORY 1200 1300   Y7   BA 014 TRI    0
5 LHR ORY 1300 1400   Y4   BA 016 TRI    0
6 LHR CDG 1400 1455  F5Y0  BA 044 TRI    0
>BBBB
START YOUR ENTRY WITH   N  -ENTRY CODE TO BOOK FROM AVAILABILITY

CORRECT - NOW MAKE THE ENTRY TO BOOK 2 F CLASS SEATS NEAREST TO
ARR TIME IN PARIS AT  1200
```

```
KB027
2FEB
1 LHR ORY 0900 1000  F4Y0  BA 006 TRI    0
2 LHR CDG 1000 1055  F3Y4  BA 042 TRI    0
3 LHR ORY 1100 1200  F0Y7  BA 012 TRI    0
4 LHR ORY 1200 1300   Y7   BA 014 TRI    0
5 LHR ORY 1300 1400   Y4   BA 016 TRI    0
6 LHR CDG 1400 1455  F5Y0  BA 044 TRI    0
>NBBB
AFTER N -ENTER   2   -THE NUMBER OF SEATS WANTED.

CORRECT - NOW MAKE THE ENTRY TO BOOK 2 F CLASS SEATS NEAREST TO
ARR TIME IN PARIS AT  1200
```

```
2FEB
1 LHR ORY 0900 1000  F4Y0  BA 006 TRI    0
2 LHR CDG 1000 1055  F3Y4  BA 042 TRI    0
3 LHR ORY 1100 1200  F0Y7  BA 012 TRI    0
4 LHR ORY 1200 1300   Y7   BA 014 TRI    0
5 LHR ORY 1300 1400   Y4   BA 016 TRI    0
6 LHR CDG 1400 1455  F5Y0  BA 044 TRI    0
>N2BB
AFTER  N2 -ENTER CLASS WANTED  F

CORRECT - NOW MAKE THE ENTRY TO BOOK 2 F CLASS SEATS NEAREST TO
ARR TIME IN PARIS AT  1200
```

```
2FEB
1 LHR ORY 0900 1000  F4Y0  BA 006 TRI    0
2 LHR CDG 1000 1055  F3Y4  BA 042 TRI    0
3 LHR ORY 1100 1200  F0Y7  BA 012 TRI    0
4 LHR ORY 1200 1300   Y7   BA 014 TRI    0
5 LHR ORY 1300 1400   Y4   BA 016 TRI    0
6 LHR CDG 1400 1455  F5Y0  BA 044 TRI    0
>N2FB
NO - AFTER  N2F  -END YOUR ENTRY WITH   2   -LINE NUMBER OF
BA042  -THE NEAREST FLT TO ARR TIME 1200 WITH 2 F CLASS SEATS.
CORRECT - NOW MAKE THE ENTRY TO BOOK 2 F CLASS SEATS NEAREST TO
ARR TIME IN PARIS AT  1200
```

Figure 5

VJ36

```
5  1  2FEB
5  2  1 LHR ORY 0900 1000   F4Y0   BA 006 TRI      0
5  3  2 LHR CDG 1000 1055   F3Y4   BA 042 TRI      0
5  4  3 LHR ORY 1100 1200   F0Y7   BA 012 TRI      9
5  5  4 LHR ORY 1200 1300     Y7   BA 014 TRI      0
5  6  5 LHR ORY 1300 1400     Y4   BA 016 TRI      0
5  7  6 LHR CDG 1400 1455   F5Y0   BA 044 TRI      0

1   RECID-VJ36
1)
```

```
2 1 CORRECT - NOW MAKE THE ENTRY TO BOOK 2 F CLASS SEATS NEAREST
   TO
2 2 ARR TIME IN PARIS AT  1200
3A1 N
3B1 2
3C1 F
3D1 2FEGM
4A1 START YOUR ENTRY WITH   N  -ENTRY CODE TO BOOK FROM AVAILABI
    LITY
4A2
1I)
```

```
4B1 AFTER  N  -ENTER   2   -THE NUMBER OF SEATS WANTED.
4B2
4C1 AFTER  N2  -ENTER CLASS WANTED   F
4C2
4D1 NO - AFTER  N2F  -END YOUR ENTRY WITH   2   -LINE NUMBER OF
4D2 BA042  -THE NEAREST FLT TO ARR TIME 1200 WITH 2 F CLASS SEAT
    S.
    >
```

Figure 6

FRAME UHBD

The student sees:

```
    BA 813/29MAR -BALDERN/LMR
 1 3BALDERREN/LM    MAMEDI        2 3BADERN/HMR/L    AHSEDI
 3 2FELDEN/FHR/G X AHSHAN         4 1ALDERN/LMR      AHSEDI
NO MORE NAMES
)

THE LIST BACK - YOU NOW RETRIEVE ANOTHER PNR  -  DO NOT RETRIEVE
A NAME NUMBER YOU HAVE ALREADY TRIED.
```

The trainer wrote:

```
5 1    BA 813/29MAR -BALDERN/LMR
5 2  1 3BALDERREN/LM    MAMEDI        2 3BADERN/HMR/L    AHSEDI
5 3  3 2FELDEN/FHR/G X AHSHAN         4 1ALDERN/LMR      AHSEDI
5 4 NO MORE NAMES


1    RECID-UHBD
2 1
2 2 THE LIST BACK - YOU NOW RETRIEVE ANOTHER PNR  -  DO NOT RETR
IEVE
1)
```

```
2 3 A NAME NUMBER YOU HAVE ALREADY TRIED.
3A1 *
3B1 1*EOM
3B2 2*EOM*GOTOUHBF
3B3 3*EOM*GOTOUHBG
3B4 4*EOM*GOTOUHBH
4A1 NO - START YOUR ENTRY WITH   *   FOR DISPLAY - TO RETRIEVE A
    PNR
4B1 NO - AFTER  *  -END YOUR ENTRY WITH NUMERAL  1  2  3 OR 4
    TO
1)
```

```
4F2 RETRIEVE A PNR FOR A NAME NUMBER YOU HAVE NOT ALREADY TRIED.
)
```

Figure 7

9.5   Figure 7 shows an example of a frame which attempts a high level of simulation of the live system and therefore requires multiple branching.

    The student may reasonably enter any of the following: *1, *2, *3, *4. All these options are therefore treated as right answers; because we are simulating we have to provide a separate response for each possible right answer.

    Examine the check fields in the course writer's version. The first field, 3A1, has only one option, an asterisk *, because all the right answers begin with an asterisk. If the student has not begun his answer with * he receives a conventional error response specified in 4A1.

    The second check field, 3B, looks for four possible alternatives, 1, 2, 3 or 4. If the student has not entered any of these in the second character position of his answer he will again receive a conventional error response as shown in 4B1 and 4B2. However, if he has entered one of the possible right answers he will be sent to another frame which will contain a display appropriate to his answer.

    If he has answered *1 he will simply be sent to the next frame in the group. If he has answered *2 he will be sent to VHBF and so on. To keep a record of branching sequences of this kind the course writers usually sketch a route map. Figure 7 is an example of such a route map featuring the frame VHBD which we have just analysed. Notice that the shortest path through the sequence is to answer YES on frame VHBA and *4 on frame VHBC. Any other choices could involve as many as five additional frames.

    Once again we have shown a relatively simple example, but it illustrates the amount of planning required to present in UTS what the live system can do automatically and the way in which the structure remains hidden from the student.

10.0   Other features of the system

10.1   To keep within reasonable bounds our account of the UTS system and of the Reservations course, we have confined ourselves to describing the most distinctive features of both. To go into greater detail would require of the reader a fund of very specific technical and airline knowledge which he is unlikely to have or to want. In this section we conclude our account of the system by describing two features which are particularly important in their effect on students' attitudes to their training.

10.2   RANDOM ACCESS

    To gain access to the 'library' of UTS courses, the student must first sign into the BABS system as a training agent (see 4.2.1 above). He then enters the code UTS START, which, in effect, takes him out of training agent mode and into the UTS library.

Once he is in UTS he has random access to any frame in any course in the system. He can use the entry SKIPTO — — — — to display any frame, eg SKIPTOXXXX will display frame XXXX.

The student, therefore, has three ways of exit-ing from any particular frame:

☐ he may enter the 'correct' response and be automatically progressed to the next frame specified by the course writer;

☐ he may sign out of UTS and leave the course (temporarily or permanently) at that point;

☐ he may enter SKIPTO ???? and be taken to the frame of his own choosing.

However, the random access, or, SKIPTO, facility does not exist to enable students to skate over a course without bothering to make proper responses. In any case, they could not do this, even if they wished to, because students do not have access to a complete listing of all four-character frame identifiers. The facility exists to serve three important purposes.

10.2.1 It enables a student to resume his work on a course at the exact point where he left off. A student working through a course may need twenty or more sessions spread over a period of weeks. At each session he must sign in and sign out of the UTS library. At its present stage of development, the UTS system keeps no permanent record of how far the student has progressed. When a student signs out of UTS the system reveals the identifier of the frame he is on (see 10.3 below), and he is then responsible for recording that frame identifier so that he can SKIPTO it when he resumes the course.

10.2.2 It enables the student to exercise some control over his own study, and to find his way back to his own course if he accidentally goes astray. In either case he will need to use the index for his course.

Figure 8 shows the first few lines of the index for the Basic course. The student in UTS can display this index at any time by entering SKIPTOBASI. Similarly SKIPTOADVA, SKIPTOAIRP, SKIPTOROMA will display the indexes for the Advanced, Airport and Roma courses; in each case the course code is used as the frame identifier of the relevant index. The index shows the title of each block in the course and the identifier of the *first* frame in the block.

Using the index and the SKIPTO facility, the student may exercise his own judgement in a number of ways.

At any time he may revise any block which he has previously studied.

If he thinks he already knows a particular topic, he may go straight to the relevant 'self-test'. If he passes it, he need not study the preceding block(s).

BABS INDUCTION COURSE - BASIC INDEX

```
*    MANDATORY ENTRIES AND ENTRY CODES.................SKIPTONES0
*    CREATING THE ITINERARY BY DIRECT SEGMENT ENTRIES..SKIPTONES1
**   ENTERING PASSENGER INFORMATION....................SKIPTONES2
**   USING END ITEM KEY...............................SKIPTONES3
**   DISPLAY FACILITES AND END ITEM....................SKIPTONES4
***  ERROR RESPONSES AND END OF TRANSACTION CHECKS.....SKIPTONFS1
**   COMPLETING THE BASIC PNR - SELF TEST.............SKIPTONFC0
)
```

```
**   NAME ENTRIES - BABS OPERATING MANUAL FORMAT.......SKIPTONGS0
**   NAME AND GENFAX ENTRIES FOR INFANTS AND CHILDREN..SKIPTONGS1
***  CANCELLING/CHANGING NAME ENTRIES - BASIC..........SKIPTONHS0
***  CANCELLING/CHANGING NAME ENTRIES AND GENFAX
     ENTRIES CHILDREN/INFANTS - BASIC - SELF TEST......SKIPTONHC0
**   AVAILABILITY REQUEST ENTRIES.....................SKIPTONIS0
***  READING AND BOOKING FROM AVAILABILITY - TYPE 1/0..SKIPTONJS0
***  HOW BABS CHOOSES FLTS FOR AVAILABILITY DISPLAYS...SKIPTONJS1
**   DISPLAY MORE MORE AVAILABILITY ENTRY.............SKIPTONKS1
)
```

```
***  CREATING A PNR USING AVAILABILITY DISPLAYS.......SKIPTONLS0
*    SEGMENT CONTINUITY - DATE ORDER..................SKIPTONMS0
**   INSERTING AND CANCELLING SEGMENTS................SKIPTONMS1
**   SEGMENT CONTINUITY GEOGRAPHICAL ORDER............SKIPTONMS2
*    EOT CHECKS NAMES/SEGS............................SKIPTONNS0
**   AVAILABILITY/CANCELLING/INSERTING SEGMENTS
     SELF TEST.......................................SKIPTONNC1
***  AVAILABILITY DISPLAYS - FLIGHT TYPES 0 1 AND 2...SKIPTONOS0
**   QUOTASALES - FLIGHT TYPES 0 1 AND 2.............SKIPTONOS1
)
```

Figure 8

If he has to break off his study in the middle of a block he may start again at the beginning to regain continuity. If he has opted to repeat a block (see 8.2) he is free to change his mind.

All of these 'freedoms' assist in motivating the student. The training may have been produced at a great distance by a hidden hand, but the student is still treated as a person who can be trusted to make important decisions about his own training needs.

10.2.3   Finally, the SKIPTO facility enables trainers or local supervisors to construct special courses using any *ad hoc* combination of blocks in the library. This method is regularly used to satisfy special requirements which are not durable enough to justify being allocated a course code and being built into the structure of the Reservations course.

10.3   SIGNING-OUT DISPLAYS

```
GOOD - YOU HAVE NOW COME TO THE END OF-
                                    USING END ITEM KEY

IF YOU WANT TO REPEAT THIS PART OF THE COURSE - ENTER  **  AND
YOU WILL BE TAKEN BACK .......

..IF YOU WANT TO CONTINUE - ENTER YOUR ...COURSE CODE NOW...
>UTSEND

UTS ENDED AT NE04. 60 FRAMES COMPLETED - ERROR PERCENT 10
```

The student has come to the end of a block and has signed out using the entry UTSEND. The bottom line shows the system's response to this entry. It confirms that he has signed out and gives the four-character identifier of the frame. It also gives the total number of frames the student has completed at that sitting, ie since he last signed in to UTS, and his 'error percent'.

The term 'error' in this context means an entry which has failed to progress the student to another frame. While the student is signed-in to UTS, the system keeps a tally of the number of frames he has completed and the number of entries he has made. If the student has completed 100 frames and pressed the 'Enter' key 150 times, then 50 of his entries must have been 'errors'. In this particular example the system will compute his 'error percent' as 33, ie 33 per cent of his entries were errors. It is arguable that the true error percent should be 50 per cent on the grounds that 50 of his entries must have been corrections of previous errors, therefore, *at first attempt* he made 50 correct answers and 50 wrong ones. However, the argument is largely academic because we discourage the students from attaching any importance to the error percent, except when it relates to a block which has been designated as a self-test.

The officially sanctioned use of the error percent display is in conjunction with the self-tests. We have seen, in 8.5 above, that when the student works through a self-test he is told only whether he has passed or failed. However, he can obtain a mark for a self-test by zero-ing the frame and error count at the beginning of the test (by signing out of UTS and then signing in again), then completing the test and signing out at the end. The frame count and error percent display will then refer to the test only; and the error percent, deducted from 100, gives the student's mark for the test. This method of marking is used for continuous assessment of the student during the course, and the marks may be kept as a permanent record of the student's performance.

However, when the students are learning rather than being tested they ought to regard the 'error' responses not as a discipline but as an assistance, ie as *remedial* responses. If they need more assistance or additional explanation they should not be inhibited from evoking error responses just because it will 'look bad' on their error percent when they sign out. Furthermore, in a branching sequence a student may make a number of choices which are 'wrong', but which nevertheless take him on to another frame. Wrong entries of this kind will not even be registered as errors by the system because they do not evoke an 'error response'.

All this is carefully explained to the students, who nevertheless persist in taking a close interest in their error percents and in introducing a competitive element into their training. It is apparent that this form of feedback, for all its imperfections, has a powerful motivating effect on the students, as well as encouraging them to be more accurate in their entries and to study each frame carefully.

11.0   The benefits of the course

11.1   Obviously we have not the space to mention everything that could be said about a course which took over two man-years to prepare. Perhaps some readers have already thought of additional ways of exploiting the system. However, most of the benefits of the course will be evident from what we have already said.

11.2   To summarise the benefits of the course:

    ☐ It is available at all times, and at all places that are on-line to BABS.

    ☐ It requires minimum assistance from a supervisor or trainer.

    ☐ It embodies the experience of many trainers and the feedback from many students to form an adaptive and largely self-motivating course.

- ☐ The medium is ideally suited to the subject matter.
- ☐ The course can easily be kept up to date. There is, in effect, only one copy of the course, ie the copy which is held in the central computer. When this one copy is amended the course is amended simultaneously for all students in all locations.
- ☐ It promotes a uniformly high standard throughout the airline.

11.3   Finally, the cost benefits are huge. Suppose the course has a life of five years, and the target population (approximately 5,000) has an annual turnover of ten per cent. (Both of these assumptions are rather modest!) Then the total number of students trained would be 2,500. Without the facility of completing their BABS Reservations training on-site they would need to come to London for a ten-day course. Many of them are in London already; so suppose only 1,250 had to have accommodation and allowances for ten days. The total cost of this at current prices would be in excess of £250,000. All this has been saved at the expense of two man-years of trainer time.

3.9 Computers in Military Training

ROGER MILES

Miles, R (1977) Computers in military training, *British Journal of Educational Technology* 8: 242-52. Reproduced with permission of the author and the editor.

Introduction

Educational technology as a whole has gained much from research and development in the Armed Services; computer-assisted learning (CAL) is no exception. Though small, the work in the Armed Services has been a vigorous and important area of the National Programme in the United Kingdom. After a slow, cautious start, six military feasibility studies and two development projects funded by the Programme have created several activities which show strong signs of becoming operationally worthwhile. Those responsible for this work have also contributed to the overall strength of the National Programme by illuminating significant differences between education and training as well as adding to emerging generalisations about CAL. This co-operation has been most welcome since workers in a high cost area like CAL can ill afford to ignore opportunities to benefit from the experiences of others.

When the National Programme began in 1973, the Armed Services were already using computers in training in several ways but not in the tutor role. Although they had played a considerable part in pioneering programmed learning, the Services did not go on to replace the teaching machine with the computer terminal. What did evolve from the programmed learning work was a general adoption of a systems approach to the development and management of training, aimed at maximising the job relevance, effectiveness and efficiency. This approach treats teaching machines and computers as just two of the many devices available to assist training where appropriate.

National Programme funds have enabled the Armed Services to broaden their experience of computer applications as well as expanding existing work. The Programme has also provided a forum for the three Services to share views and experiences and to examine together the lessons to be learned from other areas and countries, notably the USA where experience is substantial.

This paper will be accurately reflecting the current situation if it depicts a wide variety of applications, many of them small activities at an early stage, set in a background of cautious but strong interest in the military potential of computer-assisted and computer-managed learning.

Current applications

Without question the major use of computers in military training is in simulations of vehicles, equipments and systems. Inclusion of these simulators in CAL may seem surprising because the computer's primary role in the simulator is creating the fidelity of the situation: it does not directly regulate the learning process. However, simulators can dramatically improve the learning experiences available to students, and the ways they are used do raise some important general questions for CAL. Furthermore, there is a distinct trend towards giving the computer more responsibility for monitoring and controlling student progress in training simulators (Miles, 1975, 1977). Hence computer-based simulators must be an important part of any review of computers in military training.

SIMULATION

Substantial efforts have been devoted to building highly realistic simulators in which difficult and dangerous tasks, such as landing an aircraft, can be practised safely and less expensively than in the real vehicle. Vehicles other than aircraft are increasingly being simulated for training as operating costs rise. The Army's Chieftain tank simulator has achieved useful savings in running costs and simulators are being developed for other Army vehicles. Ship simulation is a growth area at present with both civil and military applications.

Particularly striking developments in recent years have been the system simulators and tactical training environments such as those used by the Royal Navy's School of Maritime Operations. A faithful replica of the operations room of a ship, fed by computer information, provides procedural and skill training facilities which can be carefully planned and closely monitored. In the tactical trainer, on the other hand, equipment realism is less important since the emphasis is on decision making and assimilation and interpretation of information. The realism of the flow of combat information is the important factor which the computer helps to create.

It seems certain that such complex and expensive simulator installations will be used increasingly in the future. The value of the tactical trainer for practising tactical appreciation and action against a variety of threats is obvious and will increase as the power and variety of weapons available to hostile forces grow. Similarly the role of procedural trainers for operator and team training will grow. Simulation will be the only way to give experience of some types of action conditions.

One can identify three issues which affect the success of simulator training: these are simulator design, instructor training and evaluation. Firstly, it is recognised that an equipment designer, concentrating on the engineering problems of building a simulator, may omit important considerations or give them too low a priority. Research has shown that the optimum simulation for training may not require the highest degree of engineering fidelity. Since high fidelity simulators are very expensive, there are important financial benefits in identifying where and when cheaper simulations and part-task training devices can be used. Secondly, instructors should be trained to work with simulators because they present special situations and are not identical to the real equipment.

The third issue is the important question of how to evaluate a simulator application. Simulator effectiveness cannot be predicted from existing knowledge because of the incompleteness of psychological understanding of the learning process and our limited ability to anticipate the optimum man-machine interface for any given system. Much is known which can guide the development process, but ultimately the value of a particular simulator must be determined by a specific study. This raises a second difficulty because formal scientific methods which make comparisons under controlled conditions are of dubious value in complex real-world situations. Introducing a simulator into an existing training organisation can be a major change in a dynamic social situation. Experience has shown that comparisons between old and new training methods are frequently naive in design and produce spurious or inconclusive results (Holland, 1961). New methods of evaluation are evolving through a shift from experimental research methods to intensive studies of specific examples and a different approach to creating a conceptual framework upon which to base generalisations (Cronbach, 1975).

Since the Armed Services have major investments in training simulators it follows that their design, use and evaluation are matters of considerable importance. The same point can be made about other aspects of computer-assisted learning, but the high costs and widespread use of simulators give this area priority and require that every effort be made to ensure they give value for money.

COMPUTER-ASSISTED LEARNING

Whilst the Armed Services have not applied the tutorial style of CAL, they have developed a range of activities in which the computer aids teaching and learning. This work is in military colleges and advanced technical training establishments, not in basic training.

At the Royal Naval College, Greenwich, the Department of Nuclear Science and Technology has been using a computer since 1969. Initially it was used for analysis of laboratory experimental results and a system for on-line analysis of data from multi-channel analysers has been developed recently. However, the major application has been in digital modelling of complex engineering systems for design studies by advanced students.

After an informal association with the National Programme's Engineering Sciences Project, the College has received funds to assist the introduction of CAL packages on various topics. Some are being transferred from the Engineering Sciences Project and others produced locally.

The Royal Naval Engineering College, Manadon, uses CAL in several ways. For example, the Marine Engineering Department has a propulsion system simulation which allows students to investigate the interaction between system elements and observe transitory effects

361

which are difficult to measure in real life. Simulations and graphical displays are also used in control engineering, telecommunications and electronics; statistical programmes are used in engineering management courses.

With help from National Programme funds, the Electrical Engineering Department of the Royal Military College of Science, Shrivenham, is expanding its use of CAL packages for teaching topics in control engineering. Computer generated graphical displays of, for example, frequency response diagrams, give students valuable insight into system behaviour without them having to rely on textbook illustrations or make vast repetitive calculations to draw their own. This project is also co-operating closely with the Engineering Sciences Project.

Another Army establishment, the School of Signals, Blandford, uses computer simulations in advanced communications courses to give guided practice in system control and operation. These simulations were produced locally and run on Hewlett Packard 3000 computers.

A National Programme-funded study at RAF Locking is exploring the use of CAL for training maintenance technicians in fault finding and diagnostic skills on complex equipment such as airfield radar. Large equipment like radar is very expensive and so is a scarce resource in training establishments; there is limited opportunity for hands-on experience and trainees spend much of their time in classroom instruction or studying manuals. The CAL system simulates faults on the radar and provides guidance and practice in their location. Thus CAL gives trainees additional experience of fault finding and provides a valuable bridge between classroom work and practice on the real equipment.

Obviously CAL of this type cannot be a complete substitute for training on the real equipment; trainees must learn a system's geography, manipulation of test equipment and safety procedures on the actual equipment. However, CAL may be a better means of meeting some training needs than providing additional equipment. A preliminary report from this study suggests that a CAL system may be a viable alternative to new equipment costing £35,000 or more (Parker & Knight, 1976).

COMPUTER-MANAGED LEARNING

Several military establishments have developed computer-managed learning (CML) systems for handling student records, test marking and trainee performance analysis. The scarcity of individualised free-flow training schemes has meant that the routing function which the computer has in many CML systems has not been required. Changes in training organisation may make individualised training schemes economically attractive and create a need for computer routing but current applications are confined to testing and record-keeping.

An interesting project at the Army Apprentice College, Arborfield, has developed a training quality control system on a mini-computer. This system builds up profiles of trainee performance which facilitate identification of training weaknesses and inform staff of remedial needs. Benefits of this system come from fewer relegations and failures and consequently more trained personnel produced. The computer also marks objective tests by means of an optical mark reader and analyses test items, thus achieving savings on routine clerical jobs. A small system for test marking and analysis has also been developed at the Royal School of Military Engineering, Chatham, to assist record-keeping and quality control.

The National Programme and International Computers Limited have co-operated in the creation of a large general purpose CML system known as CAMOL (Computer Assisted Management of Learning). The RAF Staff College, Bracknell, assisted in the design of the CAMOL system and, helped by a National Programme-funded systems analyst, developed a modest but very effective automated diagnostic assessment system for students starting the Basic Staff Course. After examining the CML systems available in this country and the USA, the Army has commenced a trial implementation of the CAMOL system in the Trade Training School, 8th Signal Regiment, Catterick. Staff and equipment are partly funded by the National Programme but Ministry of Defence funds are providing the medium-sized computer necessary for this work. The computer will initially be assisting testing, record-keeping and report production; it will perform some important functions previously prevented by shortages of staff and time. Also computer use for routine tasks should release instructor time for more tutorial duties and create opportunities for reductions in clerical staff. Furthermore the enhanced record-keeping and report-production facilities of CAMOL should help management to make the best use of training resources.

The Catterick project is an important trial of the CAMOL system's value to military training and could lead to its wider adoption elsewhere. The Arborfield system could also have wider application as an aid to student achievement measurement. In recent years, there has been a significant growth of objective testing and a more sophisticated approach to performance assessment in military training. This trend should continue and increase the need for computer support for the statistical work involved.

Another clear trend is the increase in short, specialist courses as a variety of new equipment is introduced and reductions in manpower reduce the need for the longer career courses. Thus there will be an increase in the number and variety of tests used with the many small groups undergoing different training at any one time. The substantial assessment and training management problems presented by this situation could stimulate greater use of CML systems.

ADMINISTRATION

Even now, fitting all the required courses into a workable training programme is a demanding task for staff of many Service training establishments. Thus it is not surprising to find that a number of them have tried computer methods for scheduling courses, timetabling and resource allocation. The Royal Naval College, Greenwich, has developed computer methods of calculating staff loadings to assist course timetabling and allocation of syndicate groups; a timetabling program for one department is also being developed. A staff loading program,

developed in 1973, is used at HMS Collingwood and may be enhanced
to analyse use of classroom and laboratory facilities; computer assistance
for timetabling and longer-term scheduling is also being considered. A
small project to develop a scheduling system for the Royal School of
Military Engineering, Chatham, had made considerable progress when it
ended prematurely. A small local project at RAF Cranwell produced a
working system successfully. Some time ago Headquarters Training
Command, RAF Brampton, and the Royal Military College of Science,
Shrivenham, co-operated on studies of computer timetabling methods.

Whilst some of these local developments have been reasonably
successful none of them has produced a computer system capable of
scheduling the large training centres. Discussions between the Ministry
of Defence and the National Programme resulted in a feasibility study
of computer scheduling for a very large Army training establishment —
the School of Electrical and Mechanical Engineering, Bordon. A
commercial organisation, Oxford Systems Associates Limited (OSA),
was commissioned to undertake this work because of its experience with
computer methods in industrial job-shop scheduling and school
timetabling. This study ended on 31 December 1976 with feasibility
established but considerably more effort required to produce an
operational system. The Ministry of Defence is now reviewing the
requirements in this area before deciding on further development.
Meanwhile the National Programme has funded OSA consultancy to
assist RAF Locking with enhancement of their locally evolved system
which shows considerable promise.

Computer-assisted methods may produce better schedules in terms
of more even loading of resources and provide more flexibility.
Smoother loading would lead to important savings of expensive
resources and better working conditions for students and staff.
However, mathematicians and computer scientists have given
considerable attention to timetabling and scheduling problems without
being entirely successful. Many problems remain to be solved and the
part which the computer can play in this aspect of training management
is by no means clearly established. Nevertheless it is an important topic
for further research and development since the benefits achievable with
an operational system are very substantial.

TRAINING DEVELOPMENT

All three Services use a systems approach to training development and
provide specialist personnel to guide and assist the training organisation
in using instructional technology to best advantage. At the core of this
work is the analysis of military employments to ensure that training is
wholly relevant to jobs, a time-consuming activity involving large
amounts of data collection and data processing. The Royal Navy has
used a large American computer package for occupational data analysis
(CODAP) to assist the process (Nicholl, 1975). Wider use of this system
is being considered and the other two Services have run trials with it.

A difficulty with the CODAP system is that it requires a very large
computer. Furthermore, because it was designed for occupational
analysis it includes functions not always required in a job analysis for

training. Thus smaller computers have been used for specific analyses of job data. This is likely to increase as more powerful small computers become more widely available. However, CODAP or a similar system could be an important aid to manpower planning as well as training because it provides comprehensive analysis and job comparison facilities. Already HMS Collingwood is developing a Training Requirements and Management Planning Information System (TRAMPIS) to forecast the requirements for certain types of training and resources needed to meet them.

An important factor in the design of training is the assessment of potential trainees. Computer support to personnel selection work is being used at the Army Recruit Selection Centre, Sutton Coldfield, and such activities may expand in the future. Computer analysis of tests of ability and attainment can reduce tedious clerical effort and facilitate data storage.

The vital area of training validation has received relatively little attention as yet, but the computer's ability to store and analyse training and job performance data has obvious applications. HMS Collingwood is using the computer to manage course records and to analyse training results and reports of subsequent performance at sea.

Thus the computer is already assisting training development activities and considerable scope for expansion is apparent. All three Services are viewing the computer within the general framework of the systems approach to training. This has many advantages: it facilitates identification of places where computers are needed rather than cheaper training aids and uses existing training development expertise in creating effective computer applications.

However, computing is a sophisticated technology requiring specialised knowledge. Computing facilities and expertise are being made available to training development personnel; for example, the Army School of Instructional Technology has recently been specifically tasked with this area of interest and computing expertise has been brought into the Ministry of Defence (Army) committee responsible for instructional technology. Similar fusions of computing and training interests are developing informally in the Royal Navy and Royal Air Force. A focus of interest for computer applications to training development and the wider use of computers throughout training is emerging in each service.

Towards the 1980s

The number and variety of current activities indicate the existing importance of computers in military training and provide a foundation for predictions of future growth and expansion. However, this progress could be handicapped unless training authorities are given ready access to expert help and guidance. Computer applications require special provision of resources. Thus in reporting the conclusion of a study on 'Computers in military training in the 1980s' (Miles, 1977) considerable attention was given to the organisation and resources needed to facilitate worthwhile applications.

Another important task in the future study was to examine the many computer applications in the American Armed Forces and identify lessons to be learned from that experience. Generalisations are always dangerous and can be particularly misleading in this area because US and British military training are organised very differently; a computer application which has proved cost effective in America may not be useful in the UK. Nevertheless the possibilities for transfer of some methods need to be considered as will be seen from the following brief overview of the major current activities in the US Armed Forces.

American military training authorities have been researching and testing various computer applications for quite some time, CAL since the early 1960s and simulations since well before that. Sherron (1976) reports a study of future computer uses in the US Armed Forces which included a comprehensive review of current activities. He concludes that feasibility has been established and that cost effectiveness in operational situations is the current issue. Several systems are being used in specific applications prior to more general implementation and there is a substantial programme of research and development planned.

The largest and most interesting computer-based training system in the US Navy is the computer-managed instruction (CMI) system at the USN Air Base, Memphis. It became operational in 1974 and is the result of seven years' developmental work by the Naval Technical Training Command. The system is designed to manage the movement of large numbers of trainees through totally individualised free-flow training schemes. None of the instruction comes from the computer, which is concerned with test marking and analysis, routing and record keeping. This system is also used in the Basic Electricity and Electronics Schools of the Naval Training Centres at San Diego and Great Lakes. Currently about 4,000 students are on the system at any one time; this figure is planned to rise to 18,000 by 1980. Research and development is under way to improve efficiency and specify a second generation system.

US Army experiments with computer-assisted instruction began in the mid-1960s at the Signal School, Fort Monmouth. (The Signal School has since moved to Fort Gordon.) This work led on to plans for a large-scale prototype Computerised Training System (CTS) built around six mini-computers with a total of 128 terminals.

The CTS is planned to support over 5,000 trainees per annum and will provide a mixture of instructional and management functions as students move through free-flow training and assessment of a highly individualised form. Both instructional material and tests will be on-line; also instructors will be able to amend materials or add information at terminals. The instructors will be responsible for helping and counselling individuals and writing courses and tests for computer presentation. Subject to satisfactory results from the Fort Gordon trial, it is intended to introduce CTS to other Army schools.

The most significant CAL activity in the United States Air Force is undoubtedly the Advanced Instructional System (AIS) being developed at Lowry Air Force Base, Colorado. This eight-year project, costing over $11 million and due to end in October 1977, is creating a multi-media individualised instructional system which incorporates elements of computer-assisted and computer-managed learning. In fact, one of the four courses being developed, for weapon mechanics, involves only ten per cent CAI; in this course the computer's main function is to route students through use of various instructional resources. Results already show that considerable reductions in course time may be achieved. A seven-week inventory management course was run on the system in 1975 with the last five weeks self-paced. Over 3,000 students completed the course with an average time saving of thirty-eight per cent which was calculated to be worth $1.2 million.

Each American Service is pursuing its own sizeable programme of research, development and trials of CAL and CML. An interesting Army Research Institute research project is attempting to incorporate training material within an operational weapon system. The Tactical Fire Direction System (TACFIRE) which will give artillery units automatic data processing in the field includes an on-line computer. CAI materials on several fire control operations have been produced for use with TACFIRE and tested in trials. Since equipment costs are covered in purchase of the tactical data system this 'embedded' training system concept could be a financially attractive form of training. It also has the important advantage of enabling more training to be done in the field unit rather than central schools.

There is substantial co-operation between the US Armed Forces and the major civilian developments in CAI, namely the PLATO and TICCIT projects. The TICCIT system (Time shared, Interactive Computer-Controlled Information Television) developed by the Mitre Corporation has been used by the Air University, Maxwell Air Force Base, and in two US Navy Air Bases for training crews of the Viking anti-submarine aircraft. The PLATO (Programmed Logic for Automatic Teaching Operation) system developed at the University of Illinois is the best known and most widely used CAI system in the USA. Its uses in Air Force training include vehicle maintenance and medical training. The Army Ordnance School has used PLATO on several courses and it has been tested in a number of other Army and Navy applications. This experience is highly relevant to the British Armed Services since both PLATO and TICCIT may soon be marketed in Britain.

Much of the American CAL work is within patterns of training rarely used in British military training. In Britain there is less individualised learning, a much smaller number under training, more norm-referenced rather than criterion-referenced assessment, and broader course content. The latter important point stems from the fact that the two structures of military employment are different, the US personnel tending to have much narrower specialisations than their British counterparts. Thus it would be most unwise to assume that methods or systems cost effective in the American situation would be directly transferable and equally beneficial. Nevertheless there is much to be learned from monitoring the American experience. For example, the use of CAL for electronic maintenance training seems likely to grow in both countries. Also the increasing emphasis on management rather than tutorial applications in the large American systems such as CTS will make them more relevant to the British situation.

The future study also considered likely developments in the tasks and equipment of military personnel in an attempt to identify training needs which could benefit from computer support. It was seen that, despite recent large reductions in defence spending, Britain's commitment to the western alliance will maintain her need for powerful forces competent in the full range of military skills. The severe limitations on personnel and resources will make the quality and efficiency of training more important than ever. Furthermore, the increasing complexity of weapon systems and other equipment will demand new levels of skill and place greater responsibility on the individual. Some new equipment, for example new communications systems, is introducing radical changes in military thinking and so creating new training needs.

An overriding consideration throughout military training is the need to keep the maximum numbers of personnel operational at any one time. Decentralised methods which bring training to the operational unit instead of men returning to schools assist attainment of this objective. Computers could be an important means of delivering well designed, on-the-job training, particularly for those working on systems which incorporate computers.

Conclusion

Computers are being used in British military training in several ways; there are firm indications of future expansion and scope for development of new applications. Much of the current development parallels activities in civilian education; there is the same emphasis on simulation and management uses of the computer. By comparison the American Armed Forces make much greater use of computers and are a rich source of suggestions and guidance. However, whilst the total British military training effort is considerable, it is almost certainly too diversified to employ the large centralised computer-based systems used by several American military training establishments. Other aspects of the American work have much more relevance and could, for example, greatly assist the likely growth of CAL for maintenance training. The 'embedded' training concept is another important common interest because it addresses the important objective of providing more training in the operational unit rather than at centralised schools. Thus computers are an established feature of some parts of military training; in others their value has yet to be demonstrated.

Finally, it is very noticeable that the military approach to CAL shows a much better integration of CAL within educational technology than occurs generally in civilian education. This arrangement provides a supportive climate for CAL development but also exposes the work to close scrutiny alongside other methods and media within a systematic approach to meeting training needs. Several of the military CAL projects provide examples and information which some elements of education and industrial training may find helpful, but the value of this general approach to computer applications has wide significance.

References

Cronbach, L J (1975) Beyond the disciplines of scientific psychology, *American Psychologist* February: 116-27

Holland, J G (1961) Evaluating teaching machines and programs, *Teachers College Record* 63 1: 56-65·

Miles, R (1975) Computers in simulators in the armed services. In R Hooper and I Toye (eds) *Computer Assisted Learning in the United Kingdom: Some Case Studies.* London : Council for Educational Technology

Miles, R (1977) *Computers in Military Training in the 1980s.* Technical Report No 18. London : National Development Programme in Computer Assisted Learning

Nicholl, C J (1975) The use of computers in occupational analysis in the Royal Navy. In R Hooper and I Toye (eds) *Computer Assisted Learning in the United Kingdom: Some Case Studies.* London : Council for Educational Technology

Parker, G R and Knight, K R (1976) Can computer assisted learning reduce the cost of equipment training?, *RAF Education Bulletin* 13: Autumn

Sherron, G T (1976) *An Examination of the Manpower and Personnel Implications Emerging from the Instructional Use of Computers by the Military Services in the 1980s.* Washington DC : Research Report to the Industrial College of the Armed Forces

Epilogue: Next Year, Jerusalem! The Rise of Educational Technology

DAVID HAWKRIDGE

Hawkridge, D G (1976) Next year, Jerusalem! The rise of educational technology, *British Journal of Educational Technology* 7: 7-30.
Reproduced with permission of the author and Councils and Education Press.

What this paper is about

'Next year, Jerusalem!' was and still is the yearly declaration of hope for millions of Jewish people. For centuries at a time there seemed little chance for many Jews to celebrate the Passover actually in Jerusalem. Yet the hope was sustained.

Educational technology has been characterised by a similar pattern of hope during its brief life as a field of endeavour. Each year many have been willing to declare, at conferences and courses, in papers and speeches, to county education officers and kindergarten teachers, that educational technology holds out much of promise. This is right: a young field should contain plenty of optimists. Its members ought to be proselytising among those who see change in education as a threat rather than a boon. The Jerusalem of improved education is well worth hoping for, and technology may be able to hasten the day when that goal is reached. On the other hand, educational technologists' hopes have been dashed many times, as this paper will show. There have been an incredible number of false starts.

Without a doubt, there must be many readers of this journal [the *British Journal of Educational Technology* in which this paper first appeared] who have argued with their colleagues about the origins and nature of educational technology. Certainly there have been several *BJET* papers offering views (for example, Ely, 1970; Holroyde, 1971; Dieuzeide, 1971; Chadwick, 1973). After much discussion, the Council for Educational Technology issued an official statement about its field of interest and so did its predecessor, the National Council for Educational Technology. Quite recently, Rowntree (1974) provided us with a book on the subject in relation to curriculum development.

There are some who wish that these debates would come to an end. They would prefer to see a body of theory grow to support a strong, apparently absolute view of the nature of the field. They feel that if physics is physics, then why should not educational technology be educational technology, for all to see. They call for an end to the ambiguity they cannot tolerate.

This paper will not end the ambiguity in people's minds about educational technology; indeed, it may well add to feelings of uncertainty in the continuing debate. It will note the downfall of some principles and practices which were honoured at one time or another over the past fifteen years. A few sacred cows' tails may be twisted. At best, it will enrich the debate. For some readers, it may offer some interesting leads and references, since the historical approach allows for the inclusion of many topics. For others, there may be the intellectual excitement of perceiving new trends and links.

The structure of this paper is very simple. After a short section on definitions, there are three longer sections which provide the historical perspective. No historical account of the rise of educational technology will be unblemished; there are too many deadly sins historians commit, and a paper cannot possibly compete with, say, Saettler's (1968) classic book. Nevertheless, these three sections are vital. First, there is what we might call the period of pre-history, for which the paper can offer no more than a catalogue of milestones with some commentary. Secondly, there is the period of educational technology's infancy. From the time of B F Skinner's (1954) article up to around 1966, programmed learning and programmed instruction (the two terms were interchangeable for most people) held the stage. Still the term 'educational technology' was rarely heard. Where it was used, it was used vaguely, as a generic term covering programmed learning and a cluster of loosely related studies, such as those on computer-assisted learning. Thirdly, we must count as adolescence the period from 1966 to the present. Many of the concepts in programmed learning have shown remarkable resilience, but their use has been broadened in all kinds of ways. Educational technology has grown in breadth, if not stature, each year. Educators have been heard to complain, with dismay, that educational technology will soon encompass everything in education.

The three periods are the basis for most of this paper. It would be sickeningly anticlimactic to stop there, however, and the chance to speculate a little on the future is very inviting. The last section will be devoted to considering the next stage of evolution. Is educational technology likely to merge with other fields into general educational research and development? Is educational technology in search of a new image and a new name?

Definitions

It is very tempting to propose a cast-iron definition of educational technology, from which it might then be possible to identify the boundaries and constraints of this paper. To use such a definition, however, is to risk implying that the field is in a static state, whereas it is dynamic and shifting constantly: 'a moving target', according to Armsey and Dahl (1973).

If we start from Galbraith's (1967) definition of technology as 'the systematic application of scientific or other organised knowledge to practical tasks', then we may go on to Saettler's (1968) definition of educational technology as 'the practical art of using scientific knowledge about education'. Some may prefer Galbraith's qualifier: 'scientific and other organised knowledge'.

Educational technologists are those who seek to apply scientific and other organised knowledge to the practical tasks of education. They are people with a foot in two camps: they seek to understand the theory and to apply it. Such people were around long before anyone thought of the trendy title, of course. There has long been a need for a group of people to act as go-betweens. Educational technologists have been known to claim that there is an embarrassing lack of knowledge about learning and that learning theories abound but conflict (Bloomer, 1973). Both assertions may be true for those wanting full and certain answers. For others, exciting prospects loom out of the growing fund of knowledge about human memory, social behaviour, cost-benefit ratios and systems design — to mention but a few fields. There are other, weaker definitions of educational technology. One lays emphasis on using tools and equipment (the products of technology) to improve learning (MacKenzie, Eraut & Jones, 1970). Another claims that the processes of technology should be applied in education: automation, quality control and so on. We should note these definitions, but they are not central to this discussion.

Pre-history

If we accept the definition of educational technology as the systematic application of scientific or other organised knowledge to the practical tasks of education, then we may ask where this knowledge has come from and who in the past attempted to apply it.

Saettler (1968) writes about those he considers to have been predecessors. He justifies his choice on two grounds: first, he chooses those (see Table I) 'who actually made teaching their principal vocation'; he chooses the originators of 'the most distinctive instructional techniques'. He admits that his criteria eliminate a number of religious figures known as great teachers, and non-teaching philosophers like Rousseau and Locke who influenced education. It would be waste of space to argue about whether Saettler's list is the best. We could add, however, one or two names conspicuous by their absence, while offering some commentary on some of those he mentions.

For example, Bacon might be said to have been in favour of the systems approach: he 'seized the whole problem, stated its terms and formulated its equations'. His methods of inductive thinking, put forward in *New Atlantis* and *Advancement of Learning*, were aimed at achieving power over nature through knowledge. Knowledge was to be acquired through observation, investigation and experimentation. Without doubt, his ideas underlie much of educational technologists' thinking.

Saettler does not mention that Comenius, in his *Didactic*, called for school reform founded upon 'exact order in all things'. Comenius expected that the methods of teaching and learning would be so excellent that the desired results would always be obtained. Does that remind us of the call from some educational technologists for '90/90' performance based on criterion-referenced instruction (Ofeish, 1964)?

Locke, in *Thoughts Concerning Education* and *The Conduct of*

Precursors	Century	Contributions
Elder Sophists in Athens	5th BC	systematic instruction to groups, based on rhetoric, dialectic and grammar
Socrates in Athens	5th BC	Socratic dialogue
Abelard in Paris	12th AD	scholasticism
Comenius in several European countries	17th AD	application of Bacon's inductive method to education; anticipated many modern principles of learning
Lancaster in England	19th AD	manuals of instruction and design of classrooms for mass instruction under monitors
Pestalozzi in Switzerland	19th AD	psychologising of instruction, ie harmonising of instruction with the stages of child development
Froebel in Germany and Switzerland	19th AD	motor expression and socialisation in school
Herbart in Germany	19th AD	instruction highly systematised; cognitive elements made central; rational science of learning
Thorndike in New York	20th AD	connectionism and laws of learning; empirical-inductive development of a science and technology of instruction; mental measurement
Dewey in New York	20th AD	reflective approach to instruction; problem solving
Kilpatrick in New York	20th AD	project method; learning by doing
Montessori in Rome	20th AD	adaptation to the learner; freedom in the teacher-pupil relationship; emphasis on sensory discrimination
Burk in San Francisco Washburne in Winnetka Parkhurst in Dalton	20th AD	individualised instruction; the Winnetka Technique and the Dalton Plan
Morrison in Chicago	20th AD	Morrison Plan; worksheets and recitation
Lewin in America	20th AD	cognitive-field theory

Table I. *Precursors of educational technology (derived from Saettler, 1968)*

Human Understanding, wrote in ways that would have pleased programmed learning enthusiasts confronted with teaching adults from minority groups in the United States Job Corps in the sixties: he took little account of heredity and considered the mind as a blank which had its powers and virtues 'worked into it by the formation of habits'. These habits were inculcated through practice and discipline, he said. Locke might have approved of a linear programmed text designed to shape behaviour, since he wrote of the mind being like wax, to be moulded and fashioned as one pleases. On the other hand, he might have rejected programmed learning as too bookish and unlikely to train the character.

Rousseau, as a romantic, would scarcely have seen eye to eye with educational technologists, yet like them he was strongly in favour of the learner participating actively. He also said that education should be based on a knowledge of the learner.

Herbart's propositions were based on analyses of instruction. In his *Educational Doctrines* he gave instruction and the techniques of the classroom high importance. He proposed four steps: (1) secure attention and interest; (2) provide related examples (association); (3) establish the rule (systematisation or generalisation); (4) apply the rule (application). Educational technologists will recognise this inductive method of teaching, and those who were engaged in programmed learning in the 1960s will recall the egrul approach (example plus rule), and its converse, the ruleg approach, adopted in linear programmes (Evans, Glaser & Homme, 1960).

Spencer's principles are now so familiar to educators that it is hard for them to realise that he was pronouncing upon a new scientism. He wanted knowledge and learning to be based upon experience rather than upon vague abstractions. He saw scientific analysis as offering the final explanation of all things. Educational technologists have perhaps drawn from his philosophy their belief in empiricism.

Some of the notions of Comenius and Rousseau, of Herbart and Spencer, would be violently attacked if they appeared today in *BJET*. Educational technology is derived indirectly from their thinking, however, even if more modern names like Thorndike, Dewey and Skinner are the ones that spring to mind. The body of organised knowledge used by educational technologists contains these early ideas.

Saettler (1968) rightly contrasts Thorndike and Dewey. Thorndike theorised and investigated along scientific lines. Dewey was the pragmatist whose hypotheses were never submitted to scientific experimentation. Both made contributions which were taken up, half a century later, by educational technologists. For example, writers about programmed learning were pleased to quote a passage from Thorndike's *Education: A First Book* (1912):

> If, by a miracle of mechanical ingenuity, a book could be so arranged that only to him who had done what was directed on page one would page two become visible, and so on, much that now required personal instruction could be managed by print.

Such points of technique were trivial, however, when set beside Thorndike's monumental writings on connectionism and the laws of learning. His Law of Effect said that the connection between a situation (stimulus) and behaviour (response) is strengthened only if some success or satisfaction follows the response. This principle of reinforcement lay behind a great deal of work by Pressey, Skinner, Glaser and others much later. Thorndike also devoted much effort to the development of a science of instruction, on which a technology could be based. It was Skinner's (1954) view that Thorndike had not succeeded, yet Thorndike's achievements in studying both animal and human learning were surely part of the foundation for Skinner's own work.

What have educational technologists taken from Dewey? Dewey, as a pragmatist, believed that something was good only if it proved itself in experience, if it was conducive to social progress. His social objectives were far more acceptable than Thorndike's and his views dominated education in the United States for many years, backed up by the powerful Progressive Education Movement. Probably Dewey would have been against programmed learning since he abhorred the notion of a programme determining the route of learning for the pupil. On the other hand, he considered the classroom to be very much a social laboratory, an environment to be explored by his pupils. It was the school's business to select the experiences which would prove most valuable to the pupils, and to provide the right environment within which these things would be learned. Dewey (1917) described mind as a quality of behaviour, to be learned, and rejected dualistic theories of mind and body. Mind was the quality of behaviour which appeared in the conduct of the individual when outcomes were anticipated and thus became controlling factors in the ordering of events. In these views he would have the agreement of many educational technologists today. They would appreciate much in his book *Sources of a Science of Education* (1929), but at the same time would go beyond it and away from it, towards behaviourism and Skinner.

Watson is known as the first behaviourist, although Thorndike shared many of his ideas. For him, consciousness was an unusable concept, and he based all his studies on the experimental analysis of human behaviour, using techniques developed from similar studies of animal behaviour (Watson, 1924). Behaviourists believed that there were scientific means of predicting and controlling human behaviour. These views led them to declare that teaching could be described in terms of presenting the correct stimuli in order to elicit the desired responses from pupils. Through atomistic analysis, behaviourists such as Tolman and Hull built up theories of learning (Tolman, 1932; Hull, 1943).

Skinner set out to gather systematic observations about behaviour in order to gain an understanding of how it could be controlled. His emphasis was essentially a practical one: he did not attempt to develop an alternative theory of learning but sought a repertoire of techniques. He displayed distrust of behaviourism as such in an article (Skinner, 1950) which concluded: 'Theories are fun. But it is possible that the most rapid progress toward an understanding of learning may be made by research which is not designed to test theories.'

Skinner devoted considerable attention to animal behaviour, but later turned to human learning, including verbal behaviour (Skinner,1953, 1957). He considered humans to be adaptive social organisms, continuous with the rest of the biological universe. Human learning he saw as the ability to adapt to one's environment. We are moving ahead too fast, however; before we reach Skinner's famous 1954 article that marked him as a progenitor of programmed learning, it is essential to touch upon several other major contributors to the stream of thinking and doing which is now called educational technology.

Pressey's (1926, 1927) testing machine is well known, but his sole contribution to educational technology probably lay not so much in his machine as in his strong belief that an industrial revolution in education was about to dawn, bringing great benefits of more effective and more efficient learning (Pressey, 1932). He pursued this dream for several decades, although he had little time for programmed learning or for teaching machines when these came along. Even his own machines were thrown away in favour of a small card with blobs of ink on it; the learner erased the blob over the answer he thought correct, and underneath was a symbol that told him whether he was right. Simple, cheat-proof and, above all, cheap. During the sixties he also advocated adjunct auto-instruction as an alternative to programming (Pressey, 1964; Pressey & Kinzer, 1964). This technique employed self-corrected quizzes as adjuncts to various types of instructional material, in more than one medium if appropriate.

Another contribution to educational technology may have come from those who developed individualised education in the United States. Burk and his colleagues in San Francisco devised 'self-instructional bulletins' which could be used by pupils to study at their own rate on an individualised basis. Two of his students amplified his system in Illinois some years later, into what came to be known as the Dalton Plan and the Winnetka Technique (Parkhurst, 1922; Washburne, 1932). The essence of both schemes lay in clarity of objectives, alternative routes and rates of progress for individual learners, and a high degree of feedback. Devising materials suited to different styles of learning and different characteristics of learners was explored throughout the elementary school curriculum. For example, Washburne and his associates Vogel and Gray (1926) stated three of their aims as follows:

1. To make a clear re-statement of the school course in terms of units of achievement.
2. To develop diagnostic tests to measure this achievement and point out weaknesses.
3. To develop self-instructive, self-corrective practice materials for pupils to prepare for the tests.

There is no doubt that educational technologists in the late sixties built on these ideas when individualised education projects such as Individually Prescribed Instruction (IPI) and the Program for Learning in Accordance with Needs (PLAN) were set up (see Cooley & Glaser, 1968; Glaser & Nitco, 1970, on IPI; Flanagan, 1971, on PLAN).

Educational technologists designing these projects depended heavily, too, on the work of Tyler on objectives in education. As early as 1934 Tyler published a book on achievement testing (Tyler, 1934) which raised issues regarding the specification of objectives during curriculum development. Achievement tests could be valid only if they matched closely the objectives set for the pupils. Tyler continued his interest in objectives in later publications (1950, 1964), although he never took up the behaviouristic position of Mager.

Finally in this section we must make some mention of the growth of psychometrics. The psychometric field deserves attention because it has provided some of the tools of measurement needed by educational technologists for diagnosis and assessment, and contains ideologies they have seized upon. We have already mentioned Pressey's interest in using testing to provide reinforcement through self-diagnosis. The development of psychological tests of achievement in the period up to

1954 was rapid, and these tests were constructed on scientific principles many of which could be adopted by educational technologists. Unfortunately, it turned out that few programmed learning experts were trained in psychometrics and a number of facile debates were carried on. A facade of rigorous quantitative testing was to become important to educational technologists, in spite of Skinner's own disinclination to depend on 'mechanised statistics' (Koch, 1959): 'Statistical techniques serve a useful function, but they have acquired a purely honorific status which may be troublesome. Their presence or absence has become a shibboleth to be used in distinguishing between good and bad work.'

What we see at the end of this pre-history is a confluence of ideas, none of which by itself could provide a basis for educational technology. We might speculate that all that was required in the early fifties was a suitable hopper into which these ideas could be streamed. We might even suggest that Skinner turned out to be the spigot through which the ideas spouted in an eclectic jet aimed at dislodging many established educational practices. Was the jet fluid first named 'programmed learning', then 'the systems approach to learning', and finally 'educational technology'?

Infancy

'We are on the threshold of an exciting and revolutionary period, in which the scientific study of man will be put to work in man's best interest. Education must play its part. It must accept the fact that a sweeping revision of educational practices is possible and inevitable.' With such evangelising zeal did Skinner write in his 1954 article, 'The science of learning and the art of teaching'. 'From this exciting prospect of an advancing science of learning, it is a great shock to turn to that branch of technology which is most directly concerned with the learning process — education.'

Educational technology was about to be born. Skinner saw four serious shortcomings in the educational system:

1. the reinforcers used were still aversive
2. they were used too long after responses had been elicited
3. the progression towards the required behaviour was poorly arranged
4. reinforcement was provided too infrequently.

He suggested that few teachers, if any, could remedy these shortcomings working alone with a group of pupils, and proposed that machines might be employed to perform most of the functions the teacher could not perform, as well as some of those she could. He tried to forestall criticisms by denying that 'an essentially human intellectual achievement is being analysed in unduly mechanistic terms', and by pointing out that the machines would free the teacher to begin to function 'through intellectual, cultural and emotional contacts of that distinctive sort which testify to her status as a human being'. Skinner saw programmed learning and teaching machines as part (if not all) of an overall improvement in teaching techniques. He claimed that insufficient attention had been paid, by those attempting to improve education, to

377

the improvement of technique. He suggested that educational television, for example, was no exception, being only a way of amplifying and extending *old* techniques.

> Texts garnished with pictures in four colours, exciting episodes in a scientific film, interesting classroom activities — these will make a school interesting and even attractive . . . but to generate specific forms of behaviour these things must be related to the student's behaviour in special ways.

The principles on which his teaching machines were based were:

1. reinforce the student's responses frequently and immediately
2. provide for the student to be in control of his learning rate
3. make sure he follows a coherent, controlled sequence
4. require participation through responding.

After studying the pre-history of educational technology, we can now see fairly clearly that Skinner was proposing a detailed application of his own particular brand of a science of learning, through the use of technological devices. Programme the learner, he said, by book or by machine. He set an example by programming his own course on the analysis of behaviour, both in book and machine forms. Marvellous! Here was a scientist interested in education and actually doing something about it! Just what so many had been waiting for.

Following Skinner's lead, programmed learning mushroomed in America, and soon afterwards spread to Britain and other countries. We shall not trace its development in any systematic fashion. Hartley (1974) has written a recent review of the research for those interested. Instead, we shall pick up two themes already referred to in the last section: behavioural objectives and psychometrics. After dealing with them, we may find that a few selected artefacts will offer an interesting basis for commentary.

Bloom, of the University of Chicago, was chairman of a committee which attempted to set out a taxonomy of objectives in the cognitive domain. The committee was set up following a meeting of interested persons during the 1948 convention of the American Psychological Association and met annually from 1949 to 1953. Its members were all college or university examiners who considered that such a taxonomy might be useful, in higher education at least. Some of them went on to produce a further taxonomy in the affective domain, and one for the psychomotor domain was also planned. But the book Bloom edited became famous.

The importance of this committee's work cannot be overlooked. The book (Bloom, 1956) is now in its sixteenth printing and has influenced curriculum development at all levels. Much of the thinking behind it was taken first into programmed learning and later into the mainstream of educational technology. Mager (1962) offered the training man's version, and emphasised the need for behaviourally-stated objectives, but Bloom's committee led the way for those in education. Significantly, the taxonomy was dedicated to Tyler. Probably neither Tyler nor Bloom thinks of himself as an educational technologist, yet the 'organised knowledge' about objectives provided by these two was assimilated into the systematic approach to the design of learning advocated by programmed learning enthusiasts and educational technologists.

Having decided to set objectives for learners, programme writers sought ways to judge whether learners had reached them, which brings us to the psychometric issue of criterion-v norm-referenced testing. We have already seen that the precursors of educational technology were looking for techniques for learning to perfection, as it were; some were even ready to ignore the genetic inheritance and to declare that if only the right instruction could be devised, all pupils would learn what was being taught. Norm-referenced tests, the main type developed for American schools during the period of pre-history, were based on assumptions contrary to these views. They were tests intended to show where a pupil stood in relation to a given universe, usually his peer-group, and in many cases the statistical work behind their development assumed a normal distribution of abilities among pupils. Criterion-referenced testing started from the assumption that a given task could be achieved at a given criterion level by all those who had been appropriately taught. By and large, programmed learning was to take into its practice criterion-referenced tests, since these matched the principles enunciated regarding objectives and testing by leaders like Mager. A full understanding of the differences between the two types of tests has continued to elude many practitioners, however, in spite of excellent articles in journals devoted to educational measurement (for example, Hambleton & Novick, 1973).

Now let us turn to examine a set of artefacts which together serve to illustrate six major phenomena belonging to this period of infancy (see Table II).

ARTEFACT 1

Lumsdaine and Glaser's *Teaching Machines and Programmed Learning: A Source Book* (1960):

> Hailed as the bible. A compendium of articles, originally intended as a source book on 'educational automation', ie teaching machines, perhaps to hasten the industrial revolution in education, at least in America. Pask the only British author included. Depends heavily on materials from the Pressey and Skinner stables, but ranges quite widely into Crowderian (branching) programming, Pask's adaptive machines, and related areas of psychology.
>
> Contains an interesting speculative article by Finn in which he writes 'both the mass instruction systems and the technology of individual instruction — teaching machines — are gathering terrific momentum', and 'instructional technology is here to stay'.
>
> Many of the papers not contemplative but reports of experimental work.

Lumsdaine and Glaser's source book became just that. It performed a great service and was widely purchased because it drew together many papers which were relatively inaccessible. Now industrial trainers, education students, and Armed Services training personnel were able to read library copies of this 724-page tome. For many of them it was probably their first introduction to Crowder's ideas on 'intrinsic'

Phenomena	Artefact(s)
1) Attempts to widen the scope of programmed learning and thus to widen the audience to whom the messages were being issued about educational reform à la Skinner.	1, 3, 5, 7
2) Well advertised trials of certain machines and texts, aimed at showing that proven products were being offered rather than mere inventions or writings.	2, 3, 5, 7
3) Efforts to convert the élite, whether in universities or foundations or commercial companies, in order to increase the backing for programmed learning.	2, 4, 5
4) The selling of programmed learning as a panacea for at least some educational and training ills; large profits expected.	3, 4, 7
5) Searches for scientific evidence to support the techniques being employed.	2, 4, 6, 7
6) Popularisation of programmed learning among teachers and trainers, principally through seminars and workshops, but supported by a plethora of newsletters, local and national.	3, 4, 7

Table II. *Listing of phenomena belonging to the infancy of educational technology*

programming, which were incorporated into TutorTexts and AutoTutor teaching machines. Crowder wrote that he wanted to automate the classical process of individual tutoring. Like Skinner, he broke down the material to be learned into small segments (but not as small as Skinner's) and tested understanding at the end of each segment. Instead of expecting the pupil to write down his answer (a constructed response, if we recall the jargon), Crowder inserted a multiple-choice question. If the pupil selected the wrong answer, he was routed to a page containing remedial material, and then tried the question again. If he selected the right answer, then he went on to the next segment. Crowder claimed that his programmes were adaptive to the learner's behaviour. In a rough sort of way, they were. His Skinnerian critics tended to point out that if his segments of instruction were properly designed, the pupils would be able to answer the question first time.

Pask, meanwhile, had been developing much more sophisticated notions of adaptive teaching machines. He started to publish papers on automatic teaching around 1957, and was designing machines which would respond directly and immediately to learners' inputs. His Solartron Automatic Keyboard Instructor 'played a game' with the learner, being partly competitive and partly co-operative. The machine used the learner's responses to compile a model in which patterns of learning, level of difficulty, pace of learning and types of errors made were represented in dynamic fashion and controlled the presentation of new material to the learner. Pask's work was closely related to the beginning of CAI (computer-assisted instruction) at the University of Illinois where Stolurow and Bitzer were experimenting in the SOCRATES and PLATO projects; in all three cases these researchers were seeking ways in which the versatility of electronic switching mechanisms could be harnessed to provide vastly flexible programmes of learning, based on adaptation to learners' responses.

Finn was Professor of Education at the University of Southern California in Los Angeles at the time, and President of the Department of Audio-Visual Instruction of the National Education Association. From these heights he surveyed the audio-visual movement and found that programmed learning was good, particularly in machines. Perhaps he was the first to coin the term 'instructional technology'.

ARTEFACT 2

Kantor and Mager's *Klystrons* (1961):

> By-product of a research project at Varian Associates, manufacturers of electronic equipment, this programmed book was first tried out on 'adult young ladies', either employees or wives of Varian employees.
> Preface says the book was revised until 'at least seven consecutive individuals scored better than 90 per cent on the quiz (criterion examination)'.
> A question from the quiz:
> 'The cavity resonator in a *reflex* klystron serves as
> (1) catcher only
> (2) buncher only
> (3) both buncher and catcher'.
> Klystrons are electron tubes developed in the 1950s, now displaced by transistors.

It is quite understandable that Kantor and Mager should take a technical topic like this one for their experimental vehicle. Mager had a background in experimental psychology and at the time that *Klystrons* appeared was involved in industrial training at Varian Associates. The concrete, finite nature of the subject matter was highly compatible with Mager's approach to behavioural objectives. Note the developmental testing (tryout) and the criterion-referenced test, with its multiple-choice questions.

ARTEFACT 3

Programed Instruction **1** 1. May 1961:

> Journal put out by Center for Programed Instruction; ran for about four years; and contained much of interest to those more concerned with programming pedagogy than mechanics of teaching machines. Center was to become part of Institute of Educational Technology in 1964.
> First number begins: 'the school year 1960-61 can be marked down as the year when programed instruction got out of the psychological laboratories and into the classrooms. In school systems all across the nation, children and teachers received their first exposure to an embryonic but immensely promising teaching technique'. A lead article starts 'We have been cursed by all this talk about machinery'.

Programed Instruction (a spelling which has become extinct) was a proselytising newsletter, edited at first by Filep. Part of its cost was met by a grant from the Carnegie Corporation of New York. This particular number reported recent research, summer workshops to be held, and a public statement on self-instructional materials and devices released jointly by the American Educational Research Association, the American Psychological Association and the Department of Audio-Visual Instruction of the National Education Association. It also carried an article for teachers on how to prepare programmed texts. A companion article (one of a series, it turned out) was entitled 'Faulty frames' and dealt with part of Susan Markle's text, *Words*.

There is a wealth of interesting papers in this newsletter's later numbers, spanning far more than simply programmed instruction. The overall impression it gives, however, under Filep's editorship and later under Komoski, is one of hectic activity. There was always a great deal of doing: conferences and programme trials, surveys of outstanding programmes, reports from publishers on the programming boom, and messianic messages about revolutionising the school system in the United States. Not that we should denigrate the serious research also reported; most of the 'big names' in programmed learning contributed papers to the newsletter.

ARTEFACT 4

Richard Goodman's *Programmed Learning and Teaching Machines* (1962):

> Slim booklet introducing English audiences to ideas of Skinner and Crowder. Goodman's background in computing shines through. He looks forward to CAI and the prospect of teaching machines being learning machines, ie fully adaptive. Pask is mentioned in this connection, along with SAKI (Solartron Automatic Keyboard Instructor). Goodman also describes or refers to British studies; eg Reid's work at Aberdeen University on programmes about paper-making, Kay's research at Sheffield, and RAF experiments comparing teaching machines, programmed texts and conventional instruction.

Goodman began his booklet in optimistic vein: 'We are today on the verge of what promises to be a revolution in education.' His emphasis was chiefly on what teaching machines would be able to do. His own interest, as Head of the Department of Computing and Cybernetics, lay very much in this direction. Yet for many English readers, this booklet was the principal reference on teaching machines and programmed learning. The English versions of the AutoTutor and the TutorTexts dominated the market, although other devices were being designed and other companies were rushing to get into the publication of programmed texts.

ARTEFACT 5

Harvard University Committee on Programmed Instruction: *List of Library Holdings* (1962):

> Skinner was Chairman of the Committee. This was the first of a series of lists issued until 1965 under some grant. Nearly 300 items in this one, mostly for 1960-61. Details of developments between 1954 and 1960 sparse: eg Hughes Aircraft Co began to think about applying teaching machines to Air Force training in about 1958; System Development

Corp of Santa Monica conducted experiments in automated teaching at about the same time; Thomas Gilbert was writing about principles of programming continuous discourse for the Bell Telephone Laboratories in 1958; Wells Hively and a few others were interpreting Skinner's paper for particular audiences; Lumsdaine was doing and reporting some experimental work on response cueing and size-of-step; in 1959, the Earlham College Student Self-Instruction Project, based partly on PI, began; Skinner wrote several papers on teaching machines; Susan Meyer (Markle), a student of his, was testing a programmed textbook; Porter was reviewing teaching machine developments.

The Committee at Harvard was supposed to initiate academic staff into the mysteries of programmed instruction, as well as playing some role (now not clear) in the fostering of research. To an outsider, it seems to have failed in both its objectives. At least it employed a librarian for some years to collect the research literature; without doubt, Harvard now has the best archives on programmed instruction in the 1960s.

ARTEFACT 6

Schramm's annotated bibliography *The Research on Programmed Instruction* (1964):

Reports 190 studies, 165 for 1959-62. 'No method of instruction has ever come into use surrounded by so much research activity'.

Nearly half the studies dealt with presentation variables, such as branching and pacing. Nearly 30 per cent dealt with response modes — covert *v* overt, etc.

Collates research results under six headings relating to Skinnerian tenets: (1) an ordered sequence, (2) short steps and few errors, (3) constructed response, (4) immediate knowledge of results, (5) at learner's pace, (6) reinforcement.

Number of times authors get mentions: Lumsdaine 21, Sheffield 7, Eigen, Glaser, Kopstein, Maccoby, Moore and W Smith 5 each. Others fewer than 5.

'We rather expect research on programmed instruction to merge with the broader stream of research on instructional technology, to the benefit of both.'

Schramm's bibliography was greeted by some as a milestone in the progress of programmed instruction. They felt that a scientific base had been established by this review carried out by one of America's top scholars in the communications field. Although his work became frequently quoted, his provisos were largely ignored. He had noted the deficiencies in research design, the small samples, the short trials, the inadequate statistical treatment, and above all the inconclusive nature of the results. In fact, this review offered little comfort to those who wished to apply 'science and other organised knowledge' to education.

ARTEFACT 7

Tutor Age 12. March 1965:

Newsmagazine about automated teaching, edited by Rowntree and Mitchell. Reviewed PL in 1964 in this issue. Down-to-earth attitude and everyday use of machines emerging. More co-operation between developers and users, and greater concern for learner-centred learning. Systems approach being advocated. Value of film in PL, especially in colour. Worldwide interest in PL and particularly AutoTutors.

This well-produced trade journal represented the best type of commercially-sponsored publication in the heyday of programmed learning. It came close to being a learned journal, yet had a lively style which must have commended it to both teachers and laymen. In fact, some of the articles in this issue were reprinted from teachers' magazines and other journals. In between were an abstract of a thesis, advertising of AutoTutors, brief reports on symposia, and lists of TutorFilms available. The tone was hopeful and helpful without being aggressive.

After examining these artefacts and the phenomena they exemplify we may come to the conclusion that both artefacts and phenomena are the evidence of only temporary success. The artefacts served their purpose, then were cast aside. The phenomena did not persist except for the first; there has indeed occurred a widening of scope. Will educational technology, now in its adolescence if we regard programmed learning as its infancy, give rise to similar phenomena, equally shortlived? To put it bluntly, are educational technologists following a fad?

Adolescence

Towards the end of 1965 and in early 1966, I visited a very large number of individuals and institutions concerned with programmed learning in the United States and Britain. I noted a general liberalisation within the programmed learning movement. Fewer and fewer programmes were being written strictly to Skinner's original prescription, and very few indeed to Crowder's. The pure linear programme, consisting of many short frames, with a high degree of repetition, was no longer favoured. Crowderian branching was inserted into linear sequences. More programmes were appearing making use of ancillaries, such as McGraw-Hill's texts on melodic perception, which had a set of tapes. Interest in teaching machines was very much on the wane, with manufacturers of simple linear machines going out of business. Educators and psychologists were saying that the only machines which stood much chance of succeeding commercially were those which incorporated more than the written word, through using records, tape or film. Computer-assisted instruction looked a likely horse to back. 'Skills analysis', 'operational research' and even 'curriculum development' were the in-terms, along with 'behavioural objectives' and 'multi-media systems design'.

At the same time, it was astonishing to a visitor to the States to see how programmed texts were being used on a regular basis, in big business and industry. Vast numbers of 'trained programmers' had been and were being turned out by the week and the month at places like the Center for Programed Learning for Business in Ann Arbor, Michigan. The programming activities of government bodies such as the Public Health Service, the Job Corps and the Armed Services in the United States seemed gigantic compared with what was going on in other countries. At college level there had been a gradual but steady increase in the use of programmed materials. In schools the picture was less encouraging: it was hard to find widespread evidence of persistent use of programmed materials. Reports like *Four Case Studies of Programed Instructions* (Schramm *et al*, 1964) had raised more doubts than questions answered. Even the bonanza of public spending on education had not raised very high the hopes of the publishers of programmed texts for schools.

In Britain there seemed to be a time lag. British research workers were still dealing with problems which no longer intrigued the Americans. Machines were still to the fore, with journals still discussing the merits of linear *v* branching programmes and machines *v* texts. In Britain, departments of education and of psychology in the universities seemed to have led the way from the start, with commercial enterprise playing a lesser role except in the case of teaching machines. Industry, education and commerce, where interested, turned to the universities for advice and assistance, much of which was given *gratis*, of course. In 1966 there were some signs that the lead of the universities would be challenged and taken over by commercial programming companies working under contract, with the universities being left to do research. The sums being spent on this research were minute compared with America; higher education in Britain was short of funds, as usual.

At that time, in early 1966, there were few indications in Britain of programmed learning becoming generally used, whether industrially or in the educational system or in government agencies. At the 1966 conference of the Association for Programmed Learning, Thornhill (1966) asked the question, 'What future has programmed learning in British schools?' He considered programmed learning to be possibly only 'one item in the coming revolution in educational technology'. Another revolution brewing?

Few calls to battle accompanied the change of title for the Association's journal in February 1967. The editor, Annett, admitted that:

> the change in title is (necessarily) abrupt but the change of policy is gradual, reflecting a steady trend towards a wider outlook. A few years ago PL meant something fairly specific — a particular set of techniques based on the work of B F Skinner. Programmed learning has been in the vanguard of attempts to introduce a scientific attitude and scientific methods into teaching.

Annett went on, 'Teaching technology appears to be advancing on separate fronts . . . it is time we learned from each other and broadened our horizons.' The journal was now to contain articles on closed-circuit television and computer-assisted instruction as well as those on programmed learning. The name of the Association was not changed to include the words 'and Educational Technology' until January 1968; the change was made to reflect changing interests among the Association's members, and there was some pressure to drop 'Programmed Learning' altogether.

These changes in titles were accompanied by changes in the terminology being used in published papers. 'A systems approach to education and training' was urged upon all educational technologists. Different authors had rather different interpretations of what the term meant, but in general it seemed to imply a systematic (as opposed to systemic: see Pask & Lewis, 1972) analysis of all the components in a given learning situation, whether or not that situation involved programmed learning. 'Educational technology' became a more popular term too. For example, two papers by Davies (1970, 1971) emphasised first the need for proper foundations for measurement in the new field, and second the need for accountability of educational technology, perhaps along the lines of American schools' performance contracting. By 1973, the same journal, *Programmed Learning and Educational Technology*, could carry a whole issue devoted to educational technology in teacher education. The *Journal of Educational Technology*, started in 1970 and later to become *BJET*, carried a number of papers about the nature of educational technology, as we have already seen. In fact it was never a journal about programmed learning, nor did it carry much in the way of reports of experimental research involving programmes.

Across the Atlantic, much the same discussions were proceeding, but with different results. The National Society for Programmed Instruction established a committee in 1967 to consider a name change. At the 1968 Convention in San Antonio, members indulged in much breast-beating but decided to leave the name unchanged. The 1968 President of the Society, Geary Rummler, wrote later that year that there were signs that the 'educational revolution' was going underground, by which he meant that people in the programmed learning business were starting to publicise themselves less, even though their business was thriving. Instead of the NSPI taking the term 'educational technology' into its title, another organisation chose to do so. The Department of Audio-Visual Instruction of the National Education Association acquired the new title of the Association for Educational Communications and Technology during 1970. The membership voted 35 to 1 to make the change, which came in the wake of a major report to Congress.

As in Britain, there were changes in the journals too. *Teaching Aids News* was transformed into *Educational Technology*, but still without full blessings from scholars. The new fashion for writing about the systems approach gathered support. What started it all is not clear, but Silvern (1964) must have been one of the first. Writers such as Cyrs and Lowenthal (1970), who used a systems approach to curriculum design, and Gilkey and Benyei (1970), who proposed a systems approach to multi-media learning, added to the number of pages to be read without noticeably increasing understanding of how systems theory could aid education.

Considering that the United States had held a clear lead over Britain in the development of programmed learning, it was a little surprising that educational technology should assume political significance in Britain first. Brynmor Jones submitted a report to the British government in 1965 on audio-visual aids in higher education. In his report he advocated a National Centre for Educational Technology under the control of a National Council. In 1967 the National Council for

Educational Technology was set up, spanning not only higher education but also all other sectors. With a small secretariat and a small budget, the Council was obliged to operate more as adviser and liaison agent than as initiator and executor (Willis, 1972), but at least it represented official recognition of educational technology. If we speculate for a moment about the motives leading to this recognition, we will recall that this was still the period of Harold Wilson's 'white-hot technological revolution'. It was also a period of financial stringency. Lack of funds meant no National Centre; the National Centre for Programmed Learning at the University of Birmingham, set up some years earlier with government funds, was allowed to decline. The Council was perhaps a way of promoting innovation and improvement. Perhaps it was for promoting interest in a cost-effective means of education. Whatever the motives, it provided a focus for educational technology.

In the United States in the late sixties, Congress was pouring out billions of dollars for education under its Elementary and Secondary Education Act of 1965 (and later versions). Congressmen were giving more attention to education as a means of reducing social inequality than ever they had before, with Kennedy and Johnson having provided the lead. The desire to see these large sums well spent, if possible with proven results, plus high confidence in the potential of technology for America, led among other events to the appointment of the Commission on Instructional Technology, with a budget of $500,000 from the US Office of Education.

MacKenzie (1970) has provided a full account of how the Commission came into being and a valuable criticism of its report (Tickton, 1970). He noted that the Commission placed its emphasis on the potential of instructional technology for improving the quality of learning, not for making it cheaper. He also noted that the Commission had shifted away from a concern for the uses of hardware, expressed in the original terms of reference, towards interest in the development of a technology of instruction.

As a mechanism for bringing about this development, the report proposed the establishment of the National Institutes of Education, on similar lines to the National Institutes of Mental Health in the US. Within the former, there would be a National Institute of Instructional Technology.

In the event, the National Institute of Education was set up. Just one Institute. And what a rough passage that Institute has had! In more than one year there have been moves in Congress to cut its funds completely. Starved of adequate resources, the Institute has seemed to operate more as an extension of the Office of Education than as an independent agency. Its progressive outlook has not been enough to lead to the setting up of the National Institute of Instructional Technology, although there is now a National Center for Educational Technology within the National Institute of Education.

What of the Office of Education and National Institute of Education's positions today? The signs are that educational technology, under whatever guise, is healthy. Large sums have been allocated to projects that lean heavily on the application of scientific principles to learning (to return to our definitions) and the implementation of techniques of empirical testing to improve learning situations. The State University of Nebraska Project (an American modification of the Open University model: see University of Nebraska, 1973) and the Rocky Mountain Satellite Technology Demonstration (Weinberger, 1975) are but two major examples. Computer-assisted instruction is receiving considerable support too from these agencies.

Other Federal Government agencies have taken up the theme, looking to educational technology to provide solutions to some of their problems. For example, the US Agency for International Development selected educational technology as one of three priority problem areas for investigation during the seventies (USAID, 1970). The agency made a grant of $1 million to Florida State University for the development of its Educational Technology Center. Within individual countries, the agency makes grants aimed at using educational technology as a tool for educational reform (see Hornik *et al*, 1973).

Philanthropic foundations in the United States have shown keen interest too. The Ford Foundation's study (Armsey & Dahl, 1973) ranged across the whole educational field. The Carnegie Commission in Higher Education (1972) published an optimistic report envisaging a fourth revolution in learning (the last one was Caxton's) through technology, and particularly at the higher education level. The Spencer and Markle Foundations funded projects involving educational technology.

The World Bank has declared its support for educational technology (McNamara, 1970), but only for 'well-conceived projects which point the way toward more efficient and economic use of resources'. Recent rejection by the World Bank's advisers of a large-scale project for Thailand which would have employed educational technology indicates that the Bank takes a highly critical approach.

Unesco's Division of Methods, Materials and Techniques, under Dieuzeide (1971), has promoted educational technology in various ways, in association with the United Nations Development Programme. Among the best-known projects are the Indian Satellite Study and the Ivory Coast educational television project, both carried out under multiple auspices including Unesco and UNDP. These international agencies use the term educational technology in a confused way. They seek to employ the media and to develop instructional systems based on a technology of education. They also seek both to improve learning and to make it cheaper.

Something of these dual approaches was present in the discussions in Britain surrounding the demise of the National Council for Educational Technology and its replacement by the new Council for Educational Technology. Old readers of British journals on educational technology do not require explanations; those who are new to the field may wish to consult Mansell (1972) or the Report of the National Council for 1967-73 (NCET, 1973). Mansell, for example, noted that the Government certainly sought increased productivity in education, which he considered to be a labour-intensive, low-technology industry. At any rate, the new Council was intended to represent (in ways which NCET did not) both those wishing to employ the media and those developing educational technology. Improving learning was still to be the basic motive, with the hope that it might turn out to be cheaper too if educational technology was used.

Now, only a few years later, the Council is beginning to get into its stride. It is not blessed with funds galore; compared with its US counterpart, it has virtually nothing, and operates in a much less official or commercial fashion. For all that, it is the outward representation of renewed recognition by Government that educational technology may have something important to contribute to the nation.

During adolescence, educational technology has had other godfathers. The University Grants Committee, concerned with the training of university teachers, has set aside funds now used for staff often labelled educational technologists. In America, there has been some increase in the number of 'offices of instructional resources' established in State and private universities, although Popham (1974) has said there are not enough. 'Learning Resources Centres' would be counted by some in Britain as indications of progress by educational technology, as would the major projects in computer-assisted instruction both sides of the Atlantic.

It is said that to count your blessings you must know what to count as a blessing. Much the same is true for educational technology. Those who wish to boost its image can point to hundreds of manifestations of what *they* call educational technology. Others who wish to denigrate it can list equal numbers of instances where educational technology has failed, or is only peripheral or ephemeral. Dare we predict, on the basis of such subjective opinion, what will happen next?

The future

For the future we all have hopes and expectations. There are also a few certainties that we feel we can count upon. Most of us admittedly have some difficulty in deciding what we should include in each of these three categories: certainties, expectations and hopes. Certainly scientific research will continue. The fund of 'scientific and other organised knowledge' can be expected to grow. We can hope that educational technologists will draw upon this fund and seek to apply its resources. There must be control and exploitation, for humanistic ends, as Travers (1973) has indicated in an important article discussing educational technology as a political phenomenon.

What are these ends? To improve learning may be the broadly stated goal; to provide for more learning by more learners may be subsumed within that broad goal, as well as to provide for more learning at lower costs. Learning remains the basic good in our thinking, although we may disagree about *what* should be learned.

To improve learning, educational technologists require a stronger repertoire than they now have. There has been considerable confusion, as this paper has shown, because educational technologists have been eclectic without taking the trouble to understand the sources they have exploited. As go-betweens, they have been castigated by theorists for not being sufficiently theoretical, and by practitioners for attempting to apply research findings. As go-betweens, they require effective techniques grounded in strong theory.

It might be too much to expect or even hope for a resolution of the conflict between the theoretical-deductive and the empirical-inductive modes of thought (Conant, 1964), the literary and the scientific (Snow, 1964), referred to by Saettler and underlying many criticisms of educational technology. Educational technologists tend to belong to the empirical-inductive school, which is to say that by and large they are doers rather than thinkers. Lewis (1975) has recently put in a claim for more theoretical-deductive work in educational technology, however, and his words are worth quoting:

> In almost every field of endeavour — especially in the so-called 'human' sciences — people differ enormously in the extent to which they feel satisfied with the prevailing state of the art. There are people who genuinely believe that they are doing a grand job with the tools they already have at their disposal. And there are other people who believe that the tools in question are thoroughly puny and unsatisfactory.
>
> What educational technology needs, I believe, is stronger and better techniques. In the absence of additional techniques, simple-minded practitioners will go on trying to 'force-fit' existing techniques to situations in which they are not really appropriate.
>
> Who then is to devise the new and better techniques? My answer to this question is that, if the required techniques are produced at all, they will be produced by thinkers, rather than doers. I firmly believe that the future of educational technology is now in the hands of the thinkers. What is needed is a handful of experienced people, who have thought widely and deeply, and who are literally obsessed by the problems posed. These people must also have the ability to analyse and synthesise, and, in effect, to invent whole new conceptual frameworks. If they do not have this latter ability, they will be soon reduced merely to improving what already exists.
>
> I think that this radical rethinking is both a lonely and a high-risk activity.

Because such theoretical-deductive work is a high-risk activity *and* a high-risk investment, there are few engaging in it and there is little money to finance it. Yet Lewis is surely right in his analysis. Such thinking is particularly needed if we want to see humanistic values included in our application of scientific principles to education. We know far too little about humans' motivation to learn and not enough about the ways they learn from each other through different types of relationship. The ghost in the machine has not taken up much of our attention. Who has read Eisner's latest writings (1975), for example? Do we believe in what he calls 'the perceptive eye'? Are we the victims of our own purposive-rational behaviour?

Finally, what hopes or expectations may we entertain about the future of educational technology as a separate field of endeavour? We can expect to struggle for some years still in our search for identity. Hamlet said, 'O God, I could be bounded in a nutshell, and count myself a king of infinite space, were it not that I have bad dreams.' Many educational technologists have tried to bind themselves into a nutshell, protected from the rest of education, indeed from the rest of society. Others have sought to be kings of infinite space through broadening their scope to include everything. The bad dreams about their relationships with others have persisted. The time is now coming when educational technology should take its place as a specialised branch of educational research and development, retaining its identify but cementing ties with other fields instead of rivalling them.

Next year, Jerusalem!

References

Armsey, J W and Dahl, N C (1973) *An Inquiry into the Uses of Instructional Technology.* New York : Ford Foundation

Bloom, B S (ed) (1956) *Taxonomy of Educational Objectives: Handbook 1: The Cognitive Domain.* New York : Wiley

Bloomer, J (1973) What have simulation and gaming got to do with programmed learning and educational technology?, *Programmed Learning and Educational Technology* 10 4

Carnegie Commission on Higher Education (1972) *The Fourth Revolution: Instructional Technology in Higher Education.* New York : McGraw-Hill

Chadwick, C (1973) Educational technology: progress, prospects and comparison, *British Journal of Educational Technology* 2 4

Conant, J B (1964) *Two Modes of Thought: My Encounters with Science and Education.* New York : Trident Press

Cooley, W W and Glaser R (1963) *On Information and Management Systems for Individually Prescribed Instruction,* Working Paper No 45. Pittsburgh : University of Pittsburgh Learning Research and Development Center

Cyrs, T E and Lowenthal, R (1970) A model for curriculum design using a systems approach, *Audiovisual Instruction* 15 1

Davies, I K (1970) Foundations of measurement in educational technology, *Programmed Learning and Educational Technology* 7 2

Davies, I K (1971) Developing accountability in instructional systems technology, *Programmed Learning and Educational Technology* 8 3

Dewey, J (1917) *Creative Intelligence.* New York : Holt

Dewey, J (1929) *Sources of a Science of Education.* New York : Liveright

Dieuzeide, H (1971) Educational technology and the development of education, *British Journal of Educational Technology* 3 2

Dieuzeide, H (1971) *Educational Technology: Sophisticated, Adapted and Rational Technology.* Paris : Unesco International Commission on the Development of Education

Eisner, E W (1975) *The Design and Evaluation of Educational Programs.* New York : Macmillan

Ely, D P (1970) Toward a philosophy of educational technology, *Journal of Educational Technology* 2 1

Evans, J L, Glaser, R and Homme, L (1960) *The Ruleg (Rule-example) System for the Construction of Learning Programs.* Report prepared under the Cooperative Research Program of the US Office of Education at the Dept of Psychology, University of Pittsburgh

Flanagan, J C (1971) *The PLAN Educational System: a Program for Learning in Accordance with Needs.* Palo Alto : American Institutes for Research

Galbraith, J K (1967) *The New Industrial State.* Boston : Houghton Mifflin

Gilkey, J and Benyei, P (1970) The instructional unit: a systems approach to multimedia, *Audiovisual Instruction* 15 1

Glaser, R and Nitco, A J (1970) *Measurement in Learning and Instruction.* Pittsburgh : University of Pittsburgh, Learning Research and Development Center

Goodman, R (1962) *Programmed Learning and Teaching Machines.* London : English Universities Press

Hambleton, R K and Novick, M R (1973) Towards an integration of theory and method for criterion-referenced tests, *Journal of Educational Measurement* 10 3

Hartley, J (1974) Programmed instruction 1954-74: a review, *Programmed Learning and Educational Technology* 11 6

Holroyd, D (1971) Educational technology means men — or machines?, *British Journal of Educational Technology* 2 2

Hornik, R C *et al* (1973) *Television and educational reform in El Salvador.* Stanford : Institute for Communication Research, Stanford University

Hull, C L (1943) *Principles of Behaviour.* New York : Appleton-Century-Crofts

Kantor, R H and Mager, R F (1961) *Klystrons.* Palo Alto : Varian Associates

Koch, S (ed) (1959) *Psychology: a Study of a Science.* New York : McGraw-Hill

Lewis, B N (1975) Personal communication

Lumsdaine, A A and Glaser, R (1960) *Teaching Machines and Programmed d Learning: a Source Book.* Washington DC : Department of Audiovisual Instruction, National Education Association

MacKenzie, N (1970) Springboard or scaffold? The Commission on Instructional Technology in the United States, *Journal of Educational Technology* 3 1

MacKenzie, N, Eraut, M and Jones, H C (1970) *Teaching and Learning: an Introduction to New Methods and Resources in Higher Education.* Paris : Unesco and the International Association of Universities

Mager, R F (1962) *Preparing Instructional Objectives.* Palo Alto : Fearon

Mansell, J (1972) A new organisation for educational technology, *Programmed Learning and Educational Technology* 9 4

McNamara, R (1970) *Lending in Education: a Memorandum.* Washington DC : International Bank for Reconstruction and Development

NCET (National Council for Educational Technology) (1973) *Educational Technology: Progress and Promise.* London : National Council for Educational Technology

Ofeish, G D (1964) Introduction. In G D Ofeish and W C Meierhenry (eds) *Trends in Programmed Instruction.* Washington DC : Department of Audiovisual Instruction, National Education Association and National Society for Programmed Instruction

Parkhurst, H (1922) *Education on the Dalton Plan.* London : Bell

Pask, G and Lewis, B (1972) Teaching strategies: a systems approach. In Unit 9 of *The Curriculum: Context, Design and Development.* Milton Keynes : Open University

Popham, J W (1974) Higher education's commitment to instructional improvement programs, *Educational Researcher* 3 11

Pressey, S L (1926) A simple device for teaching, testing and research in learning, *School and Society* 23, March

Pressey, S L (1927) A machine for automatic teaching of drill material, *School and Society* 25, May

Pressey, S L (1932) A third and fourth contribution toward the coming 'industrial revolution' in education, *School and Society* 36

Pressey, S L (1964) A puncture of the huge 'programming' boom?, *Teachers College Record* 65 5

Pressey, S L and Kinzer, J R (1964) Auto-elucidation without programming, *Psychology in the Schools* 1 4

Rowntree, D (1974) *Educational Technology in Curriculum Development.* London : Harper & Row

Saettler, P (1968) *A History of Instructional Technology.* New York : McGraw-Hill

Schramm, W (1964) *The Research on Programed Instruction.* Washington DC : US Department of Health, Education and Welfare

Schramm, W *et al,* (1964) *Four Case Studies of Programed Instruction.* New York : Fund for the Advancement of Education

Silvern, L C (1964) *Designing Instructional Systems.* Los Angeles : Education and Training Consultants

Skinner, B F (1953) *Science and Human Behavior.* New York : Macmillan

Skinner, B F (1950) Are theories of learning necessary?, *Psychological Review* 57, July

Skinner, B F (1954) The science of learning and the art of teaching, *Harvard Educational Review* 24 2

Skinner, B F (1957) *Verbal Behavior.* New York : Appleton-Century-Crofts

Snow, C P (1964) *The Two Cultures: and a Second Look.* London : Cambridge University Press

Thorndike, E L (1912) *Education: a First Book.* New York : Macmillan

Thornhill, P (1966) What future has programmed learning in British schools?, *Programmed Learning* 3 2

Tickton, S (ed) (1970) *To Improve Learning.* New York : Bowker

Tolman, T C (1932) *Purposive Behaviour in Animals and Men.* New York : Appleton-Century-Crofts

Travers, R M (1973) Educational technology and related research viewed as a political force. In R Travers (ed) *Second Handbook of Research on Teaching.* Chicago : Rand McNally

Tyler, R (1934) *Constructing Achievement Tests.* Columbus : Ohio State University Press

Tyler, R W (1964) Some persistent questions on the defining of objectives. In C M Lindvall (ed) *Defining Educational Objectives.* Pittsburgh : University of Pittsburgh Press

Tyler, R W (1950) *Basic Principles of Curriculum and Instruction.* Chicago : University of Chicago Press

University of Nebraska (1973) *Post Secondary Education through Telecommunications.* Lincoln : University of Nebraska

USAID (United States Agency for International Development) (1970) *Priority Problems in Education and Human Resources Development — the 1970s.* Washington DC : USAID

Washburne, C, Vogel, M and Gray, W A (1926) *Results of Practical Experiments in Fitting Schools to Individuals.* Bloomington : Public School Publishing

Washburne, C (1932) *Adjusting the School to the Child.* New York : World Book

Watson, J B (1924) *Behaviourism.* Chicago : University of Chicago Press

Weinberger, C (1975) Speech to the American Institute of Aeronautics and Astronautics in Washington DC, 26 February

Willis, N E (1972) And what of the future? A survey of the work of the National Council for Educational Technology, *Programmed Learning and Educational Technology* 9 3

Authors' Addresses

Howard Barrows
Faculty of Medicine
McMaster University
Ontario, Canada

Peter Burnhill
Design Department
Stafford College of Further Education
Stafford, UK

Harry Butcher
British Airways Travel Division
PO Box 115
West London Terminal
Cromwell Road
London SW7 4ED, UK

Ivor K Davies
Dean of Education
Indiana University
Education Building
Bloomington
Indiana 47401, USA

Bernard Dodd
Senior Psychology (Navy)
Old Admiralty Building
Spring Gardens
London SW1A 2BE, UK

Brian J Essex
3 Alleyn Road
London SE21 8AB, UK

David Hamilton
Department of Education
University of Glasgow
Glasgow S12 8QQ, Scotland, UK

J Roger Hartley
Computer-Based Learning Project
Department of Education
The University of Leeds
Leeds, UK

James Hartley
Department of Psychology
The University of Keele
Keele
Staffordshire, UK

David Hawkridge
Institute of Educational Technology
The Open University
Milton Keynes
Buckinghamshire, UK

John Hegarty
Department of Psychology
The University of Keele
Keele
Staffordshire, UK

Richard Hooper
Mills & Allen Communications Ltd
Buchanan House
24-30 Holborn
London EC1, UK

F S Keller
860 Oleander Drive
Aiken
South Carolina 29801, USA

Richard LeHunte
Inbucon Learning Systems Ltd
Ancaster Lodge
Queens Road
Richmond
Surrey, UK

Brian Lewis
Institute of Educational Technology
The Open University
Milton Keynes
Buckinghamshire, UK

Kenneth Lovell
Department of Education
The University of Leeds
Leeds, UK

Susan Markle
Office of Instructional Resources
University of Illinois
Chicago Circle
Box 4348
Chicago
Illinois 60680, USA

Ference Marton
Institute of Education
The University of Goteburg
Fack
43720 Molndel, Sweden

Richard J Miles
APRE
c/o RAE
Farnborough
Hants, UK

Gerry Moult
British Airways Travel Division
PO Box 115
West London Terminal
Cromwell Road
London SW7 4ED, UK

Victor Neufeld
Faculty of Medicine
McMaster University
Ontario, Canada

Seymour Papert
The Artificial Intelligence Laboratory
Massachusetts Institute of Technology
Boston
Massachusetts, USA

Malcolm Parlett
National Foundation for
Educational Research
The Mere
Upton Park
Slough
Berkshire, UK

Gordon Pask
Systems Research Ltd
Woodville House
37 Sheen Road, Richmond
Surrey, UK

John Patrick
Department of Applied Psychology
The University of Aston
Birmingham, UK

George J Posner
111 Stone Hall
Cornell University
Ithaca
New York 14853, USA

C Sheppard
Applied Psychology Unit
Admiralty Research Laboratory
Teddington
Middlesex, UK

Marten Shipman
Director of Research and Statistics
Inner London Education Authority
County Hall
London SE1 7PB, UK

Richard E Snow
School of Education
Stanford University, Stanford
California 94305, USA

Robert Stammers
Department of Applied Psychology
The University of Aston
Birmingham, UK

Kenneth A Strike
111 Stone Hall
Cornell University
Ithaca
New York 14853, USA

Robert E Williams
The Hermitage
Alstonfield
Ashbourne
Derbyshire, UK

Index

Abbatt, F R, 74, 78, 87, 94
Abbreviations, 184
Abelard, P, 373
Aberdeen University, 382
Ability, general mental, 99
Acceptance, 23
Achievement:
    motivation, 99
    prior, 99
    psychological tests, 376
    tests, 213
Ackoff, Russell, 135
Action, 157
    skills, 15
Activity, 31
Adaptive teaching machines, 379, 380
Adjunctive programming, 255
Admiralty Research Laboratory, 195
Advanced Instructional System (AIS),
    366
Advance organisers, 88
Adventurousness, 251
Advice:
    action-oriented relationships,
    117-18
    alternative solutions, 107
    effectiveness of relationships,
    119-21
    entering relationships, 112-15
    ongoing relationships, 115-18
    prescription-oriented assumptions,
    109
    product-oriented assumptions,
    108-9
    product-process-oriented
    assumptions, 109-12
    relationship assumptions, 107-8
    system requirements, 121
    terminating relationships, 118-19
    theory, 104-22
Agenda-setting, 117
Agreements, 58-9
Agricultural botany paradigm, 205
Aims, 66
    comparing goals and objectives,
    141-4

creativity, 259
    topics, 66
AIRIMP, 331
Airline reservations, 331-58
Air University, 367
Algorithms, 53
    identification, 170
    performance, 83
Ambiguities, 184
American Educational Research
    Association, 382
American National Instructional
    Television, 139
American Psychological Association,
    283, 378, 382
Analogical concepts, 57
Analysis, 23
Anastasio, E J, 220
AND, 172-3, 178
Anderson, R C, 79, 170-3, 176, 183
Andre, T, 79
Animal studies, 37-8, 43, 243
Annett, J, 41, 153, 154, 156, 158,
    160-1, 164, 385
Anxiety, 32, 100, 102
APL, 78
Appendices, 185
Aptitude:
    measure, 100
    profiles, 102
    scores, 98
    -treatment interaction (ATI), 18,
    96-9, 102
    variables, 99
Archetypes, 15-16
    audio-visual, 20-2
    engineering, 22
    problem-solving, 22-3
Arcs, 83
    clusters, 83
Arizona State University, 284, 290,
    291
Armsey, J W, 371, 388
Army Apprentice College,
    Arborfield, 362-3
Army Ordnance School, 367

Army Recruitment Centre, Sutton
  Coldfield, 365
Army Research Institute, 367
Army School of Instructional
  Technology, 365
Arnheim, R, 253
Arnold, J E, 251-2, 254
Artificial intelligence, 57, 93
Art Work Judgement tests, 264
Art-work, programmed instruction, 234
Ashby, Sir Eric, 11, 12
ASS, 219
  evaluation, 226-8
  tension between DISS and, 226
Assessment, 43
Assimilation, 219-22
  critical mass, 222
  curriculum integration, 222
  location of projects, 221
  matched funding, 221-2
  organisational structure, 221
Association for Educational
  Communications and Technology,
  381-2, 386
Association for Programmed Learning
  385
Associations, 42, 254, 374
Associativity, 174
Atkinson, R C, 41
Atomistic analysis, 375
Attention, 374
  intensity, 49
Attitude tests, 213
Attribute/s:
  physical, 165
  prompting, 178
Audiometry, pure-tone, 238
August, G J, 184
Austin, C, 61
Ausubel, D P, 34, 37, 83
Author languages, 89
Auto-instruction, 376
Auto Tutor, 382, 384
Ayscough, P B, 78, 224
Azrin, N H, 33
Azzi, Rodolfo, 283

BABS, 332-58
Bacon, F, 372
Bahlke, S J, 256
Baker, E, 66
Barker-Lunn, Joan, 43-4
Bannister, D, 62
Bar charts, 187
Barnard, P, 183-4
Barrett, B H, 238, 243
Barron, F, 251-2
Barron Welsh Art Scale, 253
Barrows, Harold S, 34, 313-24
Bartlett, F C, 57
Bateson, G, 57
Beasley, N A, 241, 245
Behaviour:
  patterns, 198

shaping, 22
specifications, 304-5
Behavioural:
  instruction, 33
  objectives, 141, 143, 304-5,
    377, 384
  science, 13, 108
Behavioural Research and
  Development, 242
Behaviourism, 19, 57, 375
Beittel, K R, 253-4
Belbin, R M, 40, 59
Bell Telephone Laboratories, 383
Bennett, N, 36, 43
Benyei, P, 386
Berry, P C, 78, 162
Biddle, W B, 176, 183
Biggs, J B, 52
Bijou, S W, 238-40, 243-4
Biomedical problem solving, 316
Bisseret, A, 163
Bitterman, M E, 37, 43
Bitzer, D I, 220, 380
Blaiwes, A S, 185
Blank-mind themes, 272
Bloom, B S, 377
Bloomer, J, 372
Bloom-type taxonomies, 303
Blum, M L, 163
Bohr's principle, 18
Books, prices, 12
Bori, Carolina Martuscelli, 283
Bork, A M, 77, 87-8
Boutwell, R C, 174-5
Bower, G H, 39, 43
Bower, T G R, 30-1, 39
Box, H O, 38
Brainstorming, 254, 259, 261, 263
Branching, 379, 385
Brandex, Professor, 293
Brasilia, University of, 283
Bricker, W A and D D, 238
Briggs, I J, 42
British Airways:
  anatomy of a frame, 346-53
  computer-assisted instruction,
    331-58
  course design, 337-40
  target population, 336
  task analysis, 336-7
British Journal of Educational
  Technology, 370, 374, 386
British Standards Institution, 189
Brittain, W I, 253-4
Broadbent, D E, 57
Brogden, H E, 253
Brown, J S, 78, 90
Bruner, Jerome S, 41, 51, 147-9,
  172-3
Bryson, L, 106
Bugelski, B R, 30
Building, 254
Bunderson, C V, 29, 102

Burk, F, 373, 376
Burkhart, R C, 253-4
Burnhill, Peter, 182-94

Cage, John, 302
CALCHEM, 224
California, University at Los Angeles
    (UCLA), 302
California, University of Southern,
    381
Cambridge University, 223
Candour, 127
Capitals, 192
Carbonell, J R, 93
Career choice, 311
Carnegie Commission on Higher
    Education, 219, 388
Carnegie Corporation, 381
CASTE, 69
Cattell, R B, 97, 253
Center for Programed Instruction, 381
Center for Programed Learning for
    Business, 384
Chadwick, C, 370
Chains, 42, 155-6
Change, planned, 23
Chapanis, A, 163, 182
Chemical Society, 225
Children, teaching to think, 270-81
Choice, 32
Christensen, C M, 184
Clark, C H, 254
Clark, D C, 172, 174
Classical paradigm, 205
Classification, 92, 98, 170, 174, 179,
    196, 201-2
Class relations, 166
Cleary, A, 241, 244
Coaching, 117
CODAP, 364-5
Cognitive:
    feedback, 31-2
    psychology, 33, 35, 271
    structures, 82-3, 85
    styles, 35, 85, 99
    theory, 31-6
Cohen, J, 185
Coldeway, D O, 171
Cole, A, 94
Cole, Brett, 291
Coles, C R, 43
Coles, P, 184
Collins, A, 93
Colour, 192
Columbia University, 283
Combination, 254
Comenius, J A, 372-4
Commission on Instructional
    Technology, 387
Communication, 223
    existing channels, 225
Commutivity, 174
Competency-based programmes, 137-8
Complexity, 198

Computer-assisted instruction, 35, 57,
    273, 331-58, 380, 385
Computer-assisted learning (CAL),
    73-5, 219, 221-3, 226, 228, 371
    armed services, 359-69
    design problems, 87-9
Computer Assisted Management of
    Learning (CAMOL), 227, 363
Computer-based instruction,
    psychological principles, 73-95
Computer Based Learning Project,
    227
Computer-based teaching
    programmes, 84
Computerised Training System
    (CTS), 366
Computer-managed learning (CML),
    221-3, 228
    armed services, 362, 366-7
Computer science, as a school
    subject, 273-4
Conant, J B, 390
Concentrated study, 209
Concepts, 58, 170-81
    acquisition, 176, 179
    -clusters, 305
    learning, 156
    -relation diagrams/matrices, 305
    relationships, 307
    simulation and illustration, 75-7
Concerned reaction kinetics, 80
Conditioning theory, 30
Conditions, creativity, 257-8
Confidence, 109
Connectionism, 374
Conrad, R, 154
Consciousness, 375
Consistency, 60
Consultants, illuminative evaluation,
    214
Contemplativeness, 251
Content analysis, 83, 86
Content maps, 86
Contracts, 114
Control programs, 86
Convergent-divergent, 32
Conversational domain, 65
Conversations, 56-72
    computer-controlled, 67
    operating system, 68-9
    testing, 311
    tutorial, 65-8
Cooley, W W, 376
Correlates, psychological, 97
Correspondence courses, 296
Council for Educational Technology
    (previously National Council for
    Educational Technology), 370
Counselling, 117
Course development, 13
Covington, M V, 234, 255
Cowan, J, 34
CPQ, 253, 256, 264

CRAMP, 196
Creative thinking, 320
Creativity, 234
    conditions, 257-8
    definition, 251
    identification, 253-4
    increasing ability, 254
    measuring ability, 256
    objectives, 257-9
    process of, 252-3
    product, 253
    programme construction, 258-63
    programme development, 256
    programme effectiveness, 263-5
    programmed instruction, 250-69
    relevant factors, 257
    subjects, 257-8
    tests, 253
Crick, Francis, 12
Criterion tests, 102
Critical incident technique, 163
Critical mass, 222
Critical thinking, 300-1, 316
Criticism, 317
Crnic, Linda, 179
Cronbach, L J, 34, 98, 100, 361
Cropley, A J, 251-2
Crossman, E R F W, 154
Crowder, N, 254-5, 380, 382, 384
Crowderian (branching)
    programming, 379
Croxton, F, 187
Crutchfield, R S, 234, 255
Crystallised ability, 99
Cues, 198
    identification, 155
    interpretation, 155
Cunningham, C C, 241
Cunnington, M W, 256
Curriculum:
    design: objectives, 135-51
    design: Tyler-type, 303
    development, 13, 370, 384
    integration, 137, 222
    planning, *see* Planning
Cyclicity, 60
Cyrs, T E, 386

Dahl, N, 371, 388
Dale, R R, 44
Dalton Plan, 208, 376
D'Angelo, E, 300
Data:
    collection and classification,
    201-2
    -gathering, 115
    interpretation, 106-7
Davies, I K, 13, 15, 18, 28, 84, 104-22,
    131, 133, 135-51, 182, 184-5, 196,
    255, 386
Davies, J P, 162
Davies, L B, 255
Davis, R W, 133
de Bono, Edward, 19, 254

Decision-action process, 105
Decision making, 15, 155
    documentation, 132
    evaluation and illumination, 216-17
    instructional design, 195-204
    orientation, 116-17
Decisions, 10
    rules, 87, 92, 199-202
    tables, 185
    trees, 160, 162
Deduction, 312
Definition, 170, 173-4, 176-89
    by synonym, 175
Demonstrate-prompt-release, 334
Descriptors, 61, 63, 66
Development, 39, 168
Deviation, 23
Dewey, John, 136, 270, 274, 276,
    373-5
Diagnosis, 14-15, 90-2, 115, 325-30
Diagnostic evaluation, 319-20
Diagrams, schematic, 132
Dickinson, G C, 188
Dieuzeide, H, 370, 378
Difference, 32
    individual, 83, 96-103
Difficulty, 168
Dirkswager, A, 66
Discipline consultants, 322
Discovery, 149
    guided, 318
    role of objectives, 146-9
Discrimination, 31, 239-40, 242-3,
    245
    learning, 156
    multiple, 42
DISS, 219, 223, 224
    evaluation, 226-8
    tensions between ASS and, 226
Dissemination, 219, 222-6
    reasons for selection, 223
    strategies, 223-6
Distributed study, 209
DiVesta, F J, 183
Documentation, 163, 225
Dodd, Bernard T, 132, 195-204
Dogmatism, 20
Dooling, D J, 182
Douglas, J W B, 44
Drill-and-practice programs, 273
Drucker, Peter, 15, 105
Duncan, K D, 132, 154, 156, 158,
    161, 163-4, 195

Earlham College Student Self-
    Instruction Project, 383
East Anglia, University of, 139
Eddington, 19
Education:
    de-schooling, 137
    definition, 10
    purposes, 108
Educational sociology, 301

Educational technology:
    definitions, 371-2
    one, 13
    two, 13-14
    three, 14-15
Educational Technology, 386
Education Technology Center, Florida
    State University, 388
Edwards, A E, 243
Effectiveness, 120
Effect, Law of, 374
Effector response, 155
Ego, regression in service of, 251
Egrul, 374
Eigen, L D, 383
Eisner, E W, 390
Elementary and Secondary Education
    Act 1965, 387
Ellis, N R, 238
Ely, D P, 370
Emanuel, R, 234
Emerson, 141
Emotion, 32, 252
Empirics, 390
    inquiries, 167
    prerequisites, 167-8
Energy, 252
Engineering Sciences Project, 227, 361-2
Englemann, S, 171, 176
Ennever, L F, 138
Entailment mesh, 61
Entailment structure, 60-5
Eraut, M, 18, 372
Error:
    count, 344-5
    patterns, 174
    per cent, 356-7
    responses, 349, 353
Essex, Brian J, 325
Ethics, 123
Evaluation, 13
    illumination, 205-18
    nature and purpose, 108
    relationships, 111
    self-, 315
Evaluators, relationships with, 104-5
Evidence, 127
    interpretation, 127
    status, 125
Examination results, 51
Experience, 14
    past, 38-9
Experimental condition, standard, 67
Exploration, iterative, 100
Exteriorisation, 58, 67
Extraversion factors, 264
Exvia/invia, 256

Factor analysis, 214
Factors, 206
Faculty advisers, 322
Faculty theories, 272
Fading, 239, 245
Familiarity, 168

Farmer, John, 290-1
Faust, A W, 29
Faust, G W, 171-2
Faw, V E, 36-7
Feedback, 79-81, 89, 117, 157, 198,
    357, 376
Feldhusen, J F, 256
Feldman, J, 174
Feliciano, G D, 187
Fielden, John, 226
Filep, R T, 381-2
Finn, J D, 379, 381
Flanagan, J C, 163, 376
Flavell, J H, 53, 57
Fleishman, E, 196
Fleming, R, 187
Flew, A G N, 43
Flexibility, 15, 32, 310
Florida State University, 388
Flow-charts, 132, 185, 235, 326-7
Fluid ability, 99
Footnotes, 185
Ford Foundation, 302, 388
Ford, Julienne, 44
Foster, J J, 184
Fox, K, 186-7
Frame-writing, 132
Frayer, D A, 171-2, 174-5, 178-9
Frazer, Sir James, 15
Free-operant behaviour, 238
Free-operant devices, 244
Free-operant tasks, 243
Freud, S, 252
Friedlander, B Z, 238
Froebel, F W A, 373
Frohman, M, 114, 117
Frye, Northrop, 16
Functionalism, 57
Furst, Edward, 143

Gage, N I, 41
Gagné, Robert M, 34-5, 39-42, 82,
    148-9, 155-6, 171, 173, 255
Galbraith, J K, 371
Games, 259
Gardner, John, 104, 106
Gardner, W I, 238
Generalisation, 31, 183, 374
Generalists, 310
Generality, 142
Geographical Association, 225-6
Geometry, turtle, 276
Gestalt judgements, 256, 264
Gestalt school of psychology, 53
Getting-it themes, 272
Getzels, J W, 251
Ghatala, E S, 171-2, 174-5, 178-9
Ghiselin, B, 252-3
Gilbert, Thomas F, 255, 334, 383
Gilkey, J, 386
Glaser, R, 34, 43, 374, 376, 378-80,
    383
Glasgow University, 227
Glossary of Training Terms, 153

Goals, 32, 66, 142-3
  compared with aims and
    objectives, 141-4
  content, 317
  personal, 315
  process, 317
  setting, 13
Goldman, R D, 52
Goodman, Richard, 382
Goodnow, J, 61
Goodwin, A R, 185
Gordon, W J, 254
Gough Adjective Checklist, 253
Grading, 289-90, 293
Graphs, 186-9
Graph theory, 82
Graves Design Judgement Test, 253
Graves, Robert, 16
Gray, W, 376
Great Debate, 12
Green, J, 94
Greene, F M, 237
Greenfield, P M, 54
Greeno, J G, 85
Group ideation, 254
Grubb, R E, 83
Gruber, H E, 54
Grundin, H U, 79
Guidance, 147
Guilford, J P, 57, 252, 254
Gurbutt, P A, 82, 83
Guthrie, J T, 80
Guynn, Stephen J, 122

Hagaman, W D, 91
Hallman, R J, 252
Hambleton, R K, 379
Hamilton, David, 132, 205-18
Hammersley, M, 43
Harlen, W, 138
Harless, W G, 91
Harlow, H, 38
Harper, R, 241
Hartley, James, 18, 30-46, 84, 131, 136,
  182-94, 255, 377
Hartley, J Roger, 28, 73-95
Harvard University Committee on
  Programmed Instruction, 382
Hawkins, S, 187, 189
Hawkridge, David G, 29, 370-93
Headquarters Training Command,
  RAF Brampton, 364
Headrick, M W, 238
Hegarty, John R, 233, 237-48
Heisenberg, W, 19
Help, facilities, 89
Herbart, J F, 373-4
Hertfordshire County Council, 227
Heuristics, 173, 273, 307
Hewlett Packard, 362
Hierarchies, 34-5, 142
  cumulative, 34
  learning, 149

  task analysis, 156-62
  topic maps, 83
Hilgard, E R, 30-1, 39, 43
Hinde, J S, 37
Hinde, R A, 37-8
History 13-16 project, 220
Hively, W, 176, 239, 242-3, 383
HMS Collingwood, 364
Hobbes, Thomas, 145
Holland, J G, 242, 361
Holroyde, D, 370
Home study courses, 296
Hooper, Richard, 28, 133, 219-29,
  235
Horn, J L, 99
Horn, R E, 186
Hornick, R C, 388
House, B J, 238
House, E, 224
Houston, J P, 254
Howe, M J A, 33
HSPQ, 253, 256, 264
Hudson, L, 252, 254
Hughes Aircraft Co, 382
Hull, C L, 375
Hullian Chinese ideographs, 175
Hull, University of, 156
Humanities Curriculum Report, 139-40
Hume, David, 145
Humour, 252
Hunter, I M L, 39

Idea books, 256
Ideational scaffolding, 83
Identification, 259
Illinois, University, 380
Illumination, 132
  creativity, 253
  documentary and background
    information, 213-14
  evaluation as, 205-18
  decision making, 216-17
Illuminative evaluation, organisation
  and methods, 210-14
Illustration, 175
  concepts, 75-7
Imagi-craft record programme, 256
Imperial College, 222
Impressions, 127
Improvement, 23
Impulsiveness, 32
Inbucon Learning Systems Ltd, 195
Incubation, creativity, 252-3
Indexes, 33
  UTS, 354
Indian Satellite Study, 388
Individualists, 251
Individually Prescribed Instruction
  (IPI), 376
Information mapping, 186
Innovation, 57
Inputs, 157

Inquiries:
    empirics, 167
    logic, 166-7
Instance probability analysis, 179
Institute of Educational Technology, 381
Instructional:
    strategy, 83
    text, improving, 182-94
    theories, 41
Instructional designs:
    criteria for decisions, 197-201
    decision making rationale, 199-201
    decision rules, 199-202
    defining decisions, 196-7
    individual differences, 96-103
Instructional development, 13
    conservation, 98
    nature and purpose, 108
    relationships, 111
Integrated day, 208
Integrity, 123
Intelligence, 99
Interest, 168, 374
Interjudge reliability, 256
Internalisation, 51, 168-9
International Computers Ltd, 227, 363
International Organisation for
    Standardisation, 189
Interpersonal skills, 215
Interventions, agenda-setting, 117
Interviews, 115, 163, 212-13
    personal, 309
Intrinsic programming, 254
INTUITION, 69
Invia, 256
Isomorphisms, 61
Isotype system, 189
Italics, 184
Item analysis, 102
ITRU, 196
Ivory Coast educational television
    project, 388

Jackson, P W, 251
Job aids, 162-3
Job analysis, 152, 364-5
Jobs Corp, 384
Johnson, D M, 173
Johnson, L B, 387
Jones, Brynmor, 386
Jones, H C, 18, 372
Journal of Educational Technology
    see British Journal of
    Educational Technology
Judgement, 10, 256
    art, 256
    criteria, 253
    deferred, 254, 259
Jung, C, 15, 24
Justification (explanations), 308, 310
Justification (typography), 190

Kant, I, 24

Kantor, R H, 381
Kapota, K J, 242
Kay, H, 382
KCR, 79-80
Keller, Fred S, 234, 282-95
Kellerisation, 171
Keller Plan, 33, 234
Kelly, G A, 57, 63
Kelly Grids, 309
Kennedy, J F, 387
Kibaha Training School, 329
Kiernan, C C, 33
Kilpatrick, 373
Kinzer, 376
Klausmeier, H J, 171-2, 174-5, 178-9
Kneller, G F, 251, 254
Knight, K R, 362
Knight, M A G, 195
Knight, Wilson, 16
Knowledge, 19
    organisation, 210
    previous, 81, 88, 98, 118
    process, 148
    product, 148
    specifications, 304-5
Knowles, M, 30
Koch, S, 377
Koestler, A, 252
Kogan, M, 220
Kogan, N, 251, 254
Kolb, D A, 117
Komoski, K, 382
Kopstein, F F, 383
Kotarbinski, T, 303
Kuhn, T S, 18
Kulhavy, R W, 79, 173
Kulik, J, 33

Laboratories, relevance of results,
    37-8
Lacey, C, 44
Lachman, R, 182
Laing, R D, 57
Landa, L N, 171-3, 178
Lateral thinking, 19, 254
Lawrence, P J, 255
Learner:
    characteristics, 197, 199
    control, 85-8
    -based programming, 254
Learning, 47-55
    different kinds, 39-41
    goals, 86
    improvement, 389
    integrated, 320-1
    interaction with teachers, 43
    laws of, 37-42, 374
    meaningful, 83
    natural process, 32
    outcome, 49
    principles, 30-3
    problem-based, 315-17
    progress, 319

resources, 318-19
self-directed, 314-15, 319
sequential, 316
small-group, 317
strategy, 52, 83, 85-6
style, 57, 318
tasks, analysis, 88
theory, 30-46, 301, 372, 375
to learn, 57
Learning Resource Centres, 389
Leeds University, 74, 77, 80, 82, 84,
86, 91, 94, 224, 227
Legibility, 189-90
LeHunte, R J G, 195-204
Leith, G O M, 40
Leplat, J, 163
Levinson, F, 241
Lewin, Kurt, 40, 105, 373
Lewis, Brian N, 28, 136, 235, 296-312
386, 390
Libraries, personal, 319
Lindsley, O R, 238, 243
Linear programming, 384-5
Lines, spacing, 189
LISP, 273
Locke, J, 372-3
Logical prerequisities, 166
Logic, inquiries, 166-7
LOGO, 78, 273-4, 279, 280
London Business School, 227
Lovell, Kenneth, 28, 73-95
Lowenfield, V, 253-4
Lowenthal, R, 386
Lumsdaine, A A, 379-80, 383
Luria, G R, 57, 69

Maccoby, E, 383
Macrae, C, 94
McCulloch, W S, 56
MacDonald, B, 223
Macdonald-Ross, M, 136, 182, 189-90
McGraw-Hill, 384
McGuire, C, 251
McKeachie, W, 43
MacKenzie, N, 18, 372, 387
Mackie, A, 255
MacKinnon, D W, 251, 264
McMaster Philosophy, 313-24
MacMaster University, 313-24
McNamara, R, 388
Mager, R F, 185, 254-5, 376, 378-9,
381
Mair, J, 63
Malpass, L F, 237
Man: A Course of Study, 208
Manipulation:
data, 313
educational personnel, 206
Manpower planning, 365
Mansell, J, 388
Mapping, 86
information, 186
Marking, 222, 362-3, 357, 366

Markle Foundation, 388
Markle, Susan, 132, 170-81, 382-3
Marshall, A E, 245
Martin, H C, 177
Marton, F, 43, 47-55, 57
Maslow, A H, 252
Massachusetts Institute of
Technology, 209, 213
Matched funding, 221
Matching-to-sample, 239-40, 243, 245
Maxwell Air Force Base, 367
Mayer, R E, 85
Mayes, J T, 241
Means-ends model, 136, 142
Mednick, M Y, 252
Mednick, S A, 252, 254
Melton, A W, 40
Memory, 58
extensions of, 319
long-term, 155
rote, 308
short-term, 155
span, 99
visual, 99
Merrill, M D, 83, 86, 171, 174,
179
Metaphors, 21-2
Meyer, Susan see Markle, Susan
Military training, 359-69
administration, 363-4
CAL, 359-69
CML, 362, 366-7
training development, 364-5
Mill, John Stuart, 145
Miller, C M, 43
Miller, G A, 57, 155-6, 183
Miller, R B, 154
Mistakes, learning from, 318
Mitchell, R, 383
Mitre Corporation, 367
MMPI, 253
Mnemonic-concrete strategy, 52
Models, 15-16, 17-18, 59, 63, 67, 319
Modesty, 127
Modification, 225
Modularisation, 225
Modules, 337-8
Mogford, K, 246
Montessori, M, 270, 373
Moore, Professor O K, 293, 383
Morgan, J H, 245
Morgan, J S, 220
Morgan, R P, 220
Morpheme, 173-4, 176, 178-9
Morphisms, 61 see also Isomorphisms
Morrison, A, 373
Moseley, D, 241
Motivation, 13, 31, 81, 259, 278,
357-8
Muhimbili National Teaching
Hospital, 327
Multi-media systems design, 384

Multiple-choice exercises, 320
Multiple-choice teaching
machines, 343-4
Muzzey Junior High School, 278-81
MYCIN, 92-3
Myers, R F, 256

National Centre for Educational
Technology (proposed), 386-7
National Centre for Programmed
Learning (University of
Birmingham), 387
National Council for Educational
Technology (latterly Council
for Educational Technology),
221, 338, 370, 386-7
National Development Programme
in Computer Assisted Learning
(NDPCAL), 94, 219-27
National Education Association
see Association for Educational
Communications and Technology
National Foundation for Educational
Research, 141
National Institute of Instructional
Technology, 387
National Institutes of Education, 387
National Institutes of Mental
Health, 387
National Programme on Computer
Assisted Learning, 226, 228, 235,
359, 361-4
National Programme, UNCAL, 220
National Society for Programmed
Instruction, 386
Naval Technical Training Command,
366
Naval Training Centres, San Diego/
Great Lakes, 366
Naylor, J C, 163
Nebraska, University of, 388
Needs, 137
Negatives, 184
Neufeld, Victor, 313-24
Neurath, Otto, 189
Newson, E, 44
Newson, J, 44, 246
Nicholl, C J, 364
NIH Syndrome, 224
NIM, 273
Nitco, A J, 376
Nodes, 83
head, 63
Novick, M R, 379
Nuffield Foundation, 139
Numerical data, presentation, 185

Oakeshott, Michael, 137
Objectives, 319, 376, 379
behavioural see
Behavioural: objectives
Bloom-type taxonomies, 303
compared with aims and goals,
141-4
creativity, 257-8
curriculum design, 135-51
definition, 131, 136
general, 142-3
justification, 144-6
personal, 320
process of planning, 135-41
relevancy, 144-5
role of discovery, 146-9
specific, 143-4
statement of, 88
worthwhileness, 145-6
see also Performance: objectives
Observation, 23, 163, 212, 309
Ofeish, G D, 372
Ohmann, R M, 177
Olton, R M, 255
Open University, 221, 227, 234-5,
296-312
doubts, 298-9
economic aspects, 297
educational implications, 298
social and humanitarian
aspects, 297-8
indices of quality, 302-11
Institute of Educational
Technology, 301
Operant conditioning, 22, 27
Operational research, 384
Operations, definition, 156
Optics, 60
Organisation, 31
Organisational structures, 43
Orientation, 99
Originality, judgements, 256
Orlando, R, 238
OR relationships, 172, 174
Osborn, A F, 254
Osgood, C E, 61
O'Shea, T, 93
Outcome, level, 50
Oxford Systems Associates Ltd, 364

Pacing, self-, 255
Packham, D, 241, 244
Pages, size of, 189
Paired experiment, 58-9
Papert, Seymour, 58, 78, 234, 270
Paradigms, 15-17, 21
agricultural botany, 205
classical, 205
objective, 18-20
social anthropology, 205
subjective, 18-20
Paragraphs, identification, 192
Paramedical staff, training, 325
Parameters, 206
Parker, G R, 362
Parkhurst, H, 373, 376
Parlett, Malcolm, 43, 133, 205-18
Parnes, S J, 254
Pask, Gordon, 28, 33, 35, 56-72, 81,
83-6, 379-80, 382, 386

Patients, simulation, 76
Patrick, John, 152-64
Pattern recognition, 309
Perception, melodic, 384
Perceptive eye, 390
Perceptual features, 31
Perceptual speed, 99
Performance:
    algorithm, 83
    assessment, 363
    contracting, 208
    criteria, 315
    objectives, 93
    trainee analysis, 362
Perry, Walter, 235
Perseverance, 252
Personal:
    construct theory, 57, 63
    contact, 224
Personalised system of instruction
    (PSI), 33
Personality, 31
    teachers and students, 43
    tests, 213, 264
    theory, 32, 36-7, 301
Peters, Richard, 10, 145-6
Peterson, P L, 100
Peterson, R W, 54
Phillips, D C, 15
Physical Sciences Program Exchange,
    227
    Piaget, Jean, 39, 43, 53, 56-9,
    138, 148, 270, 272
Pie charts, 187
Planning:
    expedient, 139-40
    piecemeal, 140-1
    systematic, 136-8
Playtest, 238
Poetry, concrete, 273
Politics, 123
Polonius, 127
Poole, R, 19
Pop-ed culture, 272-3
Popham, J W, 388
Popper, Karl, 136-7, 140
Portability, technical, 225
Porter, D, 383
Porteus, A, 100
Positivism, 127
Posner, George J, 35, 132, 165-9
Post-tests, 85
Poulson, S C, 52
Poulton, E C, 57
Practice, relationship with theory, 27
Prediction, 23
Prerequisites:
    empirical, 167-8
    logical, 166
Pre-school provision, 43
Presentation:
    sequence, 35
    skills, 225

Pressey, S L, 254-5, 374-6, 379
Previous experience, 81, 88, 98, 118
Probability:
    analysis, instance, 179
    theorems, 91
Problem/s:
    analysis, 105
    boxes, 319, 321
    classes of, 23
    definition, 106
Problem-solving, 14, 34, 155-6
    capabilities, 306
    clinical medicine, 325-30
    procedures, 309
    teaching, 77-9
Procedures, 169
Processing, level, 50
Proctors, 33, 286-9, 293
Products, evaluation, 259
Program:
    design, 225
    exchange centres, 225
Program for Learning in Accordance
    with Needs (PLAN), 376
Programmed instruction, 42, 195
    knowledge of results, 259
    novelty, 259
Programmed Instruction, 381-2
Programmed learning, 131, 137, 143,
    208, 371, 374, 378
*Programmed Learning and
    Educational Technology,* 386
Programmed Logic for Automatic
    Teaching Operation (PLATO),
    367, 380
Programmed texts, 33
Programmes, linear versus
    branching, 385
Programming languages, 78
Programs, knowledgeable, 89
Progressive Education Movement, 374
Progressive focusing, 214
Proportionality, 54
Propositional relations, 166
Propositions, connected, 58
Prose, improving, 182-6
Psychology:
    computer-based instructions, 73-95
    structural, 57
    see also Gestalt school of
        psychology
Psychometrics, 376-8
Public Health Service, 384
Punishments, 41
Purdue creativity programme, 256
Purpose, 32
    concept of, 154

Quality, indices of, 302-11
Queen Mary College, 227
Queens College (NY), 290
Questioning, 58, 183, 251-2
Questionnaires, 213, 309

Radio, Open University, 296
Random Access, 353-6
Rawson, M, 94
Ray, W S, 251
Recapitulation, 308
Recognition procedures, 309
Recommendations, structural, 117
Reflectiveness, self-conscious, 147
Regression lines, 100
Reid, L 185, 382
Reinforcement, 31-2, 240-3, 282-95
    mutual, 288
    tokens, 238-9
Relationships:
    constructive, 110
    interpreted formal, 58
Relevance, 32
Remote Association Test, 254
Renewal, 23
Repetition, 31
Replication studies, 127
Reproduction, learning strategies, 52
Research:
    audience considerations, 124
    influence, 124
    responsibilities, 123-7
Resnick, L B, 34, 43
Resource person, 321
Resources, allocation, 110-12, 363
Response, Law of Effect, 374
Responsibility, 19, 32
Results:
    immediate knowledge, 255
    knowledge, 259
Retardation, teaching machines, 237
Rewards, 41
Richardson, E, 14
Rickards, J P, 183-4
Rimland, B, 97
Robin, A C, 33
Robinson, F G, 34, 183
Robinson, K E, 145
Robson, J, 77, 87-8
Rocky Mountain Satellite Technology
    Demonstration, 388
Rogers, C R, 36-7, 250, 253
Role specificity, 127
Rorschach tests, 253
Rosenberg, B, 243
Rote-memory, 308
Rothenburg, D, 220
Rothkopf, 176, 255
Rousseau, J-J, 372-4
Rowntree, D, 370, 383
Royal Air Force, Brampton, 364
Royal Air Force, Cranwell, 364
Royal Air Force, Locking, 362, 364
Royal Military College of Science,
    Shrivenham, 362, 364
Royal Naval College, Greenwich, 361,
    363
Royal Naval Engineering College,
    Manadon, 361

Royal Navy, military training, 364
Royal Navy School of Maritime
    Operations, 360
Royal School of Military Engineering,
    Chatham, 363-4
Rubenstein, R, 78
Ruleg, 374
Rule learning, 156
Rummler, Geary, 386
Ryan, A, 126

Saettler, P, 371, 373-4, 390
Säljö, R, 43
Sampling, 213
Scandura, J M, 33, 57
Scanning function, 154
Scatter-plots, 100
Scepticism, 20
Scheduling, 363
Schein, E H, 114, 117
Schiller, J C F, 252
School of Electrical and Mechanical
    Engineering, Bordon, 364
School of Signals, Blandford, 362
Schools' Council for Curriculum and
    Examinations, 12, 138-9, 147,
    220, 224
Schramm, W, 383, 385
Schutz, H G, 187
Science 5/13 Project, 138-9
Scoring, 260-1, 264-5
Scott, B C E, 69, 76, 85
Searles, J E, 303
Self, J A, 93
Seligman, M E P, 37
Semantic scales, 61, 309
Sensitivity, 15, 147, 238
Sentences, 183-4
Sequencing, 34-5, 81, 132, 165-9,
    240, 255, 316
    rules, 159-61
    see also Task sequencing
Serialists, 32, 85
Sesame Street, 175, 177, 179, 208
Seymour, W D, 153
Shackel, D S J, 255
Sheffield, F D, 383
Sheffield Polytechnic, 224
Shepherd, A, 162
Sheppard, C, 195-204
Sherman, J G, 284
Sherron, G T, 366
Shipman, Marten D, 28, 43, 123-7
Shuford, E H, 66
Shumway, R J, 174
Sidman, M, 239-41, 243
Signal learning, 42, 155
Silvern, L C, 386
Simon, H A, 252
Simons, H, 43
Simulation, 163
    armed services, 360-1
    British Airways, 334-58

concepts, 75-7
models, 90
packages, 89
Simultaneous-contrast techniques, 42
Singleton, W T, 153
Skilbeck, Malcolm, 144
Skills analysis, 153, 384
Skills, interpersonal, 215
Skinner, B F, 22, 27, 79, 156, 237,
239-45, 254-5, 371, 374-5, 377,
379-80, 382-5
Skinner box, 38, 238, 270
SKIPTO, 354, 356
Sleeman, D H, 93-4
Smedslund, J, 54
Smith, E B, 182
Smith, W, 383
Snow, C P, 390
Snow, Richard E, 28, 34, 44, 96-103
Social:
factors, 38
psychology, 31-2
science, influence on education, 127
situation, 32
Social-anthropology paradigm, 205-7
illumination evaluation, 207-10
Social Science Research Council, 94
Sociologists:
influence of, 123
numbers, 124
Sociology, 43
Socrates, 146, 373
SOCRATES, 380
Solartron Automatic Keyboard
Instruction (SAKI), 380, 382
Solomon, C, 78
SOPHIE, 90
Sophistication, 166
Sophists, 373
Space, 165
Specialists, 310
Spencer Foundation, 388
Spencer, H, 374
Spoken discourse, 47-55
Sprecher, T B, 253
Staats, A W, 240-1, 243
Stammers, Robert, 152-64
Stanford University, 220
Starr, M K, 17
Statistical techniques, 377
Stenhouse, Lawrence, 139
Stimuli, 375
availability of reinforcement, 243
control, 238
Law of Effect, 374
-response (SR) theory, 31, 33, 36,
42, 79, 155
Stoddard, L T, 239-41, 243
Stolurow, L M, 380
Stordahl, K, 184
Strategy, 39
Stratified blocks, 337
Stratton, R P, 173

Strauss, A, 53
Streaming, 313
Strike, Kenneth A, 35, 132, 165-9
Strong Vocational Interest Blank, 253
Structures, 31, 42
Stryker, R E, 187
Students:
aptitudes, 98
behaviour, 83
error patterns, 174
performance, 110
performance data, 75
records, 362
selection, 322-4
Study, distributed/concentrated, 209
Subjects, creativity, 257-8
Suppes, Patrick, 220
Surrey, University of, 227
Svenson, L, 51
Swanson, 174
Swift, D F, 125
Swift, Jonathan, 9
Symmetry, 174
Synectics, 254
Synonyms, definition by, 175
Synthesis, 23
Systematisation, 374
System Development Corp, 382-3
Systems analysis, 14
System-theoretical prescriptions, 303

Tables, 186-9
Tactical Fire Direction System
(TACFIRE), 367
Tait, K, 94
Task:
complexity, 89
difficulty, 81-2, 88
family grouping, 198
features, 197
frequency, 198
nature, 198
sequencing, 88
size, 198
Task analysis, 13, 102, 131, 152-3
hierarchies, 156-62
recording, 161-2
sources of information, 163
Taxonomies, 154-6
Bloom-type, 303
Taylor, C W, 253
Taylor, T R, 76
Taylor, W, 124
TEACHBACK, 69
Teachers, interaction with
learners, 43
Teaching, 117
inductive method, 374
methods, 43
mode, 85-7, 89
strategy, 86
system-theoretical prescriptions,
303

Teaching machines:
adaptive, 379-80
for severely retarded, 237-48
matching-to-sample, 243
multiple-choice, 241
Teaching Aids News
see Educational Technology
Team teaching, 208
Television:
closed-circuit, 385
Open University, 296
teaching by, 222
Tennyson, R D, 174, 179
Terrace, H S, 239
Tests, 289, 311, 343-4, 379
conversational, 311
creativity, 253-4
data, 213
empirical, 388
marking, 222, 362-3, 366
objective, 363
projective, 253
psychological, 376
self-, 354, 357
Textbooks, learning from, 43
Thematic Apperception Test, 253
Theory, relationship with practice, 27
Thinking:
inductive, 372
teaching children, 270-81
Thomas, L F, 61
Thoresen, C E, 33
Thorndike, E L, 373-5
Thornhill, P, 385
Thought, theoretical-deductive/
empirical inductive, 390
Tickton, S, 387
Tilmann, P W, 171-2, 174, 176, 178
Tilles, S, 109-10
Time, 165
Time-shared Interactive Computer-
Controlled Information Television
(TICCIT), 86, 367
Timetabling, 363-4
Tokens, as reinforcers, 238-9
Tolman, E C, 40
Tolman, T C, 375
Topic maps, 83
Topics, 58
Torrance, E P, 251, 254, 256
Torrance Tests of Creative Thinking,
254, 256
TOTE units, 156
'Touch Tutor', 239, 241-6
Toy libraries, 246
Toys, 246
Trade Training School, 8th Signal
Regiment, Catterick, 363
Training:
analysis, 152-64
embedded, 368
valuation, 365

Training Requirements and Manage-
ment Planning Information
System (TRAMPIS), 365
Transactionalism, 57
Transactions:
explore, 66
tutorial, 65-8
Transformation, learning strategies,
52
TRANSLATOR, 6, 202
Translators, 199
Travers, R M, 389
Treffinger, D J, 256
Trochaic meter, 174, 179
Trow, M A, 207
Trust, 109
TTCT, 264
Tuition, levels of, 306-11
Tutor Age, 383-4
Tutor Films, 384
Tutorials, conversations and
transactions, 65-8
Tutoring, CAL, 74-5
Tutors, 317-18
Tutor Texts, 382
Tyler, R W, 376, 378
Tyler-type prescriptions, 303
Typography, 34, 184, 187, 189-92

UNCAL, 225
Underlinings, 184
Understanding, 31, 59-60, 308, 311
levels of, 306-11
nature and control, 57
UNESCO, 388
Unilever Ltd, 227
United Nations Development
Programme, 388
United States:
Agency for International
Development (USAID), 388
Air Force, Lowry Air Force
Base, 366
Armed Services, 366-8
Army School of Signals, Fort
Monmouth/Fort Gordon, 366
Navy Air Base, Memphis, 366
Office of Education, 387
Unit planners, 322
Universal training simulator (UTS),
334-58
anatomy of a frame, 346-53
course benefits, 357-8
internal organisation, 340-6
random access, 353-6
University Grants Committee, 389
Use, frequency, 169

Value, 141
isolation, 137
judgements, 131
systems, 131
Van Horn, R W, 36

Varian Associates, 381
Verbal Association, 156
Verification, creativity, 253
Versatility, 252
Visualisation ability, 99
Visual memory, 99
Vogel, M, 376
Vygotsky, L S, 57-8

Walker, R, 223
Wallach, M A, 251, 254
Waller, R, 190
Wallis, D, 41, 195
Wants, 137
Washburne, C, 373, 376
Wason, P, 184
Watson, L S, 238, 375
Weber, J C, 91
*Webster's III International
    Dictionary,* 177-8
Weinberger, C, 388
Weir, S, 234
Welford, A T, 57
Wertheimer, M, 53
Whalley, P, 187

Wholists, 32, 85
Williams, Robert E, 234, 250-69
Williams, Roger, 96
Willis, N E, 387
Wilson, Harold, 387
Winnetka Technique, 376
Wisdom, 135
Wolverhampton Polytechnic, 227
Woodford, F P, 33
Woods, Pat, 43, 81
Wood, R, 141
Wooley, F R, 174, 179
Words, spacing, 189-90
Work study, 154
World Bank, 388
Wright, P, 183-7
Wringe, Sally, 140
Written discourse, 47-55
Written material, design, 132
Wulff, J J, 162

Yamamoto, K, 254
Youtz, R P, 253

Zen, 19